Gabriela Cunninghame Graham

Santa Teresa - Being Some Account of her Life and Times

Vol. II

Gabriela Cunninghame Graham

Santa Teresa - Being Some Account of her Life and Times
Vol. II

ISBN/EAN: 9783337112875

Printed in Europe, USA, Canada, Australia, Japan

Cover: Foto ©Lupo / pixelio.de

More available books at **www.hansebooks.com**

SANTA TERESA

BEING SOME ACCOUNT OF

HER LIFE AND TIMES

TOGETHER WITH

SOME PAGES FROM THE HISTORY OF THE
LAST GREAT REFORM IN THE
RELIGIOUS ORDERS

BY

GABRIELA CUNNINGHAME GRAHAM

Vol. II

LONDON
ADAM AND CHARLES BLACK
1894

Teresa de Jesus

SANTA TERESA

CONTENTS

CHAPTER XV
LIFE IN THE ENCARNACION — JOURNEY TO SALAMANCA — FOUNDATION AT SEGOVIA . . . 1

CHAPTER XVI
THE FATE OF THE CONVENT OF PASTRANA . . . 32

CHAPTER XVII
HISTORY OF CASILDA DE PADILLA — FOUNDATION OF VEAS . . . 41

CHAPTER XVIII
SUPERABUNDO GAUDIO . . . 90

CHAPTER XIX
LETTERS FROM TOLEDO . . . 125

CHAPTER XX
FROM AUGUST TO CHRISTMAS DAY 1577 . . . 182

CHAPTER XXI
FROM JANUARY 1578 TO CHRISTMAS DAY . . . 204

CHAPTER XXII
LA VERDAD PADECE PERO NO PERECE — 232

CHAPTER XXIII
DIOS É VOS — 248

CHAPTER XXIV
ANTES QUEBRAR QUE DOBLAR — 281

CHAPTER XXV
EL ORO FINO SE ECHARÁ DE VER EN EL TOQUE — 309

CHAPTER XXVI
THE CROWN OF THORNS AND ROSES — 341

CHAPTER XXVII
NOT TO A STRANGE COUNTRY, BUT TO HER NATIVE LAND — 368

CHAPTER XXVIII
THE PATRON SAINT OF SPAIN — 394

CONCLUSION
INVENI PORTAM — 409

EPILOGUE — 443

CHAPTER XV

LIFE IN THE ENCARNACION—JOURNEY TO SALAMANCA—
FOUNDATION AT SEGOVIA

In the meantime the nuns of the Encarnacion, backed up by many influential people of the town, prepared to resist the noxious control which the visitor and Carmelite chapter had forced on them against their will and without their sanction. Their bitter hostility to Teresa arose from many reasons. Had she not risen, out of their knowledge, into fame — and to small minds (and the majority of minds are very small) can any one they have known and been familiar with commit a greater crime? Is it not a personal insult to themselves—an impalpable derogation from their merits? When, indeed, shall a prophet get honour in his own country? Moreover, had she not blackened her offence—she, this Teresa de Ahumada, who had lived with them for more than thirty years—by inaugurating a Reform which was little less than a treason, at the very least an act of base ingratitude to the Order she had been nurtured in, a slight to the Encarnacion in particular, and an obvious reflection on themselves? Neither had they any mind to be shorn of their privileges, to be rudely shaken up from their supineness and exemptions—exemptions that Popes had sanctioned, — by this stern and rigorist who would surely never rest until she had reduced them to a rule and discipline they had not professed and did not feel inclined to admit. Hunger was bad, but to be forcibly transformed into a model of virtue like San José was worse. No, not they! they would soon show the visitor and his prioress that it was not so easy to tamper with the liberties of the Encarnacion as they thought. They bespoke the assistance of a number of gentlemen of the town, and prepared to resist Teresa's entry by main force. The visitor himself felt an uneasy qualm as the moment approached.

Accompanied by the Provincial, Fray Gaspar de Salazar, and another monk, sent with her by the visitor in case it came to blows, Teresa re-entered her old home.

In the low choir of the convent—that choir to-day so tranquil and dreamy—which faces the high altar, the Provincial convoked the frowning and angry sisterhood, and read to them the patent of Teresa's election by the visitor and chapter. Their conclusion was the signal for the wildest uproar. Many rose up and defied the patents, vomiting forth accusations and insults against Teresa. The minority seized the cross and formed in procession to receive her, whilst the two monks effected her entrance by sheer force. Then arose an unholy Babel; a shrieking of women's tongues, a frenzied excitement, which it is hard to imagine as having taken place within the tranquil walls of the Encarnacion. Some chanted the *Te Deum*; others breathed maledictions against their prioress and him who sent her there. The Provincial, beside himself with rage, stood in the midst of a pandemonium he could neither restrain nor control, surrounded by fainting, hysterical, excited women. During the progress of this wild scene Teresa remained humbly kneeling before the altar. She now rose. With a smiling face she mediated between the wrathful Provincial and his no less furious and rebellious subjects. She expressed her sympathy with the nuns for having a prioress forced on them against their will and begged the Provincial not to wonder at anything they said, for they were right not to desire a prioress so unworthy Concealing her intent, she approached those who had fainted either through excitement or weakness of the heart, and stroking their faces gently with her hands in compassionate tenderness, it was noted that under her soothing and magic touch they recovered consciousness and strength. When, however, she was confronted with these miracles and others like them, she attributed them to the great virtues of a relic of the Lignum Crucis she bore on her person: " All to dissemble," adds Yepes, "that which the Lord had placed in her hands." Such was her stormy entry.

The Provincial, however, although he had effected Teresa's entry, left the revolt still raging behind him when he shook the dust of the Encarnacion off his feet that October day. The most obstinate and defiant only waited for an opportunity to flout her authority. They plotted amongst themselves to resist her orders by insolence, and, if necessary, by blows. Teresa was not ignorant of these intentions when she held her first chapter. As the sisterhood, however, gathered together in the choir to meet their prioress, a strange hush fell upon them; some averred afterwards that they trembled, for, enthroned in the provincial stall, they saw, not the obnoxious intruder, whom they had come to insult and set at nought, but the benign and beautiful image of Our Lady of Clemency, holding in her hands the convent keys; at her feet serene and confident sat Teresa de Jesus. Overawed by her profound humility, they listened in silence, as she rose and gently addressed them. The words which fell from her lips welled from her heart to meet the exigencies of a fleeting moment. It was not a set oration, but one most potent. They were perhaps afterwards preserved by the pen of some sister who was present, although the dissimilarity of style to Teresa's has caused them to be regarded as apocryphal; but the spirit which informs them, so firm, moderate, and gentle, is verily her own:

Ladies, mothers, and my sisters, our Lord has sent me to this house to undertake this post by reason of my obedience, one which I as little expected as deserved. This election has given me great distress, not only because it has forced duties on me that I may not be able to fulfil, but also because it has deprived you of the control which you possessed over your own elections, and given you a prioress against your will and taste, and such a prioress that she would do well if she succeeded in learning from the least one of you the many virtues she possesses. I come only to serve you, and to administer to your pleasure as far as I am able; and to this end I hope that the Lord will help me greatly. For as to the rest, any one of you can teach and reform me. For that reason consider, my ladies, that what I can do for each one of you, I will do it willingly, even to the shedding of blood, and giving up my life. I am a daughter of this house, and a sister of your graces. I know the circumstances and necessities of all, or of the greater number; there is no reason to dread one who is so entirely yours. Do not fear my rule, for although I have lived until now, and ruled amongst Discalced nuns, by the Lord's mercy I know well how those who are not should be governed. My desire is that we should all serve the Lord with suavity; and that we should do that little enjoined on us by our Rule and Constitutions, for the love of that Lord to whom we owe so much. Well do I know how great is our weakness; but although our works do not reach so far, let our desires do so; for the Lord is pitiful, and will order it so that, little by little, our works shall rise to our intentions and desire.

Teresa had surprised them into silence, and that pause of hesitation and suspense, which she knew so well to turn to account, gave her the victory. Those haughty and indomitable nuns, many of whom belonged to the noblest families of Castille, were vanquished. They who had been the most refractory, voluntarily placed the yoke which had seemed so unendurable upon their own necks. They it was who brought her the convent keys, and requested her to distribute the offices of trust as she thought fit. So true is it, as she herself says, that everything is best achieved by love.

And not only was Teresa *suaviter in modo*, but *fortiter in re*, as a gay young gentleman, belonging to one of the noblest families of Avila, found to his cost. More persistent than the rest who had been wont to spend the sunny afternoons dangling around the convent gratings, infuriated at the failure of all his efforts to see a particular nun, he demanded to speak with the prioress herself, and took her roundly to task in no measured or courteous language. Teresa listened to him in patient silence, reasoned with him gravely, and then menaced him sharply and decisively with the king's displeasure. If his shadow fell again across the convent doorway, she would, she said, make the king cut off his head. When he retired, discomfited and dismayed, from the interview he himself had sought, he averred there was no jesting with the Mother Teresa, adding sorrowfully that, as for him, he had done with nuns, and that the palmy days of the Encarnacion were over.

Her other measures were equally energetic and radical, although so masked over with deference for her subjects that, surprised to find themselves captives, they proposed of their own accord those measures which she secretly desired. "It is right, mother," said the humbled nuns, amongst whom were some of the most refractory, "that your reverence should have the keys of the wheels and parlours, and choose such and such persons for office." "Since so it appears to your reverences," she answered, "let it be so."

With the Commissary's approval she sent for two of her Discalced friars, Fray Juan de la Cruz and Fray German de San Matias, to take charge of the services and the souls of the nuns of the Encarnacion. Isabel Arias, a first cousin of her own, on whose co-operation she could rely, was summoned from Valladolid, where Maria de Bautista (afterwards so famous) substituted her as prioress. The temporal affairs of the convent began to improve under Teresa's wise administration. She herself was beholden to the convent for nothing beyond a ration of bread, and we find her writing to her sister Juana to send her a few reals to provide for her most urgent necessities. Even with the alms sent her by her powerful friends, Doña Maria de Mendoza, and that Doña Magdalena de Ulloa, "the almsgiver of God"—the friend and mother of Don John of Austria—it was a perpetual struggle to keep the wolf from the door. "With the great want I see in the Encarnacion," writes Teresa, "I can save nothing."

Besides the constant care and responsibility entailed on her by a large and poverty-stricken community—"This house of the Encarnacion is seen notably to make my health suffer; please God I may gain somewhat by it"—this feeble and elderly woman, suffering from habitual ill-health, her nights consumed by fever, which left her at two in the morning only to make way for the shivering fits of ague—("it grieves me to see myself so useless, that I do not and cannot leave my corner except for Mass")—never lost sight of the scattered communities she had founded, kept up a ceaseless correspondence with them, advising, directing, and consoling, "So that I might see," she adds, "that, as St. Paul says, all is possible in God"

Scarcely able to cope with her innumerable occupations and trials, not the least amongst them her enormous correspondence, she felt that sense of loneliness, of complete isolation, which often weighs so heavily on those whose genius or aspirations interpose a bar between themselves and their fellows. It is scarcely a complaint, scarcely more than a sigh, which breathes imperceptibly through her familiar letters. "I miss you very much here," she writes sadly to her sister Juana, buried in the little town of Galinduste, near Salamanca, where she and her husband were wont to pass the winter (on account, as we shall hear farther on, "of the excellent fires"), "and I find myself alone." The cold, hard winter of the upland Castilian town sorely tried the ailing woman. "God deliver me from it"—she refers to Galinduste—"and even from this also." "My native place," she adds to Doña Maria de Mendoza, "has agreed with me in such a way that it does not seem I was born here. At one and the same time I have so little health (and I laugh sometimes at myself that in spite of it all I do everything), and I am left without a confessor, and so much alone, that there is no one with whom I can converse for some little consolation; but I must be so circumspect in everything, although, as to what concerns bodily comfort, sympathy has not been wanting, nor thoughtful people."

But if she lives in solitude,—the solitude which is perhaps the inexorable fate of those greater than their age,—it is sweetened by the love and respect she has conquered from her nuns. "When I see them so tranquil and good, and certainly so they are," she writes feelingly to Doña Maria de Mendoza, "it hurts me to see them suffer [from hunger]—the change in them is so great as to praise God for it. The most wilful are now the most contented, and the kindest to me. This Lent neither man nor woman, not excepting even parents, has visited the convent, which is a strange thing for this house. . . . Truly there are here great servants of God, and nearly all of them are improving. My prioress works these marvels. That you should see it is so, the Lord has ordered my state to be such, that it seems as if I had only come here to abhor mortification, and to consider my own comfort alone."

Although she never for a moment shrank from her responsibilities, her words to Father Ordoñez, in reference to the foundation of a school for the education of maidens in Medina del Campo were surely dictated by her own experience of the difficulties to be encountered in the government of a large community. It must be remembered that when she took up the reins in the Encarnacion the relaxations that had driven her from it had ended in complete disorganisation. More than eighty nuns fought for preference, and filled the cloister walls with their often not edifying chatter. By degrees Teresa herself had drained off the purer and more conscientious spirits to swell the Reform, and only the residuum was left. "It is as different," she writes, "teaching girls, and managing a great number of them together, from teaching boys, as white is from black. . . . I have experience of what many women together are like. God deliver us."

Whilst Teresa thus defined a sharp line of demarcation between the sexes, which, so all unconsciously in her own case, she had annihilated so gloriously, she wrote her brilliant and witty answer to the friars of Pastrana, who had challenged her and her nuns to enter with them the lists of a spiritual combat. This Cartel de Vejámen, now become famous, veiled a deep current of lofty intention under the jesting terms of knight-errantry. In this spiritual combat, suggested by the celebrated Gracian, who two years before had entered Pastrana as a novice, which was in Teresa's case at least a combat of wits, the monks measured themselves against a powerful and merciless antagonist. Thus were the two people, afterwards destined to wield such an enormous influence over each other's lives and the future fortunes of the Order, first brought into contact, little recking the closeness of the ties which time was to forge between them, and which "death itself was powerless to loosen."

The prologue is dainty and humorous:

Having seen the cartel, our strength did not seem sufficient to enter the lists with champions so brave and valorous, as they were certain of victory, and of leaving us entirely despoiled of our possessions, and even perchance so cowed as to be unable to do what little we can. Seeing this, not one of us signed, and Teresa de Jesus least of all. This is entirely true, without a trace of fiction.

We agreed to do what our strength allowed us, and, after a little practice of these feats, it might be that, by the favour and help of those who should desire to take part in them, we may be able to sign the cartel a few days hence. It must be on condition that the maintainer being, as he is, buried in those caves [an allusion to the caves of Pastrana], the first dwelling places of the primitive friars of Pastrana], does not go back from his promise, but that he sallies forth into the field of this world, where we are. It may be that finding himself always at war, where it is necessary for him always to keep his armour buckled, and never relax his attention, nor enjoy a moment in which he can rest with security, he may not be so furious, for the one is as different from the other as action is from words, for we understand a little of the difference between them. Let him sally forth, himself and his companions, and leave that delightful life; it may be then that, as soon as they do so, they will stumble and fall, and that it may be necessary to help them to rise; for it is a terrible thing to be always in danger, and laden with weapons, and hungry. Since the maintainer provided food so abundantly, let him send the provisions he promises without delay; for to vanquish us by starvation will gain him but little honour or profit.

Each of the nuns offers up a merit in exchange for some virtue to be gained by the prayers of the knights of Pastrana. Thus Beatriz Juarez (she was probably Teresa's infirmarian, for the whole of this strange and characteristic document is instinct with subtle irony) bestows two years of what she has earned in curing very troublesome patients to him or her who shall offer up a prayer each day that the Lord may keep her in his grace, and grant her not to speak unadvisedly.

Teresa de Jesus takes up the challenge last in quaint and humorous spirit.

Teresa de Jesus says: That she will give to any of the Virgin's Knights who shall every day offer up a most determined resolve to bear all his life with a stupid, vicious, gluttonous, and ill-conditioned superior [she was herself the prioress of the Encarnacion], the day he shall do so, the half of what she has merited that day in the communion as also in the many sufferings she endures; which, in short, all told, will be little enough. He must consider the humility of Christ before his judges, and his obedience even to death on the cross. This contract is to last for a month and a half.

Teresa's residence within its walls sheds to-day its greatest glory over the imposing embattled convent of the Encarnacion. As her influence still lingers in a thousand details, so in like manner it may be that, if they could but render them, those massive walls still conserve the tones of her voice, as of those of the generations of nuns who have passed away to their eternal rest under the cloister slabs. Strange it is that the inanimate should live, whilst the vitality it enveloped, with its passionate throbs, its world-embracing aspirations, its strange mixture of the human and the divine, should be swallowed up in darkness, and leave no record. It is hard to penetrate the quaint and fanciful body of legend which has sprung up about this period of her life, formed in equal parts of fact and fancy, but so inextricably blended as to be impossible to separate. The Virgin of Clemency still looks down on the curious gazer into the obscure depths of the Coro Bajo which faces the High Altar, with the same benignity as when she quelled Teresa's first unruly chapter. From that day to this, like the Visigothic Archbishops of Toledo, who never again occupied the throne where it is said San Ildefonso perceived the vision of the Virgin, no prioress has dared to profane the priorial stall, so doubly consecrated,—consecrated by an inanimate figure,—consecrated far more by the hand whose severed portions have been scattered as a benediction over the world.

Here in this shady locutorio, where behind the wooden lattice flits a glimpse of some white coif, cutting a straight line over a pallid brow, and luminous eyes; where the sun streams in through an open casement and sleeps on the red brick floor, so cool, so full of a rural quaint simplicity which is mingled with I know not what dignity and stateliness of another epoch, Beatriz de Jesus entering suddenly, testified to having seen Teresa and San Juan de la Cruz floating in mid-air in ecstasy. That little narrow grating, submerged in obscurity, where the nuns communicated, tradition sanctifies as the spot where Christ celebrated his espousals with Teresa de Jesus. As with Sta. Inés,[1] Sta. Cecilia, St. Catherine of Alexandria, here the faithful devoutly believe that Christ pledged his mystic troth to Teresa de Jesus.

And in very truth she saw,—or fancied she saw (and are not the two identical, oh! ye of little faith?)—those great things which had been promised to her as she knelt in the little hermitage of Medina del Campo.

In those moments when, in her own figurative and sublime language, her soul rose above itself on to its own house-top, soaring to heights alone inhabited by the brooding presence of the divinity:

I saw Christ, represented to me as at other times in an imaginary

---

[1] Perhaps better known to the English reader as St. Agnes.

vision, in the interior of my soul, give me his hand, and say to me: Behold this nail, which is the sign that from this day henceforth thou shalt be my bride. Until now thou hadst not merited it. Henceforth thou shalt watch over my honour not only as thy Creator, and King, and God, but as my spouse in very truth. My honour is thine, and thine mine.

Now she sees the heavens open and reveal the enthroned Divinity, in all its glory, and is surprised to find that the vision which had seemed to her so transitory has lasted two hours. On the Day of the Assumption she watched the Ascent of Christ into heaven, and the joy and solemnity of the celestial court as he took his place amongst them.

These visions, however, sensual as are many of the elements which form them, and their evolution distinctly and easily traceable—that of the celestial court is moulded on Ezekiel and the Apocalypse, as her fancy of the animals supporting the throne distinctly proves—are mingled with others, truly the most wonderful she ever used, which show the curious mixture of poetic and delicate feeling, combined with an intuitive perception of philosophical abstractions and psychological analysis, which is so characteristic of her intellect, and separates her by a world from the aberrations of the Quietists.

Being, with the rest, at Hours, my soul was suddenly suspended, and every part of it seemed to me to be like a clear mirror whose back and sides, top and bottom, were all absolutely clear, and Christ our Lord, as I am accustomed to see him, in the centre of it. It seemed to me that I saw him clearly in every part of my soul as in a mirror, and this same mirror (I know not how) was entirely sculptured in Christ himself by a communication (that I cannot describe) of exceeding love. I know that this vision did me great good whenever I thought of it, especially after communicating. I understood that when a soul is in mortal sin, this mirror is covered with a dense mist, and becomes very black, so that the Lord can neither be represented in it nor seen, although he is ever present giving us life and being; and that in the case of heretics, it is as if the mirror was shattered, which is much worse than if it was only darkened. The way in which it is seen is very different from any description of it, for it is very difficult to make any one understand it. But it has done me great good, and filled me with sorrow for the times when my sins darkened my soul so much that I could not see this Lord!

In the nomenclature of the mystics, in which sometimes I can distinguish the voice of a distraught Plato,—high philosophical contemplations, driven into a thousand aberrations by the attempt to reconcile them with, and force them into, the narrow limits of Christianity,—this representation of the mirror was an *imaginary* one, since it united dimensions, with light and a centre; all these things being counterfeits of, or bearing some resemblance to, corporal ones. In the intellectual vision, on the contrary, the soul rises to the comprehension of things in themselves, in their essence,—seizes on the archetypes of ideas, when all image is superfluous.[1]

In her vision of the Diamond, without using any philosophical subtleties of language, she gives an example (perhaps unconsciously) of the intellectual vision, clearer than any definition:

> Being once upon a time in prayer, it was represented to me like a flash, although I saw nothing formed, still it was a representation with all clearness, how all things are seen in God, and how all are contained in him. . . . It seemed to me, I repeat, although I cannot be certain, that I saw nothing; (still something must be seen, since I am able to give this comparison) but it is in a way so subtle and delicate that either the understanding cannot reach it, or I do not myself understand these visions, for they do not appear imaginary, and in some of them something of this there must be, but rather that as the faculties are suspended, they cannot shape it afterwards in the way the Lord then represents it to them, and wills that they should enjoy it. Let us say that the Divinity is like a very lustrous diamond, larger than all the world, or like a mirror, in the same way as what I said of the soul in the former vision, saving that it is in a manner so transcendental, that I cannot express it: and that all we do is seen in this diamond, it being so fashioned that it includes everything within itself, because there is nothing but what is contained in this magnitude. It was a fearful thing for me to see in so brief a space, so many things together in this clear diamond, and most grievous whenever I think on it to see what ugly things were represented in that lovely clearness as were my sins.

On St. Stephen's Eve, during the first year of her rule at the Encarnacion, as the voices of the nuns intoned the magnificent strains of the Salve Regina, Teresa, kneeling in the choir, wrapped in ecstatic devotion, saw the Queen of Heaven flutter down, surrounded by a multitude of

---

[1] This is at all events what I can seize as being the schoolmen's meaning, for I must put myself into Teresa's category (in which I think she far outstripped both schoolmen and philosophers) when she says, "As for mind, soul and spirit it is all one to me."

angels, and by some strange transmutation fill the place of the wooden image in the priorial stall ("at least it seemed to me that I saw not the image, but our Lady, as I say"), whilst the invisible forms of the angels (whose presence she felt and did not see) clustered above the carved heads of the choir stalls, and wreathed themselves about the lectern.

These were the visions which illumined her cares while the two years of her term of office were fast drawing to a close in the Encarnacion, where five years later, such the devotion and affection inspired by the austere benignity of her rule, those same nuns, with the same independent and insubordinate spirit they had on a similar occasion directed against herself, will unanimously elect her prioress, and carry their suit against the angry Provincial who refuses to confirm it, before the Royal Council Chamber, then the supreme Court of Spain, suffering imprisonment and the severest punishments rather than yield a jot of their pretensions.

For towards the end of July 1573, the old wayfarer, her frail and ailing body sustained by her brave and resolute spirit, once more found herself on the way to Salamanca, where the necessities of her daughters so urgently claimed her presence, that they had obtained Fernandez's permission (who happened to be there at the time) for her to return to them. Before she started, towards the middle of June (although she had written to him before), she addressed the first of her letters that has been preserved to "the Sacred Cesarian Catholic Majesty of the King our Lord." The nature of the service she sought from Philip is unknown, but the letter itself forms a curious link between the life of the Carmelite saint and the history of the House of Austria. For "our lady the queen" and the prince to whom she refers, for whose long life the community of the Encarnacion and the convents of the Reform offer up their supplications, are that Ana of Austria, Philip's fourth wife, who should by rights have become the consort of the unfortunate Don Carlos, and her son, the infant Don Fernando who, a baby of one year old, had just been proclaimed heir to the Spanish throne in the monastery of San Geronimo el Real. "On which day," says Teresa, "we offered up especial prayer. . . .

A great alleviation it is for the trials and persecutions rife in it, that God our Lord possesses so great a defender and prop of his Church as is your Majesty." So she addresses the strange and much-misunderstood man—a man without parallel in history, for none have ever been so belauded and so vilified; a man, in whom it is difficult to separate what was imposed on the monarch from the spontaneous tendencies of the individual, so intimately are they connected; whose gloomy fanaticism, as it touched on the one side the lowest depths of superstition, is on the other the outcome of the noblest qualities of the Spanish character. His desperate struggle with heresy, so full of tragedy and bloodshed, displaying all the chivalrous sentiment, the sombre passion, the exalted devotion to an idea of a Loyola (an idea drunk in at the founts of mysticism, but ferocious in the effects which are its logical outcome), was a quixotic enterprise, but surely not one devoid of grandeur.

On the eve of her journey she wrote to the Jesuit Ordoñez as to the establishment of the girls' college in Medina. "I should like," she says, "to have much opportunity and health to say some things which, to my mind, are important. And such has been my condition,—incomparably worse than before, that it is all I can do to write this. . . . To-morrow I start, if I am not taken ill again, and the illness must indeed be serious to prevent me." So did the brave and resolute spirit sustain her frail and ailing body.

The simple pages of Master Julian de Avila (her companion on this expedition as on so many others) flash to us, so to speak, this sixteenth-century journey with its vivid details, showing to us for a moment, as in the obscure depths of some magic mirror, the quaint picturesqueness of a life which has almost faded not only from existence, but whose meaning also has almost faded from the mind,—the mind which preserves latent for so long those mysterious impressions of heredity ready to be stirred into life by some chance impulse, but which the railroad, and the commercial ugliness of the nineteenth century will soon altogether obliterate.

The little party consisted of Teresa, Fray Antonio de Jesus, Master Julian de Avila, and Doña Quiteria of Avila, a nun of the Encarnacion, and afterwards its prioress. They travelled on donkeys. To avoid the suffocating midsummer heat, as intense on these upland plateaux as the cold is great in winter, and which was hurtful to Teresa, they left Avila about nightfall, intending, as is still the custom in hot weather, to travel all night. Mounted on their donkeys (how many generations of nuns and donkeys have passed in and out of the gateway of the Encarnacion!), these nuns of the sixteenth century, so cloaked and caped to the eyes that, as they flit through the gloaming, they look for all the world like a group of Moorish women on a road in Morocco to-day; to the imminent peril of their necks, clatter down the narrow street, as steep as a precipice, composed in equal parts of boulder and cobble-stones, that leads down to the bridge; fading past some little square more open than the rest, where a torchlight sheds a ghostly gleam on shadowy houses and yawning gateways, clustered round a cross with a boulder for its pedestal. Before them, dark and sombre against the light of the evening sky,—the light that still ripples uncertainly on the river,—lies the hill up which winds the road. Once on the summit, whence the strange silhouette of the walled mediæval town lies sloping down to the river in the breathless repose of the summer night, they are in the vast rolling prairies and "descents" of billowy forest, that sweep uninterruptedly away to Alba.

A region unintersected by roads: at most a little sandy path frayed by the feet of generations of donkeys, scattered over with huge crags and boulders,—gray and strange enough, in the sunlight, but which when touched with the moonbeams take the most fantastic shapes.

Here the imagination forges a phantom city, there a looming tower. I too, like Teresa, have ridden over these plains by night, a belated traveller, between the small hours of the night and morning. The vast solitude, the open, unending expanse of earth and sky; the immense masses of rock, jagged, and rounded, and angled; the midnight sky of a depth and serenity peculiar to the heavens of Avila, where even the stars gleam larger and more brightly than elsewhere, leave an impression never to be effaced.

As a beginning to their journey, before they got to

Martin, a little hamlet not far from Avila, Fr. Antonio de Jesus, who was probably nodding with sleep, and was at the best but an indifferent horseman, had a bad fall from his donkey. Says Master Julian:

It was God's will, however, that he did not hurt himself, either in this or in many others he has had on journeys connected with the business of the Order. With us travelled a waiting-woman belonging to a lady [probably to Doña Quiteria]. A little farther on, I saw her fall from her mule with such violence that I thought she was killed, and God delivered her, so that she escaped without the slightest injury. And as we travelled on in the dark, for night had now closed in, we lost the donkey on which was packed the money [500 ducats, the dower of Ana de Jesus, the purchase money of the house at Salamanca] and other provisions for the road, and it did not turn up again all that night; so that what with the tumbles, and looking for the donkey, together with the great darkness, it seems to me it would be after midnight before we arrived at the posada. I would not eat any supper, although I think I needed it, but thought it better not to break my fast, so as to be able to say Mass on the morrow. In the morning a lad set out to look for the donkey, and found it lying a little to one side of the road, untouched and his burden intact. Whereupon we had a mind to go and say Mass in a neighbouring hermitage, called Our Lady del Parral. We got there in good time, but found nothing in the Hermitage to say Mass with. I was forced to go to the village at some distance from the Hermitage, for the necessary things, but the Curate was not at home, and there was no one who could give us them.

In short, the whole morning slipped away in comings and goings, and sorely against my will, I found myself, not only unable to say Mass, but supperless and breakfastless to boot, and tired out with the journey. And although the Holy Mother remained without communicating—for this her journeys never prevented her from doing—I did not feel it so much as I should have done; for, as if I had not had trouble enough about it, they made merry at my expense, and well they might.

The next night our loss was greater even than that of the donkey; in spite of it carrying, as they said, 500 ducats. It happened that as we were again travelling by night, and the darkness was very great, our people divided into two companies; he who accompanied the Holy Mother, for to save his honour, I will not mention his name [Fray Antonio?], left her and the Lady Doña Quiteria, who is now prioress of the Encarnacion, in the street of a small hamlet, to wait there until the rest came up, so that they might all join and not be separated; in such wise that when the others did appear, and he who for the sake of going in search of them had abandoned the saint and her companion, returned to look for them, he could never hit on the spot where he had left them; and as the darkness was so great, he missed it so completely that, twist and turn as he liked, he did not find them; and as he said they must have gone on ahead, we travelled on a good space until we came up with those in front. We said to one another:

Is the Mother there with you?
They answered:
No!
Is she not travelling with you?
How should she be if she was travelling with you?
What has happened?

So that we all found ourselves in double darkness—that of the night which was great, and that of finding ourselves without our Mother which was incomparably greater. We knew not whether to turn back or to go forward. We began to shout—no answer. Again we were forced to separate, some to look for what we had lost, the others to shout to see if from anywhere there came an answer. After being in this distress a considerable time and he who had left them most of all, as we were turning back to retrace our steps, behold our Holy Mother coming towards us with her companion and a labourer, whom they had taken from his house and given four reals to, to put them on the right road. He indeed had much the best of it, for he returned home with them in great glee, and we in greater at having once more found all our treasure, and right merrily we trudged on, recounting our adventures. We alighted at an inn where there were so many muleteers lying on the floors that we could not take a step without stumbling over pack-saddles and sleeping men. We found a place for our Mother and the nuns (I do not believe it was more than six feet), so that, to make room for them all, they had to stand up all night. The only merit these posadas possessed was to make us long to get out of them as quickly as possible.

And if it had only been the fatigue, the sleepless nights in poverty-stricken resting-places, haunted by muleteers and fleas, the fierce heat which increased her fever, or the winter's sleet and bitter winds, others too have suffered these for the sake of realising a cherished fancy—of seeing some spot lost to the world; but she, this woman nigh on sixty, in pursuance of her lofty object, of the Idea which absorbed her life, had furthermore to suffer the criticism to which these journeys subjected her, and the scandal they gave to the social prejudices of her age. If she had warmer partisans and more devoted followers than ever woman had, she had antagonists (as who has not who is worthy of them?) as bitter and as strong. Many were of the opinion of the papal Nuncio, Sega, when at a later date he inveighed against her as a restless, roving woman; many very learned and virtuous people (amongst them some of the gravest doctors and professors in Salamanca), who, however much they loved and admired her for her virtues ("for I believe," says Master Julian, "that no living person could but love her"), disapproved and condemned her going about from place to place instead of staying quietly in the retirement of her convent. "It is as if they who are not thirsty should contemn a person for drinking; for if they who murmured at her knew the great necessity which spurred her on, they would no longer have done so, even if they had seen her start for Jerusalem." Nevertheless, she had only to see and speak with her greatest detractors, to turn them into her fastest friends, to make them defend her cause against all comers. In the case of her confessors this was especially remarkable. She owed it to a great extent to her own consummate diplomacy,—a diplomacy she scrupled the less to exercise (for although it had been one of her besetting foibles as a child and maiden, she had ceased to care at this period what the world thought of her), inasmuch as it was to forward the Reform, and the Reform and Teresa were now identical. In it she had submerged her individuality, for it she lived; to work for it seemed to give her a fictitious strength, which deserted her when the occasion for effort was over. If she wished to be thought good, if she wished that men should think well of her, it was for the sake of her Reform; that through her at least,—she who was its foundress, and who was responsible for its existence, —no reproach should reach it, no diminution of the lustre which began to give forth so bright and pure a light. "For this cause," says Yepes, "she desired to be esteemed and honoured; and whereas formerly she had fervently supplicated our Lord to remove the opinion men held that she was a saint, yet when she saw the favours God had bestowed upon her, and the many things he had entrusted to her, and how he had chosen her to be the instrument of resuscitating this Order, the constant care of her life was that no imperfections should be noted in her."

Thus it was her custom, on her arrival in a place, as she did on this occasion in Salamanca, to seek out men of weight and learning, and make them her confessors. By this means those who had been prejudiced against her by what they had heard and were disposed to be adverse to her, were infallibly won over, and thenceforth invariably assisted her with their influence, and encouraged her in her projects. Chief amongst the backbiters of Salamanca was one Fray

Bartolomé de Medina,[1] a distinguished lecturer of the University. Teresa never rested until he had heard her in the confessional; to listen to her, and to become her willing servant, was all one. She left him full of amazement, but filled with so profound a respect and love for the woman he had vilified, that it seemed to him a favour little less than divine to be summoned by Teresa when she needed him in Alba. When one of her nuns, to whom he was talking at the torno at Alba, happened to mention her as Mother Teresa, it so angered the old man that he scolded her roundly for her want of reverence, and ordered her in future to speak of her by no less a title than Our Mother Foundress.

The business that had called Teresa to Salamanca, and into which she at once plunged with characteristic energy, was the purchase of a house. The preliminaries had already been adjusted between the prioress Ana de la Encarnacion and the owner, subject to Teresa's approval. It was the only one available in all Salamanca; but besides the price, which they had arranged to pay by degrees, it was necessary to lay out more than a thousand ducats to make it habitable. None of them had dared to face so great a responsibility without Teresa, and so they had waited until she arrived with the precious donkey which bore the first instalment of the price. "None of her daughters," she says in the Foundations, "had been called upon to suffer more than the nuns of Salamanca." For three years they had lived in a ruinous house, before which ran an open sewer, which made it damp and cold. It was out of the way, and alms did not flow in; whilst, greatest of all troubles to the devout nuns, they were deprived of the consolation of the Sacrament on the humble altar of their little church. On the other hand, the house they were about to purchase was almost as bad, and the little band of newly-arrived travellers were filled with dismay —all except Teresa, whose phenomenal daring in such cases was proof against all difficulties. Undaunted by the cost, or by the question how she was to get the money to pay for it, she at once concluded the sale, subject to certain conditions which were to keep the good sisters in a constant ferment of disputes

[1] This Fray Bartolomé de Medina was a very notable person in his day; nor is his manual of the Confessional entirely obsolete in this.

and lawsuits for the next ten years of their lives. The owner of the house was one Pedro de la Vanda, "a knight of good quality although not rich and of indigestible condition." When Teresa arrived in Salamanca he was absent from the city; but although the king's consent (necessary in such cases) to annul the entail was not yet arrived, he had consented to give them possession, and allowed them to set to work on the walls which were to shut in the life of the Carmelites from the outer world. Spurred on by the threats of the owner of the one they occupied, who signified his intention of enforcing payment of another year's rent if they were not out of it by Michaelmas Day, the preparations were pushed on with all haste. Teresa from the window of her cell acted as overseer, and kept her keen eyes on the workmen. Sometimes she ordered wine to be fetched for them; and a legend grew up on the strength of the assertion of one Pedro Hernandez, a carpenter, that on one occasion it had been mysteriously increased. On Michaelmas Eve, before it was daylight, and against the advice of some of their well-wishers, who deprecated their haste—"When needs must, advice is not always easy to follow, if it does not assist," says Teresa—amidst torrents of rain, the nuns moved their few and humble belongings. It had been published throughout the city that the touching ceremony of the Consecration was fixed to take place on the following day, and every one was prepared. Towards afternoon the rain came down so heavily as to make the translation of their possessions from one house to the other almost impossible. Worse still, it poured through the ill-roofed chapel, lustrous with fresh whitewash, and flooded the pavement below. "I tell you, daughters, I fell into great imperfections that day; as it was already known, I knew not what to do, but I was in a grievous state, and I said to our Lord, almost complainingly: That he should either not bid me undertake these works, or that he should remedy that necessity. The good Nicolas Gutierrez" (he whom we have before seen assisting her when she first founded in Salamanca), "in his equable manner, as if there was nothing wrong, bid me gently have no anxiety, for God would remedy it." And so it was; for when St. Michael's morning rose, calm and radiant, over the world of Salamanca; amidst strains of triumphant music, and with great solemnity, Teresa saw raised above the heads of the hushed and expectant crowds—amongst them the most powerful nobles and greatest ladies of Salamanca —the Host, which consecrated alike her convent and her labours.

The next day, as if to temper their joy and triumph, arrived Pedro de la Vanda himself. Oblivious of the condition that the house was to be paid for by instalments, he now demanded full and instant payment. The convent rang with his angry voice. Even Teresa's persuasive tongue failed to control his ungovernable rage; the nuns cowered before his violent gestures. They offered to forego all they had spent, and abandon the house: but this he would by no means hear of, having no mind to lose so good a price.

Three years later the question was still unsettled, and the purchase in abeyance, and for another ten years the disputatious and ill-conditioned knight was a constant thorn in the flesh to the poor nuns. Time, which removes all landmarks, has demolished this. It stood close to the great palace of Monterey, and the house of the Conde de Fuentes, who rased it to the ground to make room for a magnificent convent of Reformed Augustinian nuns. As the curious visitor stands in the lofty and silent nave of the convent church, he treads, perhaps without knowing it, on the site of that humble chapel where Teresa knew so many commingled emotions of doubt and joy. In vain she endeavoured to alleviate her daughters' sufferings by transferring them to another house. She failed to effect it, and the foundation of Salamanca weighed on her to her death. Small wonder that the mild pen of Master Julian (he notes plaintively how he was employed from Our Lady of August to St. Michael's Day, "spending much money with many workmen until the convent was concluded, with its cells, refectory, and church, and all other essentials pertaining to a convent") distils unwonted bitterness:

> I strongly wished that they had taken the counsel given by Christ to his apostles, that when they were not received in one town, they should go to another, and that they had shaken off even to the dust that stuck to their feet, so as not to carry it away with them; which, for me

at least, it was impossible to do, since I had swallowed it and sweated it, with the bitter draughts that blessed soul gave us about his house the whole time until we fled from it. God forgive him. Amen!

Teresa still hoped, however, when at the end of five months she set out to pay a visit to her nuns of Alba, that the matter would be satisfactorily settled. "This business of Pedro de la Vanda," she writes to Bañes, "seems as if it would never finish: I believe that I shall have to go first to Alba so as to save time, for the matter is ticklish, being a dispute between him and his wife," . . . and she adds, "the love of God can bear much, for if there was anything in it that was not [the love of God—Teresa's style is singularly elliptical], it would already have been settled."

Her letter from Alba to her prioress of Salamanca, Ana de la Encarnacion, breathes a rustic calm, a serene pleasure in the natural beauties around her, such as is felt by one who, leaving some dusty and noisy town, and along with it his cares, suddenly finds himself transported into some country hamlet, tranquil, green, and sleepy. She had looked forward to its peaceful seclusion to restore her shattered strength, and the event proved that she was right, for she speaks of being better than was her wont.

Jesus be with your reverence [she writes]. Let me know how you and all are, for well would I desire to be able to enjoy you there as I do these here. I think that here I shall have fewer cares, and I have a grot which looks on to the river, as does the cell also where I sleep, so that I can enjoy it from my bed, which is a great delight to me. I am better to-day than I am wont. Doña Quiteria, still with her fever, says she misses you all. . . . To-day the duchess [of Alba] sent me this trout: it seems so good that I have hired this messenger to send it to my father the master fray Bartolomé de Medina; if it should arrive at dinner-time, let your reverence send it to him by Miguel at once, and the letter along with it; and if later, nevertheless do not fail to send it to him, to see if it will induce him to write a line. Let your reverence fail not to write how you are, and be sure to eat meat these few days; tell the doctor of your weakness, and do not forget to remember me to him. . . . Tell Juana de Jesus to let me know how she is, for her face was very thin when I started. . . . If Lescano [the messenger] should ask for anything, give it him, as I said that if he wanted anything, your reverence would give it him, for I will pay you. I am sure, however, that he will not ask it.

The letter of a loving mother, to whom the slightest

detail connected with the well-being of her children is precious, with a sly, humorous thrust at the grumpy Fray Bartolomé de Medina, whom she has determined to conquer; her courteous inquiries for her friends, the Countess of Monterey and the wife of the corregidor; giving us too a glimpse of the messenger—ragged surely, swarthy, and good-tempered, who, in spite of his rags and poverty, bore the nuns' messages for nothing, and would probably have spurned the bare thought of payment. A strange, ill-assorted, democratic society, such as it still exists in these old-fashioned, old-world places where the nineteenth century has not carried its abominable vulgarity. A letter, too, that only a Spaniard could have written—and that a Castilian—with its kindliness, sobriety, and fun, tinctured with an old-world grace and stateliness that has gone with the age in which it flourished.

But she was not long to delight in the lovely plains and poplar-fringed river of the Tormes. Teresa had been visited in Avila by Doña Ana de Ximena, the widow of Don Francisco Barros de Bracamonte, whose name proves him to have belonged to the noble family of the Bracamontes of Avila. Isabel de Jesus, who had taken the habit two years before at Avila, was this lady's cousin. It was this visit which probably suggested to Teresa the idea of founding in Segovia. The noble widow, who had found but little happiness in life, felt impelled by an irresistible impulse to seek in the obscurity of the cloister what had been denied to her by the world. On her return home she and her cousin Andrés de Ximena devoted themselves to securing the license of the bishop and city of Segovia, which was conceded to them with ease. Unfortunately, however, the bishop's promise was a verbal one. The news reached Teresa in Salamanca. To receive it and a divine locution at the same time bidding her to found was all one. If the locution was a self-deception; if for words inspired by the Divinity she mistook the fervent impulse which gave her no rest,—an impulse felt by lower and less enthusiastic minds in matters on which hang merely material interests, an interior voice which prompts them to do this rather than that,—it was a wholly unconscious one. She was convinced that it was next to impossible even to imagine that Fernandez, who was averse to further foundations, would allow her to desert her post of prioress of the Encarnacion until her term of office was over. "As I was thinking on this," writes Teresa, "the Lord told me to tell him about it, for he would bring it about." Fernandez was then in Salamanca. She wrote to him pointing out how, as he already knew, she had received a precept from the General to found whenever a suitable occasion presented itself; that the city and bishop of Segovia had admitted one of her convents, and that she only awaited his permission to found; that she informed him of it to comply with her conscience, but whatever his decision she would remain content. To her amazement and contrary to all expectation, the visitor interposed no objection. She at once charged her friends at Segovia to set about hiring a house, for her past experiences in Toledo and Valladolid had shown her the advisability of not looking out for a permanent one until she had taken possession. This for many reasons, chiefly indeed that she had not a "blanca" to buy one with, since once the convent was made she depended on God to send her both money and a house to her liking.

On the 8th February 1574 she signed the convent accounts for the last time, and, wasted with fever and sickness, full of trouble in mind and body, she set forth for Medina, with Doña Quiteria of Avila and a nun she took from Alba. She was joined at Salamanca by Isabel de Jesus and a lay sister, both natives of Segovia. She was escorted from Alba by one who appears for the first time in our pages—Antonio Gaitan, one of those anomalous characters so frequent in this history, a gentleman of illustrious birth who, sickened of the world's vanities, of which he had drunk freely, devoted his life to God's service. He shares with Master Julian (although Father Julian was the first) the glory of having been her companion in her longest and most toilsome journeys, and of having lightened hardship and hunger by his unselfish and gentle humility. He undertook the most menial office if necessary, more willingly than any servant. "It is well, daughters," says the grateful Teresa, oblivious of the spell her own personality had cast over these men, "it is well that you should remember them in your prayers, and you would most willingly do so, if you knew the wearisome days and nights, and the hardships of the road that they endured." In Avila the band of travellers was swelled by the addition of another nun and Fray Juan de la Cruz. It is needless to say that Master Julian was of the party. It was March when they set out to cross the bleak mountains of the Guadarramas, the barrier between the two Castilles. On the 18th they arrived in the grand and stately city of Segovia—the grandest and stateliest in Spain. Tired and dust-stained, under cover of night and with all secrecy, they entered the house that had been taken for them. Friendly hands had prepared for their coming, and they found the house provided with many little necessaries, and the church decked and arrayed in readiness for the morrow; so that on the following morning, on St. Joseph's Day, Teresa's favourite and best-loved saint (and the fact filled her with the most intimate satisfaction), the little bell which had now ushered in so many foundations rang in another. Julian de Avila said the first Mass, and placed the Host upon the altar. And then came that contradiction which Teresa looked upon as the best test of the value of her work. During the course of the journey, when Master Julian asked Teresa for the license, and he heard that she had nothing but the Bishop's verbal promise, his heart sank within him, and he already anticipated difficulty with the Provisor (or vicar substitute), the Bishop being then absent in Madrid. His forebodings were but too well founded. When the Provisor heard what had taken place, his fury was boundless. His ecclesiastical dignity thrown to the winds, he sped to the convent church, where he found a canon of his own cathedral saying a Mass. This canon, who happened to be the Bishop's nephew, and afterwards became the Bishop of Guadix and Baeza, struck by the cross over the doorway, and finding on inquiry that it belonged to a freshly-founded convent of Discalced Carmelites who had just arrived, and had only that very morning taken possession, and said their first Mass, entered the humble chapel, and after kneeling a moment before the altar in adoration, sent his page to ask permission to say a Mass. "He was in the midst of it when

the Provisor broke in upon him in a towering rage with the rough exclamation: 'You had better have left it unsaid!'"
"Well do I believe," says Master Julian, ascribing to another what his own feelings would have been under the like circumstances, "that, however great the canon's devotion, it left him at that moment." He next looked about him for the offenders. The nuns had already retired, and Master Julian, who was a witness of his tempestuous arrival, considering that prudence was the better part of valour, discreetly hid himself behind a staircase there happened to be in the gateway. "The Provisor fell, however, upon St. John of the Cross: 'Who has placed this here, father?' said he. 'Get it all cleared away at once; indeed I have a good mind to send you to prison.' And I believe it was only his being a friar that saved him, for I am convinced that if it had been me, I should certainly that time at least have gone there. Nor would it have been strange that I who had so often shut up nuns, should have been shut up for once myself, although, as they did it from choice, they do not feel it so much as I should have done." The *naïf* Father Julian is not exempt from a sense of shame as he reflects on his cowardice, and in a bolder tone he adds:

After all, I did not flee from the dungeon, but only hid myself so as to avoid being sent there. The Provisor made such haste to undo all that had been done that St. Joseph's night, that this great tempest did not pass over. He sent an alguacil to prevent any one saying Mass, and he sent a priest of his own to say one in order to consume the Host. The mother and sisters were doubtless witnesses of the ease with which their labours were undone. When I escaped I went to the Jesuits' college to relate what had happened; and although the rector did all he could, and went straight to speak with the Provisor, he made no impression on him. He went about in search of the persons who had been present at the granting of the license, and after much contention about the matter it was agreed that a judicial inquiry should be instituted as to how the license had been given. Now with this it seemed the matter was settled. We stated our case before the notary with very reliable witnesses, and so the Provisor could not avoid granting the license for saying Mass, although he refused to allow us to have the Host; and in this he was right, for the house was a hired one, and the chapel was in the gateway; and as to this our Mother was also agreed, as she knew that the mere fact of saying Mass was enough to take possession. In the midst of this great tempest our Holy Mother showed her great valour, for she was neither agitated nor overwhelmed, nor did she lose heart. On the contrary, she spoke to the Provisor with great boldness, mingled with great courtesy, so that it could be seen that the Lord helped her.

For nothing could quell or cast more than a momentary shadow over her indomitable spirit. When the Provisor took the extreme resolve of posting an alguacil at the church door, she merely wondered why, as it could only frighten those within; and she herself attached no importance to anything that happened when once possession had been secured. The motive for this outburst on the part of the Provisor, who acted like a veritable jack-in-office, was ruffled dignity at not having been himself consulted; and "if he had been," says Teresa, one of the shrewdest judges of character, "we should have sped worse than we did." She owed much to the friendly offices of the good canon, whom she doubted not that God had led to her convent that morning. With that strange mixture of worldliness and sanctity so conspicuous in her, she reminded him of the obligations he was under to assist her—obligations imposed on him by kinship (which in the Spain of that day formed a link as strong as in the patriarchal ages of the world), her cousin Doña Maria de Tapia being his aunt. Thenceforth, as long as she remained in Segovia, he acted as her chaplain and confessor.

What struck him most particularly in her upright and generous character (and his testimony is not without importance, from a man who seems to have been particularly single-hearted and truthful), was her silence about herself. From which fact, and the things he afterwards heard about her, he concludes, in his letter to the General of the Order, dated 1606, that as they had already gone through so many searching ordeals, and she was now sure of herself, she had no longer any motive to divulge them to the directors chance threw in her way, shrinking, as she always did, from being taken for a saint. The impression she left on him was the indelible one she left on all whom accident or their good fortune brought under her influence. On the day he received the news of her death, the accidental sight of one of her books (the *Camino de la Perfeccion*, which he had made one of his servants copy out for him unknown to the saint), which had for long been mislaid, and then strangely reappeared, affected him so strangely that he fell back in the arms of a brother ecclesiastic, moved to floods of tears.

Almost at the same moment that Teresa established a new house of her Order in Segovia, that of Pastrana, which had cost her so many bitter moments, was undone. The exactions, the folly, and the caprice of its unfortunate patroness, who, on the death of her husband, Ruy Gomez, in 1573, in the first violence of her grief, insisted on assuming the habit of the Discalced Carmelites, and entering the community of Pastrana, had led to this extreme resolution. As may be supposed, from the very first an incompatibility existed between the good nuns of Pastrana and their self-imposed inmate—an incompatibility which, as every one foresaw it must, presently grew into an insurmountable antipathy. Mariano, whom she had forced to give her the habit at her dead husband's bedside,—not a very clean one, according to the chronicler,—uneasily conscious of the coming storm, made all haste to set out for Andalucia. When the prioress (that Isabel de Sto. Domingo who was so scandalised in Toledo at Teresa's conferences with the ragged Andrada), ruthlessly roused from her slumbers at two in the morning by Fray Baltasar de Jesus knocking at the convent gates, heard from his lips that the princess—come to bewail her widowhood within its walls—was on the road to Pastrana in a cart (she had refused to come in her coach), she exclaimed, "The princess a nun! Then I give up this house for lost!"

There were, no doubt, faults on both sides: it would seem to be the prerogative of religion to develop all the hardness and rigidity of human nature. These good sisters who had renounced their lives could be as stern and rigorous as they were generally sweet, gentle, and beneficent. And although we must allow considerable latitude to the account given by the chronicler, who, actuated by a natural, to some extent a laudable, instinct to glorify his Order by showing that the fault was all on one side, still the nuns seem never to have forgotten the fact that the princess was their patroness, and that they owed many favours to her hand, and to have borne her freaks as gently and patiently as possible until they could bear them no longer.

The first demand of the princess when she arrived with her mother, the Princess of Mélito, at eight in the morning, was that the habit should be given to two of her waiting-women; and when the prioress replied that she could not comply without the superior's consent, she asked imperiously, "What right have the friars to meddle with my convent?" After consulting with the prior of Pastrana, Fr. Baltasar, it was resolved to do as she wished. A more harmless freak, but one which probably gave great offence to these quiet, retired women, reared in the strictest obedience, was to insist on sitting in one of the lowest places in the refectory, instead of accepting the seat of honour which had been reserved for her close to the prioress. It was proposed, after some consultation with her mother, to set aside part of the convent for her use, and that of her servants, where she could receive her visitors without interrupting the discipline of the community, whilst she herself could enter whenever she liked by a private door. This she refused. The day after the celebration of her husband's obsequies, the Bishop of Segorbe and other great personages arrived to pay their visits of condolence. In spite of the prioress's remonstrances, who begged her to receive them at the grating of the church, the princess insisted on the gates being thrown open, and the convent turned into a miniature court. The indignation of the nuns may be imagined as they thus saw their tranquillity invaded, not merely by the bishop and a train of lordly visitors ("for lords do not think they are lords if they obey laws," remarks the chronicler with dry acumen), but by their men-at-arms and lackeys. The rest of her conduct was on a par with this. She insisted on having two secular women to wait on her, and refused with disdain the offers of the worthy prioress, who proffered her services and those of the community, especially of the two novices to whom she had herself forced them to give the habit.

Teresa was appealed to, and wrote to the petulant and self-willed princess, but in vain. The great lady who made the nuns serve her on their bended knees and address her by her titles, was in no mood to listen to reason. The prioress and two of the most aged nuns of the community solemnly warned her that if she persisted in her conduct there was no help for it but that they should leave the convent. In high dudgeon she retired to a hermitage in the convent garden, where, from its being outside the cloister boundaries, none of the nuns could go to her. Still obedient and anxious to conciliate her, they sent her the two novices, who were not as yet so strictly shut out from the world, to wait upon her. Here the stern, weird old hermit Catalina de Cardona (whose life, even for an age steeped in romance, is particularly strange and striking) paid the Princess of Eboli a visit. On her return one night from singing Matins with the nuns in the choir, Catalina, herself a woman of highest rank, with the familiarity of age and old friendship (in former life she had been long a trusted inmate of Ruy Gomez's household), told her bluntly to beware how she treated the nuns, for, said she, "as I was at Matins I saw angels amongst them, guarding them with drawn swords." But the princess was not to be so easily terrified by the mystic threats of the old visionary. At last open hostilities broke out. She abandoned the hermitage and betook herself to a house close by, where she dwelt in seclusion, still wearing the garb of the Carmelites ; and presently, as might have been foreseen, she took up her abode in the gaunt, gray old palace which stands protecting the walls of Pastrana, facing the lovely vega and the jagged spurs of the sierras of Cuenca. Worse than all, with a breach of faith impossible to excuse, whatever the reasons she may have felt she had for her bitterness against the community, she ceased making the allowance that had been assigned to it by Ruy Gomez. Her grief had already subsided, and, either unable or unwilling to recognise that the inflexible laws of convent discipline should be more imperious with a few poor humble women, who subsisted on her alms, than her own capricious and imperious will, resenting their firmness, the alms ceased, and she left them to struggle alone as they best might with their necessities.

After an anxious consultation between Teresa, the Provincial, Fr. Angel de Salazar ; Fr. Pedro Fernandez, the visitor ; Bañes, and Fr. Hernando de Castillo, it was decided that, after requesting the princess once more to attend to the necessary sustenance of the convent, the only alternative was to abandon it. Fr. Hernando, an old and trusted confidant of Ruy Gomez, was the bearer of the embassy. But she broke out into such violent invectives against the nuns that it was easy to see that all she desired was to be rid of them. The Provincial, Fr. Angel de Salazar, was sent to Pastrana, and once more he and Fr. Hernando returned to the palace on their ungrateful mission. This time the princess, feigning illness, refused to see them, and the servants made no secret of their mistress's intentions. On hearing this, Teresa, then in Salamanca, instructed the prioress as to what she was to do. And although the nuns professed themselves willing to suffer rather than abandon their house, she replied that there was now no help for it, as the heads of the Order had decided otherwise, and to go on slowly making preparations, so as to be in readiness to leave it when she should write to them from Segovia, whither she was on the eve of her departure.

The princess was but ill prepared for this trait of resolution and energy on the part of those whom for more than a year she had tortured with her caprices. The prioress sent for the corregidor and a notary, in whose presence she delivered up to the former all the jewels and presents the princess had ever given them. With the inventory in her hands she checked them off one by one till the number was complete. The rumour got about that the nuns were going. The princess affected to be deeply distressed, and sent the corregidor to tell them that she would place guards at the convent gates. The prioress answered that it was now too late. The princess (with a touch of humour truly delightful) then signified her consent, if they would agree to take with them the two unfortunate waiting-women, she being now anxious to get them off her hands. This, they replied, they would do in the case of Ana de la Encarnacion, who was needy and portionless; but as to the other, who was better off, her Excellency might arrange about her even as she thought fit.

The Princess of Eboli never darkened Teresa's life again, and her strange, meteoric individuality, full of passion and uncontrollable impulses, has flitted across the pages of my history for the last time. Henceforth she is swallowed up in the dark gulf of state intrigue of the age. Her unhappy passion for Antonio Perez, and its consequences, I have already dwelt on. As she disappears, and the horizon of her life grows dim, I feel a strange, inexplicable sympathy for that proud, headstrong, self-willed character (for if she sinned she suffered more). Her strange and pathetic fate was a meet ending to her restless, agitated life. But in justice to the dead, let me try to exonerate her memory from the charge which has darkened her fame from that day to this, —that in an impulse of pitiful and malignant revenge she denounced Teresa's book of her Life to the Inquisition. It has never been proved that she did so. The only argument of any weight that has been brought in support of such a charge, is that no one was so likely, considering the circumstances, to have done so as she, and that it was so denounced by a woman and a lady of high rank. Impetuous and uncontrollable as she was, if she denounced it at all, it would have been when the motives for her anger against Teresa and her nuns were still fresh, and rankling in her mind. If I have read her character aright, she was incapable of patiently waiting for an opportunity to do so black an injury in cold blood. Plunged as she was in the vortex of the court life of her time, Teresa and her nuns must long have faded from her brain at the date (1579) when she is supposed to have made the denouncement.

A strange and picturesque type of the great lady of the period, she flashed for a moment over the life of the great foundress, and both of them have now become phantoms, to all except a few enthusiastic searchers into the past, on the dim background of Tradition and History!

CHAPTER XVI

THE FATE OF THE CONVENT OF PASTRANA

IT was early in April (according to Lafuente) when Master Julian and Antonio Gaitan arrived in Pastrana to finish the last sad work of demolition, and bear the nuns to Segovia. They kept their mission as secret as possible. After speaking with the prioress, who was on the look-out for them, and anxious to be gone, they hired five carts to take the nuns and such few treasures as they could call their own. When they had concluded the preparations, and laid in their little stock of provisions for the journey the day before they started, at the last Carmelite Mass which was to echo through the little church which a few hours thence would be full of the silence of emptiness and desolation, the Host was solemnly consumed. So as not to rouse the princess's suspicion, they were to start at midnight. But in spite of their precautions it got to her ears, and she sent one of her household "to say many things" (we can well imagine what they were), which it was perhaps as well that the fearful ears of Master Julian were spared, the shower of abuse falling instead on Fray Gabriel, a Discalced Carmelite of Pastrana.

At midnight a little procession of closely-veiled nuns, escorted by priests and friars, sallied out from the convent gates, which closed on their retreating forms for the last time, and like shadows lost in the greater shadow of the night, wended their way up the silent and irregular street (the convent which still exists—the home of another religious community—lies in a hollow) which led to the outskirts of the town. The five carts were waiting for them on the summit of the hill. "And as no one was with us, and we crept on in silence, half-fleeing as it were, although not from God, but from men, it seemed like the flight of David, when he fled barefoot with his followers before Absalom; save that we had no Shimei to curse us, but God, who accompanied us, aiding us, and comforting us; for in this case it needed as much courage to flee as in others to attack." It is Master Julian who speaks, and tells the story in his own charming and gossiping fashion.

"When we arrived at where the carts were waiting, which was at some little distance from the town, we all placed ourselves in marching order; and, so that danger of sea (!) as well as of land might not be wanting, on the second or third day of our journey, we had to cross a river, which I think is the same as that which passes by Alcalá de Henares. It is generally crossed in a ferry-boat, but the drivers, who knew the country well, said that they would not go in the boat, which was at some distance off; that they could easily cross by the ford, and that all our company could go and cross in the boat. Afraid that there might be some difficulty, I stayed alone with the drivers, and entered the river on horseback, which to all appearance was not very deep. Upon this the five carts enter in single file; when the front one got to a deep and narrow current there was in the middle of the river, which in that place was very wide, the mules refused to enter, and the more the drivers urged them on, the more they held back, and if they made a few steps forward they sank and knelt down as if they were going to the bottom. I shouted to them to turn back, but even had they wanted to, it was now impossible. I found myself in great distress, and with none to help me, for all the others had gone save the carters and the nuns. As for the poor nuns, some of them seemed about to faint; whilst the drivers shouted to the mules, the nuns must have also shouted to God. The Lord willed that by pure dint of shouting and strength one of the carts got through. When this, which had the best mules, was drawn up in safety on the bank, the mules were unyoked, and attached to each cart by turns, so that with the help of four mules all the carts crossed safely; and thus were we delivered from this danger, although I resolved never again to believe drivers in a matter of such importance, who, to save themselves the trouble of yoking and unyoking their mules

(Master Julian might also have added, to save the expense; for the ferry-boat charges, being private monopolies, are to this day extravagantly high in Spain), "refused to go in the boat and put themselves in great peril."

The chronicler has it that at the very moment when the nuns saw themselves in imminent danger of a watery grave, Teresa requested her daughters in Segovia to pray for them. No doubt she repeated the request as often as she thought of the travellers exposed to all the perils of travel, when travel was full of danger. Nevertheless the inference drawn by the chronicler is obvious.

After several more days of constant journeying, often retarded by other mischances and hardships, left by Master Julian at the bottom of his inkpot, the travellers emerged from the vast deserts and shaggy pine forests, to-day as wild, desolate, and deserted as they were then, between Guadalajara and Segovia, which they entered on the 4th or 5th of April. Teresa received the wanderers with heartfelt joy; and Master Julian and Antonio Gaitan, their mission ended, returned to their several homes, highly pleased at the success of their labours in so good a cause, and more than ever resolved to follow their Mother wherever she should see fit to lead them.

Nor was the foundation of Segovia accomplished without a sore struggle. Julian de Avila and Antonio Gaitan, before they departed, had bargained for a house, but in such a sorry state as to draw from Teresa the remark that she knew not where their eyes were when they wanted to buy such a place. When she at last found one to her liking (it still remains, spite of all the changes of time, the home of her daughters), she found herself plunged head and ears in contentions and lawsuits. The cathedral chapter held a mortgage over the house, and insisted on being paid. The Franciscan friars and the monks of the Order of Mercy objected to the vicinity of another convent, subsisting like themselves on the alms of the faithful. However, the canons' mouths were shut with money; the Franciscans calmed down; and a few days before Michaelmas the nuns stole into their new house, unperceived by the mercenaries who still persisted in their suit. Nevertheless, they too, seeing that their enemies were in possession, were glad to hold their peace for a gift of money.

It may be asked how it was that a woman who of herself was nothing and had nothing, beyond her staff and her rosary, came to have the administration of large sums of money,—and that at the very time when she was writing to her niece, Maria Bautista of Valladolid, to get some one to lend her a few reals to relieve her most pressing wants in the Encarnacion, until such time as she was paid the money sent her by her brother ("whether it be little or much," she writes, "get it for me!"); how it was that she arrived in Segovia without a farthing, and in a few months bought a house which cost 4600 ducats, besides being able to defray the expense of making it fit for the purposes of a convent?

It must be remembered that there was then no lack of titled and wealthy novices, who accounted it a privilege and a glory to lay their rank and their riches on the altars of a convent. Nor can we judge of this strange century from a modern standpoint. In those days the cloister by no means implied the frigid dearth of affection and human interest which a northern mind and a Protestant standpoint instinctively attach to it. Even now, if it were not for the constant poverty which menaces every moment of their existence, the life of a Spanish community is by no means a mere round of dull, sour, monotonous discipline and observance. Merry enough eyes gleam from under the white coif; shrewd and voluble tongues, and no less nimble wits, discourse behind the iron grating as freely as if it did not exist. The nuns have their visitors—the bishop; their own chaplain; old, sundried, wrinkled priests; great ladies, who entertain them with a mixture of profanity and godliness; shabby Beatas, with whom they bemoan their ailments and crunch sweetmeats. For it is the imagination which forges these grim spectres that haunt the northern intellect. And the Spaniard has little or none; he cannot dread what he does not see; what has for him no concrete existence. In those days especially, when the existence of great ladies in their vast palaces, regulated by a severe ceremonial, was in itself monastic (even now amongst the aristocracy of Spain, who adhere to the old traditions, the women of the family dress and live like

Beatas), the transition to the cloister was by no means great. In the case of Teresa's foundation at Segovia, as we have seen in that of her previous ones, she set forth dependent on what the Lord might send her—and it never failed to come in the shape of well-dowered novices. In Segovia she bought the house with the dower of the widowed Ana de Ximena and her daughter, Maria de Bracamonte, who were quickly followed by a wife, Mariana Monte de Velosillo—she entering the cloister and her husband the priesthood on one and the same day.

In temporal affairs Teresa was as shrewd and competent an administrator as she was great in spiritual ones. As poverty never stood in the way of her accepting a novice—" I never remember my not receiving one who gave me satisfaction "—and as rank and riches, even if supported by the recommendations of her most esteemed confessors, could never cross the pure threshold of her convents without being accompanied by the qualifications she so rigidly exacted, so, although she kept a keen eye on virtue, it was no less keenly fixed on the dower. "In Medina," she writes to her absent brother, Lorenzo, "one has entered with 8000 ducats, and another is about to enter here (Toledo) with 9000, and this although I asked nothing." "May the Lord reward you for the alms you have decided to bestow on the convent you enter," she wrote to Isabel de Jesus; "for it is a great deal. It will be a great consolation to your grace to do what the Lord counsels, to give yourself to him, and what you have to the poor for his sake. And, considering what your grace has received, it does not seem to me that you could have given less than what you do; and since you give all you have, it is not a little that you do, nor will your reward be small." Again, speaking of another nun, she says, "Yesterday we gave the habit to a maiden of very good disposition, and I believe she will have something, and even a great deal, with which to aid us. She is just the thing for us." Again, writing from this very foundation of Segovia, she mentions to Maria Bautista that she has just heard of a nun of excellent parts with a dower of 2000 ducats, "which will help to pay for the house."

Yet, withal, so profoundly disinterested was she for herself and her convents that, at a later date, seeing the mischief in the inevitable relaxation in convent manners and discipline introduced into them by the admission of women of high rank, she came to the firm determination to admit no more. Nor does her sanctity lose, but rather gain, by this mixture of worldly forethought and shrewdness, without which she could not have impressed herself as she did upon her century. The ecstatic would have wearied us to death long ago by the monotony of her raptures. Human nature refuses to be kept so long at such a strain. It is the twists and turns, the cranks and idiosyncrasies, the angles here, the asperities there, that we love to explore,—poor mortals ever bent on dissecting our own devious nature, which as constantly escapes from us. To many minds the skeleton of an apple-tree, jagged and gnarled, and covered with rough fruit spurs, often exercises a more powerful fascination than the regular branches and pyramidal form of the tall and stately larch.

September was wearing to its close before the nuns established themselves in their new home. The day after she had seen them settled she set forth for Avila.

Increasing years, infirmities, and cares have begun to tell their tale upon her. For the first time she begins to complain of failing sight, and to lean more heavily on the staff (the gift of her brother from the Indies) which supported her steps through the convent corridors. To Maria de Bautista she describes herself as so worn out and old as to startle her. Death has thinned the first ranks of the Carmelite nuns. Isabel de los Angeles has passed away in Medina, and Beatriz de la Encarnacion at Valladolid. It would be impossible, without drawing out this book to too great a length, to dwell on the virtues of these her humbler followers. Their end was such as had been their life. Isabel de los Angeles caught consumption from a sick nun she was nursing, and lingered for six months. On the day she died, to the astonishment of the nuns, who had left her prostrate with pain and agony, they found on their return from Mass that she had mysteriously rallied. When they questioned her she told them that the Mother Teresa had been with her, who after gently stroking her face and blessing her, had said, "Daughter, do not be silly, and have no fear, but great confidence in what your Spouse did for you; for the glory is great, and be sure that to-day you shall enjoy it." It was noted afterwards (memory and desire play strange tricks) that at the moment she passed away, Teresa (in Segovia) fell into an ecstasy, and saw the scene that was at that moment passing far away at Medina del Campo.

So great was the hold she had taken on the imagination of her enthusiastic disciples that few who had known her in life failed to see her presence in that mysterious moment when they hovered between two dim and unknown eternities. And to this day, those who enter her rule still assert and believe that their last hours are soothed by the radiant presence of their great foundress and exemplar.

It had been Teresa's intention, if she could have found time, to proceed to Valladolid, where Maria de Bautista had not been without her cares. Sleepless nights spent beside the sickbed of a dying nun, and the tiresome contention in which she saw herself involved with the relatives of a novice, still little more than a child, had filled her with that longing for repose which at times sweeps over the most actively inclined. "You would not have better health, but worse," replies Teresa (who, strangely enough, considering her agitated and restless life, constantly asserted that her natural inclination lay towards solitude), "if you enjoyed the tranquillity you speak of; and this I am sure of, because I know your character, and so the thought of your labours does not distress me; you have got to be a saint in some way; and to desire solitude is better than to enjoy it. . . . Do not be vexed with me, for I have already told you how much I should like to come: it would be false to say that I do not desire it. So many great people and so much bustle will be a great fatigue to me; but I will go through all to see you." What, however, she had dreamt was possible in July had become impossible in September. The foundation of Segovia had kept her longer than she had bargained for. She consoles her prioress gently for the inevitable disappointment. Her niece would only be startled to see her so old and worn out. After all, her visit would soon come to an end, like everything in life, and she entreats her not to let it pain her, although in her pain she finds consolation for her own at being obliged to start for Avila without seeing her. She holds out hopes of being able, when the Lord so disposes, of making her a long visit; "for to see each other for so short a time is a great weariness; the time all slips away in visits, and we lose our sleep for the sake of talking." For a fresh foundation was already engaging Teresa's thoughts—that of Veas. Besides which, only seven or eight days remained before her term of office expired in the Encarnacion; and her presence there was unavoidably necessary. Nor did she lose a moment; for the day following that on which she placed her daughters in the peaceable possession of their house, she bent her footsteps homewards.

Outside Segovia, a narrow street winds down to the great Dominican monastery, which stands in a bower of foliage close to the lovely stream of the Eresma. Teresa must have surveyed with more than usual interest the splendid shrine, built by the Catholic kings over the famous cave, lost amongst the cliffs and underwood of the river bank, which was the scene of the penances of that other great founder of an Order, Sto. Domingo of Guzman.[1] Here she tarried, it would seem, as was the custom of all travellers in that age, to seek a benediction on her labours and journey at the hands of one with whom, in spite of the century that rolled between them, she felt a spiritual kinship. It was not the first time she had visited it, for it was here on St. Albert's Day (the 7th August), as she approached the altar to communicate, that, according to the chronicler, she had seen Christ on her right hand and St. Albert on her left. Presently Christ disappeared, leaving her alone with St. Albert, to whom she commended her nascent Order. It was then that St. Albert counselled the separation of the new and vigorous offshoot from the ancient stock, and its formation into a separate province. The basis for this legend may be small enough, but it conclusively proves that even at this period Teresa was nourishing the thought which afterwards came to be an accomplished fact, viz. the erection of the Discalced Carmelites into a self-governing body. Now, ere she bade farewell to Segovia, and the mules which were to bear her to Avila waited at the monastery gate

[1] Better known to English readers as St. Dominic.

as she once more knelt in prayer in the saint's cave, she had other visions, perhaps the more carefully preserved by Yangues, who was present, as they were flattering to the Order of which he was a member. We must accept the narrative for that of a man who, however excellent, was deeply tinged, as all were, with the superstition of the age, when piety did not stop at a little pious exaggeration—even a little pious fraud (unconscious enough)—to serve a pious purpose.

After remaining for half an hour in prayer, to the wonder of the prior and monks who accompanied her and waited to bid her farewell, Yangues noticed that her face was flushed and radiant, and wet with tears. She replied to his inquiries that Sto. Domingo had appeared to her in great splendour and glory, and had promised to favour her Order. After shriving his great penitent, Yangues led her to a little chapel which contained a carved image of the founder of his Order. Here, he says, Sto. Domingo appeared to her again, and told her of the great conflicts he had waged with devils in that same spot, and the celestial favours he had there received. "And when the mother asked him why he always appeared to her on her left hand" (and now the Dominican's account becomes a little suspicious), "because, said he, the right hand belongs to the Lord, and the holy Mother also added that the image of the glorious Sto. Domingo that stood in the chapel was the very portrait of the saint himself."

But the journey was no vision, but a very real thing; and presently the monastery, buried amongst the stately poplars that tower against the rocky eminence, which in that place completely shrouds the city from view, faded from her sight, and the mules' slow tread mingled with the murmurs of the river, rushing through the hollow at her feet.

CHAPTER XVII

HISTORY OF CASILDA DE PADILLA—FOUNDATION OF VEAS

ON the 30th of September Teresa left Segovia. She arrived at Avila in time to resign her three years' term of office as prioress of the Encarnacion.

In spite of the wishes of the community, which would fain have elected her a second time, she used her influence in favour of Isabel de la Cruz, and retired to San José, where for a brief space she once more took up the reins of government. Her daughters, however, did not enjoy her presence long, for towards the close of the year we find her in Valladolid, where the state of her convent filled her with the most heartfelt satisfaction. Of two novices especially, the entrance of one of whom at least—for the other was but a poor peasant girl—must have caused a profound sensation in the little world of Valladolid,—she writes in enthusiastic praise. This was Casilda de Padilla, the youngest daughter of the Adelantado of Castille[1] and Doña Beatriz de Acuña, who a few months before, at the age of thirteen, after a long struggle with her family, had made her escape from them and assumed the habit of a Discalced Carmelite nun.

The history of this girl plunges us back into that strange century of fierce fanaticism and religious ardour. Sprung from two of the noblest houses of Castille (her father was Adelantado of Castille, and her mother a sister of the Count of Buendia), she was the youngest of four children, three of

---

[1] An adelantado was originally the governor in time of peace,—in time of war the captain-general—of a frontier province. As time went by this title became invested in the noble family of the Padillas, to whom Philip II. granted the title of Counts of Santa Gadea. Padilla, the hero of the Comuneros, was a member of this family.

whom had so well responded to the virtuous impulses implanted in them by their mother—she had been left a widow early in life—that, unhesitatingly bidding farewell to a world they had scarcely entered upon, they buried their youth in the cloister. At seventeen Antonio, the heir, spurned his titles under foot and entered the Society of Jesus; the sister who succeeded him in his estates, valuing them as little as her brother, resigned them in her turn and became a nun; the third elected to live a life of chastity and edification with her mother; and Casilda alone was left to carry on the traditions and heritages of her race. The last hope of two proud and ancient families, she was barely ten or eleven when her kinsmen procured a dispensation from the Pope and married her to her uncle, her father's brother.

"The Lord did not will," writes Teresa, "that the daughter of such a mother and the sister of such brothers should be any more deceived than they, and so it came about as I shall now relate. Scarcely did the child begin to delight in the clothes and ornaments of the world, which conformably to her rank were enough to captivate the fancy of one of her tender years, than the Lord began to give her light, although then she did not understand it. After spending the day very happily with her husband, for she loved him more dearly than his age seemed to warrant, a great sadness came over her, when she saw how the day had ended, and that so must all days end.

"She began to feel so great a sadness that she could not hide it from her husband, nor did she know the reason of it nor what to say to him, although he asked her. At this time he had occasion to take a journey, which took him to a great distance from home, and as she loved him so dearly, she felt it greatly. But now the Lord discovered to her the reason of her grief; that it was to incline her soul to what will never end, and she began to think how her brother and sisters had taken the safest road, leaving her in the perils of the world. This on the one side; on the other the thought that she had no remedy,—for she knew not as yet that her betrothal did not hinder her becoming a nun,—distressed her greatly, and above all the love she bore her husband prevented her taking a resolution, and so she struggled with her grief. As the Lord willed her for himself, this love gradually lost its hold on her, and the desire to abandon all grew stronger. At this time she was moved solely by the desire of saving herself, and seeking the best way of doing so, since it seemed to her that if she were plunged farther in worldly things she would forget to solicit those of eternity, for at so early an age did God inspire her with this wisdom to seek how she might gain that which has no ending. . . . She began to discuss it with her sister. The latter dissuaded her from what she looked upon as a childish whim, and told her that the fact of being married did not interfere with her salvation. She answered then, Why had she left it [the world]? And some time passed away during which her desire grew ever stronger, although her mother dared say nothing, for she, perchance, it was that warred against her with her holy prayers."

It was at this time that the poor little distraught and melancholy child went with her grandmother to see a lay sister take the habit in Teresa's convent. From that moment she fell a victim to the irresistible and relentless attraction of the cloister, and her fate was decided.

". . . One morning, when she and her sister accompanied her mother to the convent, as chance would have it they entered inside the monastery, little thinking that she would do what she did. When she found herself inside no one was able to cast her out. So did she weep and plead to be allowed to remain that every one was amazed. Her mother, although secretly glad, was in fear of her kinsfolk, and would fain have got her away so that they might not say she had persuaded her to it, and the prioress also was of the same mind, for it seemed to her she was too young, and further proof was needed. This happened in the morning; they were forced to remain until the evening, and sent for her confessor, the Father Master Fray Domingo (Bañes). . . . He saw at once that it was the spirit of the Lord, and helped her greatly, enduring much from her relatives on that account. He promised her to assist her to return some other day. With great persuasion, and for the sake of her mother, so that no blame might attach to her in the matter, she went away this time. Her mother secretly began to acquaint her kinsmen with what had happened, so that if it came to her husband's ears he might not charge her with having concealed it from him.

"They said it was a childish freak, and that she should wait until she was older, as she was not yet turned twelve. She asked them how it was that they accounted her old enough to be married and left to the world, and yet not old enough to give herself to God. From the things she said it was indeed patent that it was not she who spoke in this. It could not be kept so secret but that her husband was warned of it; when she knew of it she could not endure to wait for his return; and one day—it was the festival of the Conception—being in her grandmother's house, who was also her mother-in-law, and knew nothing of this, she implored her to let her go with her governess to divert herself a little in the country; her grandmother, in order to please her, sent her in a cart with her servants. She gave one of them money, and begged him to wait for her at the convent door with some bundles of vine-shoots; and she made them take a roundabout road so that they brought her close to this house. When she got to the door she told them to ask for a jug of water at the torno, and that they were not to say who it was for, and she got down in great haste: they answered they would bring it to her out there; she would have none of it. The vine-shoots were there already; she told them to tell the nuns to come to the door to get them, and placed herself close beside it, and as soon as it was opened she slipped inside, and ran to embrace Our Lady, weeping, and begging the prioress not to cast her out. Loud were the shouts of the servants and the blows they battered on the door: she went to speak to them at the grating, and told them that on no account would she come forth, and bade them take the news to her mother. The women who accompanied her were objects of compassion; as for her, she cared little for it all. When the grandmother heard the news she at once sped to the convent. In short, neither she, nor her uncle, nor her husband, who, when he came, did his utmost to speak to her at the grating, did more than torment her by their presence, and leave her more firmly resolved than ever. . . . When her husband and kinsmen saw how little good it was to try to get her out of her own free will, they resorted to force; and so procured a Royal Warrant to get her out of the monastery, and constrain the nuns to set her at liberty. During all this time, which was from the Conception until Innocent's Day, when they took her away, she remained in the monastery without taking the habit, performing all the observances of the Order as if she had received it, and with the utmost happiness. On that day, when the 'law' came for her, they took her to a gentleman's house. She was borne away, sobbing bitterly, and asking why they tormented her, since nothing they could do would change her resolution. Here monks as well as other persons—some because it seemed to them a freak; others because they wished her to enjoy her rank—did their utmost to persuade her. . . . When they saw it was no good, in order to detain her for a time, they placed her in her mother's house, who, now wearied of witnessing such disturbances, instead of helping her at all, was, as it seemed, against her; her confessor's opposition also was extreme, so that except God she had no one on her side in whom she could confide but a waiting-woman of her mother's. So she passed through great tribulation and distress until she accomplished her twelfth year, when she found out that since they could not prevent her being a nun, they were thinking of taking her to the convent where her sister was, on account of the life not being so strict.

"No sooner did this come to her knowledge than she resolved to take any means whereby she might accomplish her intent: and so one day, when she went to Mass with her mother, being left in the church whilst her mother was confessing in the confessional, she begged her governess to go and ask one of the padres to say a Mass for her, and when the coast was clear, put her chapins in her sleeve, gathered up her skirts, and set forth with all haste for the convent, which was at a great distance off. Her governess, as soon as she found her gone, ran after her, and when she got close to her, besought a man to detain her: afterwards he said that he was powerless to move, and so did nothing. She had barely got within the outside gates of the convent, and shut the gates and begun to call, than the governess arrived,—but by that time she was already inside, and they at once gave her the habit, and so ended the good beginnings that the Lord had placed in her."

"Although we look for much from Estefania, who to my thinking is a saint," writes Teresa to Don Teutonio de Braganza, "Sister Casilda fills me with astonishment, for surely I find her one both inside and out: if God keeps her she will be a great saint, for that it is his doing is clearly seen. Her vocation is great—more than seems possible at her age. Her happiness and humility so great as to astonish me!"

So far Teresa, and one scarcely knows which to admire most: the indomitable resolution, the force of will, the sly cunning displayed by a child of scarcely more than eleven years, in the prosecution of her object; the folly of a grave Dominican and man of letters like Bañes, finding in the escapades of the self-willed culprit the "spirit of God," and lending her a hand to defy her relatives; or the seriousness and good faith with which Teresa chronicles misdemeanours for which an easy and simple act of grace might seem to have commended itself as the most apposite and efficient remedy. At all events Casilda got her will, and the feud she bred between the nuns and the two most powerful families of Valladolid, who considered, and perhaps with reason, that they had been unjustly defrauded of their last remaining representative in the direct line, was so bitter as to defy even Teresa's attempts to heal it.

Precocious sanctity, like precocious genius, is rarely trustworthy! Little more is known of the Adelantado of Castille's daughter, whose renunciation of her rank and vast estates to join the sisters of Valladolid must have excited so profound a sensation in the little world of her day. Her claim to the notice of posterity begins and ends with the childish tragedy—the last scene of which was enacted when at sixteen she made her final profession—a profession which Gracian himself delayed in order to receive the vows of so illustrious a subject. In after years—once at least—Casilda was elected prioress: a post she no doubt owed as much to her birth and social position, to which a religious community is as susceptible as the rest of humanity, as to her merit.

But whatever her excellences—and they may have been

many—she obscured them in the eyes of the Order on which her entrance had cast a brief and fugitive lustre by abandoning it to enter a Franciscan convent at Burgos. It is possible that the disputes between her family and the community (for so far was Teresa from establishing concord that in 1579 we still find them haggling over the payment of her modest dowry of 2000 ducats) may have prompted a step which, it is said, she afterwards bitterly regretted.

However this may be, few of Teresa's nuns could boast as did Casilda when, as a middle-aged woman, she gave her deposition for the saint's canonisation in 1610, that one of the earliest, as it must undoubtedly have been one of the most cherished, memories of her childhood was of being cradled and ofttimes soothed to sleep in the arms of the great Teresa de Jesus.

At all events her conduct became a tradition of her house. In the following century more than one noble dame of her race and line obscured or enhanced their dignity (it is merely the point of view that makes the difference) by becoming inmates of Teresa's convents.

Teresa's visit to Valladolid was but of short duration. Solicited on every side by proposals of fresh foundations, she was now bent on accomplishing those of Veas and Caravaca.

She was sixty when she set forth on the longest and most remarkable of all her journeys. Hitherto her wanderings in the cause of her Reform have been restricted to her native province; she is now to carry it into the heart of Andalucia. "Until now," says Master Julian with a touch of pathos, "our mother had only travelled in the vicinity of Avila—journeys of twenty to thirty leagues each; but when years were beginning to tell, and infirmities to increase, then she began to undertake the longer ones of from fifty to a hundred leagues." For the first time—or is it fancy?—a sigh of melancholy, of craving for rest, a certain note of weariness exhales from her letters; if such a word as melancholy applies to a spirit of resignation in which there is no sign of weakness or faltering courage,—gentle and serene as some breathless day in autumn. Rather is her tone that of one whom material success can no longer either deceive or elate,—nor disillusion sour;—of one whose experience of the past has taught her to look for nothing from the future.

It is for the young and inexperienced traveller, to encourage him to fresh exertion, that hope casts its glittering mirage over the dusty road of life; with the buoyancy of youth and the weight of years the illusory glow vanishes, and he finds himself face to face with a gray and relentless destiny, and with the strange fact that the endless revolutions of the world have not taught wisdom to her children. But Teresa has arisen to a loftier altitude, where the mind has ceased to need all such fictitious aid; in her own unrivalled expression, "her soul was securely seated on its own house-top." What matter if all is a shadow: whether in the theological sense or one philosophical; what matter if life is but a fleeting and unsubstantial phantasmagoria, if through the gloom one star alone, the star of Duty, casts its pale fine radiance to the outskirts of eternity, and she can say like the magi of old, "Vidimus stellam ejus in oriente, et venimus."

It is the highest state to which humanity can attain, to which but few have attained, for it is even a reflex, however dim and obscured, of the calm impersonality of the Divinity.

> Blessed be God [she writes to her friend Doña Ana Enriquez, the Duchess of Alba], that we shall rejoice in him securely for Eternity, for certainly we can count on nothing here, what with these absences and changes. With this looking forward to the end, I endure life; they say that mine is full of trials, but to me it does not seem so.

Fame—and she is now famous—but imposed on her a more transcendental sense of responsibility,—but bound down her life and will more firmly with the ligatures of duty. She is, as she writes to Fr. Luis de Granada, placed before the eyes of the world, "a great trial for one who had lived her imperfect life."

In the letter she addresses to Don Teutonio de Braganza, Archbishop of Ebora, from Valladolid, on the eve of her long and perilous journey, we feel the weight of increasing years and infirmities: "Truly" (she refers to her journeys) "it is one of my greatest trials, and to see besides how ill they are thought of. Oftentimes I think how much better it would be for me to remain quietly in my retreat, if it were not for the General's precept. At others, when I see how the Lord is served in these houses, all I can do seems to me but little." Even, she goes on to say, the journey to Salamanca seems to her too sore a burden for her feeble strength. "I should like to find myself there," she adds, "but unless it be for a foundation the journey is very irksome to me and I would not take it unless I was ordered to."

Thus she wrote on the eve of what was to be the longest and in many respects the most memorable journey of her life, with foundations pressing her on every side; in this same letter she expressly mentions four, none of which, however, she saw accomplished, and it was long before she was fated to find herself back in Avila. "I shall start from here," she tells Don Teutonio, "after Epiphany. I shall return to Avila by way of Medina, where I do not think to stay more than a day or two; and in Avila the same, for I shall go on at once to Toledo. I should like to get this business of Veas done with."

Before following her on her journey it is necessary, since she herself has done so,—to devote a few words to the two women to whose devoted efforts the convent of Veas owed its existence.

Like that of Casilda de Padilla, the history of the sisters of Veas, who, long before Teresa appeared on the religious history of the age, resolved to devote their lives to the strictest order they could found, is chiefly interesting for the curious insight it affords into the workings of the inner social life of the period.

With a few unimportant variations, the history of one of these pious Beatas might do duty for all. For one luminous detail which throws light on the manners and customs of the age, we must wade through the same dreary repetition of miraculous conversions, omens, miracles, and supernaturalism. Even Teresa herself becomes but heavy and leaden reading. And yet underneath it all there runs a deep undertone of real beauty and pathos—the pathos of humble virtue and heroism; which rises sometimes into a clarion note of courage and defiance both admirable and enthralling.

Twenty-seven years ago, before Teresa began to make a stir in the world, there lived in Veas, a little town situated amongst the first rising slopes of the Sierra Morena, a gentleman, Sancho Rojas de Sandoval. His worldly property was considerable, and both he and his wife[1] were of illustrious birth and unsullied ancestry—"old Christians and of unblemished blood," as Teresa forgets not to record. Amongst other children they had two daughters—the future foundresses of Veas. The eldest of these, Catalina, was fourteen when she first felt the mysterious call that changed the current of her life. Until then nothing was farther from her thoughts than to leave the world: on the contrary, so highly did she esteem herself, that none of the marriages proposed to her by her father seemed good enough for her. One morning in the silence of her chamber—which was next to that of her father, who was still asleep—she was musing on one of these offers of marriage, "one that was better than she could have hoped for," and had just said to herself, "With how little is my father contented, so long as I marry a mayorazgo, I, forsooth, who think to be the beginning of my race," when her eyes chanced to fall on the inscription over a crucifix hanging on the wall. Suddenly, even as she read, the "Lord changed her entirely." "It seemed," says Teresa, "as if a light entered her soul, which enabled her to see the truth, just as if a dark chamber had been flooded with the sun." By one of those sharp and sudden revulsions that are amongst the strangest and most mysterious problems of psychology, the beautiful and haughty girl was transformed into a humble and contrite penitent, oppressed by the enormity of her sins, her sole anxiety to redeem them by a life of poverty and chastity. In the hushed tranquillity of that early morning, whilst the rest of the household were still asleep, did Catalina fight out and decide her destiny.

When she awoke from her trance, "for the Lord suspended her," Catalina was a changed being. Between her and the past lay an abyss of terrible and intervening emotion. "She at once vowed to devote herself to a life of charity and poverty, and would fain have seen herself in such subjection, that for the sake of being so she would gladly have been taken

---

[1] She belonged to the illustrious house of Tamames, which has since given a ducal title to Spain.

to the land of the Moors." At this moment (at least, such is the narrative Catalina related to Teresa after the interval of many years) there was a noise in the room above so great that it seemed as if the whole house was coming down, and horrible howlings, which so terrified her father that he rose from his bed, slipped on his clothes, and with his drawn sword rushed into his daughter's room like a madman, to see what it was. After searching an inner room and finding nothing he bade her go to her mother, as she must not be left alone, and told her what he had heard; "Which clearly shows," moralises Teresa, "how much the devil suffers when a soul he has made sure of escapes his clutches."

From this moment the girl, whose impatience of control had led her to spurn the fetters of matrimony as an intolerable burden, becomes the humblest, the most submissive of penitents.

To spoil the beauty that drew suitors to her feet, she wet her face, and stood exposed in the corral (courtyard) to the mid-day sun. At night when they slept she kissed the feet of those over whom during the day she had exercised the authority of a mistress. She spent the hours of sleep in prayer, and the morning sun still found her on her knees. During a whole Lent, strange symbol of the moral combat within, she wore her father's coat of mail next the skin. The desire of her life was to become a nun, but this her parents would not hear of. It is strange that such submission, such self-abasement, such humility, which to the profane at least would seem the sentiments of all others most calculated to soften the heart and call out the tenderest impulses of our nature, should generally transform those who experience them into bits of adamant, insensible to the pleadings of affection or the claims of duty. It would seem that sanctity and humanity are sworn foes. Despairing of obtaining her father's consent to her entering a religious life, at the end of three years she assumed the habit of a Beata.

Nor was the strange and terrible series of heterogeneous maladies she suffered from for seventeen years—fever, dropsy, heart and liver disease, a cancer in the breast, consumption—enough to quench her resolution. Together with her younger sister Maria, who at fourteen also assumed the

Beata's habit, she taught the poor children of Veas to read and sew, until, the pride of the parents revolting against receiving a gratuitous benefit, the good work was put an end to. At length, when the death of their mother—the worthy knight had preceded his spouse to the grave by some five years—left them free to follow their inclination, the two pious women, bent on carrying out the idea of their lives, determined to devote their patrimony to the foundation of a convent.

Twenty years before the day on which Catalina witnessed the crowning triumph of her life—at least, so she told Teresa in Veas,—she had had a dream of mysterious and significant import. She thought she was traversing a narrow and dangerous path along the brink of a deep precipice, when she saw a friar, who, beckoning her to follow him, led her to a house filled with nuns, and lighted only by the burning tapers they carried in their hands. When she asked them to what order they belonged, they were all silent and raised their veils from their smiling and happy faces, and the prioress, taking her by the hand, said, "Daughter, you too are wanted here," and showed her the Rule and Constitutions. One is not surprised to learn that after twenty years Catalina was still able to recognise Fray Juan de la Miseria as the friar of her dream, and Teresa and her companions as the prioress and nuns who had smiled upon her slumbers. A similar felicity of memory enabled her to write down what she had seen of the Rule and Constitutions, and that with such singular precision that, when years after she showed them to a Jesuit, he, with the simple and unquestioning faith that has always distinguished his order, unhesitatingly recognised them as those of the Discalced Carmelites.

Whereupon Catalina at once despatched a messenger to Teresa, then in Salamanca, to urge her to start at once for Veas — "since the house was waiting, the foundress alone was wanting." "On making inquiry of the man" (it is Teresa who speaks) "he praised the country highly, and with reason, for it is exceedingly delightful and the climate is good; but as I thought of the many leagues between it and Salamanca, it seemed to me impossible, the more so as it was useless to think of it without the Apostolic Commissary's license, who, as I have said, was averse to, or at least no favourer of these foundations, and so I was about to refuse without saying anything to him about it. Afterwards I bethought me that since he was then in Salamanca, it was not right to do so without asking his advice, on account of the precept our most reverend father general, Rubeo, had imposed on me to found wherever I could. As soon as he saw the letters, he sent to say that it did not seem worth while to discourage them; that he had been edified by their devotion, and that I might write to them that, provided they could get the Council of Orders[1] to sanction it, the foundation should be proceeded with; nevertheless that I might be certain that it would not be granted, for he knew of other places belonging to the comendadores, which had been years endeavouring to obtain a license for the same purpose, but without success." Fernandez's answer was, in short, equivalent to a polite refusal,—as indeed he intended it to be. But the astute old friar had overreached himself. The energy and resolution of a bedridden woman scattered his precautions to the wind, and the Apostolic Commissary had reason to regret that, instead of being betrayed into a conditional consent, he had not given a direct negative. " I sometimes think of this," says Teresa, " how against our will we become the instruments of carrying out what our Lord devises, like Fray Pedro Fernandez, the Commissary, in this case; and so when the license was obtained, he could not refuse his."

For four years Catalina and her friends had left no means untried to get the Council of Orders to grant the license, but in vain. When the messenger reached Veas with Teresa's answer her recovery seemed hopeless—the license also. Her kinsfolk implored her to abandon an attempt which seemed to them little short of madness, the more so as it was in vain to hope that any monastery would admit a confirmed invalid within its walls. The sick woman, reassured by an inward conviction, or rather by what amounts to the same thing in mystical theology, " a voice that spoke within her," boldly

[1] A council founded by the Catholic kings, composed of a president and various knights elected from amongst the different military orders of the kingdom. As Veas belonged to the knights of Calatrava, the consent of this tribunal was absolutely necessary before the foundation could be proceeded with.

replied, that if within a month she regained her health she herself would go to Madrid for the license.

On St. Sebastian's Eve, within a few days of the expiry of the term she had proposed, Catalina, to the speechless astonishment of her relations, rose from the couch to which she had been confined for more than half a year, and from which she had scarcely stirred for eight, to all appearance sound and strong. "At this time," writes Teresa, "she had suffered from continual fever for eight years; she was consumptive and dropsical, with such a consuming fire in the liver that it was perceptible even through her clothes, and burnt up her chemise, a thing I should never have believed had I not had my information from the doctor. Besides these ailments she also suffered from a cancer in the breast, gout in the joints, and sciatica. So base am I," she adds, strange mixture of superstition and common sense as she was, "that unless I had had it from the doctor, and those who lived in the same house with her, it would not have been too much to think that there was somewhat of exaggeration." Catalina sped to court, unopposed by her kinsmen, overawed, as well they might be, at such activity on the part of one who had twice received extreme unction. It was a miracle, and they respected it. And it is strange indeed what miracles hope can work, and how the near prospect of the fulfilment of the ardent longings of a lifetime can infuse fresh vigour into an enfeebled frame, and give it a temporary lease of life and strength.

After three dreary months spent in prosecuting what seemed a hopeless suit, during which she experienced all the sickness of hope deferred, she had recourse to the king himself, and such was the esteem in which he held Teresa's character and abilities that he had only to learn that it was for one of her monasteries, to grant Catalina's petition on the spot. And thus was Fernandez, who had thought it quite safe to despatch a conciliatory and consolatory reply to sustain the hopes of the foundresses at Veas, so long as the prospect of a license seemed to lie in the dim future, triumphantly hoist with his own petard.

Towards the middle of winter the intrepid old woman once more set forth upon her travels. Once again the

covered cart, under the convoy of the Castilian priest and the
Salamanca gentleman, crept over the snowy plateaux of
Spain, and little did the wild herdsman dream as, standing
motionless against the sky, he watched the progress of the
little cavalcade over the treeless plains, ere it became a speck
amongst the other specks on the horizon, that it bore one
before whose glory that of Santiago himself should pale and
lose its lustre. At Medina she gave the habit to Doña
Elena Quiroga, the Cardinal Archbishop of Toledo's niece.
At Toledo and Malagon she broke her journey to rest, and
inspect the interior discipline of her convents. At Malagon
the little band was further increased by the addition of a
priest "of the very religious ones, much given to prayer,
retirement, and mortification" (so remarks good Master
Julian), Fray Gregorio de Nazianceno, who accompanied
them to Veas, where Teresa gave him the habit and solemnly
received him into her Order. After leaving Malagon they
turned aside from the direct road, so as to pass through
Almodóvar, where Fray Antonio de Jesus was then treating
for the foundation of another monastery. In this town Teresa
lodged in the house of one Marcos García and Isabel Lopez
his wife. As is still the custom in patriarchal Spain, their
eight children were called up to be inspected by the stranger.
Teresa raised her veil, and after looking at them attentively
one by one, she said to their mother, "Your Grace, mistress,
possesses amongst these eight, two, one of whom will be a
great saint, a benefactor of many souls, and the Reformer of
a great Order, as time will show." And then raising her right
hand, she placed it on the shoulder of Antonio Lopez (the
narrator) and said, "Little saint, remember that you will
need much patience, for many are the rude blows you will
receive in this valley of tears. What say you to that?"
And he replied, "I will have all I can." And again she
repeated her question, "But what if the blows be very great,
what say you?" And then she went on: "Time will show
that when one of these eight shall have been dead five years,
it shall still be seen which one of them it was." At least
so runs the story related, most firmly believed in, and as
solemnly ratified by Antonio Lopez, one of the eight
who stood before the saint that day,—in the evidence for his

brother's beatification, when failing memory had dimmed its real details, and the alchemy of time and years transmuted them into others more in accordance with the event. Still the simple pathos of its telling makes it interesting, although as evidence of Teresa's miraculous gifts of prophecy, it would be quite as convincing if the Carmelites did not tell it one way and the Trinitarians another. For one of those self-same children, Fray Juan Bautista de la Concepcion, *did* afterwards become the reformer of the Trinitarians, although the opinion of his own order is divided as to the share he took in it, and was beatified by Rome. And not merely in his case, but in that of his sister as well, who afterwards became a pious Beata, attached to the Carmelite Order, was Teresa's prophecy fulfilled; for when five years after her death her tomb in the friars' church of Almodóvar was opened, her body was still found to be entire. It would be interesting to know how far these predictions were altered in after years to suit the event by an order jealous of their reputation, and not over-scrupulous in their measures for establishing it.

Prophecy or no prophecy—and I for one do not abase the greatness of this woman by attributing to her the arts of a soothsaying gipsy—it shows how strangely she impressed herself on the imagination of her age, and how those whose lives she crossed in childhood regarded the grandiose figure; how the touch of her hand, the sound of her voice still lingered in their memory from youth to age—its most precious records, until the tomb sealed them up for ever; and she herself, one of the majestic traditions of Spain, had become to the generation that took the place of that which dimly remembered somewhat of Teresa the woman—a consecrated fetish, devoid of passion, sex, humanity,—on the gilded altar of a church. That her popularity was growing; that her name has already become a talisman to the crowd, may be seen by the tendency of her nuns—she was accompanied by two of her cleverest prioresses, Ana de Jesus and Maria de San José—to consider their hairbreadth escapes on this perilous journey as so many miracles. On the last day's journey after leaving Almodóvar, the drivers lost their way amidst the wild passes of the Sierra Morena. Hemmed in on every side by savage peaks and precipices, they dared neither go back nor forward. The nuns invoked the assistance of San José, and sure enough, as if in answer to their prayers, a distant voice from the bottom of the valley warned them of their peril and directed them to safety. "I know not," said Teresa, as the muleteers went to look for their invisible benefactor—some wandering shepherd who, himself unseen, had seen and noted their danger—"I know not why we let them go, for it was my father José, and they will not find him." Verily, Faith is sometimes better than Reason, for the muleteers, not to be outdone, affirmed with oaths (as indeed we may be sure they did) that from that moment the mules sprang forward as if they trod on air, and stony heights and horrid precipices had been enchanted into level plains.

Before they got to Veas still another miracle happened, that the Venerable Mother Ana de Jesus has not forgotten to record in her evidence for the saint's canonisation. In order to cross the Guadalimar it was necessary for the nuns to alight from the carts and ford the current on mules. But scarcely had they got to the edge of the water when, without knowing how, they found themselves on the other side, leaving every one transfixed with amazement that, on account of the merits of his servant, the Lord made them invisible bridges.

And if it pleased these holy women in after years to consider the natural effects of blinding terror as a miracle, and, losing sight of the sure-footed mules, to attribute their passage across the rapid current of the Guadalimar to supernatural agency, who shall gainsay them? The illusion is harmless enough, and the disregard of the actual benefactor merely human, for, after all, if a horse is a feeble thing to save a man's life, the same may be said of a mule.

It is most probable, as it lay on the way, and she would surely not pass without visiting one of the principal houses of the Reform in Andalucia, that she rested a day or two at La Peñuela. Thence to Veas it is about two days' journey. The landscape now was no longer the familiar arid uplands of Castille, in which earth seems to become a paraphrase of the immensity of the sky. Aloes—the remains of Arab cultivation—now began to send their spiny tufts of dull cobalt blue against the bright red marl of the soil, whose dazzling brilliance under the sun was almost insupportable. The accent too had changed, and with it the manners of the people. If Teresa noted these things she has left no record of it.

The fame of her miracles, losing nothing in the transmission, had sped before her to Veas, and it may be that she partly owed to them a reception more gay and joyous than any she had yet received. And yet, if the veil could have been snatched from eyes blinded by the passions and foibles inherent to humanity (alas for humanity, the same to-day as then!), and they could have seen wherein lay the real miracle,—the untiring constancy, the unflinching will of the woman bent and tortured with infirmities, who feebly exclaimed, as she sallied forth from Malagon, and contemplated the long and arduous journey before her, "Lord, look to it thou, that I may have strength to bear it,"—I doubt whether instead of joy, it would not have filled them with the profoundest sentiment of sadness. None less than she has needed the glamour of the supernatural to take her place amongst the great ones of the earth. And yet I question whether the bulk of her pious votaries now are one whit more enlightened than her admirers were then, and whether one paltry miracle "cooked up" by pious fraud does not far outweigh the heroism of her life, the genius of her writings, the strong current of rectitude and honesty which underlies even the greatest vagaries of her mysticism, the charm and fascination of her wonderful personality. But away such thoughts on this day of joy! Let us from this nineteenth century descend into the tranquil streets of the little town, and watch, unnoted spectators, one of those scenes of simple and contagious rejoicing and devotion, than which even now, when shorn of much of their splendour and of much of their enthusiasm, nothing is more thrilling or stirs the heart more strangely.

To-day the little town has aroused itself from the apathy in which it lies dully absorbed for the greater part of the year, except on some such occasion as this. The vineyards and the oliveyards are deserted, and there is an unwonted stir in the air of this tranquil winter's day. Presently a troop of horsemen,—of the knights who shed a lustre over the grim old houses, which now stand like spectres of a more dignified past, as useless to their descendants as the rusty swords which then dangled by their side,—ride out amidst groups of eager peasants to meet the cart which bears Teresa and, passaging their horses ["haciendo gentilezas"] before it, conduct her in triumph to the gates of the church. Presently the bells in the tower burst out into merry and repeated chimes; the crowd breaks into acclamations; hoary-headed men and women murmur blessings on the saint of Spain—not yet a saint except in their imagination —whom, like Simeon, they have lived to see; some drop down on their knees in the dust; the clergy motionless, a white blot against the shadow of the porch. For there it comes, that travel-stained and humble vehicle, slowly creaking into the market-place, surrounded by its bodyguard of mounted gentlemen; and from it alights—and now a hush of expectancy creeps over every person there—the bent form of a woman, veiled from head to foot, who leans somewhat heavily on her stick, as one by one, priest and gentleman and peasant,—and methinks her eyes are bent more kindly on the last than on any of the rest,—kneel to kiss her hand and seek her benediction.

Then the great silver cross is raised on high in the searching rays of the February sun; the pulse of a whole people throbs simultaneously as the triumphal chant of the *Te Deum* unloosens their pent-up emotions; as slowly winding through narrow streets, every casement gay with silks and velvets, and the ground strewn with flowers and sweet-smelling rushes, the procession threads its way to the ancestral home of Catalina Godinez, to which that day was to add a more imperishable blazon of glory than the knightly arms of her forefathers, mouldering from its angles, inasmuch as it was to shelter the great Teresa de Jesus, and become the eighth convent of her Order. It was the Day of St. Matthias, and the pious virgin of forty-one remembered, not without a thrill of awe, that it was on that same day twenty-seven years ago that she had first felt the mysterious impulse which had been the magnet of her life.

"If now we did not wish for you, and cast you out into the street, what would you do?" asked Teresa in her quaint and funny way, as she gave the two sisters the habit, and accepted the renunciation of all they had. "We will serve your reverences," they answered, "in the porteria, and if you did not give us food we will ask for alms for the love of God."

Teresa's entry into Veas was the first of those triumphs which we shall soon see repeated in Seville, Palencia, Soria. The days are over when she entered Medina like a thief in the night; and the days are still to come when her feast-day will become the occasion of national rejoicings, such as in life she never could have dreamed of.

※   ※   ※

It was in Veas that Teresa first met the man with whom her life was thenceforth to be so intimately blended. It was the prologue to the stormiest and most agitated portion of her career, which from this moment takes a fresh development. Hitherto we have watched her founding her convents of nuns as busily as of yore she built up mimic ones in her father's garden. Henceforth we shall follow her, as, beaten on by storms and tempests, the victim of active persecution (for the finger of malice points most readily at those whose station or virtue makes them most conspicuous), she stands ever at the helm, guiding the frail bark of her Reform into the desired haven.

In order to understand the fierce struggle into which her meeting with Gracian was at once to plunge her, and on which the Descalzos are now called upon to enter if they would save themselves from total extinction; in order adequately to follow her history, which is now that of the Order she has herself raised into being, it is necessary briefly to retrace the progress and development of the Discalced Carmelites since the day that Fray Juan de la Cruz and Fray Antonio de Jesus,—"her friar and a half," as she called them with loving satire,—resuscitated the Primitive Rule of San Brocardo de Jerusalem; that Rule which first sent forth its reflex from a Syrian mountain, in a lonely straw grange lost in the brown immensity of a Castilian landscape.

Within the space of four short years nine monasteries have sprung into existence, four in Castille and four in Andalucia, and one of them—that of San Juan del Puerto—abandoned. A college has been founded at Alcalá de Henares for the instruction of Carmelite novices.

How had it all come about? With the same laborious slowness as life itself; oftentimes startling us by its cumulative results,—taken in its isolated acts day by day, nothing ; taken as a whole, tremendous, awe-inspiring. Year after year has seen a monastery founded ; has seen the Descalzos take firmer root and enlarge the circle of their influence : at first a grain of mustard-seed nourished in obscurity,—now a forest tree, young, vigorous, full of sap and vitality.

We have seen how, barely eight months after the foundation of Duruelo, Teresa had, in another distant corner of Castille, given the habit to the three men—as oddly assorted as any three ever thrown together by Fate—who were to found the second monastery of her Order : Ambrosio Mariano, Fray Juan de la Miseria, and Fray Baltasar Nieto, thenceforth Fray Baltasar de Jesus.

The first of these, Mariano—sometime diplomatist, soldier, courtier, statesman, man of science, of lively wit and caustic tongue that bit like acid ; sharpened by a long experience of all sorts and conditions of men ; hot-headed and impetuous ; fertile in expedients ; unscrupulous, not cursed with too nice a conscience—shall play no inconsiderable part in this history. Fray Juan de la Miseria, who on this occasion as on all others followed the example of his countryman with dog-like fidelity,—a gentle, harmless being, noted for little except his simplicity, unostentatious virtue, and blear-eyed portraits of Teresa—is, we feel, already predestined by that very goodness and guilelessness to the obscurity of humble effort in the background. Nieto is a man of different stamp. An Andaluz, he has grown old amongst the Observants ; amongst them has arisen into fame as one of the most eloquent preachers of the peninsula. His accession, a triumph for the Descalzos, brings with it the enmity of the great and powerful Order, who cannot regard with equanimity the desertion of so illustrious a subject. To-day, when all these cloister rivalries are silent, his character stands out from the dim background of the annals of the Descalzos for the jealousy with which he fostered calumnies against one whose only fault seems to have been his pre-eminence.

On a hot July day these three made their way up the steep and sandy path to the hill, a quarter of a league to the south of Pastrana, where a hermitage which crowned its summit—and had been for generations an object of devotion to the town-people—was thenceforth to witness the devotions of more than three generations of friars. A rejoicing multitude sallied forth with them from the gates of the old walled town of Pastrana, to escort them to the spot which was soon to be celebrated as the site of the second and most famous monastery of the Order.

It was a wild, lovely spot, this hillside of Pastrana, abandoned to rough forest and scrub. Beneath it lay a green and fertile valley; far in the distance gleamed the blue Sierras of Cuenca. Its after history was that of all the houses reared by the Carmelites. When night stole over the scene of the day's triumph, and the voice of the last straggler had died away in the distance, the three solitaries took refuge in a cave, where hitherto the wild shepherds of the district had sheltered themselves from the tempest and the midnight cold. On the morrow the sound of axe and spade and mattock might have been heard ringing through the sweet solitudes, scaring away the wild doves from the sylvan retreat, where they and the nightingales had hitherto been the only inhabitants. A few rough sheds of pine were propped up against the dove-cot walls. Primeval wilderness was transformed by dint of the ceaseless toil of these laborious contemplatives into a blossoming garden. Terraces rose one above another on the sandy slopes; and the tender green of vine-shoots and pleasant orchards gradually took the place of rough brushwood and tangled thicket. The nimble-witted Mariano displayed the engineering skill which had been in request with princes, and astonished his companions by his success in conducting water from a spring near the town on a lower level, to the top of the hill, so as to irrigate the highest of the terraces. He also excavated an underground passage through the face of the hill between the dove-cot on the slope, which was as yet the best abode they knew, and the little chapel on the summit. Here on this peaceful hillside they renewed the traditions and stern monastic discipline of the cenobites of the Thebaid. Each brought to the common stock that particular art or office that he excelled in most. Their privations were extreme. They lived on the herbs culled from the hillside until the garden repaid their labours with its produce. Cabbage and lettuce and sorrel, sod in water and so ill prepared,—such the carelessness or piety of the cook, that the particles of dirt grated on the teeth—was their ordinary fare, to which on festivals, as a special treat, they added a little oil. Hunger and necessity alone could break and swallow the bread made by the monkish baker, scarcely more skilful or less devout than his brother the cook. Beside the crust of bread and the bowl of unpalatable vegetables, a skull on a plate of ashes preached its significant lesson. Some there were who mingled their food with wormwood and ashes; others, to whom the heat seemed a weakness of the flesh, threw cold water over it.

Many there were who, besides the obligatory fasts, fasted continuously on bread and water. There were men who for twelve months together had tasted nothing but a bowl of soup and bread and water, and yet screened their abstinence with such scrupulous care that none remarked it. One forgot the use of language, and had to make use of signs; a novice on his deathbed asked leave to raise his eyes on high before they closed for ever. Benches and stools were long unknown amidst the first friars of Pastrana. And yet these men—their emaciated bodies bearing the bleeding marks of the scourge and the unhealed sores of the cilicium, who flitted about in unbroken silence, their eyes fastened on the earth—worked harder with their hands than the rudest labourer; and the vast monasteries built by these half-starved friars, their orchards and their gardens, are still a surprise and charm to the traveller who comes across them in the remote and forgotten corners of Spain. Not a breath; no change of posture betokened weariness in those bodies of bronze, in which the will had been annihilated and destroyed. They despised all support. Human Reason was as dead as the will.

The voice of the superior was the voice of Christ; the signal of the bell the signal of heaven. Dead to life, its joys, its sorrows, earth ceased to exist. Day and night from the little chapel on the height the watchers before the Host sent up a continuous stream of supplication for the Church, the Pope, the King and Kingdoms of Spain, their benefactors the Dukes of Pastrana; and they who had laboured all day at the roughest toil often spent the night in vigil, prostrate before the sanctuary.

The original monastery of Pastrana has long been swept away: for the building which now rises on the crest of the hill was erected long after Teresa and her primitive friars were dead; the Carmelites have faded into night—have become an anachronism; but as the dreamer lies on the hillside of Pastrana, under the shadow of the tall pines—the descendants of those felled by the friars—and the doves flap heavily in and out of the pigeon-cot, the only sound that breaks the mid-day silence—it may be forgiven him if for a moment the primitive friars, who built with their own hands that famous monastery, cease to become blurred and misty images in a monastic chronicle, and live to him once more in time and space.

For a moment he too becomes the retrospective victim of the strange fascination exercised on the imagination of their century by men who, fired with all the ardour of an older and sterner world, suddenly burst on the religious horizon of the age, at the very moment it most demanded them. Their unfamiliar garb, their bare feet, the unbroken silence in which they lived; their preference for the wildest and remotest spots; the stern asceticism and unobtrusive heroism of their lives, made a profound impression on their contemporaries which is still not wholly obliterated.

One can fancy the strange awe and veneration with which the simple country people, who saw with amazement men, some of whom had been great in station and the world, labouring with their hands harder than they themselves, greeted the advent in their midst of these cowled solitaries.

As the rude arriero passed that spot at night (I speak of Pastrana) he stopped his mule with almost superstitious awe to listen to the deep-toned litanies and matins of the friars, as they mingled with the song of the nightingale and the musical croaking of frogs, and all the inexplicable sounds of a southern night. The good neighbours of Pastrana slept but the more serenely if, carried on the breeze, the faint tinkle of the convent bell broke in upon their midnight slumbers. They crossed themselves and fell asleep again, secure that whilst they slept the friars prayed.

Nor were these feelings confined to the narrow circle of their rustic neighbours. Ruy Gomez, their powerful benefactor, carried their fame to court, to the ears of King Philip himself, profoundly rousing his interest in the struggles of a handful of friars to reassert the original rigidity and discipline of Mount Carmel on Spanish soil.

In the meantime, in that other corner of Castille, a third monastery has been founded by their brethren of Duruelo. About a league's distance across the desert plain,—the path now diving through oak woods, now following the meanderings of the streamlet, whose mendacious title of Rio al Mar so rouses the ire of the chronicler,—leads to a little town, Mancera de Abajo. The shields which hang from the pillars above the aisles of the church—strangely grandiose for so small a place; the same shield repeated over the grim front of the mediæval Casa de Ayuntamiento, its top story, supported by carved wooden posts blackened by time, jutting over the lower,—have lost all meaning for the rural inhabitants who look upon them daily. But down there by the river, in the bottom, at the other entrance to the town, a mill, still working, built of quarried stone, of solider and stronger architecture than the cluster of houses above—the ruins of a palace, tell to the curious in such matters,—to him who can read sermons in stones,—the past history and the life and manners of that dead and gone Mancera, and its inhabitants of Teresa's time.

Then that mass of stones, out of which all shape has not yet departed,—here and there a heavy moulding surrounds a vacant casement, framing sky and empty space; the gateway of honour, still massive and imposing, defies time;—was the feudal dwelling of a great family, a branch of the Toledos, Dukes of Alba. Around them, far away to Alba, stretched their wide domains. They ruled with a rod of iron, or beneficently, according to the mood of each successor, the little township on the hill. The dispensers of justice, lords of gallows and knife—Señores de Ahorco y Cuchillo—retainer, hind, and peasant tremblingly obeyed their behests.

Don Luis de Toledo, lord of the Cinco Villas, possessor of these fair estates, and dispenser of happiness or misery to these humble lives, attracted by the fame of the friars of Duruelo, had also ridden forth ruffling in his velvets on feast-days and Sunday mornings, under an incandescent sun, to pour his sins and woes into their ears. He pressed upon them, and they reluctantly accepted (so affirms the chronicler, in his desire to excuse the voluntary abandonment by his dead predecessors of the humble straw grange) a church he had built within a stone's-throw of his palace walls, to be the shrine of a famous altar-piece brought by his grandfather from Flanders, and bequeathed by him to his descendants as a family heirloom.

A well, a few brick walls rising amidst the arid surface of the soil, are all that attest to-day the passage of the Carmelites across the obscure history of Mancera.

Even in those days—although it must be remembered that when there were virtually no coaches, much less railways, and every man rode, no place was more remote or difficult of access than another—it was an out-of-the-way corner, and there was nothing to bring either travellers or traffic. For us the interest of the Monastery of Mancera ends on that June day of 1570, which shone on a devout procession of monks, who, abandoning the cradle of the Order, wound a wavering line across the plain, until, disappearing over the crest of the hill, they are lost for ever in oblivion.

Teresa's licenses (they were limited to two) expired with the foundation of Pastrana. It was useless to expect any further concession from the General, whose intention, far from embracing any serious increase of the Reform, seems to have been to make this little band of men of austere life and rigid virtue merely his instruments for introducing amongst the regular Carmelites a severer discipline and a more conscientious conception of their Rule—the little leaven, in fact, that leaveneth the whole lump. The farther progress of the Order was at an end, had not its development been favoured by an unforeseen combination of circumstances.

In 1570, the Pope, at Philip's request, had as we have seen vested the supreme control of the Spanish Carmelites in two Apostolic Visitors. The power of these Visitors was absolute and unlimited. Both were Dominicans, men of high position and acknowledged virtue. To Vargas, prior of the Dominican monastery of Cordoba, was entrusted jurisdiction over the province of Andalucia; that of Castille was vested in Fray Pedro Fernandez, prior of Talavera de la Reina.

By Philip's desire, and commissioned by the Nuncio, Fernandez's first visit was to Pastrana. He arrived before the convent gates—he and his companion on foot, driving before them a donkey which bore their cloaks—and the chronicler has not forgotten to record the words (so flattering to his Order) in which the old man rebuked the ill-concealed astonishment produced by the entry in this humble fashion of one holding a post of such supreme dignity. "It ill becomes him," he is reported to have said, "who comes to visit saints, to travel like a layman." Strange to find sanctity expressing surprise at conduct which would have seemed, of all others, most natural and inherent to it!

Fernandez had no cause to complain of his reception; the friars received him with every mark of joy and veneration. It was Lent when he arrived, and it was noted that he fasted on bread and water, and followed the Rule with as much rigorous punctiliousness as if he too would fain have enrolled himself amongst the restorers of the ancient fervour of the prophets. After some days spent in these pious exercises, he disclosed his commission before the convent chapter. Although he said it did not extend to the Descalzos, nor were they bound to submit to his visit; not only had the Nuncio ordered him to receive their obedience if they saw fit to give it, but the king himself was desirous that they should do so. After a brief conference, the friars unanimously signified their submission.

The reward of their judicious conduct on this occasion was a license to open a college at Alcalá de Henares, a license he made no difficulty in conceding, but which the Provincial of the Carmelites was powerless to give, and which the General would most certainly have refused. What share in it the influence of Ruy Gomez had is not certain. On the 1st of November 1570, the college bought and endowed by Ruy Gomez for the maintenance of eighteen students was solemnly opened in Alcalá. A year later, by virtue of the powers vested in their prior, Fray Baltasar de Jesus, by the visitor Fernandez, who had appointed him Vicar-general of the Descalzos, the friars of Pastrana took possession of the hermitage of Altomira, on the topmost peak of the sierra that divides the provinces of Toledo and Cuenca, within a day's journey or less, as the crow flies, from Pastrana. A wild, strange spot, perched like an eagle's eyrie far above the clouds; in summer lovely with the loveliness of these deserted uplands of Spain, a tangle of dwarf arbutus and aromatic shrubs; in winter storm-tossed, inaccessible, its paths blocked by snow for months together. With these foundations the new Order leaps out of its obscurity into the light of day, and enters on a fresh phase of its existence.

On the occasion of the opening of the Carmelite college Fray Baltasar de Jesus had roused all Alcalá with his eloquence; people, students, grave professors of the university and masters of theology alike flocked to hear the old man, who wore the garb of an anchorite of the desert, and in whom, according to the chronicler, it seemed that the spirit of St. Paul and the silvery tongue of Apollo had once more come to life. Crowds, vibrating with curiosity and excitement, gathered at the corners of the streets to watch the strange little band of Discalced students as they trudged to and fro between their college and the lecture halls. Their bare feet, their downcast eyes, their meagre and ragged habit barely reaching to the naked ankle; their hands meekly folded over their scapularies; the half-understood asceticism of their stern lives, appealed powerfully and irresistibly to the imagination. Fray Pedro Fernandez said truly, when on his visit to Pastrana he exhorted the friars to continue as they had begun,—that the mute mortification of their lives preached a more eloquent sermon than could be heard from any pulpit.

The Discalced Communities became the theme of every tongue. Every day young and ardent men, some of them graduates of the University, and nearly all men of bright promise, were drawn as by a magnet to the sunlit hill of Pastrana. People sped from far and near, led by curiosity or devotion —the former often more potent than the latter—to get a sight of the seven friars who braved the winter tempests up there on the wind-swept height of Altomira; and some there were whose idle curiosity decided the course of their lives, and stayed their wandering feet for good beside the humble shrine of Our Lady of Succour.

To-day a hare, a rabbit, starting from the perfumed tangle, alone disturbs the immense solitude of Altomira, where the friars dwelt. An eagle circles round the Moorish watch-tower which springs from the narrow promontory of rock on the extreme edge of the summit, and still sweeps the vast horizon with something of its old stern defiance. The groined roof and massive pillars of the hospederia, a little below it, which once belonged to the Knights Templars, uninjured by the passage of centuries, may yet serve to give a night's shelter to the *impertinente curioso*. A little farther down the ridge a mass of formless ruins shows where the Carmelite monastery once stood. Time or a tardy sentiment of remorse has, however, spared the little hermitage which was their church; and between the bars of the wooden grating which protects the entrance the Virgin still beams benignant. Once in the year she receives the homage of the villagers from the towns and villages dotted round its base, and the path trodden by Moors, Templars, and friars is trodden once more. Then as night sinks over the sierras she is left alone smiling into space on the wind-swept ledge, until another year shall bring her votaries to her feet again. The friars have followed Moorish adalid and Christian Templar, and faded with them into the past, but they still live in the wild legends of the country-side, and at dead of night (so they say who have heard it) the breeze carries to distant hamlets the tinkling of the bell which once summoned them to Matins.

Even stripped of the exaggerations and hyperbole of the chronicler, the history of the seven friars who, amidst the simple rejoicing of the neighbouring peasantry, climbed these Alpine solitudes to take possession of the wild windswept peak of Altomira, proves one of the most romantic pages in the monastic annals of this or any other age. Here, on the topmost summit of the sierra, above the clouds which rolled over the world below, in some rough sheds they reared under the lee of the hermitage walls and parcelled out into cells and offices, these men braved the winter storms and tempests. As they slept the snow fell down on them through the interstices of the roof; not only the passes but the church door was blocked up by snow for days together. On a winter's day a strange little procession of monks, headed by their gray old prior, might be seen trudging over the snowy waste to fetch wood and water from half a league and a quarter of a league's distance. The drops of water froze hard upon their habits; their hands to the handles of the jars. They chipped out the wine in the wine jar with a knife, and both wine and water had to be melted before hot embers before they could be used for Mass. The friars defied the rigours of the first winter they spent on those barren heights on a few beans boiled in water, so as to save their scanty store of oil for the Host. And yet from that mountain fastness, covered with eternal snow, inhabited only by wolves and friars, amidst the shrieking of the winds which drowned the brothers' voices in the choir and beat fearfully around their fragile dwelling, threatening its destruction, as sweet a perfume of prayer and pure lives ascended into heaven, as from the sunlit hill of Pastrana. The fame of the anchorites of Altomira sped through all Castille.

So did the Descalzos in Teresa's phrase appear from night to morning. Hitherto their obscurity, the meanness and poverty of their origin, had protected them from attack. The moment was now arrived when they were to be called upon to fight tenaciously for bare existence. It was to be the last great struggle which expiring mediævalism was to make against the new era which was stealthily building up the Europe of to-day; it was the last resolute stand against the disturbing influences of new thoughts and new ideas, the last attempt to reanimate and vitalise the exploded aspirations of a previous age; it was the last time that the sound of the voice of one crying in the wilderness was to ring through Spain; it was a Quixotic effort, for Time is inexorable, and what he has condemned to be cast into his wallet, he in his ceaseless march towards the future remembers no more.

The Descalzos have begun to make a stir in the world. The men of most worth, of purer lives and higher aspirations, were fast deserting the old Order to swell the ranks of the new.

When the Carmelites at last woke up to the fact that their best and most conscientious subjects were being gradually drafted into the Reform, the mischief was done. Henceforth it is to be war to the knife between the old and the new; the conservatives—grown fat on hereditary traditions and prerogatives, so much conventional lumber,—striving in vain, strong in nothing but impotent hatred, to annihilate the dangerous march of the innovators, fresh and strong, inspired for a moment with the generous sap of old strivings that they had made new. And so they too take their place in the dreary cycle of all human things, ideas, and strivings: as certainly as human life, until stagnation and decay remove them from the world's face for ever. The battle-field was to be Andalucia, and not Castille; and it was Vargas, the dignified prior of Cordoba, Apostolic Commissary of the Carmelites of Andalucia, who first threw down the gauntlet on behalf of the Descalzos.

Amongst those Carmelites who had changed the white of their Order for the spare habit of the Descalzos were several Andaluces. These, according to the chronicler, awoke so glorious an emulation in those they left behind them that they often mooted amongst themselves, and consulted their superiors (especially Fray Francisco de Vargas, Apostolic Commissary) as to how they might extend the Reform to their native province. Not finding amongst the little band of would-be reformers any one capable or zealous enough, or of sufficient reputation to warrant his being entrusted with so grave a charge, Vargas wrote to Fray Baltasar de Jesus, and earnestly besought him to proceed to Andalucia with the object of introducing the Reform into his native province, thereby repaying the benefits he had received from the Mother Order. He offered him, moreover, any one of the Observant monasteries that seemed most suitable for the purpose, and warned him not to bring as his companions any renegades from the Observance, as this might give the Calzados a pretext for opposition. The old prior of Pastrana, busy in Castille with his monasteries and the affairs of his eminent patron, Ruy Gomez, whose inseparable confidant and counsellor he had now become, having paid but scant attention to the Dominican's letters, Vargas, now more bent than ever on his cherished scheme, seized the first opportunity that chance presented to him of putting it into execution. His plan was to turn out the Observants from one of their monasteries and replace them by Descalzos. It being impossible for the Apostolic Commissary himself directly to make so open an aggression on the rights of the body it was his commission to reform, but certainly not to despoil, he looked about him for instruments. These he presently found in two Discalced friars, one of them Heredia, an Andaluz, and a renegade from the Observance, who on their way to Granada happened to pass through Cordoba and stopped to show him their patents. Instead of allowing them to proceed on their journey, the wily Commissary ordered them to take up their lodging in the Carmelite monastery, and not to leave Cordoba without seeing him again. Next day, when they came to solicit his farewell benediction, after informing them that in Andalucia they were now his subjects, and that he counted on their obedience to fulfil his orders, he laid before them his cherished scheme. Fray Diego de Heredia interposed a feeble resistance: the Commissary of Castille, he said, would take it ill that, after asking for a limited license for a particular business of his own, he should remain in another district, and that for such a length of time as the nature of the undertaking required. At last, talked over by Vargas, who promised to write to Fernandez and obtain his consent, the two friars, perhaps nothing loath to be detained, accompanied him to Seville to take possession of the monastery of San Juan del Puerto—a wild, beautiful spot between Niebla and Huelva, to-day abandoned to reeds and sea-birds.

This injudicious and arbitrary act filled up the measure of the Observants' wrath. They were now thoroughly exasperated, nor did the fact that those most active in the spread of the Reform in Andalucia were deserters from their own Order, act precisely as a salve to their wounded feelings.

Meanwhile the Reform spread as rapidly in Andalucia as it had done in Castille. Encouraged by Vargas, and with his sanction, an Observant monk of Granada, of illustrious birth but little learning—a combination not rare in those days—stirred up by Heredia's example, after discalcing himself and adopting the habit of the Carmelite Reform, trudged off on foot to Madrid to get the royal sanction to a second foundation in Granada.

On the way he fell in with Fray Diego de Leon, titular Bishop of Columbria, an island, explains the chronicler, anciently celebrated in Scotland (by which description I should scarcely have recognised the islands of Sodor and Man), who from the ranks of the Carmelite Observance had risen to the episcopal dignity. The two were old friends, had lived long together in the same monastery, and when the Bishop noted the change of habit and expressed his surprise, Fray Gabriel told him of his plans. As they travelled along together, the Bishop informed him of some hermits who lived at La Peñuela, a lonely spot in the heart of the Sierra Morena, whose mode of life resembled that of the Descalzos he had seen in Pastrana and Alcalá. The monk laboriously made his way to Madrid,—through that old-world Spain, which some luminous detail is always flashing upon us, and which as constantly evades us. The king was hunting amidst the pine woods of Balsain near Segovia. Another twenty miles for sore feet and aching bones. No matter! thither the intrepid old friar followed. With little difficulty he procured an audience (for the monastic habit was ever an open sesame to the royal presence), and obtained all he desired.

From Madrid, following the Bishop of Columbria's advice, he went to Alcalá, and thence to Pastrana. But the good old man was fain to return to Andalucia alone. For Fray Baltasar de Jesus, on whom he had fixed to make the foundation of Granada, interposed Ruy Gomez, with whom he had so ingratiated himself on account of his abilities that the prince would not hear of his leaving him; and to thwart him he said was to run the risk of losing the favour of the powerful favourite, not only for himself, but for the Order. This was in October 1572. In the meantime Fray Gabriel trudges back again to Granada, and on his way turns aside to visit the hermits of La Peñuela, whom (the Council of Trent having declared all such associations irregular) he easily induces to join the Descalzos. After giving the habit to one of the hermits, whom he bears along with him as a companion, he proceeds to Jaen to get the Bishop's license. This was refused, but, so as not to return empty-handed to La Peñuela, he petitions the city of Baeza for a donation of land for the monastery, and is made happy with 50 fanegas (something like 50 acres) close to the hermitage walls. After a visit to Granada he returned to Madrid, to get the donation of Baeza confirmed. He found Fray Baltasar de Jesus still in the house of Ruy Gomez, ministering to him in a serious attack of illness. He again pleaded that no time should be lost in undertaking the foundations of Granada and La Peñuela, and of thereby doing so signal a service to the Order. The old prior replied (I fear me he was a time-server, and that the favour of Ruy Gomez was dearer to him even than the Reform) that to leave the prince at such a critical moment was to risk all; that he must even wait until his master's returning health allowed him to make the journey under brighter auspices. Fray Gabriel obediently retired to Pastrana, where he waited throughout Lent of 1573, until towards the close of it the prince's recovery enabled him at last to bear off with him to Andalucia the Prior of Pastrana, whose presence alone was needed to turn the foundations of La Peñuela and Granada into accomplished facts. The journey was planned with the greatest caution and dissimulation. The prince himself procured the license from the Provincial of the Observants, Fray Angel de Salazar, who, if he had known the real object it was wanted for, would certainly never have granted it, on the plea that he was sending Fray Baltasar into Andalucia to treat with his son-in-law, the Duke of Medina Sidonia (he who lost the Armada), on private business of his own. The

Provincial's eyes might have been opened had he known that secret orders were at once issued to various Andaluz friars, seceders from the Observance, to set out immediately for Andalucia. To avert suspicion they were to travel in couples; some were to remain in La Peñuela; others were to go on to Baeza and Jaen, there to await instructions.

At Granada the heads of the expedition were cordially received. The young Count of Tendilla, son of the Viceroy of Naples, a kinsman of the Princess of Eboli, and governor of the Alhambra, lodged them in his own house. Vargas hastened to transfer to Fray Baltasar de Jesus his own commission as Apostolic Visitor. After rejecting the Archbishop's offer of a house in the Albaicin, which the "hardness of these people, vanquished rather than convinced" (the chronicler refers to the Moriscos), prevented them from accepting; on the 19th of May the Descalzos took possession of the hermitage of the Holy Martyrs founded by the Catholic Kings, and little more than a month later, on the 29th of June, that of La Peñuela was solemnly consecrated to Our Lady of Mount Carmel. What more Fr. Baltasar might have achieved had not the news of the serious relapse of Ruy Gomez, then lying at the point of death, recalled him in hot haste to Madrid, is not known. He arrived in time to cheer the sick courtier's last moments, and to escort the widowed princess to Pastrana.

It was then that he made over the commission he held from Vargas to a young man, who but two or three months before had taken the vows at Pastrana. It is vain to speculate as to what were the prior's motives when he singled out Gracian (whom he afterwards regarded with bitter jealousy) for such a post. Probably he would have chosen Mariano if Mariano had been ordained, and the tragedy of Gracian's life might have been averted. The duel for life or death between the Observants and Descalzos was now to be fought in grim earnest. The weapons of the weak against the strong are dissimulation and intrigue, and the Descalzos made good use of them. To circumvent the sullen and powerful Carmelites, they resort to every sort of trickery, deception, and ruse. Having risen by the General's favour, and owing everything to him, aware that he is against their further extension, they resort to the Commissary General to secure their object. When the latter has served their turn, and there is nothing further to be got out of him, they at once make use of his subordinate. They had hoodwinked Salazar once,—it might not be so easy to do so a second time. So Mariano seeks Salazar, the Provincial, and tells him a cunningly-devised story as to his presence being required in Seville to conclude some urgent affairs he had left pending there when he joined the Order. The simple Provincial was no match for the wily Neapolitan. It never occurred to him that two lay friars (for Mariano artfully concealed the fact that his companion was to be no other than Gracian, whose talents would already seem to have pointed him out as a conspicuous figure in the Order, and the good old Provincial never dreamt of asking) should be bent on a deep-laid scheme for the extension of the Reform, and he willingly sanctioned the expedition.

Without losing a moment, in the month of August the two travellers set out for Andalucia, Mariano himself nothing loath to shake the dust of Castille from off his feet before the breaking of the storm, which, he astutely foresaw, his having given the habit to the Princess of Eboli must sooner or later bring upon the Order and himself. Their progress was barred, however, in Almodóvar by a mandate from the General, insisting on Mariano's taking orders. This done, in September, dreading every moment lest the Provincial's orders for their instant return should overtake them before they reached the frontier, where they considered his jurisdiction over them at an end, they made all haste to Granada. Here they were cordially received by Vargas, who, after taking a few days to satisfy himself of Gracian's ability, at once made over to him his own powers of Apostolic Visitor of the Carmelites of Andalucia. His commission, however, was to be kept a profound secret unless circumstances should render it imperatively necessary for him to produce it. Lending a deaf ear to the incensed Provincial's impotent threats, whose orders for their instant return to Pastrana, under pain of the severest punishment, reached them whilst they still lingered in Granada; and provided with two separate patents—one for the government of the Descalzos, the other for that of the Observants,—the last only to be produced in case of extreme necessity, they bent their steps to Seville. Their first act was to restore the monastery of San Juan del Puerto to its original possessors. It was quickly done. Mariano and Gracian arrived before the convent gates at the same time as did the Observants commissioned to receive it. A chapter was convoked in which Gracian warned the friars of his intentions; to prevent any disturbance in the town, he enjoined on them absolute silence under the severest censures. At midnight of the following day, after singing Matins in the choir, Gracian marshalled his little band of monks, carefully excluding all those who had joined from the Observance, and marched them off on foot to Seville, where they arrived on the afternoon of the 2nd October, and, at Gracian's request, were permitted to take up their abode in the Carmelite monastery. But things had gone too far to be quietened by a tardy act of concession, which the Observants looked upon rather as a sign of their rivals' weakness than anything else. If for a time they allowed the Descalzos to shelter themselves in an upper part of their monastery, they could not long conceal the ill-disguised contempt and dislike with which from the heights of their antiquity and aristocratic traditions they looked down on the pestilent innovators who in their turn pretended to be the only exponents of the primitive traditions of Mount Carmel, and they soon came to an open rupture. But, however much the Observants longed to be rid of their unwelcome guests, they were equally determined that they should not, if they could help it, establish themselves elsewhere. They succeeded in preventing them from founding in one hermitage, and were likely to do so again, when the Archbishop, who in these domestic squabbles espoused the cause of the Descalzos, and even offered them a room in his palace, gave them that of Our Lady of Refuge, on the western bank of the Guadalquivir, which, buried in trees by the river side, and rarely disturbed by traffic or wayfarers, seemed to have been destined by nature for the abode of contemplatives. On the eve of Epiphany of 1574 the Descalzos, unperceived by its inmates, stole softly out of the Observant monastery, and two by two took their way to the hermitage. After solemnly chanting Vespers they assembled in the hermit's grot, where they were met by the Archbishop's steward and a notary. A friar, who at the bishop's desire was there for that purpose, then handed over the keys to the alguacil, who in his turn delivered them to Gracian; with which simple ceremony the hermitage, its gardens, and all that belonged to it passed into the possession of the Descalzos.

The news of the foundation fell among the Observants like a bomb. Our Lady of Refuge was one of the most famous images in Seville. As the stately galleons and caravels, their gay pennons and streamers dangling languidly in the hot sun of Andalucia, sailed slowly down the river, ocean-bound, their last salute before it faded from their sight was for the battlemented shrine where the Virgin kept watch over the lives of storm-tossed mariners; and again on their return laden with the gold of the Indies, castellated poop and stately mast were wrapped in a film of smoke, as they hove in sight of the white walls gleaming amongst the orange trees.

The shrine itself was filled with votive offerings of seafaring folk. The tablets which covered the walls were full of their strange deliverances and escapes from the jaws of death and peril of the deep seas; of marvellous and reassuring apparitions of the Virgin to her votaries, in answer to their agonised prayers in awful nights at sea, when the great ship, buffeted by winds and waves, creaked and groaned in her distress like a soul in pain.

The Observants, furious at the march that had been stolen on them, and at the obnoxious foundation having risen under their very noses; far from dreaming that at that very moment Gracian was virtually the head of the Order, and could do with them what he willed, haughtily demanded an explanation of his conduct and satisfaction for the insult. They chose as their ambassador the most influential member of their community,—strangely enough, that same Fray Diego de Leon, the Bishop of Columbria, who had exhorted Fr. Gabriel de la Concepcion to visit the pious hermits of La Peñuela. He and the sub-prior made their way to the hermitage. They asked Gracian by what right he had dared to admit a foundation without the Provincial's consent, in express contravention, moreover, of the General's mandates, and insisted on his producing his patents and letters so that the Observants might judge for themselves of their validity.

There were two courses open to Gracian: to produce his Brief and anticipate the storm which was inevitable, or to let things take their course. There was nothing now to be gained by temporising: it could not have gone worse with him than it did, and would have vastly strengthened his whole future position in the Order. But this was for a bolder or more vainglorious man, and Gracian was neither. He preferred to drift with the tide, and leave it to circumstances to open the eyes of the Observants. Perhaps, too, he himself was scarcely satisfied as to the validity of his commission; and he was reluctant, whilst still a chance remained of conciliating the General, to cut it off for ever. His answer to the Bishop was, that his authority for making the foundation and that by which he had restored San Juan del Puerto to the Observants was the same, and it was unreasonable to accept it in the one case if they rejected it in the other. For the rest, his patents were in the hands of the Archbishop, who on the strength of them had given him the hermitage and sanctioned the foundation, and to him he referred them. Upon which the Bishop, checkmated, returned to his convent no wiser than he had left it.

As might have been foreseen, it was not long before the Observants either knew or suspected the real state of the case; that Gracian was acting in virtue of the powers transferred to him by Vargas; and their anger centred on the men who, they felt, constituted by their talents and energy a veritable danger to their body. They wrote to the General (already sufficiently incensed against the visitors for interfering, and against the Descalzos for accepting their intervention in the affairs of an Order he looked upon as peculiarly his own) to urge upon him the necessity of obtaining from Pope Gregory XIII. an instant revocation of the commissions held by Fernandez and Vargas. If this was done they would soon make short shrift of the Descalzos.

Vargas, who as Provincial of his Order happened to be in Seville at the time, convinced that the Carmelites meant war to the knife, made haste to be beforehand with them. He wrote to the king warmly defending the friars of the Reform. This letter he sent to Madrid, by the licentiate Padilla, a priest formerly employed by Philip in the Reform of the Orders, until his harshness and "terrible condition" made it expedient to employ him no longer. Finding his occupation gone in Spain, he had proceeded to Seville, with the intention of embarking for the "Indies," there to convert the "infidels." Happily for the bodies of the infidels, however, if not for their souls, he was robbed of all he had in a posada, and forced to take refuge in the Discalced Carmelite Monastery of the Remedios.

The Pope revoked the commissions granted to Fernandez and Vargas, although the revocation was not made public until May of the following year, when the chapter general of the Order, sitting at Plasencia, issued its virulent decrees against Teresa and her friars. What they were, we shall see later on.

It is possible that had the Carmelites laughed quietly and done nothing, the world would never have heard of the Descalzos; that they would, after founding a few more convents, when the vitality which moved them had died away, have been gradually reabsorbed into the Order from which they sprang. But pride and jealousy had placed the matter on a footing the Observants had little anticipated,—no one is wise before the event,—and raised it into a species of state question between the courts of Rome and Spain. They had not counted with the determined obstinacy of an irresolute man. It was at Philip's request that Vargas and Fernandez had been appointed. To revoke their commission might also be looked upon in the light of a personal insult to himself. Gracian and Mariano were well known to him: he had watched the university career of the former with marked interest, often inquiring when he was to be made a doctor. Mariano he had repeatedly employed. It was besides a direct attack on the ecclesiastical autonomy of his kingdom, and true to the policy of his great-grandparents, Ferdinand and Isabella, he never brooked the interference of Rome in the church matters of Spain. If he was not, as was his father, the *preux chevalier* of Catholic Christendom, he tacitly considered himself what he accounted it heresy for Elizabeth to style herself in England, the head of the Church in his own dominions. His spies kept him well informed of all that went on at the Papal court, and the news of the revocation reached his ears as soon as it was made. More than once he had found himself in direct antagonism to Rome, and had boldly held his ground; he had no intention of flinching now.

The king and the shrewdest politicians of his kingdom, Covarrubias, the President of the Council; Quiroga, Grand Inquisitor, and afterwards Archbishop of Toledo; Don Luis Manrique, his chief almoner; his secretary, Gabriel de Zayas, laid their heads together (as great as any in Christendom, adds the chronicler) to devise the best means for parrying a stroke in which they not only saw the destruction of the Descalzos, but an encroachment on the rights of the throne. Padilla was consulted. Vargas, he said, already trembling at the opposition he had raised, having cooled in his projects of Reform, had transmitted it to the Father Master Gracian, "a man of great parts, letters, and ability, but somewhat fearful of attempting it," as the authority he held from Vargas did not seem to him sufficient, and in any case had now been revoked by the Head of the Church. If anything was done, it must be done quickly. The Carmelites had left one vulnerable point in their armour; they had neglected to secure the revocation of the special powers held by Ormaneto, the Papal Nuncio in Spain. If Ormaneto was now made to anticipate the publication of the Brief by issuing a counter one re-invalidating the commission held by Vargas and appointing Gracian his substitute, the Observants would be rendered powerless. Gracian, being warned by a relative of these intentions regarding him, and advised to come to court to give the benefit of his advice and experience, after preaching his Lenten sermons in Seville to enormous and enthusiastic audiences, and leaving Mariano in charge of Our Lady of Refuge, set out after Easter for Madrid, accompanied by a lay brother, who, having been formerly engaged in business, was well acquainted with the roads. On this occasion it was that, hearing of Teresa's presence in Veas, he determined to turn aside that he might see and converse with the foundress of his Order.

It is now time to devote a few words to the man who, by a strange caprice of fate, has become the central figure of the Order, and whose history forms one of the most extraordinary pages in the already extraordinary annals of the Descalzos. Born in Valladolid, when Valladolid was still the court of Spain, Fr. Geronymo de la Madre de Dios, better known as Gracian, was now a little more than twenty-seven. Diego Gracian de Alderete, his father, son of the chief armourer of the Catholic kings, became in his turn, and in a different capacity, an old and trusted servant of the House of Austria. First as secretary to the Emperor Charles V., who armed him a knight, and declared his children and descendants nobles, and then as Philip's, he did them both good service in the "interpretation of languages, accounts, crusades, and affairs of great importance, confidence, and secrecy, on account of his unequalled skill in languages, Latin, Greek, and others." He had been a traveller too, and had studied at the University of Louvain under the learned Luis Vives, where the Flemings altered his name of Garcia into Gracian; and Gracian it remained, and was transmitted in due course to his children. Later on his love of letters brings him acquainted with the Polish ambassador, a man of literary tastes like himself, whose daughter he presently marries, she being then twelve years old. The ambassador returns to Poland, and, "like the excellent Christian he was, gets himself ordained, and becomes successively Bishop of Cumas and Viernia." And the secretary buckles down to the business of life, and the struggle to maintain a large and increasing family.

But nature had done more for the Catholic kings' chief armourer's son than even his majesty Charles V. could do in those faded parchments with their leaden seals. One of the most sympathetic figures that flit across this history—seen as in a glass darkly—is that of the good secretary, scholarly, gentle, bountiful, a noble type of the Castilian gentleman. At his death (he died quietly reciting Greek and Latin verses of devotion) it was noted that where others in his position left large fortunes and estates to their descendants, he left nothing except an unblemished name, having spent all he had in charity. Something more he left: translations of Xenophon, Isocrates, and Plutarch, a History of the Conquest of the African cities on the coast of Barbary—still to be found on the dusty shelves of old Spanish libraries—rescue the name of Diego Gracian Alderete from the oblivion which has fallen on his personality.

The Polish ambassador's daughter, Juana Dantisco, proved a worthy helpmeet of the husband who, when she was old and wrinkled, could still pen a tender distich to the face whose beauty had captivated him in youth. Of their large family of thirteen children, Gracian was the third son. Trained in the school of the Jesuits, his university career was a series of uninterrupted triumphs, and already augured for him as brilliant a one in the world, when, to the good secretary's sorrow, who had intended his son to follow in his own footsteps, and depended on him to help his brothers and sisters on in life, Gracian turned his back on the honours he might legitimately have hoped to achieve in the world, and at the age of twenty-three insisted on entering the priesthood. It is more than probable that he would have joined the Jesuits —themselves anxious to secure so bright a subject—had not some unforeseen delay, together with the advent of the Carmelite students in the schools of Alcalá, diverted him from his first intention, and altered the whole course of his career. In vain he struggled against the influences which were drawing him to his Fate. In vain he drew the curtain over the tender face, which now seemed to him full of reproach, of the only mistress he had ever vowed to serve—an Image of the Virgin; a succession of apparently insignificant circumstances,—the rustic answer of an old woman whom he reproved for her excessive mortifications; a sermon the nuns of the Convent of the Image asked him to preach in praise of the antiquity of the Order of Mount Carmel—were the obscure causes which finally led him to embrace the vocation which was to be at once the glory and perdition of his life. Gracian had inherited to the full all his father's scholarly tastes and love of curious erudition, in which at a later date he sought consolation for the disasters of his life; and we can imagine what it was like,—this first sermon of a young, clever, enthusiastic man, enamoured of his subject, and exceedingly eloquent by nature. Bristling with learning, perhaps not altogether free from the alembicated conceits which were the literary vice of the period, it electrified all who heard it. He achieved a stupendous triumph similar to that which greeted him in Brussels, when towards the close of his life he preached on the same subject (the glories of Our Virgin of Carmel) before the Archduke Albert and the Infanta Clara Eugenia of Spain. All Alcalá rang with the praises of the young and eloquent orator; his admirers painted his name in red ochre on the walls of the church; nay more, so powerful its effect on one at least of his audience,—the Master Roca, a distinguished graduate of the University,—that he straightway went off to Pastrana to become a novice, and as Fray Juan de Jesus—the rock of bronze—took a prominent part in the erection of the Descalzos into a separate province, as we shall see farther on. A visit to Pastrana did the rest. The nuns were captivated by the strange and winning charm of the young man who, to the lustre of talents which had filled the schools of Alcalá with amazement and admiration, added a singularly sweet and fascinating personality, and a discretion far beyond his years.

The good nuns stoutly attributed the accession of so eminent a subject to their prayers; Teresa, more humbly, to the Virgin, who had, she said, guided her son to her most favoured Refuge. However it may be, certain it is that Gracian paid a visit to Roca at Pastrana, which impressed him so profoundly that without returning to Alcalá, he remained there as a novice.

It would seem from his own statement that the jealousy which pursued him through life, and eventually drove him from the Order, began from the very moment he entered it. Strange that the cloister should breed feelings so little akin to holiness! Those who had already professed, his seniors in years and experience, saw themselves passed over in favour of the man who, still but a novice himself, was in the prior's absence entrusted with the charge of thirty others.

Teresa herself unconsciously administered food to the incipient rancour by enjoining her prioress of Pastrana to give him (whom she said it had cost her a year's prayers to win) the same obedience that they rendered to herself.

Withal Gracian wavered: his family were bitterly opposed to the step he had taken; it had brought his mother to the verge of death; when time healed the smart, all she could be induced to say was that she had not given her son to the Virgin, but that the Virgin had taken him from her: his delicate constitution suffered severely from the asperities of the Rule. Three months before he irrevocably took the vows, he was sorely tempted to abandon a vocation so contrary to the real bent of his character, and, but for the encouragement of Isabel de Santo Domingo, it is probable that he never would have taken them.

It is difficult to disentangle truth from falsehood in the web of accusation, calumny, and extravagant eulogy, of which Gracian has alternately been made both victim and subject. It is often a mere blind accident of Fate that makes a man famous or consigns him to infamy. Had he entered the Society of Jesuits his name would have gone down to posterity, linked with those of Laynez and Salmeron. In an evil hour he turned aside to join the Descalzos. Perhaps in those very qualities which make him much the most lovable and sympathetic of Teresa's friars—much the most human—we may find the secret of his ruin. His novitiate barely concluded, he found himself, fresh from the scholarly tranquillity of a University, plunged into a movement when the feud between the Observants and Descalzos ran highest; the leader of a faction, a post for which nature had eminently unsuited him. He lacked nerve, decision, promptitude, self-confidence. He vacillated and weakened at the most critical moments, when a bold front and steady hand would have swept away every obstacle and ensured a certain victory. That very facility and yieldingness of disposition, that very candour and freedom from suspicion, the loftiest note in his character, as it was its greatest charm, became his greatest curse, inasmuch as it made him the prey of intriguing and unscrupulous men (and Gracian was neither), who, after using him as the instrument of their ambitions, basely turned and rent him. He was a student, not a fighter; a man of letters with a tendency to religious mysticism, but not an ascetic; his genial and benevolent nature often led him to consider as of minor importance those trivial details of discipline in which the more limited brains of his monkish compeers placed salvation or perdition. Alternately wavering between the advice of others and his own judgment (which was generally sound), he was incapable of adhering to a consistent line of action. Still all generalisations are eminently imperfect, and it may be doubted whether a bolder man, or one more obstinate of purpose, would have done better, or even so well as Gracian. His consummate tact; the instinct that led him to prefer conciliation to open warfare, stood him in good stead in the difficult position in which he had been placed, and helped to carry the Descalzos over many a slippery pass. Yet a great man,—far greater than the narrow despots who hounded him from the Order,—he rises immeasurably above them in the hour of his disgrace. The magnanimity, the constancy he displayed in circumstances of all most fitted to put them to the test, proves how keenly Teresa had gauged the character of him whom above all others she loved and venerated, and Pope Clement VIII. was perhaps not far wrong when he exclaimed, struck by his humility and forbearance, "Verily this man is a saint!"

It was in Veas that Teresa first beheld him with whom her life was thenceforth to be so intimately linked. Her interview with him was one of the profoundest joys of her life. Never had her heart gone out so completely to any one as it did to this young friar, who stirred it as it had never been stirred before. From that moment she vowed to him a passionate and touching devotion which ended only with her life. All praise seemed to her inadequate for one who, to her thinking, "bettered all praise," and in whom she had at last found, or fancied she had found, the only man capable of assuming the generalship of the Order; one whom she could associate with herself in the cares and trials fast becoming a heavy burden for her declining years; a confidant to whom she could unbosom her most secret soul, and on whose ready sympathy she could count for help and direction: nay, more than this, a disciple willing to defer his judgment to her own; a spiritual successor to whom she could bequeath her lifelong work.

It is with an unwonted outburst of enthusiasm,—strange, perhaps painful to watch in a nature so strong and robust as hers; trained by a lifetime's repression to keep her slightest emotion under rigid control,—that she writes to her cousin, the prioress of Medina:

> Oh, my Mother, how I have longed for you these last few days! Know that to my thinking they have been the best of my life, without exaggeration. The father, Master Gracian, has been here for more than twenty days. I assure you that even now I have not fathomed his worth. To my eyes he is perfect. . . . What your reverence and all of us must do now is to beseech God to give him to us for our Superior. At last I shall be able to take some repose from the management of these houses. For such perfection mingled with so much suavity I have not seen. May God support and keep him, for I would not for anything have missed seeing him and conversing with him. He has been waiting for Mariano, who to our delight was long of coming. Julian de Avila has lost his heart to him—so have they all. He preaches admirably.

Thus she unconsciously reveals to us the hidden depths of her passionate and tender character, still throbbing as faithfully to all the impulses of affection as if the cloister had never set its iron seal upon her humanity.

His delicacy of constitution; the softness and sweetness of his disposition; the peculiar charm of his manner, perhaps his very defects, the antithesis of her own decided character, gave him a special claim on her maternal solicitude and tenderness. With this there mingled a touch of faded sentiment. He was her Pablo, her Eliseo (Elisha, an allusion to his premature baldness): she his Angela, his Laurencia. In his hands she becomes as submissive as a child, meekly resigning her will to his. She did for him what she had never done before in the case of any of her confessors; she vowed to obey his voice as that of God; to give him her undivided and entire obedience: she gave her conscience into his keeping, to do with it as he listed, in this complete surrender of herself to a wisdom she accepted as superior to her own.

Nor, whatever his enemies may have asserted, did Gracian ever prove himself unworthy of her generous confidence. There is nothing to show that her love for him ever changed, or that her last few months on earth were clouded by the shortcomings of her favourite and best-loved son. Nay, it is more than probable that had she lived longer she would have shared his downfall. Teresa was too great for her century. Even now it is not the Teresa I am endeavouring to set forth—Teresa the high-minded, Teresa the human, Teresa the woman—who is loved and reverenced by her pious votaries, but a garbled image, decked and obscured with tinsel and paper flowers, and swathed about with strange superstitions and puerile miracles, through which we must not let the sunlight penetrate for fear of exploding the monstrous creature of distorted fancy.

That she was not blind to his defects—she was far too shrewd—never was there such a strange blending of earth and heaven as this woman, whose character is still a problem; that she endeavoured with a woman's tact to supplement by her own experience and profound knowledge of character the easy kindliness and misplaced frankness of temperament, which often exposed him to misconstruction; to infuse energy and decision into counsels that were often timid and irresolute; that she recognised how the most elevated quality of his character—his rare freedom from suspicion and inability to penetrate the base motives of others, which often imparted to his conduct a certain tinge of unpracticality, often laid him open to the attacks of his enemies, is certain. But for all this, I think she loved more than less. Never were reproof, censure, hints which it was quite admissible for an old woman, who had grown old amongst monks and nuns and their ways, to administer to a young and inexperienced man entering on an untried world full of pitfalls, more delicately, more tenderly given. Whilst life lasted she stood in the breach between him and his enemies, shielding him under the ægis of her reputation,—for few could deceive her,—and from the first she felt the buzz of malicious jealousy which threatened him, and after her death compassed his downfall.

And yet it is on these self-same distorted shreds of her letters, violently wrenched from their context, that Gracian has been sentenced and condemned for more than three centuries; and so sorely pushed were his enemies for more substantial evidence as to be forced to the expedient of making Teresa express her disapproval from heaven, through the mouth of the visionary Catalina de Jesus, the foundress of Veas.

It was without a protest, without a murmur that at Gracian's bidding she hastened to do what she declared nothing would ever induce her to do—to found in Andalucia, for which she had all the instinctive and inherited dislike of a true Castilian. The fact is that at Veas she had already done so, apparently without knowing it; for when Maria Bautista, her advice-loving prioress of Valladolid, had pointed out to her in one of her letters some months before that Veas was in Andalucia, a province expressly omitted from the General's commission, Teresa had answered that it was not that Veas, but one five leagues from Segovia, where she then was. Instead of starting for Caravaca, as she had intended; instead of spending the fierce summer heats in the beloved repose of San José, as she had looked forward to—" What a much better summer," she writes to the prioress of Medina, " should I have spent with your reverence than in the heat of Seville "—she unhesitatingly abandoned her own judgment to the voice of obedience, and even, it is said, in the face of a direct revelation, took the road to Seville, which was to be to her her Garden of Gethsemane!

" In short," she writes to D. Alvaro Mendoza, " we set out for Seville in the coming week, Monday—fifty leagues. I believe perfectly he would not have forced it upon me, but he wished it so strongly that if I did not go I should have felt some scruple that I had not fulfilled obedience as I always desire. As for myself it has distressed me, and moreover it has not pleased me much to go with this heat to pass the summer in Andalucia."

CHAPTER XVIII

SUPERABUNDO GAUDIO

IT was close on Easter [1]—*Pascua florida*—flowery paschaltide—when the little band of Castilians set out to traverse what seemed to them the "fiery furnace" of Andalucia, and the ramshackle carts once more creaked along the dusty road, a thin white streak on the calcined landscape. How they longed for the cool plateaux and sierras of Castille, she and her nuns, as they panted in the suffocating atmosphere of the cart! They who had never been so far from home before, oppressed by the strange-featured country around them, exiles and wanderers in an unknown and unfamiliar land. Some alleviations of their sufferings they *did* find in dwelling on the superior torments of hell. "I assure you, sisters, that as the sun fell full upon the carts, to enter them was like being in purgatory. Sometimes, what with thinking on hell, at others that we were doing something and suffering for God, these sisters travelled with great content and cheerfulness; for the six who went with me were such that I think with them I would have even dared to go to the land of the Turks." One of the nuns she thus eulogises was that Maria de San José, Da. Luisa de la Cerda's waiting-woman, who, having abandoned her kinswoman's palace in Toledo to follow the fortunes of the foundress, is presently, as prioress of Seville, to become one of the most prominent figures of the Order.

Hell and the land of the Turks: so it seemed, or worse, to the woman of sixty, her brain conjuring up the miniature

---

[1] So says Master Julian, but he must mean either Ascension Tide or Pentecost, which in the year 1575 fell, the first on the 12th, the second on the 22nd of May. By this count the journey to Seville took them a fortnight or ten days at least.

of a gray town cropping up amidst gray boulders, walled
and grim ; around it waste moorland and streams ; mountain
peaks tipped with snow ; dark and mysterious at sunset ;
covered with silvery haze in the light of early morning ; where
the powerful sunlight heals rather than oppresses ; and down
in the valley where gleams the Adaja, a streak of silver, an
old rambling convent ; behind it the evening sky, molten
of all precious jewels—the topaz, the turquoise, and the
amethyst.

On this journey to Seville [writes Master Julian—but he had
travelled thither before in his adventurous youth, and felt not the same
homesickness, the "saudades" of his mistress] there were noteworthy
incidents which, as they have been related by our mother, I shall not
mention here. The heat with which we started, it being close on
Easter, was so excessive, that the provisions we brought with us from
Veas, and which were to have lasted several days, could not be eaten
the following day. The mother took with her a large pig-skin full of
water for the journey, but so great was the scarcity of water that at a
venta on the way the smallest jugful cost two maravedis each, being
dearer than wine. I know not whether it was at this same venta or
another, that some perverse people so sharpened their tongues at fr.
Gregorio's expense, who had just before taken the habit in Veas, that
his conduct on that occasion was more than enough to test his virtue :
they were either fools or drunk. At last, at the end of all this, they
set on each other with knives to the terror of our nuns, who were
still inside the carts, the ground being too filthy to allow of them
alighting. At length the fighters, in dread of being taken by the
authorities, took to their heels, and left us in peace.

It is more than likely that the white venta where this
scene occurred — so rapid, so vivid in its brevity — still
gleams, carelessly oblivious of time, in the hot mid-day
sun, as it did on that day of the sixteenth century. The
travellers alone have changed. And yet, at the bidding of
a dry and scanty detail, all the strange, heterogeneous
elements which composed that picturesque, out-at-elbows,
poverty-stricken society, and nevertheless in spite of it all,
one full of a serious, old-world dignity, troop in phantas-
magoric procession before our eyes. The roads of Spain
once again swarm with that distant, faintly-discerned life
and movement. Wandering friars ; messengers on horseback or on foot—ragged Gil, or Blas, or Llorente speeding
to and fro between Andalucia and court—post from one part

of the kingdom to the other; pseudo and real pilgrims bound to distant shrines,—the cockleshell of Compostela gleaming amidst their rags; fine gentlemen and pages; swashbucklers, with mustachios twisted à la Borgoña; swarthy men who had been in the Indies and could tell strange and marvellous stories; carters and muleteers; students, ragged, thievish, and hungry—for the matter of that, so they all are; so goes on the seething medley of life and movement, some dim relics of which still remain in the group of beggars I saw the other day before the gateway of San Estéban de Salamanca, waiting with their wooden bowls for the distribution of the Sunday dole. Finery and rags, mirth and starvation; dignity gravely supported on empty stomachs; passing them all, mingling with them all, the rickety carts which bear our nuns to Seville, escorted by a Salamancan gentleman, booted and spurred, a Castilian priest, and a barefooted Carmelite friar.

Still, with all its difficulty, it is easier to reconstruct the external aspect of this Spain of theirs than that of any other country of Europe. Here, at least, civilisation has not been so busy as elsewhere effacing ancient landmarks. The dreamer who would fain penetrate himself with the distant flavour of this past epoch,—catch something of its intermittent and obscure aroma—may still dream as he threads these "caminos vecinales" winding through a maze of beautiful and ever-varying landscape—fields of green grain, ripening in the sun, full of scarlet blots of poppies; oak glades, green and silent; arid and burnt-up wastes shut in by lines of far-away mountains, blue undulations on the vast horizon —that he treads the same paths which were trodden by Teresa de Jesus three good centuries ago. Such were, indeed, the roads of Spain as she knew them, and no other. Roads in the modern sense did not exist; and the same thing might be said of the bridges, few and far between. Towns and villages were linked together by these same "caminos vecinales," little more than paths frayed by donkeys and travellers, few of them accessible to carts, following every undulation of the soil. The nearest approach to the modern "carretera" or high road was occasionally a little bit of paved causeway, left as often as not by the Moors, which ended within a quarter of a mile or less of the town to which it formed the entrance. In winter, when the streamlets were swollen by rain, neighbouring towns and villages were often cut off from each other for months together.

A journey in those days was one of very real risk and peril. Most men made their wills (and a Spaniard never makes his without extreme reluctance) before they trusted themselves to the risks and accidents of the road. And yet here are a nun and her companions, a parcel of weak women, undaunted by privation and fatigue, creaking along in an old cart through the heart of Andalucia.

Her enemies said she was a gad-about and restless woman—gad-about and restless! And, stranger than this, a modern historian, untouched by this spectacle, so all-pathetic, where valour takes the place of youth, and brave heart makes up for decaying strength, repeats the accusation in a wooden essay. So she might have been—gad-about and restless—if she had gone to please herself; although I imagine there was little pleasure to be found, except the satisfaction that comes from Duty done, to pant all day in a wooden cart without springs, and be jolted over leagues of Spanish mediæval road under the fierce June sun of Andalucia.

And so the cart and its burden creaks slowly on,—past the glories of sunrise and sunset, past the white, dusty, shrivelled-up landscape of mid-day—until, on the day preceding Easter Sunday, to the consternation of her nuns, Teresa became delirious.

> They threw water on my face, so heated with the sun that it gave little or no refreshment. Nor must I forget to tell you how bad was the posada for such an extremity; for they gave us a small room with a roof of open tiles; it had no window, and if the door was opened the sun streamed full into it. You must consider [says Teresa] that the sun in that country is not like that of Castille, but very much more importunate. The bed on which they threw me was such that I was obliged to take refuge from it on the floor. Here it was so high, there so low, that I could not lie still, for it seemed as if it had been made of sharp stones. What a thing is sickness! for it is easy to put up with anything if one has only health. In short, I thought it better to rise and set forth, for the sun of the open country seemed to me preferable to that wretched room. . . .
>
> Shortly before this, probably two days, something else happened to

us, which put us into a sore predicament, crossing the river Guadalquivir in a boat. When it came to the carts, it was impossible to keep alongside of the rope, and we had to head down the river a little, although by dragging the rope along with us, it helped us a little; but it happened that those who held it let go, or I know not how it came about, so that the boat drifted down the stream with the cart, without either rope or oars. I was much more concerned at the ferryman's distress than at the danger; we set to work to pray, all the others to shout. A gentleman who was watching us from a castle close by, pitying our plight, sent some one to lend us a hand—this whilst we still had hold of the rope, at which our brothers were tugging with all their might; but the force of the current proved too much for them, and knocked some of them down. In good sooth, I shall never forget the devotion I felt at the boatman's son: he must have been about ten or eleven years of age, but his distress at his father's plight made me praise the Lord. Nevertheless since his Majesty ever gives trials proportioned to our strength, so it was now, for the boat happened to strike on a sand-bank, on one side of which there was low water, and so we were able to get out. It was now night, and it would have gone ill with us to find the road, had not he who came from the castle put us on the right way. I did not intend to treat of matters so unimportant—for many are the tales I could relate of misadventures on the road—had I not been urged to dwell more at length on this one.

How her quaint narrative flashes the scene to us! The dusk falling over the wide bosom of the river; the red gleam of the setting sun fading behind the gray fortress on the hill; the bevy of shrieking women—she perhaps the only one silent at this moment of supreme danger—floating down the river, they and the cart, in the gathering gloom.

Before daylight, a day before the Festival of the Holy Ghost (Whitsunday), they arrived at Cordoba. They would fain have entered the town unseen and unnoticed, but (to facilitate trade) no carts were allowed to cross the bridge without a license from the governor. It would have been curious to know Teresa's impressions at sight of the Moorish town, its yellow walls whitening in the pale light of dawn on that hot May morning,—those yellow walls cracked by sun and age, and stained by time, that had once enclosed the most polished and brilliant civilisation Spain has ever known (I use the present tense advisedly). To all outward seeming doubtless, it looked much the same to her as it does to us. The Moorish water-mills in the stream; tumbled lines of flat-roofed houses rising high on the slope above the river; slender minarets and church towers, gleaming like pearls against blotches of dusky orange leaves; here and there a palm-tree, bearing with it that same dim reminiscence of the East that once upon a time brought tears to the eyes of a great Caliph of Cordoba.

One building stands out more conspicuous than the rest. What though the heavy and tasteless hand of the Christian has spoilt the delicate harmony of its lines by substituting a Renaissance bell-tower for the graceful minaret, scaly and glittering like a lizard's back, surmounted by a golden ball, from which the sun struck strange glows and sparks of fire, that had once welcomed the Moor to Cordoba—it still served to mark out the spot where stood the marvellous mosque, more famous than that of Baghdad, more gorgeous than that of Irak, once the glory and the boast of Islam. And so as they wait in the sun—the May sun of Cordoba—sparkling on the broad bosom of the river, turning all to gold, changing water-mills and tottering cabins and dirty, tortuous streets into a fairy city, making the air to quiver with its intensity, and the fleas began to bite, and the nuns peep timidly through the awnings — the expiring spirit of Gothic mediævalism looks out from the faded eyes of Teresa, its last great production, on the shell left by that other civilisation so alien to it, which it had crushed out of Spain for ever. At length, after they have waited two mortal hours (time is worth nothing in Spain), the priestly robes of Master Julian appear across the bridge. He has brought the license, but the gates are too narrow to admit the carts, which have to be sawn down, or otherwise reduced to the proper size. By this time the crowd—the crowd that is always ready in Andalucia, then as now, dirty, ragged, every rascal a gentleman, every gentleman a rascal —have gathered to stare and chatter round the stranger carts. "Pedro, dost thou see the nuns, the strangers?" "Yes, little one, how ugly they are" (everything foreign is ugly to a Spaniard, be he Castilian or Andaluz). This though the awnings of the cart were closed, and except to the eye of faith (a rare article in Andalucia), nuns ugly or beautiful were alike invisible. Fancy the scene; the jaded women, the invisible centre of attraction to Pedro, Juanito, and Ramon: ugly, bare imps chattered, withered brown hags jabbered, donkeys brayed. Old men, brown as mahogany, leaning on sticks as gnarled as their fingers, glared intently. Girls with a carnation stuck behind their right ear, their unkempt hair black and coarse as horses' tails, wrapped in gay shawls, leaned lazily out of opened lattices. The bells ring on the mules' head-stalls as they jerk back from their halters; the cocks crow from under the arms of the people going to the cock-fight; the yelp of yellow, half-starved curs, the guttural accents of the semi-Moorish crowd all mingle together in this indescribable pandemonium. "One would have thought that the Holy Father himself was to make his entrance into Cordoba that day."

Soon rumour began to be busy. An intermediate line of carts stretching far into the plain had been descried. Grave and reverend fools closely wrapped in their brown cloaks (a cloak is good in Spain against either heat or cold) laid their addle heads together, and were of opinion that all the nuns of France were coming, *vienen monjas por millones* —nuns like locusts. It was a danger, a menace to the city, to the State, to Religion. We must fetch the governor, warn the alguaciles. These cannot be nuns, they must be some heretics.

For this is an excitable population, finding in the occurrences of everyday life more marvels than many find in fairy tales.

In a church, at least, they will have a moment's peace from the curiosity and comments of the populace. So to a church they betake themselves, only to find themselves in the thick of another crowd almost worse than the one on the bridge. As ill luck would have it, it was the festival of the Advocation of the Holy Ghost, and they had been guided to the very church where it was to be specially celebrated with feasts and dancing.

"When I saw this," writes Teresa, "I was greatly distressed. If it had depended on me, we would have gone away without hearing Mass, rather than make our way through such a turbulent mob. Father Julian, however, thought differently, and he being a theologian" (not the first time that theology has been in opposition to reason), "we had perforce to abide by his opinion, for the rest would perhaps have been fain to follow mine. We alighted close to the church, and although none could see our faces, over which we always wore long black veils, it was enough to see us with them, and our white serge capes and alpargatas, to convulse every one; and so it was. That fright it must have been that drove my fever away, for certainly we all got a shrewd one. As we entered the church, a worthy man came up to me to force a passage through the crowd. I begged him earnestly to take us to some chapel; which he did, shutting us in and keeping guard over us until it was time to leave the church "—an act of courtesy for which he was well rewarded, for "a few days after he came to Seville and told a father of our Order how he believed that God had repaid him for the service he had done us, for he had come into a large fortune when he least expected it. I tell you, daughters, that although this may perhaps seem to you nothing, it was for me one of the worst moments I have ever gone through; because the excitement of the people was as great as if bulls had entered. And so I was all impatience to get out of that town: although there was no place near to pass the festival in: we celebrated it under a bridge."

Thus far, Teresa. Let us now listen to the vivacious and circumstantial narrative of her chaplain, Master Julian, who in his turn, unprotected by his theology, had come to loggerheads with the priest in whose church he was saying Mass :—

Never since Cordoba was Cordoba had festival been celebrated as it was that day. For besides the procession of priests and people, there was one of nuns, better worth seeing than all the rest, for they entered the church in procession, with their white capes, their faces covered by their black veils, whilst I sped with all haste to get everything ready to say Mass and give them the Communion. . . . It was God's will that, in spite of the curate of the church not being present, they gave me what I required. I had already begun Mass when he arrived, and I know not what possessed him, but he puts me on his stole and surplice, and places himself at the corner of the altar. I suspected that he had taken offence at my having made so bold as to administer the sacrament in his church, and that he had come to do so himself. At the proper time with great determination I turned round, and gave our Lord's body to the nuns, whereupon he said nothing. But at the church door I found him waiting for me, and he gave me a sharp reproof, asking me how it came about that I had said Mass without his leave. I replied with great calmness and serenity (if it had been before I believe I should have treated him to a little sourness), for since I had now done what I came to do, all I wanted was to get away from him and the sound of his tongue. Escape from the crowd was impossible, unless we had all remained without our Mass, for if we had gone to another church we should have been followed by a crowd throughout the city : to have left it unsaid had also its drawbacks, for we were a goodly company ; and of the two courses, I decided to take the one that was most in accordance with our conscience ; more especially as the day before, which was the Vigil, we had gone without Mass, as we had nothing to celebrate it with, at which I had felt a terrible melancholy. This being so, what should I have felt if Whitsunday had gone by in the same way ?

Delightful, prosy Master Julian, so soon, alas! about to disappear from this history, with so transparent a simplicity revealing to us his foibles, his little weaknesses, his guilelessness, and his real goodness !

At length, under the grateful shadow of a bridge, too glad to take the place of the pigs they drove out, they slept the siesta, and forgot the mortifications of that memorable morning. The Whitsun festival they there celebrated remained eternally graven in the memories of those whose fate it was to survive the great companion who had been the life and soul of it. Melancholy and discouragement fled before the magic presence of the little old woman, shrewd of eye, witty of tongue,—taking in at a glance the fun, the humour, and the folly of it ; turning their adventures into food for merry laughter. " Her very laughter was contagious, and they could not but laugh in concert."

It was on such occasions, in the unrestrained and familiar intercourse of fellow-travellers who share together all the peril and mischances of the road, that Teresa was at her best, her witty satire being followed by graver words of wisdom, but in all moods entrancing the soul of her listeners, who, listening, forgot hunger, discomfort, and privation, charmed and fascinated in spite of themselves.

Our Holy Mother [writes her faithful and constant companion, Master Julian] put fresh life into us all with her excellent and most witty discourse ; now giving utterance to things of great weight, now moving us to laughter. At other times she composed couplets, and very good ones they were, for well did she understand the art, although, unless something happened on the journey to furnish her with a theme, she did not exercise it; so that, in spite of all her prayer, it did not prevent her from holding a holy and friendly intercourse of great profit to both soul and body alike.

Would that all saints were like her!

On the 26th of May Teresa and her nuns arrived in Seville, to find, instead of an Archbishop eager to welcome her and her foundation, as she had confidently expected, and both Gracian and Mariano had led her to believe, a prelate piqued and angry that they should have come at all. Her first motion was to take possession of the small, damp, and wretched house Mariano had hired for her in the Calle de las Armas, as she generally did, by celebrating a solemn Mass. The uneasy evasions of Mariano, the delays he interposed, first revealed to her the truth, which he presently confessed, that so far from his having been able to get a license from the Archbishop, he (the Archbishop) had energetically declared that neither now nor at any other time would he countenance a foundation without endowment. The news fell like a thunderbolt on the devoted head of the fever-stricken woman and her nuns, who thus saw the extinction of the hope which had lured them over fifty leagues and more of hot, dusty Andalucian road!

Both she and her monks had made so sure of the license that they had not even taken any steps to get it. The Descalzos were high in the Archbishop's favour; had he not written several times to Teresa herself in terms of great affection? and here, when they had come to do him a service, "as such in truth it was," writes Teresa, "and so he knew afterwards, only that the Lord willed that no foundation should be made unless at the cost to me of great suffering, some in one way, others in another," he turned his back on them in dudgeon. They had not taken into account, muses the chronicler, that superiors yield to humility and submission what they do not to equality. "As to endowment," says Teresa, "he might just as well have told us not to make the monastery at all." For one thing, even if she had been able to, it was against her conscience to found an endowed convent in a city like Seville, when she had never done so except in small places, where, unless she had provided some settled means of subsistence, it was useless to dream of founding. Besides, even if she consented, how was she—she whose whole belongings were a "blanca" left over from the journey, the clothes she and her nuns stood up in, and a spare tunic or two—to endow a convent? Antonio Gaitan had been forced to borrow money to take himself and Master Julian home; the house was as bare and poverty-stricken as its inmates. Mariano had, indeed, on the night of their arrival provided some rushes to sleep on and a few plates; but they were borrowed from the neighbours, who reclaimed them next day. So that all the bed they had was the bare floor, on which they lay covered over with their capes. Had it not been for Mariano, who provided them with bread (he could do no less), they must have starved; as it was, says the chronicler, such was their patience and love of poverty, that they were better satisfied than if they had been in the tents of Ahasuerus. Where were the rich novices, or indeed any novice at all, of those Gracian had promised her? One lady, indeed, took pity on them; but, entrusting her gifts to one of those pious beatas with which Seville (and indeed all Spain) swarmed, the beata carried them elsewhere, until the lady found it out, and sent them more effectual assistance.

True, the Archbishop, importuned by Mariano, "now more submissive to his authority and repentant of the blunder," relented so far within the next three days as to allow them to celebrate Mass on Trinity Sunday, and even sent one of his chaplains to officiate, but he would allow no bell to be rung, or even hung up, unless it had already been placed.

If it had been for any other but Gracian, Teresa would quickly have shaken from her feet the dust of this rich and populous city, where she and her nuns were starving, face to face with a poverty more abject than any she had yet experienced, even in Toledo.

And yet in their misfortune one or two brave hearts endeavoured to alleviate it. A priest, Garcí Alvarez, came to say Mass for them every day, in spite of the fierce sun and the distance of his house. "If he had had it to give, we should have wanted for nothing." The gray-headed prior of Las Cuevas (this a little later), himself from Avila—of the

Pantojas of Avila—ministered to their necessities ; " And it is just, sisters, you who read this, that you should commend to God those who helped us so well, be they alive or dead . . . to this saint we owe much."

Meantime Gracian writes from Madrid, and Mariano leaves no stone unturned to move the Archbishop's heart. And at last one day (the nuns have struggled and endured as best they could for a month) a gorgeous vision in purple silk, his green hat carried before him on a velvet cushion, appears before the damp, small house of the Calle de las Armas,—great people not then, as they do now, masking the insignia of rank, to make the world more ugly, but displaying to the joy of their neighbours' vision all their gorgeous pomp and ceremony. This Don Cristóbal de Sandoval was a prelate not without ability, although it had displayed itself more conspicuously in the Council of Trent than it did now in the financial affairs of his household ; in money matters, indeed, he had shown so little as to get himself deeply in debt. Perhaps, however, it is better for his fame—which recks so little of dead men's difficulties — that he governed his diocese well and wisely, and gave much to the poor, than that he died with a balance to his credit. A martinet in all points connected with discipline or government, a stickler for his dignity, to him the head and front of Teresa's offending was that she had neglected to obtain his consent before she set forth for Seville ; although, indeed, as she drily observes, " If he had known of it before I started, I am sure he would not have consented."

At all events, he came to see her, was charmed, fascinated, won. The end of it was that he gave her his full permission to do what she liked and as she liked ; and " from that time forward he always showed us grace and favour in all that concerned us."

And so the long, hot days and short nights of the Andalucian summer wore to their close, and it was now August,—August which was to fill the heart of this old, worn-out nun with intense joy ; she who imagining that she had freed herself from all the ties of earth now prepared to welcome two at least of the scattered family who had grown up together beside their father's hearth in the old, gray fortress house of Avila. For the treasure ships which bear Lorenzo de Cepeda and Pedro his brother back home again are already anchored in the roads of San Lúcar. Lorenzo's wife he has left behind him, dead and buried in Peru, where he has exchanged the years of his youth and manhood for golden doubloons and a dyspeptic liver. But his four children are there, safe and well—Francisco, Lorenzo—the name of the third is vague—and little Teresita. The same letters which convey these glad tidings tell her of the death of another brother, Gerónimo de Cepeda, at El Nombre de Dios in the Isthmus of Panama. "Weep not for him who is in heaven," she writes to her sister, Juana, in distant Alba, "but thank the Lord for having brought these others back in safety. As to Pedro, give my congratulations to Doña Mayor (some old sweetheart) on his arrival, for I think he was once very devoted to her." In her joy, losing sight of time, and thinking of this peevish, melancholy, disappointed brother of hers, who as a soldier of fortune had pursued and never found her, still as the gallant stripling of the days of yore.

Teresita, Teresica, Teresa's little niece, at once became an inmate of the convent, her small limbs clothed in a diminutive Carmelite habit, to her father's infinite delight. "She is already here, with her habit, and seems the sprite of the house . . . and they are all charmed with her ; and she has a temper like an angel, and amuses us in recreation hours with her stories of Indians and the sea, much better than I could tell them," exclaims her delighted aunt,—that elderly Teresa, who perhaps saw in the little figure which bore her name a possible successor in the work of her life. Much consultation was held with the Doctor Henriquez as to whether Teresica could take the habit at once ; but as the Council of Trent had decreed that it was to be given to no one under twelve years of age, Teresa was fain to content herself for the present with bringing her small namesake up in the shadow of the cloister.

In October, Juana de Ovalle, her husband, and children also arrived in Seville to welcome the travellers, but Lorenzo had already gone to court, better than when he arrived, for he "came very thin and ill." In December he returned "in sufficiently bad health, although the fever has left him, having effected nothing, but as what he had (perhaps some pension) is now safe, he is well enough off. He is highly delighted with his sister and Juana de Ovalle, . . . and they not less with him."

But if thirty-three years as governor of a Peruvian town had left Lorenzo an ailing, atrabilious, and melancholy man, it had, unlike Pedro, filled his pockets with good store of ducats; and he came to his sister's aid at a critical moment.

No one would think [writes Teresa] that in a city so wealthy as Seville there should be less disposition to found than in any place I have been; so little was there that I thought sometimes it was not good for us to have a monastery there at all. I know not whether the climate itself of the country is the cause of it, for I have always heard it said that there the devil has more license to tempt than elsewhere (it is God who must give it him). . . . But never [she writes—the aspect of things without and within, alike black, dismal, hopeless, striking an unwonted chill into this stout heart]—never in my life have I seen myself more faint-hearted and cowardly than there; it is certain I did not recognise myself. Although the confidence I use to have in the Lord did not desert me, yet my disposition was so different from what it usually is since I set about these things, that I understood that the Lord partly took away his hand from me . . . so that I should see that if I had had courage, it was not mine.

In spite of the Archbishop's favour, Lent was fast approaching, and her stay in Seville was drawing to an end, and still no word of a house, nor money to buy one with, still less any one to go security for them as in other places. Teresa's great heart was full of sorrow, as she thought of her daughters left without a roof over their heads. She and her nuns betook themselves to processions to Our Lady and St. Joseph, when Lorenzo, now returned from court, "taking it more to heart than I that they should be left without a house of their own sets to work to find them one." Perhaps after all, on this occasion, doubloons and good broad pieces of eight were quite as potent as processions and orisons. A house was found, and they were all highly pleased with it, on account of the position, which was a very good one. The purchase was concluded; the deeds of sale were on the eve of being drawn up, when the owner repented him of his bargain (which was a very good one for him, notes Teresa), and the negotiations fell through: happily for the nuns; "it being so old and rotten that it would have taken a lifetime to repair it, and they might have had hard work and been sorely pushed to it for money."

So did the Lord—who had told her in her tribulation that he had heard her, and that she was to leave it to him—protect the interests of his spouses of Mount Carmel. At last they bought a house in "good condition" for 6000 ducats, little more than the price they were to have given for the site of the other. But still Teresa's troubles were not ended. The tenants of the house refused to leave it. A neighbouring monastery of Franciscans opposed their entrance. There was an error in the deed of sale, and, although it was to the prejudice of the purchasers, Lorenzo as surety was forced to take privilege of sanctuary in the Monastery of Los Remedios, to escape all the nameless horrors of a Sevilian prison: "Which here is like a hell," adds Teresa, "and everything with no justice whatever, for they ask of us what we do not owe, and of him as our security." Well might she, the old Castilian, nurtured in the honourable traditions of Avila, exclaim against the little truth and the double-dealing of the people of Seville. "The injustice customary in this country is a strange thing—the little truth, the double-dealings. I assure you it is not without reason it bears the fame it has. . . . Had my brother not been here it would have been impossible to do anything." There were other reasons why she should speak like this, as we shall presently see.

A month passed by; spring was wearing on, and the hope of possession seemed to drift farther away than ever. "Had not the deeds been drawn up so firmly," says Teresa, "I would have thanked God could they have been undone, for we saw ourselves in danger of paying 6000 ducats, the price of the house, without being able to enter it." Nevertheless one April evening, a little before the convent gates were closed for the night, arrived a messenger to say that the people living in the house, who had hitherto refused to give it up, were willing to let them enter without delay.

Trembling and in silence did Teresa, her prioress, and two nuns, a fearful company, flit through the narrow streets of Seville at dead of night to take possession of the disputed house, seeing the stealthy figures of Franciscan friars lurking in every shadowy angle and dusky corner, under black arches where some flickering oil-lamp lights up a mouldering painting of the Virgin.

O Jesus! how many frights have I passed through in these takings of possession! If one feels such fear when one goes, not to do harm, but to serve God, what, I wonder, is the case with those who are set upon doing harm both against God and their fellows! I know not what can repay them, nor what pleasure they can seek with such a counterpoise.

At sunrise next morning, the worthy Garcí Alvarez he who had toiled through the heated glow of the Sevilian streets to say Mass for them—celebrated the first one in the new house. Lorenzo was not present, being still hidden in the Remedios. Nevertheless, after some difficulty and a lawsuit, "so that trouble might not be wanting," Lorenzo, having given full security for the price, was free to superintend the construction of the monastery. Whilst he transformed the rooms into a church, busied himself with the workmen, and arranged all so well, that when it was finished "there was nothing left for the nuns to do," Teresa and her daughters remained shut up in some lower rooms—strange life that of these Carmelite foundresses!—living on good Lorenzo's bounty, who, for the matter of that, had provided for their wants for long; "for since every one did not know it was a monastery, on account of our living in a private house, we got but few alms, except from the sainted old prior of Las Cuevas of the Carthusians, a great servant of God."

Another month passed away, and all was ready. Teresa, ever averse to giving any one unnecessary trouble, was for placing the Host on the altar as quietly as possible. Not so the good Garcí Alvarez and her worthy countryman, the old prior. "They could not," she writes, "have taken the matter more to heart if it had been their own" (nay, I am sure these simple souls did so look upon it, and that each of them was morally convinced that if it had not been for himself alone the convent would never have been founded). And so they betake themselves to the Archbishop, and the three, laying their heads together, decide that the Host shall be carried from a neighbouring parish church with great solemnity; and the Archbishop orders his clergy and several confraternities to assemble and the streets to be decked.

None of Teresa's foundations took place with greater pomp and ceremony than this of Seville. On the 3rd of June 1576 a procession passed through the Sevilian streets, the like of which—at least so affirmed the aforesaid gray-headed prior of Las Cuevas—had never been seen before. From every narrow casement, so dark and mysterious with its stern gratings of twisted iron, hung gorgeous velvets and silks; the narrow Moorish streets below were gay with flowers, and thronged by myriads of curious spectators. Down below they passed: the great Archbishop bearing the Host, under the pall of cloth of gold and silver borne by cathedral dignitaries, sweeping from light into shadow; followed by pursy canons, their shoulders bending under the weight of broidered copes stiff with Gothic embroidery. Then came brotherhoods and confraternities, in their diverse coloured robes and insignia; choir boys and acolytes, scarlet robes and lace stoles dazzling in the sun; torches gleamed, censers swung, minstrels filled the air with triumphant music, banners waved. Never since Seville was Seville, says the old prior of Las Cuevas, who to-day breaks through the customs of a lifetime to walk in the throng on purpose to do honour to his countrywoman —one Teresa, a founder of convents—had the like been seen before.

And what words shall describe the labours of the good Garcí Alvarez? the altars and quaint conceits, fountains of orange-flower water and the like, with which he decked the church and cloisters? or that most moving scene of all, when the saint in the rear of the procession, throwing herself down on her knees before the Archbishop, implored his blessing, and he, never surely greater than in that moment, fell on his knees likewise, humbly imploring hers? "Consider how a wretched old woman like me must have felt to see so great a prelate kneeling before her. See here, daughters, the poor discalced nuns honoured by all, so changed was everything from the time when it seemed as if, for them, there was even no water in the river, although it is full enough. The crowd was excessive." As the Archbishop raised the Host above his head and consecrated Teresa's labours, the air was rent by volleys of artillery, and rockets and fireworks flashed and blazed into the sky, lasting until it was nearly night.

And a notable thing happened—at least so said all who saw it. An accidental explosion of some gunpowder nearly set the cloisters aflame, "it being a great marvel, too, that he who bore it was not killed." And behold! the crimson silks and yellow damasks which adorned the cloisters were not even scorched, as if no such thing had been, although the stones underneath were blackened with the smoke. "All were amazed at the sight; and the nuns (thrifty nuns!) gave praises to God that they would not have to purchase fresh silks and damasks. It must have been the devil, angry at so great a solemnity having been made, fain to avenge himself in something, and the Lord prevented him. May he be blessed for ever and ever! Amen!"

Such was the scene that took place in that month of June 1576 when the sixteenth century was already drawing to its close, before that flat-roofed house, which exists to this day, now, as then, its white impenetrable façade dotted irregularly with windows of all sizes, shutting in the mysteries of so many lives, and still preserving the secret of the strange and moving scenes it has seen during the course of the centuries, in the Calle de la Pajeria, opposite to the gardens of the Franciscans.

Other events, too, filled her life during this year's sojourn in Seville. It is to them she refers in the *Fundaciones*. "The gravest trials I suffered I do not set down here: for it seems to me that, with the exception of the foundation of Avila, . . . none has cost me more than this, on account of most of them being inward ones."

We have seen by what steps Gracian had been chosen by Vargas as his substitute in Andalucia; how Pope Gregory XIII., Pope Pius V.'s successor in the papal chair, had, at the instance of the General of the Carmelites, revoked the patents of the Dominican Visitors, Fernandez and Vargas; how this blow was swiftly parried by the Papal Nuncio, Ormaneto, who, having first assured himself through the Pope's secretary that the brief in no way curtailed his authority as Nuncio and legate à latere, nor yet his more special commission to reform the Orders, by virtue of his Apostolic powers superior to the General's, reinstated Vargas in his commission on the 22nd September 1574, and consequently Gracian, whom Vargas had invested with his powers. In April of 1575 Gracian received the Nuncio's mandate to proceed to Madrid to take possession of the fresh brief that had been made out in his favour. In May of that same year the general chapter of the Carmelites at Plasencia publicly revoked Fernandez's and Vargas's commissions, and fulminated their edicts against the Descalzos. The Observants were to admit no visitors unless appointed by the General, and to resist any unduly elected. The Discalced convents of Andalucia, and such of those in Castille as had been founded without the General's license, were to be broken up within the space of three days, under pain of the Apostolic penalties and censures, assisted, if needs be, by secular force.

Here then the situation: on one side the King, the Papal Nuncio, Teresa, and her excommunicate, disobedient, rebellious friars; on the other, the Pope, the General, and the powerful Order of Carmelites.

The air had long been full with the first faint rumblings of the storm. It had now broken with a vengeance. When Gracian arrived at Madrid, the Carmelites refused to give shelter in their monastery to an excommunicated man; upon which there are high words between the Nuncio and the Provincial, Fr. Angel de Salazar—" Let them (the Carmelites) beware before they again dared to call those excommunicated who were there at his" (the Nuncio's) " bidding" —the result being that Gracian is admitted into the monastery, and preaches at court. His brother Antonio, the King's secretary, would fain have had him refuse the dangerous commission, and, to do Gracian justice, he accepts it with the extremest reluctance, after in vain alleging the shortness of time he had been in the Order, his lack of experience, and other circumstances essential to such an office. Teresa, the nun, writes to Philip, the King, from Seville, calling on his Majesty to do her this service, of " ordering the charge of the Order to be given to a Discalced friar, Gracian, who, in spite of his youth, has made me praise the Lord for what he has bestowed upon that soul."

The King is determined, and there is no help for it but

to submit, the first act of the tragedy of his life being thus played out on the 3rd of August of 1575. What fills him with terror,—for the first part of his commission, which makes him Visitor over the Discalced communities of Castille and Andalucia, he accepts willingly enough,—is that other clause in it, whereby he is appointed Apostolic Commissary over the embittered Observants of Andalucia.

It was with very real dread, for he went in fear of his life,—a fact he had not dared to communicate to the King, —that he went to kiss the hands of the Arch-inquisitor of Spain, Don Gaspar de Quiroga, and beseech him to intercede with the King to release him from this part of his commission. But the prelate flew into a "holy fury": "Let them kill us, let them kill us!" he cried; "to whom are we to confide this business but to a man of blood and nobility, known as you are not to fear death!" So with the bezoar stone the Mother Teresa had given him hung round his neck, eating nothing but boiled eggs, lest his food should be poisoned, Gracian set forth on his three months' visit to the Reformed Convents of Andalucia. In Toledo the angry mutterings of the Observants, who declared that the Nuncio had outstepped the bounds of his authority by appointing a Visitor in the face of a Papal revocation, forced him to obtain permission to show them his faculties and warrants.

The storm rumbles on, and another element gathers in the black cloud which hangs threateningly over the devoted friar, speeding onward to his fate—the rivalry and jealousy of the Descalzos themselves. For Fray Baltasar de Jesus, in terrible dudgeon at the preference given to Gracian, avoids meeting him at Pastrana, and only returns to his "lair" when the coast is clear and the Visitor gone.

In the meantime Teresa in Seville, rejoicing in this first triumph, paves the way for her Eliseo's coming.

We hear of visits to the convent:

Yesterday the father Provincial of *los del paño* [those of the cloth. —she means the Observants] was here with a master [priest], and then came the prior, and then another master. The day before fray Gaspar Nieto was here. I find them all determined to obey your paternity, and assist you in removing anything wrong, so long as you do not push them to extremes in other things. I assure them from what I know of your paternity that you will act leniently, as it seems to me you will. Father Elias [Fray Juan Evangelista, sub-prior of the Observant Monastery] is more serene and resolute. I repeat that if you begin quietly and gently you will achieve much, for everything cannot be done in a day.

This, written on the 27th of September, is followed by another towards the end of the same year:

I assure you that your falls fill me with such pain that it would be well for you to be tied on, so as to prevent them. I know not what sort of a donkey that can be, nor what necessity there is for your paternity to travel ten leagues a day, which on an albarda [rough saddle] is enough to kill one. I am anxious as to whether you wrap yourself up warmly now that the weather is cold.... Elias is less fearful; as for me, I have lost all the fear I had before; I cannot feel any even if I wished to.

How she loves this man, young enough to be her son, distressed by his falls from his donkey, maternally solicitous as to his being warmly clothed at night in the cold Castilian climate! In his judgment and capabilities she feels unbounded confidence, guiding his steps—not by superior wisdom, for this is impossible,—but by her greater experience, riper years!

"Lorencia," she writes, "can no longer feel for her confessors as she was wont, and, as that was her only consolation, she now has none. How delicately does our Lord mortify! for she fears that with so many hindrances in the way she will enjoy but little the confessor he gives her, on account of his many occupations." And it is a curious fact that from the date he came into her life there is scarcely a letter addressed to any other director.

At last Gracian, with Fray Antonio de Jesus for his travelling companion, arrives in Seville. An anxious consultation takes place between Teresa and her friars.

Teresa, Gracian, and Fray Antonio (he less decidedly) are all for firm and gentle measures. To make full use of his commission as regards the Discalced communities, to allow the Observants to see the Nuncio's mandate,—let them have a copy of it if needs be, and give them every means of opposing it,—this, in Gracian's opinion, was the wisest course. He was overruled by Mariano, hot and fiery of temper as he was sharp and caustic of tongue. "They now possess the power, let them use it. Let Gracian force the Observants to recognise him as Commissary, and show the King and Nuncio that they had not admitted the commission for the Descalzos alone, but for the entire Order. This done, then, and then only, would it be time to soften harshness with kindness. What if the General should call them contumacious rebels? such epithets of opprobrium are glorious when shared with the Reformers of the Benedictines and Franciscans."

Gracian kissed the Archbishop's hands, paid a visit to the Deputy-Governor, the Count of Barajas, and delivered to them the royal letters of which he was the bearer, for the prudent King, foreseeing a tumult, had taken care to enlist on his side both the civil and ecclesiastical authorities alike.

On the day of the Presentation—ever-memorable day for Teresa, cowering with her nuns before the altar, praying for their Visitor's safe deliverance from the perils which, none doubted, menaced him — Gracian, accompanied by Fray Antonio de Jesus and a secretary, proceeded to the Observant Convent of Seville to present the Brief. It was read before the assembled heads of the convent, who asked for a copy to institute a plea in the ordinary form. This Gracian, acting against his better judgment, reluctantly refused to give.

A wild scene followed of uproar and confusion,—so wild and fierce that Mariano rushed off to fetch the Archbishop and Deputy-Governor,—and Teresa was overwhelmed with the news that Gracian had been killed and the monastery gates closed. The Bishop of Columbria, just returned from Rome, at length succeeded in restoring peace; and in the presence of the Archbishop and Governor the Brief was again read. The sub-prior alone, Fray Juan Evangelista—the "Elias" of Teresa's letters—signified his submission. He was at once made vicar of the monastery. The Provincial, Fray Agustin Suarez, was ordered to retire to the monastery of Osuna, and Fray Antonio de Jesus was sent to receive the obedience of the province, Gracian himself undertaking the important office of master of novices.

Such was the scene enacted in the tranquil Sevilian

monastery on that day of the Presentation 1575. In the same month, and almost at the same time, the first intimation reached Teresa's ears of the decree which had been levelled against her in the general chapter of the Order at Plasencia. Fray Angel Salazar, after publishing it in Madrid, had sent it on to a brother Observant in Seville, to convey to her, and he, thinking it would give her pain, "this being the intention of these friars when they procured it," kept it back until, hearing of it from another source, she herself caused it to be given her.

She had hoped that her journey to Seville might have been the means of pacifying the disputes between Carmelites and Descalzos. One of her first letters from Seville—of those that remain—had been to the General. If she had but known it, she might as well have written to the winds; for already, even as she journeyed over the dusty Andalucian roads, the chapter of Plasencia had decreed the extinction of the Descalzos root and branch, and the mandate was already on the way to Spain ordering her to the seclusion of a Castilian convent. This letter, dated the 18th of June, is in answer to two letters from the General, the one written in October, the other in January, which had reached her hands the day before:

> I wrote to your lordship about the foundation of Veas; and how another is asked for in Caravaca, and that they had given the license with the condition I mentioned—I also wrote to your lordship the reasons why I came to found at Seville: please our Lord that I may see accomplished the end I came for, which is to pacify these matters of these Descalzos, and to prevent them giving vexation to your lordship. Your lordship must know that I took great care to inform myself when I came to Veas that it was not in Andalucia, for it was never my intention to come here. And so it is that Veas is not Andalucia, but a province of Andalucia. This I did not know until the monastery [Veas] had been founded for more than a month. When I then saw myself in Andalucia with my nuns, it also seemed to me advisable not to leave that convent deserted and alone, and it had something to do with my coming here; but my chief object is what I wrote to your lordship, to look into this matter of these fathers; for although they justify their cause, and truly from what I know of them, they are your lordship's most loyal sons, and desire not to vex you, I cannot exonerate them from blame. Already it seems they are beginning to find out that it would have been better to have taken some other road, so as not to vex your lordship.

So she exculpates her own inadvertence in founding at Veas, and pleads with him to take Gracian and Mariano into favour. Her preference for Gracian is shown most transparently:

> We fell out about it greatly, especially Mariano and I, whose temper is very quick, for Gracian is like an angel; and had he been alone, it would have been done in another sort; and the reason of his coming here was because he was ordered to by fray Baltasar, who was then prior of Pastrana. I tell your lordship that if you knew him you would be glad to have him for a son, and truly do I know that such he is, and even Mariano also. This Mariano is a virtuous and penitent man, whose genius makes him remarked by every one; and your lordship may rest assured that he has been solely actuated by zeal for God and the good of the Order, save that, as I tell you, he has been rash and indiscreet. As for ambition, I can see none in him, save that the devil, as your lordship says, stirs these matters up, and he himself says many things that look like it. I have borne a great deal from him sometimes, and as I see he is virtuous, I overlook it. If your lordship could hear him you could not help being satisfied. This very day he told me that until he places himself at your lordship's feet he will not rest. I have already written to you how both have besought me to write to your lordship, since they have not the courage, and give you their excuses; and so here I will say no more but what it seems to me I am bound to do, since I have already written it before....
>
> Father and my lord [she continues, gentle and persuasive as only Teresa de Jesus can be, but so firm and decisive that the General might well have paused a moment to consider the nature of the woman with whom he was even then bent on waging war to the knife]—Father and my lord, at the pass things now are, it is no time for this [she refers to the decrees fulminated against the Descalzos in the chapter of Plasencia]; for this Gracian has a brother who is near the King, whose secretary he is, and whom he loves much; and the King, from what I have heard, is not averse to his taking up the Reform. The Calzados say that they know not how it is that your lordship treats such virtuous men thus, and that they would fain dwell in amity with the Contemplatives, and see their virtue, and that this your lordship has prevented them from doing with this sentence of excommunication.

She on the spot, amongst the mines and counter-mines, the bickerings and heart-burnings, jealousies and enmities, the hypocritical tongues and double faces, can form a juster judgment as to what is going on than the absent general.

> They say one thing to your lordship and another here. They [the Descalzos] go to the Archbishop and say that they dare not punish, because they [the Observants] at once go to you. They are a strange folk. I, my lord, see both one and the other, and our Lord knows that I speak truth, for I believe the most obedient now and in future will

be and are the Descalzos. Your lordship away there sees not what takes place here; I do, and tell you of it, for I know well your lordship's sanctity and how great a friend you are to virtue.

Some of them [the Observants] have come to see me. The prior especially is an excellent man. He came to see the patents by which I had founded. He wanted to take a copy; but I was fain not to give him one, so that since he saw I had the power to found, they should not institute a lawsuit. For in the patent your lordship sent me in Latin after the visitors came, you give license, and say that I may found everywhere, and such is the construction placed upon it by "letrados"; because your lordship neither fixes house nor kingdom, nor is any limit assigned, but all parts alike. And, moreover, it was accompanied by a precept which has made me exert myself more than I am able, *for I am old and weary*. . . . As to those friars they have taken [she continues, giving us an insight into the underhand doings and dissimulation of otherwise worthy, almost heroic men, and not an edifying one; the old Observant friar, for instance, the virtual founder of La Peñuela and Granada, capable of trudging twice to Madrid and back to get licenses, and yet equally capable of a lie], I have already spoken about it to Mariano: he says that Peñuela took the habit through a falsehood; for he went to Pastrana and said that Vargas, the Visitor of Andalucia, had given it him; and when it came to be known, he had taken it himself. For long they have been thinking of expelling him, and so they will: the other one is not with them now. The monasteries were made by order of the Visitor Vargas with the Apostolic authority he had; because hereabouts they hold that for the principal reformation there should be a house of Descalzos: and so the Nuncio as reformer gave them license to found monasteries, when he ordered fray Antonio de Jesus to prosecute his visit; but he did better, for he did nothing until he had besought one from your lordship: and if Teresa de Jesus had been here, perhaps this would have been looked to more; for there was no proposal to found a house without your lordship's license but what I stoutly opposed, and on this point fray Pedro Fernandez, the Visitor of Castille, acted well, and I owe him much for the care he took not to displease your lordship. The one here (Vargas) has given these fathers so many licenses and faculties and moreover supplicated them to accept them, that if your lordship could see those they have in their possession, you would know they are not so much to blame; and so they say that they have never wished to admit fray Gaspar, nor to have anything to do with him, although he has besought them greatly, nor others; and that they at once left the house which they had taken from the Order. And thus they allege many things in their defence whereby I see they have not acted so maliciously; and when I consider the great troubles they have undergone, and the penitential lives they lead, it gives me pain that it should get about that your lordship discountenances them. For truly they live good lives and in great retirement, and amongst those they have received there are more than twenty who have university degrees (*cursas, ó no sé cómo se llaman*), and who are very holy and of good understanding. And between this house and that of

Granada and La Peñuela, I think I have heard them say that there are more than seventy friars.

I know not what is to become of all these, nor how it will now appear to the world, being in such esteem as they are; but that perhaps we shall all end by paying for it dearly: for they are high in credit with the King, and the Archbishop here says that they alone merit the name of friars. For them to abandon the Reform, now that your lordship will have none of them; believe me that although you have all the right in the world on your side, it will not seem so: since you, who are a servant of the Virgin's, will not wish, nor will they consent to, your withdrawing your protection, and it will grieve her that your lordship should abandon those whose only fault is to augment her Order by their sweat. Things are now at such a pass that great consideration is necessary.—Your lordship's unworthy daughter and subject, Teresa de Jesus.

This letter, and three or four others in the same tenor, Teresa despatched from Seville to Rome. They were never answered, for even as she wrote, the thunderbolt had been hurled, and the General was in no mood to listen either to reason or probability. Towards the beginning of 1576, little more than a month after she had received notice of the decree, she made a last attempt to gain the General's ear in a truly admirable letter. We who have watched with what serenity, when ordered back to the Encarnacion, she faced the laughter of all Avila, and (so it seemed to those around her) an ignominious defeat; we who have watched her fearlessly and firmly quelling the mutiny of the rebellious nuns of the Encarnacion,—we at least shall not be surprised at the cheerfulness and willingness of her ready obedience to the decree carefully framed to give her pain (to make the affront more notorious, Salazar had purposely published it in Madrid before she herself knew anything about it), which condemned her to the seclusion of a Castilian convent, and to meddle in no more foundations. If it was a condemnation! For how little had they fathomed the depths of her nature! Had she indeed been the presumptuous, disobedient, restless woman therein described, an insult like this might have stung her to the quick! But no! her first thought is not for herself, but the Reform; her first impulse to plead not for herself but for Gracian and Mariano ("poor Mariano, sometimes so hard to understand"). "than whom I make bold to say that none of those who affirm so much are truer sons than they."

I have already mentioned to your lordship the commission given to the father Gracian by the Nuncio, and how he has now sent for him again . . . to visit the Descalzos and Descalzas, and the province of Andalucia. I know for certain that he did all he could not to accept this last, although report says otherwise; but this is the truth; and his brother the secretary was also averse to it. . . . But once it was done, if these fathers had but listened to me it would have been carried out without fixing a stigma on any one, and as lovingly as amongst brothers. . . . I am always willing to make a virtue of necessity as they say, and so I should have wished that once they (the Carmelites) were bent on resisting, they would first have considered if they could do so effectually; on the other hand [for Teresa is always impartial], I am not surprised that they are sick of so many visits and innovations as, for our sins, there have been these many years back. . . . I again repeat my supplications to your lordship, for love of our Lord and his glorious Mother . . . to reply to him [Gracian] favourably, and let bygones be bygones, even though he may have been somewhat to blame, and accept him for your true son and subject, as in very truth he is. . . . Let your lordship consider that it is for sons to err, and for fathers to pardon and be lenient to their faults. For love of our Lord I supplicate your lordship to grant me this grace. Think that it is important for many things which perhaps you, far away as you are, do not see so well as I who am here; and that although we women are not fit to counsel, sometimes we hit the mark. . . .

If there were many to commend it to! But since to all seeming he is the only one who possesses the necessary ability . . . why should not your lordship show that you are pleased to have him for a subject, so that all should know that this Reform (if it succeeds) is through you and your counsels and advice.

And she was right! The sublime contemplative, the absorbed mystic, the grandest and noblest of her friars—the farthest too from human nature—San Juan de la Cruz, was not made to cope and struggle with that atmosphere of deceit, lies, and calumny which characterised these bitter quarrels of a religious Order divided against itself. His fate would in all likelihood have been more tragic than Gracian's, whose brilliant talents, seeming to foreshadow success, were better fitted for active warfare. As for herself, the decree which was to wound her to the quick—

Would, I tell your lordship, in good sooth have been to me a great comfort and content had your lordship sent it to me in a letter, and I had seen that it was out of pity for the great labours that I (who am not for much suffering) have passed through in these foundations; and that, in reward, you ordered me to rest. Still, even although it has come to me in the way it has, it has afforded me great consolation to be able to take some repose. As the love I bear your lordship is so great, spoilt as I am, I could not help but feel that, as if to a very disobedient person, it should come in such wise that fray Angel was able to publish it at court before I myself knew anything of it. As he thought I was being unduly constrained, he wrote to me that I could alter it by having recourse to the papal camera; as if, on the contrary, it was not a great relief to me. And in good sooth, even if it were not, but a most great hardship to do what your lordship orders, it would never enter my thoughts to disobey . . . for I can say truthfully (and this our Lord knows) that if I have found any alleviation in the trials, loss of tranquillity, afflictions, and murmurings I have gone through, it was because I thought I did your bidding, and was giving you pleasure; and the same pleasure it will give me now to do what you order. I wished to comply with it at once: but it was close on Christmas, and the journey is so long, they did not let me, as they thought it was not your lordship's desire that I should risk my health; and so I am still here, although I do not intend to remain in this house for good, but only until the winter is over; *for I do not get on with the people of Andalucia.*

And so she takes her leave of him—stately, dignified, as it became the descendant of her father's house—with a touch of solemn pathos, leaving the rectification of his judgment to that Eternity which has no end: "When we stand together before God, then you will see what you owe to your true daughter, Teresa de Jesus." That was all,—the answer to the blow that was meant to crush her. She can even laugh about it with Maria Bautista: "A great benefit it will be to me to find myself away from these hurly-burlys of reforms!"; her irrepressible activity bubbling out at the end of her letter: "My life is short; I would like to have many. To-morrow is New Year's Eve."

Teresa had indeed drained the cup of bitterness to the dregs before she left this Seville—"whose people," she confesses, "are not for me"—for what seemed to her, this exile in a foreign and antipathetic country, the "land of promise" of Castille. She may well sigh, as she thinks of her laborious journeys, of the difficulties so gigantic as to dismay any but a heart so stout as hers; as with painful intensity she follows the struggles of Gracian in Seville: "Oh! the trials we suffer in these reforms! for to me has fallen a greater share of grief than happiness since he came!" Almost at the same time as she received the General's mandate to retire to a convent, she and her nuns were denounced to the Inquisition.

Let Maria de San José appear on the scene, who tells

the story. A somewhat curious personality this Maria de San José, sometime waiting-woman to Da. Luisa de la Cerda; for in those days, when the sons and daughters of the lesser nobility thought it no lessening of their dignity to swell the retinue of pages and ladies-in-waiting to a wealthy kinsman or patron, such a post implied neither disgrace nor servility, and was eagerly sought after for their daughters by noble and impoverished families—perhaps too poor to pay a dower to a convent, then a very convenient and usual mode of getting rid of a superfluity of females. Irresistibly attracted by Teresa's personal influence, she had taken the veil in Malagon six years before. A woman of decided ability, of more education than was usual in those days for her sex, her inopportune displays of erudition often aroused Teresa's good-natured satire,—Teresa, who could not by any means away with learned women. "That about Elisha is good," she says in answer to one of her prioress's letters, " but as I am not so learned as you, I do not know what you mean by the Assyrians," an expression which has passed into the Spanish language. By no means a mean authoress; leaving behind her various tercetos, that she has quaintly styled *The Garland of Myrrh*, dimmed a little by too many classical allusions, but devoid of neither grace nor tenderness, and which well might find a nook in an anthology of the ascetic literature of the seventeenth century. Teresa and her prioress, however, were not always agreed. The worst of these capable clever women was that they had a will of their own, and I fear me it often clashed with hers. Teresa complains bitterly of her coldness to her, even during this stay of hers in Seville. Nevertheless, both were too large-minded and magnanimous not to respect and admire one another, and the bulk of Teresa's letters are addressed to this very Maria de San José, who in her turn, when Death had for ever severed them, suffered exile and a broken heart in her attempt to preserve Teresa's Order as she had left it. So much for Maria de San José. Now for her story:

> At this time a great beata, in high repute for her sanctity, had entered our house, and not being able to suffer our life, unknown to our mother or to us, she bethought herself of concerting her departure through some priests to whom, to console her, our mother gave license

to hear her in confession; and when the poor thing had gone, in order to palliate her own shortcomings, she bethought herself of accusing us to the Inquisition, saying that in certain things we resembled the "alumbradas" (illuminated).

Amongst the things that either through carelessness or ignorance she said were bad, was that the sisters received the communion unveiled: it being our custom for one sister as she draws near to communicate, to pass her veil on to the next; this she said we did for the sake of ceremony. As we had not then finished the house, we communicated in a patio, which was full of sun, and to shield ourselves from it, and for the sake of being quieter, each of us after she had communicated took refuge in any corner she could, turning her face to the wall, so as to escape from the brilliancy of the sun: this she also put a bad construction on, together with many lies and false accusations against our Mother. . . . The good that came to us from this trial of being accused to the Inquisition, so that it may be seen that there is no evil which God does not turn to good, was that as our Mother was so obedient and punctual in all our prelates ordered, and desired to please the most reverend General, and he had bidden her to go to some convent in Castille and not to leave it, nor to found, nor to meddle with those she had founded, she persuaded the father Visitor [Gracian] to let her go to fulfil this obedience; and the General's orders on the one side, and the Apostolic Visitor's on the other who, opposed to her being inactive, commanded her to conclude her foundation, together with the loneliness and unprotected state in which she was about to leave us, added to the tribulation of her spirit.

And I remember me one day [adds worthy Maria de San José] that she complained to me greatly because I left her alone, and she assured me that since the afflictions of the convent of San José of Avila, she had not seen herself so hard pressed; and I soothed her by saying that her departure was not to be thought on in such a juncture, since the Inquisition was busy examining into the truth of that woman's accusations against her, for if it was necessary to take her before the Inquisition, and they came for her, and did not find her, how would it be then? "True, daughter," said Teresa, "you are right; and now I see it is God's will I should remain." Afterwards she was greatly amused at it, and often said to me: "So then, all the consolation my daughter could offer me in so deep an affliction, was to tell me that the Inquisition was coming for me!"

There were other and graver charges against Teresa and her nuns than merely communicating without veils, or even binding down the nuns and flogging them, which was another of the "great beata's" inventions. "Would to God she had accused us of nothing worse," says Teresa to Maria Bautista of Valladolid; for even the fair fame of this tired-out old woman of sixty-one did not escape, and only to hint at the calumnies against her, according to the chronicler, would be to give offence to the least modest of ears. A chance like this of venting their venom against the Descalzos in the shape of the foundress and her nuns was not to be neglected by the Carmelites, and all Seville was agog with expectation to see the *dénoûment* of the drama.

Gracian was thunderstruck when he arrived one day at the convent to find the street thronged with the mules and horses of Inquisitors, and the priestly denouncer lurking round a corner to feast his eyes on the grateful spectacle of the nuns being dragged through the streets to the dungeons of the Inquisition.

But he was disappointed! For even the Inquisitors found nothing to condemn, and the persecution of their enemies only made the virtue of the poor Castilian nuns shine forth more resplendent. It is a satisfaction to know (as Teresa does not forget to mention to Maria Bautista) that such was the pious beata's grief at leaving the convent that it upset her brain and drove her mad. Persecution not unmixed with triumph! For on the 1st of January (new style) 1576, four months before the splendid scene which crowned the conclusion of the Sevilian convent, that too of Caravaca was brought to a triumphal ending.

The foundation of Caravaca owed its origin to three maidens of distinguished birth, who, going one day to hear a sermon preached by a Jesuit, were so impressed by what they heard that, instead of going home, they took up their abode in the house of a lady, widow of an oidor (judge) in the Indies, until such time as a monastery was founded in their native town in which they could take their vows. The noble widow thereupon set aside a portion of her house for them, fixed up a wooden grating whence they could hear Mass, and sent to the Bishop of Cartagena for a license to celebrate it. She also sends off a messenger to Teresa in Avila, on the point of starting for Veas, to inform her of what has been done, and request her to undertake the foundation.

"When I saw the fervour and desire of these souls, and that from such a distance they sent to seek Our Lady's Order . . . and being informed that it was near Veas, I took a larger number of nuns . . . with the intention of going thither after I had concluded the foundation of Veas."

A difficulty about the license (Caravaca like Veas was under the jurisdiction of the " Consejo de las Ordenes "); the sudden change of Teresa's plans which took her to Seville led to its being abandoned at least for the time being. " It is true that when I had informed myself in Veas as to its whereabouts, and found that it was difficult to get at, and the road between it and Veas so bad as to make it difficult for those who should have to visit the nuns, . . . I did not care much about founding there. But as I had held out favourable hopes, I begged Father Julian de Avila and Antonio Gaytan to go there, to see if it was possible, and to cancel it if they thought fit." Whilst she had waited in Veas, therefore, the two set off for Caravaca, returning in time to take Teresa to Seville.

For the last time,—for we shall now accompany him no more (it is doubtful whether we shall even get a furtive glimpse of him again)—let us follow the priest and the worthy Gaytan over the hills and dales of this old-world Spain :

In the journey there and back we suffered much from snow and other misadventures, for I should never be done if I were to relate them all; still I will not leave untold what happened to us at the entrance to Caravaca.

We arrived at nightfall at a place called Moratalla,—very tired, for we had done a long day's journey; and the inn—for there was only one in the place—was so crowded with people that we had not room to turn round. It seems to me less painful to do the remaining two leagues, said I to my companion, than to stop here for the night. There is only one thing against it; that, as it is night, and we do not know the road, we may lose ourselves; but that we can easily remedy by getting a guide here.

He being agreed, we at once looked for a man, hired him, and set forth, bent on entering Caravaca within two hours. We were now going at a great pace, it being somewhat rainy and very dark, when we saw him, the man in front of us, flounder down a precipice, and called out : Brother, have we lost our way ?

Yes, replied the man, quite calmly, Si, Señor.

I will not repeat what we said when we heard this, and saw ourselves wandering along these impassable roads, except that my companion blamed me for it all, because, said he, as we came along I had been giving him lessons in contemplation ; the fact being that I had been telling him the commandments which were to take him to heaven, and so he thus lost his road on earth, as those often do who travel it well [the road to heaven]. And, doubtless, the real reason was that before we started the man had slung a big keg of wine over his shoulders, and must have been so drunk that he knew not whither he was going. At last, what with this misfortune of being lost, we would have nothing more to do with him, and sent him off about his business: we were left alone, not knowing whither we were going any more than if we had been blind. As we went along thus, for we had gone a long way in this fashion, we saw a shepherd's fire burning on a hill. We shouted to him to show us the way, and he, to save himself the trouble of coming down, answered: This way, that way. So that we soon lost ourselves again, and this time in such a fashion that we could not even make our way back to the shepherd; but began to seek about in vain for some sheltered nook to stop in till morning. We groped about with our hands seeking for some road; go whither it would, it was sure to lead us to a hamlet of some sort, and so when we at last found one, we hoped soon to come upon some village.

We knew not whether we were going back or forwards. We saw the form of a man, and thought we had come across some one who could direct us somewhat, and he turned out to be the very man we had dismissed, wandering about like ourselves, without knowing where. We did not feel enough pity for him to take him on with us, and so he went one way and we another, for we would not even be beholden for so much as putting us on the right road to one who had guided us so ill. At length, after we were completely tired out with walking along such a road, we heard the bark of dogs, and when we had assured ourselves that we were not mistaken, we listened to them with more attention than if it had been the best music in the world. And so it was that when we got to where the dogs were barking, we came upon the walls of the village, which we had not seen before because of the darkness. At the first house we came to, we woke up the owner from his slumbers with our shouts to ask him the name of the place. When he answered Caravaca, our soul came back again to our bodies, and we thought little of our past troubles, although we ceased not to talk of what a *cara vaca* (dear cow) it had been to us. They took us in in a posada, where we waited for daylight, to which it wanted but little.

The narration is so naïve, picturesque, and quaint that I have quoted it in full. Inimitable this glimpse of the grave Castilian gentleman and the priest wandering along in the dark, the latter so engaged in pointing out the road to heaven to a drunken man, that they lost their own. The shepherd's light gleaming red on the bleak hillside; the barking of dogs, sweeter than the sweetest music, inasmuch as it hails their approach to the sleeping town; the feeble pun on the name of the hamlet which had cost them so dear— good, garrulous Master Julian! Without knowing it thou hast left a picture painted in a few masterly strokes, bridging for a brief moment the chasm which separates thy century from ours!

The rest of the history of Caravaca is told in a few words, Teresa's:

The nuns (I mean those who were to be) were so determined, that they were able so well to gain over father Julian de Avila and Antonio Gaytan to their side, that before they left the deeds were signed. Whereupon they started on their journey back, leaving the would-be nuns highly pleased, and they themselves so much so with them and the country, that they were never done of talking of them and it, as well as of the badness of the road. As for me, as soon as I saw it all arranged, and that the license was long of coming, I again sent the good Antonio Gaytan back there once more, who for love of me underwent the labour gladly, and was, together with father Julian, set on the foundation being accomplished; because in good sooth it is to them that we must be grateful for this foundation, since unless they had gone there and made the arrangements, I should have done little enough in the matter. I told him to go, so that he might see about putting up a torno and gratings in the house where we were to take possession, and the nuns to dwell, until such time as a better one turned up. So that he remained there a long time, and as Rodrigo Moya, who as I have said was the father of one of these maidens, gave him part of his house, he stayed there a long time doing all that was necessary with right good-will. When the license arrived, I being then on the point of setting out for Seville, I found that one of the conditions in it was, that the house should be subject to the comendadores and the nuns under their jurisdiction; which I could not allow in the case of the Order of Our Lady of Carmel; and so they set about getting a fresh license, which in this case, as well as that of Veas, there was nothing left for it but to do. But the King—he who is now Don Philip, so great a friend to showing favour to such monks and nuns as he knows keep their Rule, that as soon as he knew the nature of these monasteries, and that they belonged to the Primitive Rule, he has favoured us in everything—did me so great a grace that when I wrote to him he ordered it to be granted; and therefore, daughters, I beseech you greatly always to make particular prayer for his Majesty, even as we do now.

Well, as they had to go back for the license, I set out for Seville by the mandate of the father Provincial, who was then and now is the father master fray Jerónimo Gracian de la Madre de Dios, as has been said, and the poor maidens remained prisoners in their retreat until the New Year's Day of the following year, it being February when they had sent to me in Avila. The license was brought at once with all speed; but, as I was so far away, and in the midst of so many trials, I could not go to their assistance, and pitied them greatly: because they often wrote to me in great distress, and thus it was already out of the question to interpose any further delay. As it was impossible for me to go to them, as much on account of the distance as because the foundation [Seville] was not completed, the father master Jerónimo Gracian, who, as has been said, was Apostolic Visitor, bethought himself (even although I did not go myself) of sending thither the nuns I had brought with me for that purpose, and left behind in San José of Malagon.

I took care that she in whose abilities I confided most, as being likely to carry out everything exceeding well (because she is much better than I am), should be appointed prioress, and, taking everything requisite for the journey, they set off with two of our Discalced friars ; for father Julian de Avila and Antonio de Gaytan had gone home long ago, and I was averse to bring them from so great a distance in such bad weather, it being the end of December. On their arrival, they were joyfully received by the people of the town, especially by the imprisoned maidens, the monastery being founded and the host placed on the altar on the 19th of January [old style] 1576.

CHAPTER XIX

LETTERS FROM TOLEDO

WE have watched the Reform first shaping itself in misty outline in a woman's brain; gradually growing out of the Mist until it becomes a living and potential Reality, firmly rooted in Spanish soil. The hatred and fear felt by the older Order for this young, new, ardent body that had met them so firmly and held their own so stubbornly in their first rude encounter in Andalucia had been echoed, as we have seen, in the decree fulminated by the chapter of Plasencia in May of 1575, against "certain disobedient, rebellious, and contumacious individuals, vulgarly called Descalzos, who, against the patents and provisions of the prior-general, have been inhabiting, and still inhabit, beyond the limits of the province of Castille, called the Old ... who shall be required under the apostolic pains and censures, having also recourse (in case of necessity) to the aid of the secular arm, to leave these places within the space of three days," etc. Nor did the chapter confine itself to thundering out comminations against the Descalzos from a distance. An astuter measure, likely to be far more efficacious than any threats of vengeance, was the appointment of Fray Geronimo Tostado as Visitor-general of the Descalzos, with plenary powers over the Carmelite Order in Spain. This Portuguese monk, energetic, resolute, clever, and intriguing, was to mask the cunning of the serpent with the guilelessness of the dove. He was to tickle the King with judicious flattery of his zeal for the Reform; to represent to him that his instructions were merely to redistribute. In fact, so far from extinguishing or persecuting, what could be more reasonable or harmless, or indeed more productive of good than that the posts of trust in the Calced communities should be filled by the Descalzos most worthy of them; and that others of the Calced friars should be drafted into the Discalced monasteries, the first to teach, the others to learn?

Nevertheless, this innocent and plausible system of shuffle concealed an ingenious trap. Once scattered and separated from one another in different communities—communities that we may be sure would keep a sharp watch on their actions—the Descalzos, their power broken, were no longer to be feared, whilst the General, who in his own muddle-headed way, and by his own methods, was as anxious as Teresa to cleanse out the Augean stables of the Carmelite monasteries and renew their primitive discipline, would thus achieve a double object, viz. the Reform of the ancient Order that had baffled so many of his predecessors, and the gradual reabsorption of the new.

In March of 1576 Tostado landed at Barcelona. In the following May the Observants held a chapter of the Order at San Pablo de Moraleja, at which the Carmelites and the Descalzos came to an open rupture. The chapter, after all, is but a fact imbedded in the Carmelite Chronicles, with but little fruition to be gathered from it. It is in Teresa's letters—those windows she has opened for us on the past, a past so misty and blurred—that we may catch some fugitive glimpses of these storms and tumults, of the current of human fears and hatreds that seethed beneath them.

It is the 9th of May of 1576, in Seville, and in one of its many convents, the most recently founded of them all, a nun sits writing in her cell. Wafted through the open casement comes the scent of orange-blossom from the patio below, a patio surrounded by fairy-like columns of alabaster, gleaming through dusky foliage and flowers, glittering, as the sun streams full upon them—the golden sparkling sun of Seville—like (as she says in this very letter, with prosaic Castilian imagery) "a sweetmeat made of snowy sugar." Perhaps in the distance, when she lifts her eyes from the paper—paper to-day so faded and dim—she follows the silver line of the Guadalquivir, the movement of white sails on its broad bosom, or the arabesques of the Moorish tower of the Giralda.

The letter she writes is to Mariano in Madrid. Let us look over her shoulder, all invisible to her, and read it:

The grace of the Holy Spirit be with your reverence. Oh válame Dios, and how fitted is your disposition to make one fall into temptation. I tell you, that my virtue must be great, since I do this; and the worst of it is, I fear something of it will stick to my father, the señor licenciado Padilla; since he neither writes to me, nor sends his compliments, just like your reverence. God forgive you both; although I owe so much to the señor licentiate Padilla, that, however much he may neglect me, I can never neglect him, whom I beg to consider this as addressed to him.

When I think of the perplexities your reverence left me, and how unmindful you are of everything, I know not what to think, except that "Cursed the man," etc. But, as we must return good for evil, I have desired to write this, so that your reverence may know that we took possession on Santiago's Day, and the friars have been as still as death. Our father spoke to Navarro, and he, I believe, it is who made them be quiet.

The house is such that the sisters are never done of giving thanks to God. May he be blessed for all! Every one says we got it for nothing; and so they certify that now we should not have got it for 20,000 ducats. The situation is as good as any in Seville. The good prior of Las Cuevas has been here twice (he is highly pleased with the house), and fray Bartolomé Aguilar once, before he went, for I already wrote your reverence how he was going to the chapter. It has been great good fortune to hit upon such a house. We are in a great dispute about the alcabala [a duty levied on sales or purchases]. In short, I believe we shall have to pay it all. My brother was about to lend it us, and he is looking after the workmen, for he saves me great labour. The mistake about the alcabala was in the notary [the men of law, it would seem, being as foolish in that age as this]. Our father is highly pleased with the house, and every one. Father Soto speaks most favourably of it (he has just been here), and says he will not write to you because you do not write to me. The church is being made in the gateway, and it will be very pretty. Everything is just as if it had been made on purpose. So much for the house. As regards El Tostado, a friar just now arrived, (he being a conventual of this monastery), who left him in Barcelona in March, brings a patent from him and he assumes the Vicar-generalship of all Spain. Cota came yesterday. He is lying hid in Don Geronimo's house, waiting, so they say, for fray Agustin Suarez [the Observant Provincial], who is to arrive to-day. The first two things are true, for I saw the patent, and know that Cota is here. This about the Provincial is given out for certain, and that he is coming to resume his office, and brings along with him a Motu from the Pope, which, for the objects of the Calzados, is all that can be wished for, according to what they say; and moreover the prior told me to-day that he knows it for certain from one in whom they have confidence.

So she writes on that sweet May day in Seville, and

muses, as well she may, on the ominous mustering of forces. Gracian has fled, advised thereto by "his ilustrisima señoria of our good Archbishop," the governor and the fiscal. To escape the clutches of his enemies, he is already on his way to Madrid by a roundabout road, to consult the Nuncio (for, as to visiting, it is not now to be thought of, the Carmelites are in such a state of uproar), leaving behind him Evangelista, prior of the Carmelite monastery, whom he has appointed his vicar provincial, to meet the blow as best he may. Good Evangelista, however, is full of courage. "I tell him," writes Teresa, "that as he is not one of the heads no notice will be served on him. He keeps up his spirits well, and the deputy-governor is ready to fly to his assistance if anything takes place."

As to the *dénoûment* of the comedy—like enough to prove a tragedy—we hear nothing; for on the 4th of June, little less than a month later, a week after she had witnessed the imposing ceremony which brought her labours at Seville to a triumphant conclusion, she was herself on her way to Malagon. She travelled in a coach with her brother and his children, a fact which gave room to a wicked world—ever wickeder as it grows older, so goes the commentator's odd little note at the bottom of her letters (one dreads to think the depths of wickedness it has got to by now)—to spread abroad the report that the austere and virtuous nun now kept company with squires and dames. That other little eight-year-old Teresa enlivened the journey with her childish sallies. With them too went Fray Gregorio Nacianceno, the friar to whom Gracian had given the habit in Veas.

Their way lay through Almodóvar, and in five days' time, on the second day of Easter, the travellers alighted before the gateway of the convent of Malagon.

Teresa is at once plunged into the cares and duties of her office, as we may see from the two letters she at once sits down to write to the faithful Gracian and Maria de San José. Indeed, such is the state of Malagon, and the ill-health of the nuns, that she contemplates transferring them to Paracuellos, a property of Doña Luisa de la Cerda's:

About three leagues from Madrid and two from Alcalá, so I believe, and a very healthy place, for I would fain have made the monastery there, and she would never hear of it. I am greatly averse to their going away from this, now that they are here, as it is a place of much traffic and so many pass this way; but since there is no help for it, may it please God that this may be effected, and that your paternity will be agreeable to it, as I believe you will be, for we shall not await the license and there is no other remedy; and to break up the monastery, as was done at Pastrana, is not to be contemplated for a moment. In short, if she does not answer favourably, I shall go to Toledo, to get various persons to speak with her about it, and thence I shall not stir, until this is settled either one way or the other. I arrived well, for it has been better than coming in carts, since we could travel at the hour we chose, and my brother paid great attention to my comfort. He kisses your paternity's hands, and has arrived well, and is well; he is an excellent man: if he would only leave me in Toledo and go until that business there is settled! for we should then have news of your paternity, but this there is no hope of. Teresa came amusing us all on the journey, and giving no trouble. Oh! my father, what a disaster happened to me: for, being in a parva [a shed for storing unthreshed corn]—nor did we think little of such a shelter—close to a venta, in which it was impossible to stop, an enormous lizard gets me in between my tunic and the flesh of my arm; and it was a mercy of God that it was not in any other place, for I think I should have died, so terrified was I, although my brother seized it quickly and flung it from him, hitting Antonio Ruíz on the mouth, who has been very useful to us on the journey, and Diego also; for that reason give him (Diego) the habit without more ado, for he is a little angel. The mother prioress commends herself greatly to your paternity. She says she does not write so as not to weary you. She is now up and going about; and as she is so fond of looking into everything, and so particular, it will prevent her getting well so quickly as she ought. When your paternity goes to our house [Gracian is still in Madrid, but she refers to the convent of Seville, whither he was on the point of starting], make me much of San Gabriel, whom my departure left in sore trouble, and she is an angel in simplicity, and of an excellent spirit; and I owe her much.

Order them on no account to give any one to eat in the locutorio; for this unsettles them greatly, and excepting your paternity (for this is not to be taken into account, when necessary), they do it with extreme unwillingness, and I am more unwilling still than they, and so I told them when I left, and there are many objections. And it is enough that they will not have sufficient to eat themselves, if they do it, for the alms are small, and they will not say anything, but will go without food; and this is the least. Everything is in the beginning; and this is a beginning that may lead to much evil; for this reason your paternity may see that it is of great importance, and it will console them greatly to know that you wish them to keep the rules made and confirmed by padre fray Pedro Fernandez. They are all young women; and believe me, my father, that the safest way for them is to have nothing to do with friars. Of nothing have I a greater dread in these monasteries than this: for although all is holy now, I know what it may come to if it is not remedied at once, and this makes me insist on it so much. Forgive me, father mine, and remain with God.

To Maria de San José, prioress of Seville, she writes on the same day much to the same effect—

May the grace of the Holy Spirit be with your reverence, my daughter! Oh how I should like to write at length; but as I have other letters to write, I have no time. I have told fray Gregorio to write fully all about the journey. The fact is, there is little to tell, because we travelled very comfortably, and it was not too hot; we arrived well, glory to God, on the second day of Easter.

I found the mother prioress better, although not quite recovered. Be sure to commend her to God. I have been greatly pleased with her. Often have I remembered me of the business you were left with. Please God that nothing may be wanting. For charity's sake I beg you to write to me by every means you can, so that I may always know how you are. Do not fail to write by way of Toledo, for I will warn the prioress to send them on in time, and, moreover, perhaps I shall be detained there some days, since I fear that I shall have some trouble before this business is concluded with Doña Luisa. Let all of you commend it to God, and commend me much to the mother supriora [1] and all the sisters.

See that you make me much of San Gabriel, who was almost out of her wits at my leaving you. Commend me much to Garcí Alvarez, and tell us about the lawsuit, and all the news, and above all, of our father, if he has arrived. I write to him charging him strictly that you are to consent to no person eating there. See that you do not begin it, except for him, who so much needs it, and it can be done without it coming to any one's ears; and even if it does get wind, there is a difference between the head of the Order and a subject; and his health is so important to us, that all we can do is little. The mother prioress (Brianda) will send some money with fray Gregorio for this purpose and whatever more is necessary, for truly she loves him greatly, and so does it willingly. And it is meet that he should know this; for I tell him, that you will have few alms, and that so it may happen that you will be left without anything to eat yourselves, if you give it to others. I greatly desire that you should suffer uneasiness in nothing, but that you serve our Lord much. May it please his Majesty, that it may be even as I shall beseech him! As for sister San Francisco, she must be a good historian in all that takes place relating to the friars. Coming from that house has made this seem worse to me. These sisters suffer from many trials here. Teresa came, especially the first day, downcast enough on account of leaving the sisters, she said. When she got here, she was just as if she had been with them all her life, and the night we arrived she scarcely ate her supper for joy. I am delighted because I believe her affection for us is deeply rooted. I will write again by father fray Gregorio. No more now, except that may the Lord keep and make you a saint, so that all may be so, Amen. To-day is Friday after

---

[1] Sub-prioress.

Easter. Be careful to deliver the accompanying letter to our father; and should he be absent, do not send it him except by a very sure person, as it is important.

Your reverence's
TERESA DE JESUS.

Teresa does not write to you, because she is busy. She says she is prioress, and sends you many messages.

On the 18th she again writes, in answer, apparently, to Maria de San José:—

Jesus be with your reverence, daughter mine! I assure you that if my absence gives you somewhat of pain, you indeed owe it to me. May the Lord be pleased to accept such trials and troubles brought about by leaving daughters so dearly loved; and I trust that your reverence and all of you have had good health, as I have, glory to God. By this you will have got the letters sent by the muleteer: this is a very short one, for I intended to have been here longer; and as Sunday falls on San Juan, I have cut short my stay, and so have little time.

As padre fray Gregorio is the messenger, this matters little. I am distressed about whether your reverence may not find yourself hard pressed as to the payment of those censos [interest on the bonds over the house at Seville] this year, for by next the Lord will have brought some one to pay them. A sister of Santángel [a nun of Malagon] who is here, is loud in praise of the mother prioress, and I should have liked her better than the one who entered here. She says that they will give 300 ducats of the dowry of the one here (for in August she will have been a year), and the other she says will bring as much more, so that they can pay this year. It is little enough: but if what they say of her is true, she is good even if she had nothing: and since she is from here, treat of it with our father, and if you have no other remedy, take this. The worst of it is that she is only fourteen, and for that reason I advise you to take her only as a last resource: you will see about it there. It seems to me advisable that our father should give orders for Beatriz to make her profession at once, for many reasons—and one of them to put an end to temptations.

Commend me to her, and her mother, and to every one you see, and to the mother supriora and all the sisters, especially my infirmarian. God keep me you, my daughter, and make you very holy, Amen.

My brother wrote to you the other day, and commends himself to you greatly. He is more loyal than Teresa, for he does not succeed in loving any better than you. As the mother prioress will write (with whom certainly I have had great delight), and fray Gregorio will tell you all the news, no more.

Early in July, Teresa was in Toledo.

Know that I remain here for the present [she writes to Maria de San José], for my brother started yesterday, and I made him take Teresa: for, as I do not know whether I shall not be ordered to return to Avila by a roundabout way, I do not wish to be burdened with a child. I am well, and glad to be quit of this clatter; for, in spite of my love for my brother, I was anxious for him to get home. I know not how long I shall be here, for I am still busy seeking the best way of accomplishing what is to be done at Malagon.

Her biographers have misrepresented Teresa's residence in Toledo at this time as a period of enforced imprisonment. Nothing was farther from being the case. If she departed from her original intention of accompanying her brother to Avila, it was owing to the critical position of Malagon, and the difficulty of getting Doña Luisa de la Cerda to come to an arrangement. Her further sojourn was imperatively demanded by the serious aspect of affairs in Andalucia; where—for day by day the plot was thickening—the Observants and the Descalzos were engaged in that duel for life or death which was only ended by the erection of the latter into a separate province. Gracian, who as the Nuncio's special delegate owned a superior and more immediate jurisdiction over her movements than even the General himself, desired her to remain, and his orders coincided with her own wishes; since in Toledo she could get quicker information from the scene of war in Andalucia than she could have done stuck away in Avila. Nor was the sentence issued against her by the General by any means one of enforced imprisonment, although it was then so construed by the Carmelites, to serve their own ends, as it was afterwards by the Descalzos, in their desire to make her the victim of persecution. The fact being that, although her foundations were abruptly cut short, she had perfect liberty of choice as to the convent she wished to retire to.

For indeed her presence in Toledo at this juncture is of singular importance. There, from the retirement of her pleasant cell looking out upon a garden, " cosa muy sabrosa," bidden by Gracian, not only does she conclude the history of her Foundations, but copes with her enormous correspondence, ever increasing as time goes on,—to all outward seeming a season of uninterrupted tranquillity,—in very truth the most anxious and agitated of her life. Watch her well, this old woman, as the sunlight, streaming through the little casement, creeps over the red brick floor of that pleasant cell, and outlines the laborious figure, whose pen skims over the paper so swiftly that her nuns declare she is inspired,—for it is she and she alone who is making the Carmelites totter to their foundations;—she it is, and not Gracian or any blustering Descalzo of them all, who constitutes the veritable danger that menaces that most ancient and powerful Order. Far from the fight, keenly balancing the probabilities of victory and defeat, hers is a silent *rôle*, but the greatest one of all. Alternately checking and spurring her sweet and gracious Gracian (too weak and pliant), loyal to friends and enemies alike, petted by prioress and nuns of Seville; even this rigid old disciplinarian relaxing somewhat of her austerity in his favour, allowing him all manner of privileges, "that must never be allowed to any other," who is it but the woman who stands behind him that gives his conduct that backbone, energy, and consistency in which it is so fatally lacking the moment she is dead? Who but she can conciliate the various characters of her friars, bending their activities, making their very weaknesses and defects converge to the central object? There they all are, pale enough, struggling into life again through her letters: Mariano, impetuous, violent, hot of temper and sharp of tongue; Fray Antonio de Jesus, peevish, jealous, already nursing in his breast the seeds of that animosity against Gracian and the clever capable prioress of Seville, which was to break out with such disastrous consequences after Teresa's death; Fray Juan de la Roca, inflexible as bronze itself, altering Gracian's more beneficent institutions in accordance with his own rigidity—open books (if they could but know it) to those clear, sharp-sighted eyes. They but the puppets dancing, perhaps somewhat clumsily, it is true, but dancing still, as she pulls the strings from that Toledan convent. If not, watch them when she, the principle of cohesion, is gone; each little individuality struggling to assert itself, all these heterogeneous elements she alone possessed the spell of binding together and fusing into one common action,—battling together, hither and thither in dark confusion and disintegration that no man, or woman either, shall ever piece together again.

On the 11th of July, Gracian is still in Madrid "in great tribulation, and writing very shortly,—it must be he has not time for more," she notes, always anxious to mask his failings, to Maria de San José. Tostado is also in Madrid, but his star is waning. The King has ordered Gracian to have recourse to the President of the Royal Council (Covarrubias) and Quiroga, chief Inquisitor, in all matters relating to the Order. "Please God he has succeeded in laying a heavy hand on those friars. . . . Please God all goes well. I assure you he needs all our prayers. Still he is well, and the Nuncio well pleased that he did not return to Seville."

Early in September the Descalzos reply by a rival chapter in Almodóvar to the measures taken against them in that of San Pablo de Moraleja. It is now war to the knife. Gracian, hurrying through Toledo to attend it, snatches a brief interview with Teresa. After electing four definitors—a step equivalent to severing themselves from the main body of the Carmelites—the assembled friars decide to send Fray Juan de Jesus Roca, prior of Mancera, and Fray Pedro de los Angeles, to Rome, there to circumvent the machinations of the Observants, the rest of the time being wasted by these excellent but unpractical men in a barren discussion as to whether contemplation alone, or prayer and preaching as well, should be the principal occupation of the Descalzos' life,—and this when their very existence was trembling in the balance, and not a moment should have been lost in despatching the ambassadors. Gracian, true to the traditions of his training, contended for the latter, and, seconded by Fray Antonio de Jesus, carried the opinion of the chapter unanimously with him. One only, the greatest of them all, —those present remarked that he spoke like one inspired— ventured to impugn the decision, although he owned that action could not be entirely severed from contemplation. It was as if a breath of fresh air had swept over the chapter, for the man who spoke was Fray Juan de la Cruz!

And, indeed, there is great reason not only for energetic action but positive elation. For Tostado, always seen through a glass darkly—a very phantom of a man, never emerging into bodily shape, or showing himself to us face to face,—worsted in Madrid, has fluttered off to Portugal, and left the coast clear. "Blessed be the Lord for having so ordered it!" piously ejaculates Teresa, who from Toledo keeps a sharp look-out on the movements of the enemy, and lets none of his manœuvres escape her, as she promptly transmits the jubilant tidings to Gracian in Almodóvar.

Nevertheless, there is no time to be lost. God helps him who helps himself.

That sharp old watcher in Toledo is not to be deceived by any illusory or temporary triumph:

Know that they of the Council say, that if the license [for further foundations] is to be given according to the suit at law, they will not give it unless we produce further evidence; that they have only to see a word from the Nuncio signifying his approval, to give it without more ado. An oidor [a judge or magistrate] informed Don Pedro Gonzalez of this out of friendship. Let me know by those coming from the chapter what we shall do; and it would be well for some persons of the court like the Duke or others to ask him [the Nuncio] to do so. I have suspected that he is being hampered by letters from Rome, so as not to give us these licenses. . . . I have also thought that if these [the Observants] place these false testimonies before the Pope, and there is no one there to answer them, they will obtain as many Briefs against us as they like, and that it is of the utmost importance that we have some one there; for when they see the life our friars lead, they will not fail to see the hatred, and I believe we shall do nothing until this is done; and they would bring back with them a license to found several houses. Believe me it is most important to be ready for what may happen. . . .

I have already written to you [she writes the following day] by two separate ways, how Peralta [Tostado] left for Portugal, the very Thursday your paternity arrived here. Santelmo [Olea, a friendly Jesuit] has written to me to-day that we have nothing to fear, since it is certain that Methuselah [the Nuncio Ormaneto] is set upon accomplishing our desire of getting rid of the eagles [Observants], for he sees indeed that it ought to be done. [Indeed, Tostado's absence has so daunted the ardour of the Carmelites in Toledo, that] Infante [an Observant] came to speak with me; he wanted a letter from Pablo [Gracian]. I told him you would do nothing through me, and that he should speak to you yourself: he finds himself guilty of nothing. I believe if he had any hopes of Peralta's return, he would not have been so submissive. They have written to me to-day from Seville as to the hurly-burly that is taking place there about the convent and the publication of Peralta's Brief, and how they are saying about the whole town that the butterflies [Discalced Carmelite nuns] are to be subjected.

On the 20th of September she congratulates him on his conduct in the chapter. Somehow we dimly discern whence comes that outburst of courage he presently makes proof of in Seville which wins him even the applause and admiration of his detractors.

> They arrive highly pleased [it is to be presumed she refers to the priors of Pastrana, Mancera, and Alcalá, who would naturally seek an interview with her as they passed through Toledo, on their way home from the chapter to their respective convents], and I exceedingly so, to see how well it has been done, glory to God: certainly this time, at least, your paternity does not remain without great praises. . . . He also tells me a good deal of the measures taken to procure the province, by means of our father-General, for it is an intolerable battle to go on incurring the displeasure of the head of the Order. If it can be done at the cost of money, God will give it, and the companions shall have it; and for love of God spare no diligence in starting them off without delay. Do not account it an accessory, since it is the principal thing; and if that prior of La Peñuela knows him so well, he might well go with father Mariano; but the other one would be much better, and it is now a most felicitous conjuncture. And seeing what we see in Methuselah, I know not what we wait for, since we expose ourselves to be left without any one here on our side, and to find ourselves abandoned when we least expect it.

In the meantime the balance hangs on a thread; nay, perhaps on something even less elastic—the lives of two old men, either of whom Death may remove at any moment, the Nuncio and Covarrubias, the President of the Royal Council.

It is probably to the latter, and not to the King, as has been erroneously supposed, that she refers in the following passage of the same letter as Gilberto:—

> Know that a priest, a friend of mine [Velazquez], told me this very day—for he treats with me on matters relating to his soul—that he considers it very certain that Gilberto must die shortly, and moreover he told me this very year; and that in the case of other persons, about whom he has had similar revelations, he was never mistaken. Although we can attach no importance to this, it is possible; and as it is not impossible, it is well your paternity, for the sake of the business it behoves us to attend to, should bear in mind, that it may happen, and should so act in the things pertaining to your visit as if it were not likely to last long. Fray Pedro Hernandez entrusted the execution of all his behests in the Encarnacion to the hands of fray Angel, although he himself was at a distance, and did not on that account either cease to be Visitor or to carry out his intentions.

For, whilst the friars have been arguing whether contemplation or action is the mainspring of the Barefooted Carmelites' life, Fray Agustin Suarez, believing evidently in the more immediate efficacy of the latter, has quietly resumed his office as Provincial of the Andalucian Carmelites; convoked a chapter in Ecija; despoiled Teresa's Evangelista, prior of the monastery of Seville, of his post, and sent him off about his business to join the Descalzos who had appointed him. "I never forget how the Provincial (Suarez) treated you when you were in his house [she writes to Gracian]; and I should desire, if possible, to show him we are not ungrateful. They complain that your reverence is swayed by the father Evangelista: it is also well to consider that we are none of us so perfect as to make it impossible for us to be prejudiced against some, and show favour to others; and it behoves us to take everything into account!" Better advice could scarcely have been given than for Gracian to transfer his task of visiting the Observants—and the odium of it—to the Observant Provincial Suarez. "I repeat," she writes again, "my belief in the necessity of making use of the least guilty of them, to execute your paternity's orders. The Provincial (Suarez), if he had not been corrupted, would make an excellent executioner!"

Again she returns to the most important step of all: "I beseech your paternity to hurry forward this of Rome: do not wait until the summer, for now is the fitting season; and believe me that it is advisable."

Her prudent counsels would seem to have fallen on deaf ears. Gracian rushed off to Seville, faced the turbulent and defiant Carmelites, and, aided by the Archbishop and the Deputy-Governor of the town, quelled the storm, and forced the mutinous monks to accept and obey his commission. "This once at least," writes the prejudiced chronicler, "our good father displayed greater valour and constancy than his temperament promised." So Gracian to Seville to reform the Observants—too assiduously sometimes for his own safety: "My father, do not hope to bring things to perfection by a single stroke;" whilst Teresa in Toledo, watching the course of events, warns and admonishes—alas! not often listened to—the only person of them all who had grasped the situation and formed any clearly-defined plan of action. So through her letters do we catch passing glimpses of these storms and tumults, to us—engaged in the storms and tumults of our own little world—as unreal as the medium in which they passed.

Maria de San José also plays a principal part in the drama.

All means are fair in love and war, and in those agitated days each side was intent on intercepting the other's letters. Thus, strangely enough, some of Teresa's fall into the clutches of El Tostado: "I have been troubled about the missing letters; and you do not say whether those which appeared in Peralta's hands were of any importance;" whilst on the other hand we find Gracian in possession of some of Tostado's, —how they found their way there, history omits to relate. Maria de San José is the trusty intermediary between Toledo and Seville. To her Teresa entrusts the task of keeping her minutely informed of the health and movements of this beloved son, and of the events so rapidly following each other on the theatre of Seville. In the bundle of letters so constantly speeding to and fro between Toledo and Seville, Gracian's are distinguished by two crosses. For this reason also—the danger they incur of being intercepted on the way—she refers under assumed names to those whom it would be unsafe to name outright, making an enigma impossible to unravel except by one actually in the secret. Thus Tostado figures as Peralta; Gilberto is probably Covarrubias, the President of the Royal Council; the Pope's Nuncio, Ormaneto, is Methuselah; Quiroga, chief Inquisitor, Archangel; etc.

I beg you of charity's sake [this on the 7th of September to Maria de San José of Seville] be careful to write to me what is happening when our father [Gracian] is unable to; and to give him my letters, and receive his for me; if you who are on the spot go through so many frights, you can think what it must be when one is so far away.

Happily, however, the postmaster is a Toledan, and moreover a cousin of one of the nuns of Segovia. "He has been to see me, and says he will work marvels for you; his name is Figueredo, being, as I say, the director of the posts here. We have settled it between us, and he says that, if care is taken there to give the letters to the postmaster, I shall be able to hear from you in close on eight days. Look what a great thing it would be! He says that if my packet is placed in a cover, addressed to Figueredo, the 'correo mayor' of Toledo, however many there may be in it, none of them will be lost. . . . But be careful," she adds, the old formal Castilian, "that you address him properly, and find out whether he is styled magnificent or what. For this reason

I have been delighted to remain here at this time, for in Avila there are not the same opportunities for this, and even for other things."

"For charity's sake," she repeats on the 22nd (the chapter of Almodóvar is now over, and Gracian is hourly expected in Seville), "be careful to send me news of our father, by the way I wrote you of in the letter that I sent you by his paternity. I am excessively anxious to know if he arrived well, and how it has fared with him." How it did fare with him we may vaguely conjecture from the following, written six days later: "For charity's sake write at once and particularly about what is going on, and do not rely on our father, who will not have time."

Darker fears haunted her. If those fathers of the cloth (who, like Habakkuk, seem to have been *capable de tout*) should rid themselves of their obnoxious Visitor by poison!

Teresa was not a woman to distress herself with fanciful imaginings, and it is certain that Gracian ran a very real danger of assassination or being poisoned. We have seen how from Malagon she had impressed on him that none were to be allowed to eat in the locutorio of her nuns' convent at Seville, and the same arriero who carried the letter bore another to Maria de San José containing the same injunction. An exception, however, was to be made for him, "whose health is so important to us that all we can do is but little!" . . . "Look well to it," she says to her prioress, "that you feast our father occasionally. He is as much convinced as we are that no friar is to set foot there. So much have we insisted on this point, that I would not wish you to carry it to its extremity, since I see his necessity, and how important his health is to us." But even Gracian is not to eat in the locutorio at the expense of the community. She is far too keenly alive to their embarrassments to impose on them an additional burden. What they spend on him, as well as the carriage of the letters from Seville—sometimes even we find her including the cost of postage in her own, thereby somewhat wounding the good prioress's *amour propre*—must be rigorously deducted from the forty ducats sent from San José of Avila: "and look to it, if you should run short when occasion offers to regale our father, that you let me know, and do not stand on your dignity, for if so it will not be courtesy but folly."

Repeatedly she harks back to the same theme: "Warn him not to eat with those Observant friars! I know not why he goes there, except to fill us all with anxiety. I have already told your reverence to deduct the expense from the money of San José. . . . Let the good sub-prioress, who would count water if she could, take heed to this."

But the poison reserved for Gracian was perhaps more lethal and more subtle in its working than that Teresa feared. He is surrounded by spies; his every action is watched and the worst construction put upon it. His frankness and *naïveté* of character, a certain genial imprudence which was characteristic of the man, makes him an easy prey to his enemies. He has become the victim of the most odious calumnies on the part of the Observants—calumnies which, however triumphantly he may refute them now, will hang a dark cloud round his life, and scarcely be dispersed by death.

"Your paternity will indeed do well," advises the shrewd counsellor in Toledo, "to transmit your orders (to the Observants) from your monastery, where they cannot watch whether you go to choir or not; I tell you that it is the best way of doing things. Here there is no dearth of prayers, which are better arms than the ones those fathers use." Gracian, however, reinstated in his commission by the Nuncio, pursues his course firmly.

"Greatly have I praised the Lord," writes Teresa on the 23rd of October, "for the manner in which the business goes, and the things Fray Antonio told me they said of your paternity have horrified me. Válame Dios! how necessary has been your paternity's departure; although you did no more than in conscience it seems to me you were bound, for the honour of the Order. I know not how it was possible to make public such grave accusations. God give them light, and if your paternity had only some one you could confide in, it would be an excellent thing to give them the pleasure of appointing another prior; but I do not understand it. I am amazed at him who gave such advice, as to do nothing.

It is a great thing that there are still some there who are not entirely opposed."

What these calumnies were we shall see later on. One of them at least is connected with an incident on which Teresa herself touches in her letters. With a credulity that speaks little for his judgment, the simple friar has fallen headlong into the toils of one of those religious impostors who swarmed in the Spain of that age,—a woman who got him to believe that she had an unholy commerce with the devil; whereupon Gracian defies him to single combat. "Tell him," he says, "if he thinks himself omnipotent, to come to my cell at midnight, and I will cudgel him so soundly that he shall soon see whether he is omnipotent or not." The challenge is accepted. "So he thinks to play with Lucifer, does he?" is the answer the woman brings back next day; "in less than eight days he shall find out who Lucifer is." "Within five days," Gracian wrote in the sad record of his ruined life, "began my trials, which have now lasted for more than twenty-five years, and will I believe last to the end of my life, with such entanglements, twistings, and inventions, that although I have borne them, and still bear them, I have not got to the bottom of them, nor know how else to describe them than as the inventions of Lucifer."

But Lucifer was no match for the shrewd Teresa, and when her Pablo wrote to her in his tribulation she answered thus:

As to that maiden or woman, I feel convinced that it is not so much melancholy as the devil which inspires her to practise such deceptions—for they are nothing else—so that he may deceive your paternity in something, since he has already deceived her; and so you must proceed with great reserve in this matter, and on no account go near her house, lest what happened to Santa Marina[1] (I think it was) should happen to you, for they fathered a child on him, to his great suffering. . . Consider, my father, that if she did not give you the letter under the seal of confession, it is a case for the Inquisition, and the devil can entangle you a thousand ways. The truth is, I do not think she gave it to the devil, for if she had, he would not have returned it to her so quickly; nor do I believe anything else she says, except that she must be some impostor (God forgive me!) and it pleases her to converse with your reverence. . . .

---

[1] See Voragine, "Legenda Aurea." Sta. Marina was a woman who assumed the habit of a friar, and lived as one, until the incident referred to above led to her sex being discovered.

But how malicious I am! Still it is all wanted in this life. . . . If there is anything to denounce against her (I mean beyond what you have heard in confession), be warned ; for I fear that when it comes to be more public, they will blame your paternity greatly, for having known it and kept silence. I see I am talking nonsense [O most ingenious and tenderest of diplomats!], and that your reverence knows more about it than I. . . . I repeat, my father, that you ought to try to sleep. Consider how much work you have to do, and that the weakness is not felt until the head is in such a state as to be beyond cure, and you must see how important is your health. . . .

A week afterwards :

I wrote last week to Pablo by means of the post here [the good correo, brother of the nun, "an excellent man"], in which I answered Pablo as to the tongues [the impostor spoke in unknown tongues], and consulting with José [Christ], he told me to warn him that he had many enemies visible and invisible, and to beware. For this reason, I would wish you not to trust so much in the Egyptians [the Calzados], nor in the birds of midnight.

There are other enemies, however, besides these Egyptians and night birds ; the worse inasmuch as they are of one's own house, and these wise old eyes pierce through the incipient jealousies that already begin to buzz about the devoted friar.

For charity's sake, remember me most warmly to my father fray Antonio : although it would be better, whenever you can avoid it, not to let him see how often I write to your paternity, and how seldom to him.

Indeed all the wealth of her affection is concentrated round her Paul. Perhaps, too, a touch of tender envy mingles with the love of this lonely-hearted old woman in Toledo, whose earthly ties have been so few.

God pardon those butterflies [the nuns of Seville], who enjoy so much at their ease what I enjoyed there with such great difficulty. It is impossible not to feel a little envy, but the diligence they show in ministering somewhat to Pablo's comfort, without exciting observation, is a great joy for me. I have already written them a good many foolish counsels, so as to revenge myself. Was I to deprive myself of the consolation I experience in the thought that you also enjoy somewhat, since you are so much in need of it, and your labours so great ? But my Paul is more virtuous than that, and understands me better than he did formerly. So that there may be no occasions for any shortcoming, this I ask of you, not to be their chaplain, except for that end only. So it is ; for I assure you that, if only for this, I would account all the suffering I went through in this foundation amply rewarded, and it makes me praise the Lord afresh, who did me this favour, that you have some one there with whom you may breathe freely, without having recourse to secular people. These sisters give me great pleasure (and your paternity a favour) in writing so often, for they say your paternity orders them to do so, for this alone to see you do not forget me is a great delight to me. Time will take away a little of your frankness, which I indeed see is saintly. But as the devil objects to all being saints, those base and malicious like myself would fain remove opportunities. I can converse and feel great love for many reasons; whereas not all nuns can, nor will all superiors be like my father, who puts up with so much familiarity from them. And since God has commended this treasure to you, you must not think that all will guard it like your paternity, for I tell you truly, that I fear more the robberies of men than devils; and what they see me say and do (for I know with whom I converse, and my years give me liberty) they will think they can do also, and they will be right; and this is not to cease to love them, but to love them in very sooth. And true it is that, base as I am, since I began to have daughters, I have tied myself down so tightly and watched myself so closely so as to give no cause for the devil to tempt them through me, so that, to God's glory, I believe few have been the things—very grave ones at least (for his Majesty has favoured me in this)—that they can find fault with; for I confess that I have sought to hide my imperfections from them; although so many are they, that they will have seen enough and to spare, *as well as the love I bear to Pablo and the care I take of him.*

But how wearisome I become! Let not the hearing of these things displease my father, for your paternity and I bear the weight of a very great responsibility, and must give account to God and the world; and because you know how lovingly I speak, you can forgive me and do me the grace, which I have besought of you, not to read in public the letters I write to you. Consider how minds differ; and that superiors must never speak openly about certain things, and it may be that I write about a third person or of myself, and it is not wise that any one should read them, for there is a great difference between saying what I do to you and saying it to other people, were it even my sister; for as I should not wish that any one should overhear my conversation with God, nor hinder my being alone with him, even so it is with Pablo.

Her letters to Maria de San José are of the same tenor:

I envy you greatly the ease with which you enjoy our father's company: I do not deserve so much solace, and so I have nothing to complain of . . . withal [here comes in the thrift and economy,—not for herself, but for her nuns in Seville, sorely stressed sometimes how to keep the wolf from the door, as we shall see presently]; withal, I repeat, that you order the supriora in my name to deduct all the cost from the forty ducats of San José. . . . I laugh about the way in which the good prioress will put down even the water, and she will do well, and so I desire. . . . I would wish that it should not be known in the Remedios where he eats; for no other prelate must have this door opened to him. Believe me, we must consider the future, so that we who have commenced it, may not have to give account to God

To which Maria de San José may have replied rather testily.

It did not enter my mind, I think [she adds in her letter of a week afterwards], to say he is not to eat there (since I see how great is his necessity); but, unless it is for that object, not to come often . . . rather such is the charity you do me by the care with which you minister to his paternity, that I can never repay you for it.

But in spite of all, to Teresa's distress, Gracian still continues to eat in the Carmelite monastery, and is moreover accompanied by one Fray Andrés, who cannot keep his tongue quiet. "For God's love, warn him always, and let him go to the Remedios when he has finished there, for it seems nothing less than tempting God."

For Gracian is working wonders. The nuns of Seville too have had their share in the labours of the Reform, and several of them have gone to Paterna to introduce their own discipline into the Carmelite convent there.

I envy those who went to Paterna greatly [writes Teresa, condemned to inaction in Toledo], and not because they went with our father; for I forgot that in the fact that they were going to suffering. Please God that it may be the beginning of our doing him some service. With so few as they are there, I believe they will not have to go through much, except hunger, for they tell me they have nothing to eat. God be with them, for heartily do we beseech it of him here. Send them this letter with the greatest caution, and send me theirs, if you have any, so that I may see how they get on.

This on the 26th of November. Towards the end of the same month to Gracian, full of the same subject:

I assure you that if God had not given me to understand that all the good we do comes from his hand, and how little we are able to perform of ourselves, it would not be out of the way to feel somewhat vainglorious over what your grace does. May he be for ever blessed, and his name praised for ever and aye, Amen; for the things that are taking place are enough to make one lose one's head, and the peace with which your paternity accomplishes them is what amazes me most, leaving your enemies friends, and making the Observants themselves the authors, or rather the executors, of your decrees.

I have been amused at padre Evangelista's election; for charity, let your paternity remember me to him, and to father Pablo, whom God repay the diversion he gave us with his couplets and Teresa's letter, delighting me with the news that it is not true about the cigarras [crickets Observant nuns], and the departure of the butterflies [Descalzas]. They have many enviers [the Descalzas at Paterna] for, as regards suffering, we are full of desires; God help us when we come to put them to the proof. . . . Blessed be God that your paternity has been there amidst these tumults; what would the poor things have done without you? Withal they are fortunate since now they are doing some good, and I hold in great account what you write me of the Archbishop's visitor. It is impossible but that that house will be productive of great benefit, since it cost us so dear: it seems to me that what Pablo [Gracian] is going through now is nothing in comparison to what he went through with the fear of the Aguilas [Observants]. I am greatly amused at your going about begging, and you have never told me yet who is your companion. You say that you sent Peralta's letters amongst the documents, and the packet has not come. . . . Oh, how gladly would Angela have given Pablo food when he was so hungry as you say. I know not why he seeks more trials than those God gives him when he goes about begging: it must be that he thinks he has seven souls, and that when one is done he will get another. Scold him, for charity's sake, and thank him from me for the favour he does me in being so careful about writing.

On the 3rd of December great news arrives in the old sombre convent of Toledo, which she hastens to transmit to her prioress of Seville. "I desire greatly to hear about my nuns of Paterna; I believe they will get on famously, especially with the news which our father will tell you, that El Tostado is not to be admitted; so that the Reform of the Descalzas will not end with that convent alone. God keep him, for the way in which things are now going seems little less than miraculous." It was true; for on the 24th of November a royal order had been issued, ordering Tostado to display his commission and powers within fifteen days. Evidently the Descalzos are winning all along the line.

To Maria de San José, 7th December:

You oblige me so much by the care you say you take to regale our father, that it makes me love you even more: and so, that it is done with the caution I have suggested, I am exceedingly content; for I believe that neither now nor at any other time will it be possible to treat any other so. For as the Lord singled him out for these beginnings, and they only happen once and not every day, so I think there will be none like him. . . . But neither will there be greater need than now, for like as in time of war, it behoves us to proceed with greater caution. . . . I am exceeding glad that you are beginning to see what there is in our father. I saw it from the time at Veas.

For Quiroga, Grand Inquisitor of Spain, has summoned Gracian to Madrid.

Whatever reason your paternity might have for remaining, seeing that Angel's letter [Angel is Quiroga] is so pressing, I would fain [says the shrewd counsellor], however much your work suffered for it, that you failed not to go when you have done with those señores marqueses; for, although he is not right in his conjecture, these things cannot be done by letter; and we owe him so much, and it seems that God has placed him there to help us, that even an error through his advice will do us no harm. Look to it, my father, and vex him not, for the love of God, for where you are, you are entirely bereft of good counsel, and it would give me great pain.

Her advice was as usual disregarded. Gracian let the opportune moment slip by, and still lingered on in Seville. Amongst other things we note in this same letter are the first symptoms of the mutual antipathy between Maria de San José and Fray Antonio de Jesus, only awaiting Teresa's death to break out into a flame of hot animosity.

It also pained me that the prioress says that Santoyo [Fray Antonio] does not fulfil his office of prior as he should, over and above which he shows little spirit. For God's love, tell him of it in such a way that he may know there is justice for him as well as the others. . . . I write this in such haste [we can see her sitting far into the night in the little white-washed cell, a flickering oil-lamp hanging from the wall], and the muleteer is waiting for it; and, since it is certain, I wish to impress on you again that the Royal Council has issued an edict to the effect that El Tostado is not to visit the four provinces . . . (so he told me who had seen it,—he who wrote it,—and the letter was read to me). Although I do not consider the reader a very truthful person, I believe he spoke truth this time, and had no reason to lie. In one way or another, I hope in God that all will be for the best, since he is making my Pablo an enchanter. . . . Oh, my father, and who would not desire to share these cares with your paternity? And how well you do in making your plaint to her who feels such pity for your sorrows . . . Be careful of what you eat in those monasteries.

Towards the middle of December she again writes to the man who held her so completely under his spell:

Oh, what a happy day I have had to-day, for father Mariano has sent me all your letters! . . . At last, my father, God helps you to unfurl your banners to the winds [so had those dead and gone ancestors of hers done, whose blood leaps in her as she writes], as they say: there is no fear but that you shall go forward in your great design. Oh, how I envy you and father fray Antonio for bringing about the abandonment of so many sins. And here I am with desires alone! [oh the pitiful helplessness that the accident of sex imposes on this great and valiant spirit!]. Let me know what foundation there was for the false accusation of the nun who was a virgin, and yet had borne a child, for it seems to me the greatest folly to put such a thing about as that. But none goes so far as what you wrote me the other day. Do you think it a small favour on God's part that you bear these things as you do? . . . I have been delighted with the letter which the prioress of Paterna has written to you, and the dexterity that God gives you in everything. I hope in him that they will bring forth great fruit, and it has inspired me with an ardent desire for these foundations not to cease. . . . I am thoroughly aware that there is no remedy for convents of nuns, if there is not some one to keep watch within. Oh, how desirous I am to see all the nuns rid of the control of the Calzados! The Encarnacion is in a state to praise God for! The moment I see the province effected I shall devote my life to this, for hence arises all the mischief, and it is without a remedy. Because, although other monasteries are relaxed, those subject to friars are not so bad as the ones under the Bishops, for they are terrible. And if the superiors only understood the responsibility they took upon themselves, and were as careful as your paternity, there would be a different tale to tell, and it would be no small mercy of God to have so many prayers of good souls for his Church.

What you say about the habits seems to me exceeding well, and a year hence you can make all the nuns wear them. Done once, it cannot be undone, for, although they may shout a few days, if a few are punished, the rest will calm down, for such is the nature of women, for the most part timorous. . . . I have been amused at the rigour of our father fray Antonio [this is what Maria de San José's complaints amount to]: let him understand that it would not answer ill with one or other of them [the nuns], for I know them. Perhaps their words might be freed from more than one sin, and they would even now be more submissive; for there must be leniency and rigour both, for so our Lord himself leads us, and there is no other way with the very headstrong ones.

To Mariano, 12th December:

I have only one great sorrow and envy—to see how little I am worth for all this; for I would fain be in the midst of dangers and trouble, so that to me too should fall some share of these spoils of those who knead the dough. Sometimes so base am I, that I am glad to see myself here in peace; but when it comes to my ears how you are labouring there, I am broken-hearted and full of envy of the nuns of Paterna. It fills me with intense gladness that God is beginning to get some good out of his Descalzas, for often, when I see such valiant souls in these houses, it seems to me impossible for God to give them so much, except for some great end; although it be only for the time they have been in that convent, I am full of deep content; how much more so, when I hope in his Majesty that they are to bear great fruit.

So she writes, this wonderful, many-sided woman; instructing, warning, encouraging, following every movement of her father and nuns at Seville with the most exquisite tact, the most unparalleled grace. It is in her letters, tender, pathetic, playful, humorous, always earnest and sincere, unconscious revelations of the moods and fractions of moods that made up the very human and lovable reality of Teresa de Jesus, who fought and sorrowed as deeply, and laughed as merrily (perhaps more so) as any other of her age, that she charms and captivates us most. Look not in these letters for any sign of sour disgust of life, any pretensions to superior goodness, any trace of pose. She flings herself into the minutiæ of her daily life with the keenest zest, and makes them even as interesting to us as they were to the friars and nuns who read them first. In spontaneous and simple fashion and homely phrase she paints us the very interior of convent life; nor would it seem to have been an unhappy one, nay, rather a merry and a healthy one. Simple minds and peaceful hearts, not cut off from the world, for the world entered largely into their lives—was not all Spain itself one vast monastery?—but theirs indeed the better part, and so they feel it. Innocent enjoyments, many cares—the greatest often to stave off hunger—triumphs, too—ah, how free is the mind where there is no sense of property to breed feud and discord, and the weal and woe of one are the weal and woe of the community! Certainly monasticism, as then understood in Spain and by a Teresa, was one of the noblest manifestations of national life. We see them all again, these excellent nuns, as they pass before our eyes, conjured up in a few brief phrases: the prioress of Seville with her aches and pains, blood-lettings, and purgings. Nay, we can see her as she sits at her spinning-wheel in that old dim convent of Seville, swinging her arms about so vigorously, and spinning such quantities, that "she will never get rid of that fever if she does not desist." The sub-prioress, who in Teresa's happy phrase "would count water if she could"; Gabriela, or San Gabriel, her infirmarian, whom she misses most of nights; Sor San Francisco, the excellent letter-writer, who deserves to figure in "print," struggle once more into life in these faded letters. All the little threads that made up these humble lives so long ago forgotten,—the drama of their existence becomes palpable to us. I can see the prioress, Gabriela, and San Francisco jubilant over that famous feasting with which they celebrated the Octave of the Santissimo Sacramento, sitting down each one to indite a laborious account of it, that drew from the old saint the observation "that withal she was not vexed, but exceeding glad, it was so handsome done." The constant communication kept up by Teresa with her nuns of Seville and her various convents,—the letters that pass to and fro between them and Avila,—show us a state of things analogous to nothing existing now, if we except perhaps Morocco and the East. Those roads and tracks, to-day so desolate and so lonely, were then thickly thronged with lines of travellers; recueros with their strings of laden mules sweltering along in the sun between Avila and Seville; muleteers singing as they go,—honest souls indeed, safer than the post—Spanish officialdom was always infamous,—does not Teresa expressly warn the prioress of Seville that she is only to send the cost of postage if the bearer is an "arriero," for if not, neither letters nor postage will ever appear again? The arriero's donkey not only carries letters—the bundle of her nuns in Seville is often so extensive that Teresa declares herself "delighted with San Francisco's, and all the rest, so long as they do not expect a reply"—but gifts of quinces, tollas (spotted dog-fish), fresh tunny, and other luxuries, to the old foundress in Toledo; many of them, indeed, never getting farther than Malagon, poor consumptive prioress Brianda having more need of them than she.

It is a "recuero" from Avila whom Lorenzo entrusts with the collection of the money due to him by the Sevilian convent. Watch him as he gravely stands, cap in hand, before the locutory grating, as the nuns behind it laboriously count it out to him, in greasy maravedis (to make payment easier, and the weight heavier),—scratching his head dubiously as he guards them in his sash. Lorenzo, too, writes frequently from Avila; punctiliously enclosing four reals for the apothecary who lives close to the convent, "for an ointment I think he got from him when his leg was bad."

"If you have not got the letters," writes Teresa, "pay them, and fail not to write to him, for although I send him your messages, I think he is hurt at your not doing so "—a behest faithfully accomplished by Maria de San José, for a month after we hear of Lorenzo laughing heartily at her letters, and showing them to the nuns of San José—" He will write soon, for he is very fond of you, and I also assure you that he is not more so than I am."

We have seen her directing every movement of the Reform; how acutely she has grasped the situation; how she sweeps the whole field, and marshals and directs her forces with the intuitive insight of a general! Besides this— the central theme of her life—never for a moment does she relax her rigid surveillance over her convents. Let us now watch her as an administrator.

Both convents of Malagon and Seville are over head and ears in debt. Brianda, prioress of the former, is in bed spitting blood: of her, too, we catch fugitive glances in these letters, and things are altogether so bad that Gracian suggests that Teresa herself should go there to put them right. This she valiantly resists, "since she has neither health nor charity to look after sick folk"; besides, her presence in Toledo is absolutely necessary to keep Doña Luisa de la Cerda up to the mark, for although that lady has refused to allow the community to be moved from Malagon to Paracuellos, she is building a new convent for them, "and has as good as promised 4000 ducats this year instead of 2000," in which case the master-builder promises that it shall be ready for habitation within a year from Christmas. Moreover, Alfonso Ruiz is there superintending the work, and the nuns have nothing to do; "and although I was really needed it is an evil moment, as your paternity sees, for me to go away from here." Even *in extremis* as she is, however, prioress Brianda possesses a decided will of her own; regardless of Teresa's suggestion to give the charge of the house to Juana Bautista, she has appointed Beatriz de Jesus, "who, she said, was much better: perhaps she may be, but so it does not seem to me. Neither would she hear of Isabel de Jesus as mistress of novices, they being so many as to give me great anxiety, although the latter has already filled that office, and if not very clever is an excellent nun, and has trained up good enough novices." This office, too, she confers on Beatriz, who is "very much fatigued." Teresa's greatest anxiety, however, is Seville, where the prioress is overwhelmed with censos, alcabalas, etc., and nothing forthcoming to pay them with; yet they are valiant enough, poor souls! knitting stockings, spinning, doing such work as may eke out their slender budget. Nevertheless, their only hope is in well-dowered novices, and these indeed seem difficult enough to get. Here, again, in the choosing of novices, the business qualities of the saint come out clear and distinct—so clear and distinct that one suspects she would have been an admirable dealer at a Castilian fair.

This one has a blemish; still she is not to be lightly dismissed, "as I know what it is to be in distress for money, and how hard it is to get there, if only her friends will undertake to pay her dowry of 400 ducats at once." Another is unblemished, but undowered,—still, on the principle of throwing out a sprat to catch a mackerel, even she too may be admitted; although "only for the sake of God alone can it be done, since we have as yet taken none there for charity, and he will help us; and perhaps bring others if we do this for him." A third is wealthy, but her dower cannot be counted on until her father's death. How admirably does this show that the popular idea of a saint as an ecstatic being, quite weaned from the affairs of this world, is totally erroneous. No horse-dealer could have displayed more worldly wisdom in the selection of a lot of colts from the pastures of Cordoba than does Teresa in the selection of her novices. A fourth (one of two sisters, nieces of Garcí Alvarez, both desirous of admission into the convent) is afflicted with extreme melancholy: "I was informed clearly she was mad. Besides, their father too is living, and you will see yourself in trouble before you get anything out of them." Indeed, "money down" is the saint's maxim in every case. "As regards the renunciation of the good Bernarda"—Bernarda being a would-be novice, daughter of a certain Pablo Matias, who had become surety for the nuns in the purchase of the house—"be warned; for as she has parents, her fortune will go to them, and not to the monastery; if they died before her, to the monastery. This is certain, for

I know it from competent men of letters;[1] since father and grandparents are heirs-at-law; and failing them the monastery. What they are obliged to do is to give her a dower, and if by great good luck they are ignorant of the former fact, they will praise God that you are willing to come to a settlement with them. At least, if they would give her the amount of the bond they hold over the house it would be a great thing." Which shows a very competent knowledge of law, that does not seem to be shared by the good Pablo Matias. Then she adds—this in another letter:—"You must not let him imagine you want his daughter unless she renounces" (for the same legal reasons given above). "And know that it is better she should do so for many reasons: since people in business" (the good Matias was a merchant) "are rich one day, and lose all they have the next."

She also in Toledo "keeps a sharp look-out if anything should turn up to suit you." One, indeed, with a beautful voice, does turn up; but I know not what passed between her and the saint, or if the competition was keen amongst the convents for such a quality, but she of the beautiful voice, she writes regretfully, never returned; but she still keeps Nicolao's novice, "the one of the 400 ducats and more, and plenishings," prudently in view as a last resort.

The money made my mouth water at once, for they will give it when you like, because I should not like you to touch that belonging to Beatriz's mother and Pablo, since it is for the principal payment; and if you go on gradually using it for other things, you will be left with a heavy load, which is certainly terrible, and therefore I would wish to find some remedy here. I will inform myself thoroughly of this maiden; they speak loud in her praise, and, in short, she belongs to this place. I will try and see her. I repeat to you that I would fain you did not go on selling yonder sister's "censos," but that we look out for some other means, since if not, we shall be left with the burden, and it would be a grand stroke to pay it off altogether along with what we owe to Pablo, and would relieve you. . . . Don't take the daughter of the Portuguese (or whatever he is) unless she deposits the sum she is to give in the hands of some person beforehand [excellent business capacity], for I have heard that you will not get

---

[1] In the Teresian sense, a "letrado" was one—generally an ecclesiastic,—well versed in the mysteries of canon law, which then included all other branches of jurisprudence. Its modern sense is widely different.

a "stiver" out of him, and in these times we cannot afford to take people in for nothing; and see that you stick to it.

In the meantime the Jesuits have prevented a novice with a fat dowry from entering the convent at Seville. Teresa, however, meets them on their own ground. "Endeavour sometimes," she writes, this most consummate of diplomatists, "to get some one of the company to hear your confessions, for it will help greatly to make them lose their fear of us, and, if you could, Father Acosta would be the best. God forgive them," she adds, "for with her, if she was so rich, all would have been ended, although since his Majesty did not bring her, he will look after you." A little later on we find her inculcating the same advice, when troubles were thickening around the nuns of Seville, and the prioress had fallen out with Garcí Alvarez, whose intolerable pretensions to bring whom he liked to the convent as spiritual directors were hampering her authority and filling the convent walls with discord: "An excellent custom it would be," remarks Teresa drily, who hated anything to do with Andalucia except the heat. "I am not astonished at what you tell me of your sufferings, for I myself went through much there,"—going on to suggest, with much worldly wisdom, that their best remedy is at once to make friends of the Jesuits, and get them on their side. "It will not be a small matter if the rector there would take it upon him, as you say, and would be a great help for many things. But they will have obedience, and so you must give it; for although sometimes what they say may not suit us,—still, so important is it to have them favourable, that it is well to submit. Be sure to think of things to ask them, for this they are very fond of, and rightly, for when they charge themselves with a thing they are careful to do it well. This is very important in that wretched world you are in, for when our father is gone you will be left entirely alone."

Nor were the "censos," the equivocal conduct of Garcí Alvarez, the selection of novices, the only matters that distressed the sorely-perplexed brain of Maria de San José. The notary had made a blunder in drawing up the deed of sale, and they were threatened with a lawsuit. "Be warned always," writes the cool, sensible Teresa, "that a peaceful settlement will be the best, and do not forget this, for our father wrote me how a great 'letrado' of the court had told him that we were in the wrong, and even if we had all the justice in the world on our side, lawsuits are rude things. Don't forget this."

Interest, too, in her opinion, is another "stubborn thing," and for this reason she urges on her prioress to add whatever she can to the sum required for the payment of the house—"so that you may not have to pay so much interest." In fact, the poor nuns of Seville owe money everywhere: to Lorenzo in Avila, who assisted them with the alcabala; to good Alonso de Ruiz of Malagon, who must be paid up promptly, as "his daily bread depends upon his having money to buy cattle with in Malagon." For if Teresa is tireless in endeavouring to procure likely novices for her prioress, with Castilian rectitude she keeps a sharp look-out on the interests of the creditors. "You must try, at least," she says, "to get those 3000 ducats that must be paid this year; and not to give the money to Alonso Ruiz lies heavy on my conscience, because of the little help he has there. Even if Nicolao's novice is not so perfect as might be wished, I would not refuse her." She also suggests that Maria de San José should compound with Pablo (novice Bernarda's father) for 1500 ducats, and the amount he had become surety for on the house—"for these inheritances are never good for us, since they end in nothing; and do not accept a hereditament, . . . nor let it cross your thoughts to take landed property; say that you cannot, since you must not possess an income." Although, however, they are not to accept landed property, they are not to come to terms for less than she has said; "if you could get more out of him, get it. Get some one to ask him why he wants to leave his children in the intricacies of inheriting through the convent. Even if he gave 2000 ducats it would not be much. As for the Portuguese, they say that her mother can pay the dower; she is, I believe, better than those others. In short, the money will be forthcoming; for when you least expect it, God will send you one who will bring more than you want.

It would not be ill if that captain took the high altar. Do not forget to send him your compliments, so that you may seem grateful, although you may have no reason for being so." Neither Teresa nor her prioress, however, seems to have been successful in their hunt for novices.

"I took a nun in Salamanca" [she writes somewhat ruefully—after urging upon the prioress not to wait until things are hopeless, but before she finds herself overwhelmed in difficulties, to look about her and try to get some money out of Garci Alvarez's nieces, who are about to be received in the convent, to help to pay the interest ("for that hereditament cannot be worth anything")] "who, they told me, brought her dower with her, so as to send you 300 ducats, of what you owe in Malagon, and to pay the 100 owing to Asensio Galiano, and she has not come; pray God to bring her. I assure you, you owe me much, so desirous am I to see you free from care. Why do you not try to get that money of Juana de la Cruz paid at once, so as not to be so crippled, and to get that Anegas (Vanegas = Mario de los Santos) to bring, at least, enough to pay Alonso Ruiz, which as I have already told you, since you now see his necessity, you are in conscience bound to give to him at once."

Excellent accountant—shrewd arithmetician! as interested in things of earth as in those of heaven. And yet not for herself, be it remembered, but for her convents.

And yet it is precisely this accentuated capacity for business—this rapid and sharp insight into terrene affairs, this *âpreté* for money, this acute eye for the ducats—not for herself, but for her convents—that charms me most, and furnishes the clearest proof of her greatness. To great minds, to minds impressed with a profound sentiment of self-respecting dignity, no detail that touches themselves or those connected with them is sordid or unworthy of attention. The false and contemptible pride that pretends not to taint its fingers with such a mean and insignificant thing as money, whilst underneath it is corroded by greed and envy of those wealthier than itself; that pretends to despise a sixpence, whilst it kneels down bodily before millions; that does in reality despise all the humbler duties and responsibilities of its station, was altogether unknown in that age. I have no doubt that Lorenzo (we have seen what importance he attached to the payment of four reals to the apothecary in Seville) sold his sheep and cattle personally at the fair in Avila; haggled, too; counted the money over carefully to see he was not cheated; and trotted off on his hack—his dignity not a whit impaired—to his manor-house of La Serna. For these people neither glorified nor worshipped wealth, nor yet despised sixpences, or even the humbler farthing. All this is the growth of a later age—an age without dignity, without self-respect, false at heart and rotten to the core, with its lackeys, its lickspittles, its pampered and subservient menials, its brutal and disgusting snobbishness. I doubt whether a housemaid now would not consider it beneath her to dwell, as does Teresa, minutely on the price of a piece of serge. It is the nineteenth century that has separated mankind into two classes,—the swindler and the swindled. On one side the fine gentleman, who can do nothing except through his lawyers, agents, or bailiffs, on the other the man who, sitting in his office at the head of a soap-works or sausage manufactory, too proud to sell a cake of his own soap or a pound of his sausage, is impairing the complexions and ruining the digestions of millions with his soap and sausages. Indeed, our social code has undergone a moral, or rather immoral, revision in the interests of wealth; petty swindling being still punishable, as it always was, whilst swindling on a gigantic scale is universally respected, and is, as commercialism, accounted one of the bulwarks of society.

I dwell, then, on this part of Teresa's character with peculiar pleasure—this alliance of genius and sanctity with qualities that are now regarded by ignorance and folly and the contemptible foible of despising the day of small things—whereas there is nothing small—as of baser alloy. Shakespeare leaves his second-best bed to his wife—his second-best bed; whereas to-day he would have been justly despised for knowing how many beds he had in his house, or indeed that such vulgar things existed at all. Mankind in its woful lack of imagination likes its ideal people run like candles from a mould—all one piece, either impossibly good or hideously bad; it would have a saint or a genius soaring above humanity and its affairs, in regions where such a vulgar thing as business cannot enter; likes them to save it trouble by answering to some preconceived pattern it has forged for itself in its purblind mind; would fain stretch them on its own Procrustean bed. They care not for the multifarious emotions that ruffle the face of beauty and destroy its repose, having never felt any themselves in their gross, material self-satisfaction; nor for the complex and contradictory problems of character to be observed in every one worth observing, as if the very stones in the street would not rise up against a perfectly bad or inhumanly good character. If Teresa had been a mystic alone, I should never have written her life; had she been only a clever and successful business woman, she would have had no interest for me. As it is, it is her completeness and diversity; this mixture of the terrene and spiritual; the Idealism and intense Realism of her nature, that make her to me altogether fascinating and enthralling. And all this accompanied with the greatest rectitude: no swerving to the right or to the left. We have seen how she pleads the claims of poor Alonso de Ruiz on her nuns of Seville. Although the welfare of her convents is all-important to her, the admission of a well-dowered novice the only means to stave off financial ruin, never once does she hesitate to refuse both nun and money if the candidate does not fulfil the first and most important requisite—that of being suitable for her convents. On this point she is invariably firm: read the quiet, gentle, but resolute refusal she gives the Jesuit Olea, preferring rather to incur his enmity than to palter with her duty by ordering her nuns of Salamanca to take back again a novice whom they had found unsuitable, and therefore deprived of her habit.

I believe you know already that I am not ungrateful, and so I tell you that if it was at the cost of my own health and tranquillity, it would already have been effected; but even friendship cannot weigh against a thing that belongs to conscience, since I owe more to God than to any one. Would to God it had been want of dower, for your reverence also knows [she writes to Mariano], and if not, you have only to inform yourself, of the number of nuns there are in these monasteries without any; how much more so when she has an excellent one, for they give 500 ducats, with which she can be a nun in any convent. As my father Olea does not know the nuns of these houses, I am not astonished he is incredulous; I who know they are servants of God, and the purity of their souls, will never believe they will ever deprive any one of the habit unless they had grave reasons for doing so; and as we are few, the inquietude caused by any one not suitable for our order is such, that even a base conscience would have some scruples in undertaking this; how much more so one who desires not to displease our Lord in anything. Pray tell me, your reverence, if they do not vote for her themselves, how can I or any prelate force them to take a nun against their will?

And do not think because father Olea has written to me that he has nothing more to do with her than with a person passing in the street, that he looks upon it as a matter of no importance; but on the contrary such is the charity which for my sins he has been inspired with, in a thing that cannot be done, nor I serve him, that it has given me great pain. And certainly, even though it were feasible, it would not be doing her a charity to allow her to remain where she is not wanted. In this matter I have done even more than I ought to have done, for I make them keep her another year, much against their will, so that further trial may be made of her, and so that if I pass that way when I go to Salamanca I may inform myself better of everything. This is only to serve father Olea, and for his greater satisfaction; for I indeed see that the nuns are not lying, for even in trifles your reverence knows how far these sisters are from doing so, and moreover it is not a new thing that nuns should leave these houses, for it is very often the case, and they lose nothing by saying that they were not strong enough to bear such a rigorous discipline; nor have I seen any accounted less worthy for this reason.

Warned by this, I shall be careful as to what I do in future; and so I shall not take Nicolao's novice, however much it might have pleased you: for I have got information from other quarters, and I do not wish, for the sake of doing a service to my lords and friends, to stir up enmity. Strangely enough, your reverence asks, Why did we speak of it at all then? In that fashion, we should never take a nun. I answer: Because I wished to serve you, and you gave me a different account from what I have afterwards learnt; and I know that Señor Nicolao is more desirous of the welfare of these houses than of an individual; and so made no more ado about it. . . . Do not treat of it again, your reverence, for love of God; for she has got an excellent dower, with which she can enter elsewhere, and not where, from their being so few, they must be well chosen. And if, up to now, we have not with one or other of them carried this point to such an extremity as we might, although they are very few and far between, we have suffered for it so severely, that we shall do so henceforward, and do not put us into this embarrassment with father Nicolao, for we shall only have to turn her out again. Your reverence's saying that you have only to see her to know her, amuses me. We women are not so easy to know, for you hear them in confession many years, and afterwards you yourself are amazed at how little you knew them; and it is because they even do not know themselves sufficiently enough to recount their own shortcomings; and you go by what they say. My father, when you wish us to serve you in these houses, send us nuns of good intelligence, and you will see how we shall not fall out about the dower; but without this, I can do nothing whatever for you.

If we are struck by Teresa's exactitude, shrewdness, and thrift, we are no less so by the latitude of her ideas, the moderation and width of her views as regards discipline. We may, I think, put down to a later age, anxious to exaggerate her piety at the price of her sense, the monstrous traditions that would have her crawling into the refectory whilst her nuns were at meals, saddled like a donkey under a load of stones. Such an action on her part, we may roundly dismiss at once as a fabrication. Take, for instance, her conduct in regard to Malagon. As Brianda gets worse —" God is life and can give it her"; "Dios la hizo de menos" (God made her of less), which shows how hopeless was her recovery, although indeed she eventually got better, and died at the ripe old age of ninety—the convent got worse too, and in November Teresa writes to her prioress of Seville, warning her to take example by the ridiculous and uncalled-for mortifications which, she says, " it seems that the devil teaches them under the pretext of perfection, to endanger souls, and put them in the way of offending God; know" (she writes) "some mortifications have come to my ears that they practise in Malagon, the prioress ordering them suddenly to give one another a sounding slap on the face, an invention they say they learnt here. . . . In no way order or consent to this being done there (pinches are also mentioned), nor rule the nuns with the severity you witnessed in Malagon, for they are not slaves, nor must mortification be for any other end but to do good. I assure you, my daughter, it is needful to keep a sharp look-out on what these 'prioritas' strike out of their own heads, for things now crop up that make me pitiful." To Mariano she writes — it is only an amplification of the same theme, and only shows how, even in discretion, she towered head and shoulders above her good clumsy friars and nuns in their mistaken notions of perfection—

endeavouring to abate somewhat of the rigorism which, if pushed to an extreme, threatened to cut short the existence of her friars, without attaining any useful end—

> What fray Juan de Jesus says, that it is I who wish you to go barefoot, amuses me; since I am the very person who always forbade it to fray Antonio de Jesus, and he would have erred if he had taken my advice. My intention was to enlist men of intelligence and aptitude, whom too much asperity would have scared away, and everything has been needed to mark the difference between us and those others [the Observants]. I may have said that they would feel the cold as much [with alpargatas] as if they had nothing on their feet at all. If I said anything that may have seemed like it, it was when we were discussing how ill it looked for Descalzos to be seen riding good mules, which should never be allowed except in the case of a long journey and great necessity: that the one did not tally with the other, for some young friars have arrived here who, it seems to me, might, if they had journeyed slowly, with the help of a donkey or so, easily have come on foot. And so I repeat that it is not seemly to see these Discalced lads mounted on mules and saddles.... As to the point on which I strongly insisted with our father, it was [oh! incomparable prudence] that he should see they were not stinted of food; for I bear much in mind what your reverence says, and it often gives me pain (and it did so no later than yesterday or to-day before I got your letter), since it seemed to me, seeing the way in which they treat themselves, that in two days hence nothing would be left of them.... The other thing that I besought him greatly is that he would appoint the work, even if it were only making baskets, or whatever else, and that, during the hour of recreation, when there is no other time; for it is a matter of extreme importance where there is no study; know, my father, that I am in favour of exacting much in the way of virtue, but not in rigour as you will see by these our houses. It must be because I myself am so little of a penitent.

Indeed her energetic brain is full of care as she traces these characters, to-day so faded, to-day all that remains of that complex and agitated life of hers. If Seville is head and ears over in debt, Malagon is worse. Besides a sick prioress:

> I know not what to say of so much trouble as God has given there, and with the other misfortunes, great necessity; they have neither wheat nor money, but a world of debts. I doubt whether even, please God, the eighty ducats owing to them in Salamanca, which I intended for that house, will be enough to tide them over. The expenses they have had there, and in many ways, have been heavy. For that reason, I would fain not have the prioresses of these endowed houses, or indeed of any, too liberal, for it is to come to utter ruin. The whole weight falls on Beatriz, the only one who has had good health, and she has

charge of the house, for it was given her by the mother prioress "á falta de hombres buenos"—["my husband Alcalde, for want of a better," an old Spanish proverb] as they say.

At Veas, on the contrary, all goes merrily as a marriage bell. They, too, had groaned under lawsuits, and bravely faced starvation, encouraged by Teresa, who wrote to them that it was—

To have little confidence in our Lord to think their wants should not be provided for, since his Majesty is careful to provide for the sustenance of the smallest "animalico" [little animal]. Daughters mine [and her words turned out to be prophetic], put all your care and diligence in our good Jesus, and see that you serve him, for I assure you that he will not fail nor abandon us. Also, as it is so short a time since that house was founded, it will not appear well to uproot it; wait a few years; and if our Lord does not send a remedy it will be a sign that it is his will that it be removed, and then it may be done if the prelates should think fit.

And lo! barely a few short months afterwards, in high glee, to Maria de San José she writes:

So that you may say whether my nuns cannot do as well as your reverences, I sent you a bit of the prioress of Veas's letter. See if she has not looked out a good house for the friars of La Piñuela [so Teresa spelt it]. Indeed it has given me great pleasure. Certainly your reverences would not have managed it so quickly. They have received a nun with a dower worth 7000 ducats. Two others are about to enter with as much more, and they have already received a very principal lady, niece of the Count of Tendilla, and the silver things she has already sent,—candlesticks, altar vessels, and many other things, such as reliquaries, a crystal cross,—are worth more; indeed it would be long to recount them. And now they spring a lawsuit on them, as you will see from those letters.

Such are some of the multifarious details that occupy the time and thought of the old foundress in her Toledan cell, wreathing themselves around that central object on which both her eyes and her heart are fixed. But not even for that, the successful termination of all her aspirations and labours on earth, does she relax the reins of government of her scattered convents, regulating their money matters, summing up their possibilities and a novice's dower with the precision of a chartered accountant; frugal, generous, austere, and gentle; shrewd and satirical of tongue, but melting into accents of indescribable tenderness to those she loves; as human life is but a patchwork of shreds, so are her letters, but in them we know her best as she veritably was. But for the existence of these self-same letters, I dread to think what a stupid block of nauseous cloying insipidity this great woman might have become through the pious efforts of her votaries. But there they are to all time, and in them we find her as she really lived and thought and breathed. I am only able to give the briefest and most summary idea of their contents, for they fill two respectable volumes; but in them we catch the very aroma of the past, if somewhat faintly. After the lapse of over three centuries, even such unconsidered trifles as the old-fashioned remedies ("King of the Medes" is one) culled from the quaint domestic pharmacopœia of the age, which she prescribes to her sick prioress, become invested with I know not what quaint charm and interest. The quinces and marmalade—of her own making, doubtless—that she sends to her brother in Avila, take their rank as facts not devoid of importance. Only once she touches the great current of history, and that when she writes to Maria Bautista of Valladolid to commend to God Don Juan of Austria, who has gone in disguise to Flanders as the servant of a Fleming.

In these faded letters we may construct somewhat of her own life in this sombre old Toledan convent; see some of the dead and gone forms that flit through its locutorio and corridors, all the strange old-fashioned figures,—in the world's latest fashion then,—that group themselves around her.

Early in July, Lorenzo, on his way to Avila, had left her reluctantly behind him in Toledo. Strange how in a few months this old nun has woven herself into the existence of the sombre middle-aged man, who so many years ago had watched by what was then thought to be her deathbed in Avila. Yet between duty and inclination there was no choice, and Lorenzo was fain to go without her. "Truly it has given me pain to see how everything has happened so contrary to the satisfaction he had in the thought of having me with him, and he needs me 'for many things.'" She endeavours, however, to supplement her absence by a memorandum as to those points she was most anxious he should not forget, which she gave to him as they bade one another farewell in Toledo. His sons—who, she is afraid, if they are not at once well looked after, may soon get amongst the rest of the wild youths of Avila—he is at once to place under the tuition of the Jesuits at San Gil: "I write to the rector, as your grace will see when you get there." Should the good Master Francisco Salcedo and Master Daza advise it, let them wear "bonetes" (the four-cornered caps now confined to the priesthood). He must remember that unless he goes to their houses, since they live far from that of Perálvarez, he cannot see much of Salcedo or Daza, and, moreover, it behoves that his conversations with them should be private. For the moment he is not to take a set confessor, and must have as few people in his house as possible; "It is better to go on engaging more than dismissing." She has written to Valladolid to tell them to send the page; however, since there are two of them, and they can go together, it does not matter even if they do go about unaccompanied for a short time. She reminds him that he is inclined, and even accustomed, to receive great deference, and it is necessary that he mortify himself in this, and not listen to every one, but take the advice of Father Muñoz of the Company if he sees fit, although in grave matters Daza and Salcedo are sufficient, and he may abide by their decision. "Beware," she concludes, "as to commencing things you do not immediately see the harm of, and remember that you will gain more in having the wherewithal to give in alms to God,—even as regards the world, for your sons will reap the benefit of it. For the present I would fain you did not buy a mule, but a hack fit for journeys and work; there is no occasion for the moment for those boys to go about except on foot: let them keep to their studies."

By the 24th of July the travellers arrived in Avila— the little Teresa having amazed every one by the perfection she observed on the journey. We may imagine with what childish wonder the Peruvians, Teresa and her brothers, fresh from hot Moorish Seville, looked for the first time on the gray old upland town, the cradle of their race,—no less strange to them than a place in the Yorkshire wolds would seem to a southern Frenchman, born and bred—say, in Carcassonne. We may imagine Lorenzo, world-worn and storm-tossed, wistfully retracing every feature of the familiar landscape; pointing out to them every church and convent tower and well-known corner, as the town grows larger and larger on their vision; becoming a boy once more, as the retrospective memories of his youth surge back into his brain—trifles light as air, little incidents long ago forgotten, flashing over him with all the freshness of yesterday. To his children it meant the future; to him the past, dead faces, vanished hands—all that has been and never shall be again. So he settles down; hires a house from Perálvarez, his cousin (a soldier of fortune, whom he afterwards leaves guardian to his children), and becomes once more a familiar figure in the Avila of his youth.

"Oh, how long a fortnight this has been," writes Teresa on the 24th of July. "You have consoled me much, and what you tell me of your service and house does not seem to me superfluous. I laughed heartily at the master of ceremonies [some dead and gone joke, fading away even as they laughed—vanished completely into limbo]. . . . I am much concerned about your ailment. Quickly do you begin to suffer from the cold"; for Lorenzo, inured to the tropical climate of Peru, not only misses Seville, as indeed do they all, but pines for the heat in the more rigorous climate of Castille—and yet it was July.

He is pestered, too, by needy relatives. Juan de Ovalle, out at elbows and needy, for all hidalgo as he is—peevish and touchy, conceives himself aggrieved that Lorenzo has taken Perálvarez Cimbrón into his confidence rather than himself.

He has written me a very long letter [says Teresa], in which he dwells much on how he loves your grace, and what he would do to serve you; and his whole temptation sprang from his thinking that Cimbrón was everything to you, and that you entrusted him with all your business, and that was the reason why my sister did not come. His resentment comes entirely from jealousy; and certainly I think so, because it is his nature, for I too suffered a good deal with him on account of Doña Yomar [de Ulloa] and I being friends. All his plaint is of Cimbrón. He is very childish about certain things: but he acted well in Seville, and with great good-will; and so for God's sake put up with him. I wrote to him telling him my opinion, and how much I saw your grace loved him, and that he ought rather to rejoice that Cimbrón should act in what concerned you, and pressed him to content you and to send you the money if you should ask for it; that it was better for each one to keep to his own house [an allusion to the familiar proverb, *Cada uno en su casa y Dios en la de todos*— each one in his own house, and God in them all]; that perhaps God had ordered it so, and laying the blame on him, and exculpating Perálvarez. The worst of it is, I believe he will come here, and that not all I have said to prevent him will be of any avail. Certainly I pity my sister greatly, and so we must put up with much; for, as for him, I will swear his desire to please you and be of use to you is great. God gave him no more. For that reason he makes others good-tempered, so as to bear with them; and even so must your grace do.

From Toledo, it having been Teresa's intention to accompany her brother forthwith to Avila—we have seen how it was frustrated—their things, "the trunk and all the bundles"—one can fancy the trunk, small at best, of calf-skin studded with brass nails arranged in curious patterns, probably in the centre an I.H.S. and a cross—bundles tied together, heaven knows how, for, when mule or donkeyback was the only means of transport, luggage took up as little space as possible—had been sent forward to Avila with an "arriero," and Teresica's Agnus Dei and two emerald rings are missing. "The Anusdei" (sic), she writes to Lorenzo, "is, I think, in the little coffer, if not in the trunk, together with the rings." Nevertheless they do not appear; and a month later the perplexed Teresa writes uneasily to her prioress of Seville, "whether when the things were being unpacked, or how I know not, but neither Teresa's large Agnus Dei nor the two emerald rings can be found, nor do I remember where I put them, nor if they were given to me.... Remember whether these articles were in the house when we started, and ask Gabriela if she recollects where I put them. Ask God to make them turn up." At all events, whether owing to the interposition of Providence I cannot say, she informs Maria de San José, in October, of their having been found: "Glory to God, for at first I was anxious about them."

I now tell the sub-prioress [of San José] to send the coffer to your grace [she writes to Lorenzo], so that you may take out of it the papers of the *Fundaciones*; these he is to wrap up in paper, seal, and return to the supriora, who will send them to her in Toledo—

> Together with I know not what of my companion's, and a cloak of mine (for we are in a great hurry for them); and I know not what other papers it contains, and would fain no one saw them, nor even those of the *Fundaciones*, and so I want your grace to take them out, for as for you it does not matter. The key of the coffer was broken; the lock can be taken off and kept in a chest until the key is made. It also contains the key of a letterbag, which I tell them to send your grace, for in it likewise are some papers, I believe, relating to things of prayer. These you may well read, and take out from amongst them a paper in which are written various things about the foundation of Alba. Send it to me, along with the others; for the father visitor Gracian has ordered me to finish the *Fundaciones*, and I need these papers to see what I have said, as well as for that of Alba. I do not do it with pleasure; for the moments I have free from letters, I should like to be alone and rest. It does not seem God's will. May he please to accept of it. . . . I will write about what you say to Seville, for I know not if he would get the letter. Why make such a fuss about four reals? [the famous four reals for the Boticario—"apothecary"]. If the messenger who took them found out that there was something inside the letters he would not give them. . . . I send you some quinces, so that your housekeeper may make them into conserves for you, to eat after meals, and a box of marmalade, and another for the supriora of San José, who they tell me is very thin. Tell her that she is to eat it: as for your grace, I beseech you to give none to any one, but eat it yourself for my sake, and when it is finished let me know; for here it is cheap, and not bought with convent money; for father Gracian ordered me under precept to do as I was wont, since what I had did not belong to me but to the Order. On one hand I am sorry for it; on the other (as so many things come to where I am, even if only despatches) I have been glad; for I am troubled that they cost so much, and many are those that occur.

Such the dignified, sober, self-respecting life she sketches out for Don Lorenzo, and that he no doubt lives in one of those old houses of Avila, now impossible to identify. Dressed in his suit and short cape of black velvet, like his sovereign in the Escorial, a sad hue, and one fitted for his years and melancholy, he once more becomes a familiar figure in the Avila of his youth. See him then as he takes his morning stroll, carefully keeping the sunny side of the street, gravely to inquire after the health of the good nuns of San José; or as closeted with Master Daza, Salcedo, or Julian de Avila in some little patriarchal white-washed room smelling of cleanliness and freshness, with its open beams of chestnut wood, he discourses of matters appertaining to his soul. Of Teresica, who does such honour to Maria de San José's training, we also get occasional glimpses: Gracian even snatches a moment amidst his occupations in Seville to write a letter full of fun to the demure child. For these monks and nuns were full of innocent mirth. "Do you not see how funny is his paternity's letter for Teresica; they (the good nuns of San José) are never tired of talking about her and her virtue. Julian, which is unusual, says wonders."

In September Doña Juana de Dantisco, Gracian's mother, spends three days in Toledo for the purpose of leaving one of her daughters in Cardinal Siliceo's college for maidens of noble birth. "Although I did not enjoy her company so much as I should have liked"—for the secretary's wife had many visitors—chief amongst them the good canon Velazquez—they remained great friends.

> I assure your paternity [we know to whom she writes] that God has given her the best of dispositions, and as for her abilities and good temper, I have seen few, and even I think none, like her in my life. A frankness and clearness such that I have quite lost my heart to her; indeed in this her son is nowhere. Most greatly would it comfort me to be where I could converse with them often. We got on so well together that we might have known one another all our lives. She says she enjoyed herself greatly here. God willed that she should find a lodging in the house of a lady widow who was alone with her women. She was quite at her ease, and close to this, which I accounted a great good fortune. We sent her her meals ready dressed from here.

I am sure Teresa cooked them, and saw that the little dishes were arranged "as God orders." She at least, by Gracian's request, sees Teresa's face (a privilege allowed to but few outsiders), unshrouded by the long black veil— foreshadowing the denser one with which superstition has covered her since!

> Your paternity amused me by telling me to lift my veil; it seems you do not know me! Would that I could have opened her my heart. Doña Juana had her daughter with her to the last day, who seemed to me very pretty; and it makes me sad to see her amongst those maidens, for in very sooth, as she said, she has more to go through there than [she would have] here. Right gladly would I give her the habit in this house,

with the little angel of her sister, who is as pretty a child as you need wish to see, and fat too. The Señora Doña Juana does not cease to be astonished at the sight of her. Periquito her brother, who came here with all his wits about him, does not recognise her. She is all my diversion here. Indeed so pleased is Doña Juana with all the nuns and all she has seen, that she goes away determined to send the Señora Maria [another daughter] to Valladolid as soon as may be. She went away very happy, as it seems to me, and I believe that she is in no way a dissembler. Yesterday her grace wrote me a letter with a thousand endearing expressions, and says that here she forgot her pain and sadness. . . . The day she started she says that the Señor Lucas Gracian had no return of the tertian fever, and that he is now well. And, oh! what a pretty creature is Tomás de Gracian! I was greatly pleased with him : he also came here.

And before this happy wife and mother, rejoicing in the love of her husband and numerous offspring, the old nun's heart becomes somewhat sore, and she feels a pang of longing envy. "I find, when I wonder which of the two your paternity loves best, that the Señora Doña Juana has a son and other children to love, whereas the poor Lorencia has nothing in the whole earth but this father." One of Gracian's sisters, a little child of eight, sheds the perfume of her innocent devotion through these dim gray convent precincts. Particularly noticeable in Teresa is her affection for children, and she herself would seem to have had a special fascination for them.

When Teresa joins—perhaps but rarely—her daughters in their brief hours of recreation, "your mistress Isabel," as she terms her playfully to Gracian, "jumps up from her work and sings"—no matter what she sings—the little stanza of delight scarcely bears translation. "And at other times, so absorbed in her Child Jesus and the shepherds in her hermitage, that the thoughts she gives expression to make one praise God." In fact, a certain sort of rivalry at once sets itself up between Teresa and her prioress Maria de San José as to the relative charms and virtues of these two children of the convent. "She is of a softer disposition than Teresa, and of extraordinary cleverness," remarks the old saint, as keenly observant of the character of a child as she is of that of mankind. This, however, the good prioress of Seville, who plumes herself greatly on having been the first to train up Teresica in the way she should go, will by no means admit.

It is pleasant of you not to have it that she is not to be compared to Teresa. Know then for certain, that if this my Bela had the natural and supernatural grace of the other (for truly we saw that God worked some things in her), her understanding and ability and docility, so that we are able to do what we like with her—are better. The ability of this little creature is quite remarkable, for, with a few luckless little shepherds and nuns and an image of Our Lady that belong to her, not a feast comes round that she does not make a picture of it in her hermitage, or in recreation, with a couplet or so, to which she gives such inflections that she holds us amazed. The only difficulty I have is, that I know not how to get her to fix her mouth, for it is quite devoid of grace, and she laughs very sillily, and is always going about laughing. Sometimes I make her open it, at other times close it; again, I order her not to laugh. She says, not she but her mouth is to blame; and she speaks truly. Whoever has seen Teresa's grace in body and everything, will perceive it more, for so they do here, although I will not own it, and tell her about it in secret: don't tell any one, for you would be pleased if you could see the life I lead in trying to get her mouth right. I believe, when she is older, it will not be so silly, at least the sayings that come from it are sharp enough. There! I have painted your girls for you, so that you may not think I lie about her being superior to the other. I have told you of it to make you laugh. [To Gracian]: I made your mistress Isabel write to you, so that if you do not recollect her name, hers is the enclosed letter. Oh what a lovely little thing she is growing, and how fat and pretty.

Again : " A great amusement she is to me, if it were not that this writing leaves me but little time to enjoy it. She is an angel. To-day the doctor happened to go out by a room he does not generally pass through, where she was ; although she ran away as fast as she could, when she found he had seen her, she wept sorely lest she should be excommunicated, and cast out of her house." A terrible training, this disnaturalisation of all human instincts—which can bring a child not to wish to " see her own mother, since she belongs to the world,"—but it was a training well in accordance with the fierce creed of these grim mediæval Spaniards.

Then there is Velazquez, the lettered canon of Toledo, who was better satisfied, he said, to have Teresa for a penitent than if they had given him a bishopric—a misty figure, who grows clearer by and by, when we shall meet him again as the blind bishop of Osma. " You know how Angela," she writes to Gracian, " took the prior of the Sisla for her confessor, who used to see her often, and since this began [her acquaintance with Gracian] scarcely ever.

Neither the prioress nor I could understand the cause. Once when this wretch of an Angela was conversing with José [Christ], he told her that it was he who had deterred him, the Doctor Velazquez being better for her. . . . So that, my father, she is very happy at having gone to him for confession; the more especially so, as, since she saw Pablo, with none did her soul find either consolation or joy." . . . And so the year wears on, as sitting in her cell she keeps up a constant intercourse of letters with her prioresses, sometimes writing far into the night; directs her friars; writes to great personages in Madrid (the Count of Olivares is one—to get him to write to Seville in favour of her persecuted nuns), and concludes her *Fundaciones*. " I am well," she writes to Maria de San José towards the middle of October, "and it is about to strike one, and so I will not be long. I wish to know about my good prior of Las Cuevas. Last week they sent on the tunny from Malagon, raw, and it was delicious. We enjoyed it. I have not broken a single fast-day since the Day of the Cross. You can judge if I am well or not. Our prioress of Malagon, who wrote to me she was better, did so (the saint!) so as not to pain me, for she is no such thing. To-day I have had a letter from her, and she is very ill and cannot eat, which is the worse, as she is so thin. . . . Doña Yomar (Doña Luisa de la Cerda's daughter) was married to-day. She is greatly delighted to hear how well your reverence is getting on, and Doña Luisa, who never loved me as much before, takes great care to regale me, which is not a little."

On the last day of October the *Fundaciones* are drawing to an end.

> I believe [she writes to Gracian with simple jubilation at the conclusion of her task] that you will be pleased when you see them, for it is a " savoury thing." See if I am not obedient! I think each time that I possess this virtue, for even if I am ordered to do a thing in jest I would fain do it in good earnest, and I work at it more willingly than at these letters, for such a confusion of them kills me. I know not how I found time for what I have written, and yet I have some left for Josef [Christ], who it is that gives me strength for all.
>
> I also fast, for in this country the cold is little, and so does not hurt me as elsewhere. . . To-day is the Eve of All Saints. On All Souls'

Day I took the habit. Pray God, your paternity, to make me a true nun of Carmel, for it is better late than never. . . . Your paternity's unworthy servant and true subject, blessed be God, for I shall always be so, come what may, Teresa de Jesus. . . . Already I am becoming quite a nun, pray God it lasts [she says merrily to Maria de San José—as she describes how the prioress of Caravaca has sent her that same day a serge habit, the most to her liking she has ever worn], for it is very coarse and light. I was very grateful to her for it, for the old one was too worn to keep out the cold, and they use it for chemises and all, although there are no chemises here, nor a sign of them throughout the summer, and much fasting.

Nor does the foundress in her turn forget her distant community in Caravaca. It will be remembered that the nuns for that foundation were drafted from amongst those she had taken with her to Seville.

I am just going to send to Caravaca [she writes to Maria de San José by the same recuero who is to bring back the answer from Seville as to the vexed question of the dower] an image of Our Lady I have got for them, very excellent and large and undressed, and I am having an image of San José made for me, and it will cost them nothing. She discharges the duties of her post very well.

In connection with these same images, she sends a note to some unknown person in Toledo, probably the donor of them and one of her own votaries—

The arrival of my father San José has consoled me greatly, and that your grace is so devoted to him. It will be a great consolation to those sisters, who are away there in a strange country and far from any to console them: although I believe for certain that the true consolation is very near them. For charity, your grace, do me the favour to order him [some Toledan carpenter] to take the measures of width and length, and it should be done at once, so that the case may be made to-morrow, for on Tuesday it is impossible, it being a feast-day, and the carts start first thing on Wednesday morning. And not a little do I do in giving up the image of Our Lady so soon, and I shall feel exceeding lonely without her: so that for charity let your grace make up for it with the one you are to give me at Christmas.

In another letter written at the same time to "the very magnificent" Antonio de Soria we see how scrupulously she fulfils the commissions entrusted to her.

The hundred reals and the rest, brought by the bearer of this, I duly received; may our Lord give long life to the sender, with the health I beseech of him. He takes the bed along with him; and if the Señor Sotomayor is there. I beg your grace to tell him to order it to be examined, to see that it has had no ill-treatment. . . . I am concerned that this should be such a wretched place that, although we have hunted high and low, we have not been able to find what your grace asks of me. We have searched for them everywhere, as this good man will tell you, and we have not found more than those three, and please God they may be what you want, for we were unable to make out that part of your letter in which you say how they are to be: here we call the best of them "yerba" [she refers to the silks and brocades of Toledo, famous throughout Europe, and by the term "yerba" she would seem to mean a flower pattern], and the other kind is worth nothing. Truly I have been thinking what I could send, that you cannot get there, and I do not find anything worth sending, for it would have given me great pleasure. . . . I send seven pieces in all, two of green damask and five of gold brocade.

Nor as the year draws slowly to its close does she forget her sick prioress of Malagon, whom she would fain have brought to Toledo long ago, had not the doctor "who cures us here," said that if we do so, she will not live a month, whereas she might otherwise live a year. To her she writes in tender and loving fashion:

The Holy Spirit be with your reverence, my daughter, and give you an exceeding great love of him this Christmas-tide, so that you may not feel your illness. God be blessed, for it seems to many that a happy Christmas depends on health and joys and presents; and yet on that day in which we shall give account to God, they may be evil. Of this, however, your reverence may well at this moment feel no concern, for on that bed you are gaining glory, and more glory. It is a great thing not to be worse with such severe weather. Do not be terrified at your thinness, for you have been ill a long time. The cough must come from some cold you have caught, and without seeing what has brought it on, it is impossible from a mere description to prescribe for you from here. It is better to leave it to the doctors there.

And so another Christmas found Teresa still in Toledo, a happy and tranquil Christmas, writing to her prioress of Seville to send her "confites (comfits), if they are very good, since she would like them for a certain necessity"; well too, although these days before Paschal-tide her health has been none of the best, and she is worn out with business. Nevertheless she notes with pride that she has not broken Advent. A happy and tranquil Christmas; for the cloud which menaces her Reform is as yet hidden behind the horizon, and all seems bright and clear, even as the morning light which rises sparkling over its frosty streets.

And as the old year wears to its close, and the world prepares to welcome the dawn of the new, her thoughts wander back to the home of her youth and middle age—to gray old Avila, lying so serenely there amidst the powdery snow; to Lorenzo, who by this time has taken root in his native town, and bought a property about three miles distant from it,—a country house with its cornfields, pasture-lands, and belt of scrub oak.

"It is," says Teresa to her prioress of Seville, "a termino redondo," that is, exempt from the jurisdiction of any neighbouring town or village, so that Lorenzo is in fact lord of knife and gallows in his own domain. Besides which he has rented from Hernan Alvárez de Peralta a house in Avila (one wonders which it was), "in which I heard," says his shrewd sister, "there was a room on the point of falling: look well to it." Already he is looking about him for suitable matches for his sons (this is a subject in which Teresa also takes the deepest interest, and we shall presently see her negotiating in Segovia for a well-dowered bride for Francisco), studying under the Jesuits of San Gil; whilst Teresica, in her aunt's convent of San José, plays at being prioress, and charms the hearts of the good nuns by her grace and virtue. Surely the worthy treasurer of Quito, with whom the world has sped so well, has had his heart's desire?

Perhaps who knows but he had by this purchase accomplished a dream, an ambition—that he had looked forward to this distant prospect now fulfilled of ending his days in Avila in well-earned repose and dignity, ere he too should lay down his bones beside those of his fathers and become like them, a memory—a dream long nursed in the far-away heats of Peru, as cyphering all that this world can bestow. So perhaps was his heart strengthened and his hands nerved to the fight during long and laborious years. But alas, alas! the future only becomes the present at the cost of the past. There he had left his youth behind him— behind him too the wife of his youth; and if the streamlets rushed as merrily through brown paramera and jagged pine forest, the eyes were altered that looked on them, and never more could they be the same to him as in his boyhood.

There he is, then, torturing himself with vain imaginings for want of anything better to do,—regretting barely three months after that, instead of buying La Serna, he had not laid out his money in purchasing bonds or mortgages, in those days an easy and lucrative source of income; discoursing of the state of his soul with the little knot of Jesuits and priests, amongst whom we may discern Salcedo, Julian de Avila, Master Daza, and the like. For it is to this date that we must assign that curious document the "Vejámen Espiritual," or jocular criticism, so called from an old custom long prevalent in the University of Alcalá—it was still in vogue in 1830—which formed part of the ceremonies whereby the degree of Doctor of Theology was duly conferred. The candidate made his appearance before the whole body of the University, wearing their doctorial insignia, whilst one of the two students seated on either side of him taunted him in Castilian verse with his physical, moral, and intellectual defects, and the other covered him with hyperbolical and derisory laudation.

The origin of this curious contest, in which Teresa was the judge, and Lorenzo, together with Salcedo, Julian de Avila, and Fray Juan de la Cruz, entered the lists as competitors, is said to have been suggested by a letter she wrote to her brother, in which she asked him the meaning of the words "Búscate en mi," which she had heard in the form of a divine locution. This getting to the ears of the Bishop of Avila, Don Alvaro de Mendoza, he enjoined on each one to declare what it was that God required of the soul thereby, and when they had all handed in their papers, he sent them to the saint, so that she might pronounce on them her vejámen. This she does in an acute and witty criticism, summing up in a word (perhaps without knowing it), by a subtle and delicate instinct, the various characters and tendencies of the Jesuit (Salcedo now belonged to the Company), the friar, the chaplain, and the worthy gentleman, whose leaden-footed and ponderous verses amused her most of all.

If I were not forced thereto by obedience, I would certainly not answer nor would I accept the judgeship for several reasons, although not for those given by the sisters here, who think that, since my brother enters amongst the opponents, judgment will go by favour; because my love for them all is great, as they have all helped me to bear up against my labours, and my brother only came when I had wellnigh finished drinking the cup, although he has not been without his share, and will have more if the Lord favours him. May he give me grace not to say anything that deserves their denouncing me to the Inquisition, such is the state of my head with the business matters and the many letters I have written between yesterday night and now. But obedience is all-powerful, and so, well or ill, I will do what your señoría orders.

Salcedo is far wide of the mark. The words are, "Seek thyself in me," which shows that the Señor Francisco de Salcedo errs in insisting so much that God is in everything, since he knows that he is in everything.

He also speaks much of understanding and union. We already know that in union the understanding does not act; if then it does not act, how are we to seek? I was greatly pleased with that verse of David's: I will listen to what the Lord God speaks in me, for it is important that this of the active powers being at rest should be generally understood. But as I have no intention of praising anything they have said, I say that it has nothing to do with it, since the word is not *listen* but *seek*. And the worst of all is that, if he does not retract, I shall have to denounce him to the Inquisition, which is close by. For, after the whole paper is full of: "This is St. Paul's saying," "the Holy Ghost's," he adds that he has signed his name to nonsense. Let me have this corrected at once; if not, he shall see what happens.

As for father Julian de Avila, he began well and finished ill, and so the glory is not for him. For in this case he is not asked to treat of how uncreated and created light are united, but how we are to seek ourselves in God. We do not ask him what a soul feels when it is so close to its Creator, if united with him, or whether it differs from itself or not. Since in that state I think there is no understanding left for such disputes; for if there were, the difference between the Creator and the creature would be easy to understand.

He also says: when she is purified. It is my belief that in this case neither virtue nor purification are of any avail; for it is supernatural and given by God to whomsoever he wills; and if anything paves the way it is love. But I forgive him all his mistakes, because he has not been so lengthy as my father fray Juan de la Cruz [for even he does not escape her gentle satire], who in his reply gives excellent doctrine, for him who is about to follow the exercises practised in the company of Jesus, but not suited for us.

It would cost dear if we could not seek God except when we were dead to the world. Neither the Magdalen, nor the woman of Samaria, nor she of Canaan were dead to it when they found him. He also dwells much on becoming one with God in union; and when this takes place, and he bestows this favour on the soul, he will not tell her to seek him, since she has already found him.

God deliver me from such spiritually-minded people who would leave no choice, but make everything consist in perfect contemplation. Withal, we thank him for having explained to us so well what we did not want to know. For that reason it is well always to speak of God, for we get profit where we least expect it; as it has happened with the señor Lorenzo de Cepeda, whom we are very greatly obliged to for his answer and couplets.

Lorenzo de Cepeda's is the only document that has been preserved—the only scrap of his writing indicating somewhat of his mental development. We will quote it, and then read her criticism.

So as to make up for the shortcomings of the reply [says the worthy gentleman sententiously], I will first take for my authority this saying of St. Paul's: Oh altitudo divitiarum, etc., as far as quoniam ex ipso et per ipsum et in ipso sunt omnia. Ipsi gloria in sæcula sæculorum. The reply is, then, that he who profoundly considers this fact, that God includes within himself all his creatures, and that none of them is outside of him; and that consequently God himself is in them, more than they themselves, and that he is the centre of the soul, if it is so pure as not to prevent this admirable union, it must necessarily find itself in God, and God in it."

I must renounce the translation of his verses.
To this his greater sister answers:—

If he has said more than he understands we will forgive him his lack of humility in adventuring himself amongst such lofty themes, as he says in his answer, on account of the recreation he has given us with his couplets, and for the good counsel he proffers without being asked, to practise the prayer of quiet (as if to do so depended on ourselves). He already knows the penalty to which he who does this is subject. Please God, since he is so close to the honey, some of it may stick to him, for he comforts me greatly, although I see he had good cause to be ashamed. On the whole I cannot find that any one of the papers is better than the rest, since, without prejudice, none of them is free from fault.

Order them to amend themselves [she concludes to the Bishop]. Perhaps I too will amend, if only not to appear like my brother in his want of humility. [She herself sums up the answer in two words]: All these gentlemen are so lost in the clouds that they failed by saying too much; for he (as I have said) to whom this favour shall be granted of his soul being united with God, he will not tell him to seek him, since he already possesses him.

It is to Lorenzo, then, that she writes her first letter of this New Year of 1577—for 1577, strange to say, was once a New Year. Serna—some Avilés peasant in a hurry to be off—is waiting to take back the letter. Heaven knows what little presents and tokens of affection he has brought with him to gladden her heart that day.

If at times she is impatient of her brother's claims on her time, afraid that his affection may twine too closely round her heart—" I cannot account for it, unless it is that for me the contents of this life are a weariness: it must be from my dread of attaching myself to anything in it, and so it is better to avoid the occasion"—to-day the old saint gives herself up fondly and freely to all tender and loving impulses.

After again counselling him to look well to that room about to fall in Peralta's house, she bids him send her the little coffer, together with any of her papers that were in the bundles sent on to Avila,—one bag of papers she thinks it was that went,—this to be carefully sewn up. If Doña Quiteria should send a bundle with Serna, it can come inside. She also asks for her seal, "Since I cannot bear to seal with this death's-head, but with him whom I would fain was stamped on my heart, as on that of San Ignacio." (Teresa used two seals, one with a skull, the other with I.H.S., the one she asks for here.)

No one is to open the coffer (for I think the paper of prayer is in it) except yourself, and in such a way that, if anything should catch your eye, you will not mention it to a soul. So beware, for I do not give you leave to do so, nor is it expedient; since although your grace might deem you were doing God a service, there are other drawbacks which make it impossible; and it suffices that if I hear of your grace divulging it, I shall take good care to read you nothing.

The Nuncio has sent to me telling me to send him a copy of the patents whereby these houses have been founded, and to say how many houses there are, and their whereabouts, and the number of nuns, where they come from, and their ages, and how many I think suitable for prioresses; and these writings are in that coffer, or I know not whether they are in the bag: in short, I need everything there is in it. They say he wants it in order to make the province.

I fear, however, lest his object be not to send our nuns to reform other convents, as has been broached before; and this is not good for us, for it is even now going on in the convents of our Order. Inform the supriora of this, and tell her to send me the names of those belonging to that house; and the ages of those who are there at this moment, as also how long ago it is since they entered, written in a good hand on five sheets of paper, and signed with her name.

I have just remembered that I am prioress there [once or twice, in these letters, strangely enough for such an acute and active mind, we come across lapses of memory on Teresa's part,—she often does not know where she has put things, as in the case of the Agnus Dei and the emerald rings], and that I can do it myself, and therefore she need not sign, but send me all the rest, even if it comes in her own writing, for I can transcribe it. There is no need for the sisters to know anything about it. Be careful, your grace, as to how it is sent, lest the papers should get wet, and send the key. . . .

Nor does she forget Francisco de Salcedo, to whom she advises Lorenzo to apply in all his spiritual difficulties; nor yet Pedro de Ahumada, her other brother (of whom more anon), to whom she would fain have had time to write, so as to get his answer, "for I enjoy his letters." Lorenzo is to remember her to him, as also to whomsoever else of their mutual friends he thinks best.

Tell Teresa [she adds] that she need not be afraid of my ever loving any one else as I do her; and not to keep the pictures for herself [with the exception of the ones she, the elder Teresa, has set aside for her own use], but to give some of them to her brothers. I long to see her. What you wrote to Seville about her made me praise God (for they sent on the letters to me here), for the sisters were not a little delighted, and read them during recreation, and I also; for my brother will as soon cease to live as be a gallant, and as it is all with saints everything seems to you permissible!

I know not what faint aroma of "that peace which the world cannot give" creeps through these homely joys and sorrows of convent life, and fills me with a poignant regret that such an existence should ever have been condemned by the so-called utilitarian principles of which to-day we see the failure in the ever-increasing misery, vulgarity, and restlessness of the world. Of all types of existence that have ever been consecrated by time and human longing after peace, that of the monastery seems to me the noblest, however relaxed its discipline may have become in the times I treat of. No wonder that perturbed spirits, and consciences troubled with many scruples, looked forward to its rest as a distant foretaste of the celestial repose: that young minds found in it the serene and innocent impulses, that sympathy with others, that shed a glow over the darker features of the society around them. Let us think of all this as we read Teresa's letters, looking over her shoulder, as it were, into that dim atmosphere, filled with hopes, desires, and vibrating with life and humble duties—now covered with eternal dust. There is indeed very little of herself in them. She flashes herself on us here and there unconsciously, but it is characteristic of her to fling herself into the life and doings of the little world around her.

Yesterday [she continues] we celebrated with great rejoicings the name of Jesus. God reward your grace.' I know not how to thank you for all the favours you bestow on me, if not by these villancicos I composed; for my confessor ordered me to make them merry, and I have spent these last few nights with them, and I knew not how to do so, except in this way. They have a gracious air, if Francisquito can manage to sing it. See how well they make use of me. [Then comes some advice about his methods of prayer—to be quoted farther on when that sudden flux of blood shall have rid the good gentleman for ever of his scruples and his melancholy.]

Some of the replies given by the sisters made me laugh. [The nuns of San José had also taken part in the famous contest in which Lorenzo and his companions had fared so ill.] Others are excellent, and have thrown light on what it is; for I do not think I understand it. I did no more than mention it to your grace by accident, and left the rest to tell you when I see you, if God so wills.

The worthy Francisco de Salcedo's reply amused me. His humility reaches an extraordinary pitch; for the fear with which God leads him is such, that he might even disapprove of speaking of these things in such a way. We must conform ourselves to what we see in different souls. I assure you he is a saint; but God leads him by a different road from what he does your grace. In short he leads him as one already strong, and us as weak. For one of his temper, he said a good deal. I have read your letter again. I do not understand you to say that you got up at night, but that you sit up in bed. Even this seems to me too much, for it is important to have enough sleep. On no account get up, however great the fervour you may feel, and especially if you can sleep. Do not be afraid of sleep. If you had heard what fray Pedro de Alcántara used to say about this, you would not be amazed even if you were awake. Your grace's letters do not weary me, for they console me greatly, and it would even be a comfort to me to be able to write to you very frequently; but I have so much work that it cannot be, and even to-night my prayer has suffered for it. Not that I feel any scruples about it, only distress that I have no time. The scarcity of fish in this town is a sore trouble to the sisters, and I was delighted with the sea-bream on that account. The weather is such that there is no need to send them in bread [perhaps some old-fashioned mode long forgotten for keeping them fresh]. If there happens to be any when Serna starts, or some fresh herrings, give the supriora some money to send them to us with,—for it was very well packed. This is a terrible place for us who do not eat meat, for there is never even so much as a fresh egg to be got. Withal, I was thinking to-day that for years I have not been so well as I am now; and I keep the same rules as the rest, which for me is a great consolation. The couplets which are not in my writing are not mine, for as the nuns of San José compose their own, so did one of the sisters here make these, but they seem to me suited to Francisco. This Christmas-tide during recreation we have had great store of them. To-day is the second day of the New Year.

P.S.—I thought your grace might have sent us your villancico, for these have neither head nor tail, and yet we sing them all from beginning to end; and I remember me now of one I made once upon a time when I was deep in prayer, and it seemed to relieve me, and I seemed to have more time then than now. They ran (it is so long ago that I know not now if they ran thus)—if only to show you that even at this distance from you I strive to administer to your amusement—

> ¡ Oh hermosura que ecedeis
> A todas las hermosuras !
> Sin herir, dolor haceis ;
> Y sin dolor deshaceis
> El amor de las criaturas.

> ¡ Oh ñudo, que ansí juntais
> Dos cosas tan desiguales !
> No sé porqué os desatais :
> Pues atado, fuerza dais,
> A tener por bien los males.[1]

I remember no more. What a brain for a foundress ! And yet I assure you I thought I had not a little when I wrote it. God forgive you for making me waste my time like this. I think you will be touched by this couplet, and moved to devotion ; do not repeat it to any one. Doña Yomar and I were together at the time. Remember me to her.

So the old year of 1576 wears to its close, and the new advances with stealthy strides to take its place. The stars glitter in the frosty heavens above Toledo, far above the dark outline of the convent walls. Over the waste places of the earth where man has never trod, over seas which no ship has ploughed, do they glitter too, as they have done since the world began ; sparkling as brightly, where no human eye may ever see them, as on this one

---

[1] Oh beauty that exceedest
All beauties rare !
That causest pain without a wound,
And without a pang dost sever
All love of earthly creature.

Oh knot that in this manner binds
Two such unequal things !
Why shouldst thou strive to be undone,
Since, bound, thou givest strength,
And turnest evil into good ?

little spot of the earth's surface. And yet, as she watches them through the wooden shutters of her cell, they fill the foundress's brain with specific fancies,—with I know not what pictures of Eastern plains modelled on those of Avila.

For at this season of all the year a flush of unwonted life and joy lightens up the dusky corridors and brings bright gleams into eyes faded and mortified. Before the counterfeit presentment of the opening scene of the grandiose drama of the Redemption, the hearts of these simple women are strangely stirred. They too, by the beneficence of their faith, taste somewhat of the reflected joys and grace of maternity. The little niño Jesus they have spent long hours in arranging is their child—a child that no age shall overtake, whose love shall never grow cold, whom they may for ever nurse in his pristine innocence in their bosoms. And amidst it all Teresa is alone! "You must indeed have had a happy Christmas-tide," she writes to Maria de San José, "since you had my father with you, as I also should have had in the like case, and a good New Year. Oh the ice here! There is almost as much as in Avila. . . I have been wondering what you sang at matins on Christmas Eve." . . .

CHAPTER XX

FROM AUGUST TO CHRISTMAS DAY 1577

JANUARY and February passed tranquilly away in that Toledan convent, with but little to interrupt the monotony of its existence, or rouse it out of its ordinary atmosphere of tranquil repose and humble devotion—Teresa's greatest anxiety the illness of Gracian, who, having left Seville, is now visiting the Observant monasteries of Andalucia. And yet we can fancy how the community ripples with excitement when the dusty recuero and his mules arrive from Seville, and the pious exclamations as the excellent women unpack all those good things, the generous gifts of Maria de San José. All manner of things she sends to tempt the foundress's appetite—sweet potatoes and oranges, which rejoice the hearts of the invalids; spices, orange-flower water, that the prioress of Toledo esteems as much as she does her life; old-fashioned sweetmeats, brinquinillos, confites (comfits), and the like; strange Indian resins, rejoicing in such names as Anime and Tacamaca, which Teresa will persist in calling Catamaca. Nor is this all. The foundress has but to hint to her trusty and devoted prioress the advisability of sending some little tokens of gratitude to Doña Juana Dantisco, Gracian's mother; or to lament that she has nothing to bestow on that worthy administrador of Doña Luisa's—" a man of authority, who has laboured so hard, and will labour, in the house of Malagon, and there is nothing she can think of but what he does extremely well,"—and lo! it is a sight to see the Agnus Deis, pomes, reliquaries, balsam, etc., that come on that recuero's donkey. What matter if the glass case of one of the reliquaries comes broken, and the foot somewhat twisted! An artificer soon puts it to rights, and I only hope that they gladdened the hearts of the recipients half as much as they did the giver's. Amongst them too comes a little jug,—" calderica," as the old Castilian calls it in true Avilés fashion; the prettiest one she ever saw, her prioress's special present to herself. " But do not think," she laughs, " that because I wear 'jerguilla'" (a lighter sort of serge than that generally worn by her nuns, and in her case made necessary by old age and infirmity), " I have got the length of drinking out of anything so lovely,"—and straightway she gives it away to the friendly and influential administrador. As for the orange-flower water, which I believe would have gone too had not the nuns insisted on her keeping it, " she dare swear that it was Maria de San José who packed it, it came in such good case."

Nor does the recuero return back empty. If Maria de San José sends corporals so lovely that, to Teresa's taste, they far surpass that altar-cloth sent her by her prioress of Segovia, entirely made of lace with seed pearls and garnets, worth about 300 ducats,—although she laments the sterility of Toledo (where nothing is to be got but quinces in the season, and there are much better ones in Seville), and her inability to send an equivalent,—still there are such things as bolts for choir gratings, which, although they will not please the fastidious Maria de San José, on account of their rough workmanship, still she must even do as they do in Toledo, " where we do not account ourselves any coarser in our tastes than you"; also crucifixes, which she gets some artificer to make for them in some little dark Toledan street; " they only cost nine reals, and even, I think, a cuartillo less," she writes, with great pride in her own bargaining or thrift, having in a previous letter stated the probable price at a ducat, which inclines me to believe that the artificer has also fallen a victim to the charm of the old nun, with whose personality, as Yepes tells us, none ever failed of being struck. However, there they go, exactly as they came, arriving just in time on Easter Eve to go with the recuero on the morrow, and they must get a turner to bore the holes through them in Seville.

Amongst the most noticeable of her January letters

from Toledo is the one she writes to Gracian. There has been great tribulation in Teresa's convents, for the good friar has been ill, and she had written at once to such of them as she could to commend him to their prayers. But he is now better, and as zealous as ever, finding time amidst the cares and trials of his visit throughout Andalucia to compose a manual for the confessional, "as if," writes Teresa, highly amused,—to whom it seems a very supernatural thing indeed,—"he had nothing else to do."

> Withal [she adds] we must not ask God to do miracles [she spells it miraglos, as she no doubt pronounced it, although the meticulous commentator points out that she meant to say miráculos], and it is necessary for your paternity to consider that you are not made of iron, and that many good heads in the Company [of Jesus] have gone wrong through too much work. . . . Oh! how delighted I am with the perfection with which your paternity writes to Esperanza [Esperanza is Gaspar de Salazar]; because it is advisable to write thus when the letters will be seen by others. And how exceeding right is your paternity (in what you say is needful for the Reform) that souls, like bodies, must be conquered by main force. God preserve me it, for it fills me with great joy. I should like to be exceeding good, so as the better to commend you to God; I mean that my desires and spirit might be of some avail to me; as to the latter, glory to God, I never find it cowardly, if not in things that touch Paul [Gracian].

She would fain kiss his hands over and over again, and assures him that he need have no anxiety as to her affection, "since he who joined them together was such, and the knot he tied so tight, that it will last as long as life, and death will only draw it closer."

In Seville, too, affairs are going well. Negotiations are on foot with an "excellent nun"—excellent, indeed, for not only does she bring 6000 ducats in ready money, but also tejuelas de oro worth 2000 more, whose entry will free the convent of its load of debt. "Please God there be no hitch," writes the old saint. . . . "For love of God, if she enters, bear with her defects, for well does she deserve it." In the meantime, worthy Maria de San José governs well, and wisely; sends her carefully-worked-out memorandums of their little earnings by stocking-knitting and the like, and the alms which would at last seem to have begun to flow in.

> Pray God you tell me true [writes the old saint], for I should

rejoice greatly, except that you are a fox, and I suspect you are throwing dust in my eyes, and I fear the same thing happens with what you tell me of your health, so pleased am I. Our prioress of Malagon is but so-so. I have often asked our father to let me know whether the water from Loja would be of any good brought from such a distance, so as to send for it; pray remind him of it. I sent him a letter to-day with a priest who was going to see him merely on a matter of business, and so do not write to him now. You do me a great charity in sending me his letters; but be very sure that even if there were none from him, yours will be well received; of this you need have no fear. I have now sent all your gifts to Doña Juana Dantisco, although as yet there has been no reply. In the case of people like her, it does not matter even if we spend some of the convent money, above all now that we are no longer in such need as we were at first; and even if we were, the greater the obligation she is under to the community.

Oh how vain you will be now that you are a semi-provinciala (both Seville and Paterna being now under the sway of Maria de San José). And how I laughed at the scornful way in which you say: the sisters enclose you those couplets! whilst all the time you are at the bottom of it all. And since as you say you have no one there to say anything to you. I do not believe it will be ill that I should tell you what I think from here, so that you may not grow too vain. At least you neither wish to say nor do any folly, which is very like you. Please God that your intention may be always to his service, for this of itself is not evil. I laugh to see myself over-burdened with letters, and yet sitting down at my leisure to pen such trifles. I will indeed forgive you for boasting that you will have no difficulty in managing her of the golden ingots, if you accomplish it; for I am deeply anxious to see you free from care, although my brother is making such strides in virtue, that he would willingly assist you in everything. . . .

I would have you to know that no one wears or has worn light serge here except myself; for even now, in spite of the ice, my kidneys have not allowed me to do otherwise, for greatly do I dread this ailment; and they remark on it so much, that I feel scruples about it, and as my father took away the very old one I had of coarse serge, I know not what to do. . . . Read [for is not the prioress half a provincial already?] this letter for Paterna, and if it is not right, correct it as superior of the house. I willingly allow that you will know better what to do than I.

It was with no small pride and satisfaction that Teresa had told Lorenzo and her prioress that she had not broken a fast-day since the Exaltation of the Cross. Nature, however, exacted her penalty, and the result was a severe attack of illness, which affected not only her head but her heart, as she tells her brother in the charming letter she sends him in February. She does not write herself, and indeed is getting accustomed to write by another's hand. Her only fear was lest it might have left her fit for nothing. He is not to be anxious, for she is taking care of herself in every way she sees is necessary, which is not a little, and even more than they are used to here. She is longing to get well. The mutton is so bad that she is forced to eat birds, for all the trouble comes from weakness and having fasted from the day of the Cross in September, together with trouble and age (that old age has crept in upon her is seen too evidently; but her bright and joyous spirit is that of youth), and in short she has already become of so little use, that it vexes her, "for this body of mine has always worked me harm and hindered the good I would fain have done."

One may imagine—nay, not imagine, for we know—the concern of the good Lorenzo, and how he hastens to speed off Serna with hens, eggs, and sweetmeats, and a bundle or two of the famous goose-quills, cut for her doubtless by her nephew Francisco, whom she charges with this commission, "for good ones are not to be got in Toledo, and such as there are give her great displeasure and labour." Indeed, in this very same letter, which, probably begun by her secretary, she has doubtless insisted on finishing herself, "has she not changed so many pens that Lorenzo will think her writing worse than usual, and set it down to her illness; whereas it is nothing of the sort, but only on account of the pens." Nor is the good prioress of Seville any less anxious as she burdens the recuero's mules with oranges, sweet potatoes, and fresh shad preserved in bread—anything that may tempt the sick foundress's appetite or administer somewhat to her comfort. "God deliver me," writes the grateful saint, the mother of so many daughters, "these good nuns are amazed at what you send me," for I am glad to think that if those to whom she wrote so lovingly did not immediately recognise all her greatness,—for that they will not, cannot do, such is the hard fate of humanity, until she has gone for ever from amongst them, they all love and cherish her with a devotion which shows how greatly she deserved it.

And whilst she writes of goose-quills, corporals, ebony crucifixes, sending messages to good Mistress Ospedal, the attached old servant of Francisco de Salcedo, a little cloud no larger than a man's hand is slowly gathering over the horizon, and steadily creeping nearer and nearer. For it was certain that Tostado, foiled in his attempt to visit the Observants of Seville, by the appearance of the Deputy-Governor armed with a decree from the Royal Council, is once more like a bird of ill omen flitting back to Madrid, and the family quarrels of the two branches of the Carmelites are now to be played out before the court and the world. Teresa knew full well how court favour ebbed and veered, and how small was the dependence to be placed on it. If the Nuncio and Arch-inquisitor Quiroga had managed to clip his wings and send him back crestfallen to Portugal, until he saw fit to lay the warrants for his visitation before the Royal Council,—in pursuance of Philip's invariable policy to admit no interference from Rome in the ecclesiastical affairs of his kingdom,—they might not be able or willing to do it a second time if stronger reasons should make it expedient for the King to admit his visit. Reform, indeed, must go to the wall if it interfered with graver affairs of state. It was evident that stirring times were apprehended, and that the duel for life or death between the Descalzos and Carmelites could no longer be deferred.

In Rome the Observants unopposed had worked heaven and earth against the Descalzos, and that they had been successful and were already sure of the victory might be seen from the changed attitude of their brethren in Spain, who as long as the wind blew in their faces had cleverly assumed the mask of obedience and submission, content to bide their time until a fortuitous turn of events should enable them to throw it off, and wreak their vengeance on their adversaries. Now, however, they take a bolder attitude: the prior of the Carmelites of Madrid resolutely asserts that he will resist to the utmost the foundation of any Discalced monastery in Madrid, where Mariano and his three friars have been for months manœuvring in vain to effect it, and as good as snaps his fingers in the Nuncio's face. The Nuncio, too, would seem to be wavering under the influences brought to bear on him from Rome, "where they hold him tighter than we think." "I am not amazed," writes Teresa from Toledo to her hot-headed friar, Mariano, "that you are ill, but that you are alive, according to what you must have gone through there in mind as well as body." Still he must remember that he is in the midst of enemies, and it behoves him not only to be patient and restrain that sharp, satirical tongue of his, but to retire when Passion Sunday is over either to Pastrana or the Observant monastery, so as to give them (the Observants) no loophole,— "since it is no time for monks to be outside their monastery walls, nor will any one approve of it, least of all the Nuncio, who is so strict in these matters. Consider," she adds, "that all the devils are making war against us, and that it behoves us to hope for protection from God alone, and this must be with obedience and forbearance, and then he will take it into his own hands." Now when a person's (even one so religious as Teresa) only refuge is God, I generally find that their position is pretty desperate: and I am not surprised to hear her warning Mariano that her letter is written with great deliberation, and not without substantial, and moreover very grave, motive, although it is one she cannot tell him (for fear, doubtless, of the letter being intercepted). "I am amazed at what your anger endures; but at this moment of all others prudence is needed. It is given out for certain that Tostado is coming through Andalucia; God bring him, whatever comes of it: I believe it would be better to struggle with him than with those against whom we have hitherto been contending."

And as he draws nearer and nearer the air is full of the rumblings of the coming storm.

The Observants, sniffing the battle from afar, begin to lift up their heads. Not only have they foiled the Descalzos' cherished project of founding in Madrid, but in Salamanca they have even gone to law with the Bishop for having given them a license.

And in the meantime Teresa and her nuns of Seville find themselves in the most perilous of positions, and on the brink of finding themselves in flagrant rebellion against the General. It will be remembered how, during her sojourn in Seville, she had received the General's mandate—she being at the time a conventual of Salamanca, in accordance with the patent of Fray Pedro Hernandez, the former visitor—

ordering her to retire to one of her convents in Castille, and on no account to stir from it to any more foundations. This, however, Gracian, in his capacity as Commissary-General, had overruled, detaining her not only in Seville, until the conclusion of that foundation, but again in Toledo, on account of the distracted state of Malagon. In November of the previous year, full of disquietude in view of the possibility of the Nuncio's death, she had implored Gracian to tell her what she was to do in case it did take place, and his commission be suddenly brought to an end; "since, whether we do the right thing or not," she added, "it is sure to be made public." He had apparently soothed her alarm without giving her any definite answer; for now in January matters assume a still more threatening aspect, the Observants of Toledo having got hold of the General's Brief, and being evidently bent on making the most of it against her. For the first time she realised that she had been lulled into security on the brink of a precipice, and found (what she does not hitherto seem to have suspected) that the prohibition to leave her convents included not only herself but all her nuns. So that if Gracian's commission ceased, as, in her own graphic phrase, it might do, "from one hour to another," not only she, but those of her nuns of Seville as well, who had left their cloister to reform the Observant Convent of Paterna, would find themselves in the disagreeable position of having openly and wantonly disobeyed the General, the head of the Order, and possibly, as soon thereafter as might be, safely consigned to a convent dungeon.

For, as the Observants shrewdly conjectured, this old woman alone it was who constituted their most formidable adversary, with her cool brain; the charm she exercised over princes, prelates, and those other great and noble men and women whom she so dexterously twisted around her little finger. She alone could unravel the twisted tangle of difficulty they were weaving around her, and guide that frail bark of her Reform triumphantly into the port of safety. Indeed I am inclined to believe that the rumour of the plot formed by the Observants of Seville to kidnap her and send her to the Indies, which so exercised good Maria de San José, and roused such hearty laughter on Teresa's part, was not so entirely devoid of foundation as she herself seemed to think. Without her to counsel and to restrain, to plead and to warn, short shrift indeed would those wily Observants have made with that hot-tempered, impulsive Mariano, who, in spite of all his capacity for intrigue, was always by his ill-considered words and actions getting himself and his associates into trouble; with that feeble, peevish old Antonio de Jesus; with Gracian, the best of them all, so fatally weak when it came to the point, but whom she managed to endow with her own strength of will and adroitness, so long as she stood a sheltering presence at his back. It was not to be thought that the keen-eyed Observants would let slip such an opportunity of working her ruin; and her ruin meant the annihilation of the Reform. As yet, however, the Nuncio was still alive, Gracian was still Commissary-General of the Order, and he could still issue a mandate safeguarding them from the machinations of their enemies —a mandate which, if his commission ceased to-morrow, would yet be valid, unless, indeed, El Tostado brought special powers (and this there was no reason to suppose) impugning the acts of the visitors before him. However it may be, if they are to be saved from utter extinction, it behoves them to lose no time in getting Gracian, then quietly pursuing his visit in Andalucia, to sign and seal a counter-mandate setting forth that it is entirely by his authority that she has remained in Toledo, and her nuns have reformed at Paterna, and send it to her at once in Toledo. With this document in her possession, shielding her from all eventualities and future imputations, she is safe from any attack on the part of the Observants.

It is to Maria de San José, doubtless better informed of Gracian's movements than it is possible for her to be from such a distance as Toledo, that she confides the delicate and all-important mission of forwarding her letters to Gracian without loss of time. She is at once to communicate with Fray Gregorio, and beg him in her name—"for he will do it willingly for love of her"; and indeed for love of her what is there that they will not all do?—"to send them with a sure person (Diego if he is there), it being impossible to trust them to any one but a person they are very sure of;

and he must start at once, . . . and the messenger must wait until it is done, for it can be done without delay, and bring it to your reverence, and do not send to him [Gracian] unless it be with an arriero, and pay him well for his pains." For in very truth their lives depend on the speed of Juan, Pedro, or Diego—whatever the honest arriero's name may be—who bears those letters to Granada, Antequera, Loja, or Malaga, and brings back the reply.

We may assume that the matter was concluded to Teresa's satisfaction, for in May Gracian himself arrived in Toledo on his way to Madrid, called thither by the Nuncio, anxious to see the papers relative to his visit, and to discuss the constitutions he has meditated for the firmer establishment of the Reform, with the view of convoking a general chapter, in which it may be that the separate existence of the Descalzos will for ever be ensured. And so, "well and fat," as Teresa does not forget to inform her prioress, after preaching his Easter sermon in the Convent of Las Damas Nobles, he too speeds on to court, "where it seems," says Teresa, "as if our business was doing well," following close on the heels of his rival, El Tostado, who five days before also passed through Toledo, barely spending three or four hours there in his haste to reach Madrid.

And as he does so (for news travels but slowly in those days—at the pace, you may say, of an arriero's donkey), the affairs of the barefooted friars look bright indeed to the woman he has left behind him in Toledo. "Now is the time when the prayers of all are needed," she writes earnestly to her prioress of Seville. . . . "For now with the Lord's favour we shall see the triumph of good or the contrary. Never was prayer so necessary."

Never, indeed! for even as she wrote, Fate had for ever solved the question, and in June the Nuncio was dead. Gracian had one interview with him—one interview only, in which nothing was resolved; at the second, he was lying on his deathbed. In Rome, where Reform was never relished, the wags had made merry at his expense, and ironically dubbed him Reformator Orbis; but at least poor old Reformator Orbis, who had devoted his life to purging monasteries and chastising dissolute friars, was neither grasping nor greedy, and the absolute poverty he died in might have taught a humiliating lesson to more than one simoniacal cardinal and purse-proud prelate. Philip himself paid for the funeral; and so good old Ormaneto, Cardinal Legate of the great Roman Church, disappears off the stage, where, in his little day, he had made no inconsiderable stir.

On the 2nd of July we hear of Gracian at Pastrana, "well, but full of trouble," as Teresa writes to her prioress, Mother Ana de San Alberto at Caravaca, where she too would be rejoiced to find herself, "if only to be beyond the reach of letters and business, and near those little ducklings and water, which must make her daughters of that convent feel like hermits."

No wonder that the good Gracian is full of trouble, and that the nuns of Toledo do their best to help him in such fashion as they may by prayers and devout processions; for although he has once more worsted the manœuvres of his rival, in their second encounter in that "theatre of the world" (such is the title the chronicler pompously bestows on Madrid), and forced by the King and his ministers once more to resume his difficult and onerous office, *re non integra*, sorely indeed against his will, and after pleading hard to be released from it, he stands alone in the breach, ready to fall a sacrifice either to the King's policy or his enemies' manœuvres—whichever way the breeze shall veer.

It was for this reason, doubtless, that, oppressed by an uneasy sense of the falsity and untenableness of his position, and no longer daring to detain her as he had hitherto done on the strength of an authority which was more than doubtful, he now resolved to transfer Teresa from Toledo to her primitive convent of San José of Avila. And so, towards the middle or end of July, we find him again in Toledo for the purpose of accompanying her to her native town, tranquilly cracking cocoa-nuts with the foundress and her nuns, full of childish glee and excitement at sight of the strange Indian fruit sent them by their sisters of Seville,— so little suffices to bring a gleam of joy into lives undisturbed by ambition and mundane cares. So do the infinitely little and the tragical immensity follow and precede each other in this strange tissue of alternate laughter and tragedy which goes to make up the sum of a human life. For even as they cracked the nuts, the storm was brewing. Such at least is the scene she shows us in the last letter (the last that remains) penned by her from Toledo to Maria de San José, and in which we are sorry to learn that the latter's commercial speculations have proved unfortunate, the linen (doubtless spun by herself) she sent from Seville having been hawked round the houses and monasteries of half Toledo, every one holding it all too dear at four reals, and Teresa conscientiously refusing to let it go for less.

We may imagine the leave-takings ere she sets out for Avila, for already death has been busy in that Toledan convent. Only a few weeks have passed away since some nameless nun has, in Teresa's phrase, "left them for heaven," and one voice the less rings through the little church. In the common sentiment of their loss those who are left only cling to one another more closely. We may fancy the heart-broken sobs of little Isabelita, whose joy at the brinquiños and serge from Seville are duly chronicled in these letters (poor little child, her bones crumbled to dust long centuries ago in some forgotten convent cloister!), as the last echo of the donkeys' feet dies out of the convent court, and the nuns, their faces stained with tears, once more bar the massive doors against the world and sounds of men.

We know nothing of her journey, but it is one that she remembers for many a long day afterwards, for besides old Fray Antonio de Jesus, did she not travel in the company of her beloved son? "and was not he who had joined them together such, and the knot he tied so tight, that it can only be severed with life, and death will only draw it closer?"

In August we once more find her an inmate of San José (Gracian has already left for Alcalá, to despatch the messengers to Rome), engaged in a difficult negotiation with the Bishop, Don Alvaro de Mendoza, and not only difficult, but one demanding consummate delicacy and tact. Indeed, it was no less a business than to withdraw that convent from the prelate's jurisdiction, and to place it under that of the Order, thus assimilating its discipline and government to that of the other convents she had founded.

What arguments she used we know not; nor how she managed to achieve her purpose without wounding the susceptibilities of the generous benefactor, to whom she and her nuns owed so much. Yet that she succeeded (Don Alvaro was already Bishop-elect of Palencia, and to this fact, that his episcopal connection with Avila was all but severed, his ready acquiescence in her proposal may have been greatly due), and even brought her nuns, many of whom were averse to the change, to her own way of thinking, may be seen by the letter she sent to him at Olmedo in August.

I kiss you [she writes—" your hands," she meant to say; but Teresa was as subject to slips of the pen as the most unsaintly] for the favour you do me by your letters. . . . If your lordship had seen how necessary it was for them to have as visitor one who can declare the constitutions, and knows them from having practised them, I think you would be greatly pleased, and know how great a service you have done our Lord, and benefit to this house, in not leaving it at the mercy of one who might be ignorant where the devil could and was beginning to enter, and until now without its being the fault of any one, but with the best intentions.

Do not be distressed lest we should be in necessity or want for anything should the Bishop do nothing for us, for it is better that the convents should help to bear one another's burdens than that this should be in the hands of one who never in his life will feel the same love for us as your lordship. As for the rest, if we only had you here to enjoy your company (for hence comes our pain), it does not seem that we have made any change; for we shall always be your subjects as much as ever, and so will all the prelates, especially father Gracian, whom it seems we have infected with the same love to your lordship that we bear ourselves.

Well may the simple folk of her day call her Teresa the Omnipotent. For in this same letter she achieves a double object, and procures for Master Daza—good Master Daza, who, after a laborious life, with old age creeping on him, would fain end his days in a fat cathedral canonry—the fulfilment of his heart's desire. Not only does Teresa point out to his lordship that both God and the world (when did she ever forget it?) will regard with favour the promotion of one who had done him much good service, but that it is a small matter on the eve of bidding farewell to Avila in comparison to leaving every one happy behind him. In short, the love borne him by every one is not as disinterested as that of the Descalzas of San José. And then, with the old-fashioned Castilian courtesy which never deserts her, mingled with the delicate flavour of flattery that none ever used more dexterously, she brings her letter to a close: "We are vexed that you should tell us afresh to commend you to God, for of this you ought already to have been so sure, that we feel it an affront."

In September a new disaster befell the Descalzos in the death of good old Bishop Covarrubias, President of the Royal Council, which gives the chronicler occasion to remark that in that same month, or the previous one of August, "a comet of extraordinary size appeared between the tropic of Cancer and the Arctic Circle, close to the sign of the Scales and the planet Mars, with a remarkably long tail, that seemed to us to sparkle like a star. It caused great astonishment, for not often has so large a thing been seen. Those who said it portended the death of some prince, accredited themselves with that of the king, D. Sebastián of Portugal, which took place the following year. The Carmelite Order was divided against itself, and the disturbance extended to others. Who shall know whether they were not the effects of the comet?"

And it seemed indeed that some evil star had shone on the fortunes of the Reform, and that it was to be swept off the face of the earth. All Teresa's worst fears are now realised. It has happened even as she said it would. If any proof is needed of her greatness,—her immeasurable superiority to her friars, excellent, though dunderheaded, as they were,— it may be seen in the clear, incisive manner in which she had grasped all the bearings of the struggle between the Carmelites and Descalzos, and foreseen every eventuality more than two years before in Seville, when she had written to her niece, Maria Bautista of Valladolid, that the existence of the Reform hung on the slender and precarious thread of three lives,—the Pope's, the King's, and the Nuncio's. "Whichever of them fails us," she said, "we are lost, on account of our most reverend (the General) being as he is." From the first she had warned her friars—returning to her theme with the weary iteration of hope deferred—that nothing would be done until they boldly took the war into the enemy's camp, and sent emissaries to Rome to lay the real state of the case before the Pope and General, firmly believing, as she did, that the sight of their humble and rigorous lives would be of itself the most convincing and unanswerable reply to the calumnies of the Observants. "Believe me," she had written, "that it is a great thing to be prepared for whatever may happen." Still, although it had been decided in the chapter of Almodóvar to send Discalced friars to Rome, in spite of her warnings and appeals, every day more urgent, that no time should be lost, that money should be procured, and two companions sent off without delay ("do not think it an accessory thing; since it is the principal"); in spite of her supplications to Gracian to hasten their departure before the spring came on, the foolhardy, self-willed men around her, bent not on the "principal thing," but on frittering away their energies in founding refuges for fallen (*sic*) women and hypothetical monasteries in Madrid, when their very existence and that of the Order hung in the balance, deaf to the solitary voice crying in the wilderness, let the golden opportunity slip by them for ever. And at length, her dearest hopes dashed to the ground by folly and incompetence, she was fain to write with all the sadness and bitterness of a great spirit chafing against the limitations imposed on her by circumstances and sex, the following pathetic words:—

> Know that I can do very little as to what your reverence says about going to Rome, since I have been imploring them to do it this long time, and I have never influence enough even to get them to write so much as a letter to him to whom there is so much cause to write [she refers to the General] . . . and it does not lie with our father visitor, who would already have done it. There are so many who counsel differently, that I avail little. It is painful enough for me to be able to do no more.

If, barely three months before, they had listened to her when she urged on Mariano the extreme importance of placing the Reform under the protection of some cardinal, of employing an advocate amongst the curiales, no matter at what price, to circumvent the machinations of the Observants; of getting the Spanish Ambassador to speak a word in their favour to the Pope and General, it might still have been time, and both she and they might have averted the troublous days in store for them. But nothing of this had been done, and now, when suddenly roused to a sense of their danger by the Nuncio's death, and to their own incredible folly in neglecting the so obvious precautions she had so ceaselessly impressed on them; now, when it was too late and the mischief was done, when the friendly Nuncio was dead, and buried at the King's expense, and the no less friendly Covarrubias gone to a longer consultation, can no more espouse their cause in the Royal Council Chamber, we hear of Gracian rushing off to Alcalá to hurry forward the departure of the messengers.

It is indeed too late. For the Observants have made the most of their opportunities, and the poison has worked only too well. For our "most reverend" (the General), in spite of having fallen from his mule and crushed his leg to pieces, is unfortunately for the Descalzos still alive, and every day more embittered against Teresa and her friars. The menacing shadow of Sega's presence already envelops them as with an approaching doom. For the Carmelites, enlisting on their side the powerful influence of their protector Cardinal Buonocompagni, whose creature Sega was, have left no stone unturned to gain the ear of the new legate—Philip Sega, Bishop of Ripa in the March of Ancona, and a distant connection of Pope Gregory XIII., and it is notoriously prepossessed against the Reform that he takes ship that July day of 1577 from the shores of Italy. In the meantime the Carmelites, wily and stubborn, confident in the expectation of his coming, prepare to give short shrift to the pestilent innovators. Tostado, sheltering himself behind the authority of the dead Nunico, who, he alleges, had told him with his last breath that he had revoked Gracian's commission, now no longer paralysed by fear, boldly constitutes himself, pending Sega's arrival, Vicar-General of Spain, and pours out the vials of his wrath on the disobedient friars; his commands being seconded with alacrity by his subordinates, more wrathful still.

"No further foundations shall be made, no fresh novices received into the Discalced communities. All heads and superiors of monasteries to present themselves before him to receive his instructions": so Tostado thunders from Madrid. Nor does he confine himself to thunders. As Fray Antonio de Jesus passes through Toledo on his way back from escorting Teresa to Avila, the prior of the Carmelite monastery lays violent hands on him and throws him into prison, whilst Gracian, hiding in a cave of Pastrana, is afraid to show his face, lest he too should be secretly conveyed off to some Carmelite dungeon, and there quietly assassinated.

All Madrid rings with the scandals daily taking place between the Carmelites and their brethren. Memorials defamatory of Gracian and (stranger still) of Teresa herself rain in upon the Grand Inquisitor, and penetrate into the royal closet, and these not signed by the Carmelites,—so true it is—it is one of her own proverbs, and I may therefore use it — that *El peor ladron es el de casa*, the worst thief is a domestic one. Fray Baltasar de Jesus—the aged prior of Pastrana,—whose sermons had electrified all Alcalá at the opening of the Carmelite College, who had consecrated the first foundations of the Order in Andalucia,—was one of the calumniators. He had never forgiven the man he had himself placed at the front of the Reform for having risen over his head, and it was this moment of all others that he took to wreak on him a mean and pitiful revenge, and to bespatter his fair fame with every calumny that malice and his enemies could devise.

Two years before, in Seville, Teresa's keen eyes, so doubly keen in anything that touched her " Sancto Sanctorum " (so she construed it), had seen the personal animus he nourished against Gracian ; and now it was his signature,—the signature of one of her first friars,—that the Carmelites flourished triumphantly in the eyes of the court and the world. As for the other, he was a madman, and unaccountable for his actions, and his solemn retractations were perhaps as worthy of credence as his no less solemnly attested accusations. Whereupon Teresa, stung to the quick, wrote an indignant letter to the King:

> The grace of the Holy Ghost be ever with your Majesty, Amen. A memorial has come to my notice which has been given to your Majesty against the father master Gracian, and I am amazed at the artifices of the devil and the Calced friars ; since, not satisfied with defaming this

servant of God (for such he truly is . . .), they endeavour to sully the fair fame of these monasteries ; . . . and to this end they have made use of two Discalced friars, one of whom, before he became a friar, was employed in these monasteries, and has done things which clearly show that he is often not quite right in his head ; and the friars of the cloth have made use of him and other of the enemies of the father master Gracian's (since it is his duty to chastise them), making them sign such ravings, that were it not for the harm the devil can do, I should be amused at the things they ascribe to the nuns. . . . And since it is possible to inquire into the motives of the writers of these memorials, for love of our Lord, look to it, your Majesty, as a thing which touches his honour and glory; for if they of the cloth see that notice is taken of their evidence, they will, to escape the visit, accuse him who makes it of being a heretic ; and where there is but little fear of God, it will be easy to prove it. I pity the sufferings of this servant of God, such is the rectitude and perfection with which he proceeds in all ; and this obliges me to beseech your Majesty to favour him, or to order him to be released from the occasion of these dangers since he is the son of your Majesty's servants, and it is not for himself that he suffers ; for truly he has seemed to me a man sent from God and his blessed Mother, his devotion to whom (and it is great) drew him to the Order, for my assistance : because for more than seventeen years I have borne with these fathers of the cloth, and I scarcely knew how to bear it longer, for my feeble strength was not enough. I beseech your Majesty to pardon me for having been so lengthy, since the great love I bear your Majesty has made me daring, considering that, since the Lord bears with my indiscreet complaints, your Majesty will do so also.

And as much as any appeal could move him, the King was moved by the heartfelt appeal of his unworthy servant, Teresa de Jesus, the Carmelite. Both retracted. Fray Miguel, the madman, swore before the Host and a notary that he had written nothing of the libel, but had been forced into signing it by the menaces of the Carmelites. As for the other calumnies, they were found, on being examined into by the Royal Council, equally unworthy of credence. So that, as Teresa writes to Maria de San José, "all recoils on their own backs, and turns to our good." And so old Fray Baltasar disappears into the night of his obliquity (and I for one feel a pang of regret that yonder bright June day in Pastrana should end thus) to bemoan his sin, and die an exemplary death at Lisbon.

In Avila the Encarnacion becomes the scene of an indescribable and unseemly scuffle between the nuns and the Calced Provincial—Fray Madalena, Teresa calls him—sent thither by Tostado's orders to prevent them by main force from carrying out their intention of electing Teresa a second time their prioress. And the nuns, who, to do them justice, in spite of San Juan de la Cruz and his five years' leading of them in the way of spiritual perfection, do not forget that they are sprung of the Avilas, the Muñoz, the Blasquez, the Tapias, the Aguilas,—the old conquistadores of their native town,—are not only ready to defy fifty provincials, but Tostado into the bargain, rather than abate a tittle of their rights and privileges.

I assure your reverence [writes Teresa to Maria de San José in Seville] that I believe nothing has ever been seen before like what is now happening in the Encarnacion. About a fortnight ago to-day the Provincial of the Calzados came here by Tostado's orders to preside at the election, bringing with him severe censures and sentences of excommunication against those who should vote for me, and withal they cared no more for them than if they had not existed, and fifty-five nuns voted for me ; and at every vote they gave the Provincial, he excommunicated and cursed them, and pounded [machucaba] the votes with his fist and burnt them : and for a fortnight from to-day they have been under sentence of excommunication, without hearing mass or entering the choir, even when there is no divine service, and no one, neither confessors nor their friars, are allowed to speak with them, and the most amusing part of it is that, next day after this "machucada" election, the Provincial summoned them afresh to make election, and they replied that there was no object in their making a fresh election, that they had already done so ; whereupon he again excommunicated them, called the remaining forty and four, elected another prioress, sent to Tostado to confirm it. It is already confirmed, but the rest are resolute, and declare they will not obey her [the new prioress] except as a substitute. Men of letters say they are not excommunicated ; and that the friars have gone against the Council [of Trent] in electing as prioress her who had the least number of votes. The nuns have sent to Tostado to tell him how their desire is to have me for prioress. He answers no, that if I like I can retire there, but as for prioress, they cannot hear of it with patience.

What manner of woman is this, who has so wound herself into the hearts of these turbulent and defiant nuns—the same nuns who had awarded herself some such reception five years ago—as to make them suffer imprisonment and contumely for her dear sake?

Whilst anarchy runs riot in the peaceful cloisters of the Encarnacion, Teresa, deeply distressed, writes to Alonso de Aranda, a priest of Madrid, "to find out for charity, if it is possible for Tostado or the Provincial to absolve them, and to write to Master Julian de Avila, to see if he cannot get them to obey Doña Ana." . . .

But this was not all. Against all right and reason, as Tostado's powers were still under discussion in the Royal Council Chamber, and it had not yet given its decision, on a cold winter's night (it was the 4th of December) an armed rabble of friars burst open the frail door of the little hut, which stood in a retired corner of the convent garden, where for the past five years Fray Juan de la Cruz and Fray Germán de Santo Matia had lived their simple and humble lives. For days before, in prevision of some such attack, the most distinguished gentlemen of Avila (probably Lorenzo amongst them) had kept watch and ward over the dwelling of the two friars. But the Carmelites were too wily to provoke a popular tumult, and the rumour had died a natural death. The two friars were handcuffed and marched off to the Carmelite Convent of Avila, where, after receiving a sound scourging, they were locked up in separate cells until morning. Fray Juan, however, gave his jailors the slip, sped swiftly to his hut, locked the door, tore up his papers, swallowed others; after which he calmly surrendered himself up to his pursuers, who were threatening every minute to break it open. Once more constrained to wear the Carmelite habit he had renounced seven years ago in Duruelo, he was conveyed, with the utmost secrecy, to Toledo, and Fray Germán to Moraleja.

An aggression so flagrant as to outrage every instinct of justice stung Teresa to the quick. That same night she penned an indignant appeal to the King:

> I believe it has come to your Majesty's ears how these nuns of the Encarnacion have endeavoured to procure my return there, thinking I might help them to free themselves from these friars. . . . I placed a Discalced friar, with another companion, in a house there, so great a servant of our Lord, that they are greatly edified, and the city amazed at the enormous improvement he has effected, on which account they consider him a saint, which in my opinion he is and has been all his life. . . . And now a friar, who came to absolve the nuns, has so tormented them, contrary to all reason and justice, that they are in great distress, and are still subject to the same censures as before. And

above all, he has deprived them of their confessors, for they say they have made him Vicar Provincial,—it must be because he has more capacity than others for making martyrs.

The whole town is scandalised, that, without being a prelate, nor showing any authority for acting thus (for these friars are subject to the Apostolic Commissary), they dare so much, in the case of a place so near to where your Majesty is, as if there was no such thing as justice or God. . . . I would rather [she goes on] see them amongst Moors, for even they, perchance, would have more mercy. And this friar, and such a servant of God as he is, is so thin with the suffering he has gone through, that I fear for his life. . . . If your Majesty does not order some remedy, I know not how it will end, for we have no other on earth!

And in this instance likewise Philip showed her favour. The nuns laid their plea before the Royal Council. How it was eventually decided we do not know: but certain it is that Teresa had no mind to accept the post thrust upon her by her former subjects, although they stubbornly insisted in considering the prioress elected by the minority as a mere temporary makeshift.

They have sent to Tostado [she writes], to say how that it is me they wish for prioress. He says no, that I can go there if I like, but as for my being prioress, they cannot away with it. . . . I would willingly excuse them (the nuns) if they would only leave me in peace, for I have no wish to see myself in that Babylon.

Never to my mind has Teresa presented a nobler, more pathetic figure than when, her strong and valiant spirit —great to dare and to do—chafing against the limitations of sex, "which permit her to do nothing but eat and sleep," she defends her friars and nuns with powerful and heartfelt words from persecution and calumny. It is left to her, the old worn-out nun of Avila, this poor old woman on whom for more than half a year has rained every species of persecution and calumny, to hold up the banner aloft from the midst of her seclusion—like the brave and valiant captain she was—which was to lead the struggling band of friars and nuns behind her to sure and certain victory. It was not herself she defended, Teresa de Jesus the instrument, nor yet the Reform that Teresa de Jesus had achieved. Behind her stood—unseen to all eyes but hers—a woman's figure, but a woman crowned with the halo of Divinity— Maria Sacratissima. Hers the Reform, Teresa de Jesus the humble follower, who for a moment had endeavoured to breathe a purer spirit into the Virgin's Order.

Christmas Eve approaches once more, and a frail old woman sits always in her cell at Avila. Laying down her pen, she seems at moments to be caught up into the cloud, so does her rapt face glow with a shining and radiant glory, not surely of this earth; at moments, crying aloud with tears and prayers, as she thinks of her banished and imprisoned sons. Amidst the raging of the storm, and the beating of all the tempests of heaven let loose upon that patient writer's head, on the eve of St. Andrew's Day she brings to a close and lays down the pen of the *Moradas*. In her own conception, it was far above anything she had ever written, for she says in words strangely pathetic: "It treats of nothing but him, and with more delicate ornaments and enamels, for the silversmith who made it knew not so much then. The gold is of greater purity, although the gems are not so easily to be discovered as in that other one" (her *Life*).

On Christmas Eve she fell down on the stairs and broke her arm. As she rose, she was heard to say, "Valgame Dios, he wished to kill me"; to which she heard an inner voice reply, "He did, but I was with thee." This made no break, however, in her voluminous correspondence (even in Toledo she had been forced to trust much of it to a secretary, who wrote from her dictation), embracing as it did the intricate affairs of the Order, and the private difficulties and affairs of eight convents, every one of which was more deeply in debt than the other, and all of them depending on her for advice and guidance.

CHAPTER XXI

FROM JANUARY 1578 TO CHRISTMAS DAY

THIS year of 1578, a strangely stirring one for the Reform, opens sadly for it in Avila as elsewhere. Teresa with a broken arm; the Convent of the Encarnacion—looking so peaceful in the keen light of the winter's day down in the hollow below the town—full of perturbation and distress; Fray Antonio de Jesus hidden in the cellars of Archbishop Tavera's hospital in Toledo; Gracian playing hide-and-seek, wielding an intermittent authority as the wind blew fair or foul; Mariano watching the progress of the storm from the safe shelter of the house of powerful friends in Madrid; Fray Juan de la Cruz a prisoner,—no one knows where (Teresa thinks in Rome, but is not certain). The Carmelites, all-powerful, breathing dire threats of vengeance. In the background the King and the Nuncio loom forth dimly,—the two *Dei ex machinâ* of the dark drama of intrigue and oppression, which every day becomes darker and more intricate. Events follow each other in quick succession, rousing alternate hopes and fears, chiefly the latter: for beyond the walls of Avila, in the Court of Spain itself, the struggle has commenced which will only be ended by the total extinction of the Reform, or its creation into a separate province.

In Avila, too, Teresa has much to trouble her: those poor nuns of the Encarnacion, exposed to the malicious persecutions of the Carmelites; she herself in bad odour with the Jesuits, and threatened with the vengeance of that powerful Order, who ascribe to her counsels and influence the resolution formed by Fray Gaspar Salazar (to whom years ago she had owed so much during the troublous period preceding the foundation of San José) of leaving the Society of Jesus to enrol himself amongst her friars. Such are the immediate difficulties. Her letters tell us how she solved them. As for the Encarnacion, the nuns, intimidated by the Provincial "Fray Madalena" and Valdemoro, the "terrible" friar of the Carmelites of Avila, have been terrified into signing the exact opposite of the plea they had already signed and laid before the Royal Council Chamber of Madrid; Teresa herself counselling them to obey; "for I do not think they would have done so if I had not sent to them to say that they were prejudicing their case." But she is a dangerous adversary, that little old nun of Avila, and by no means to be played with. Well may the Carmelites wish her at the bottom of the deep sea.

The Provincial, with those signatures in his wallet, already tasting the delights of an anticipatory triumph, may spur on his mule as fast as he likes over the snowy plateaux, in his haste to brandish them in the faces of the nuns' advocates at Madrid; but she is beforehand with him, and ere the friar alights at his monastery gates, I doubt not that her letter, in which she parries the stroke as best she can by making it clearly understood to Roque de Huerta, Mayordomo of his Majesty's woods and forests, and Secretary of the Royal Council, that they have been obtained by force, "so that the Council may not be misled by the representations of those fathers, since it has been a tyranny throughout," is already in that gentleman's possession.

In spite of which, however, having no mind to find herself again in "that Babylon of the Encarnacion," she is equally clear that the nuns' suit to make her prioress should not be pressed forward in the Council, and so she tells him. A warning which was quite unnecessary. Their cause dragged on its weary course amidst the usual impediments of official delays, and perhaps, for all we know, lingered on for years more.

The last we hear of the nuns of the Encarnacion is that it has reverted to its usual state — that is, laxity and disorder.

As for the Jesuits—there was no Jesuit of them all that could outwit her—to the angry remonstrances of the

Provincial Juarez and the Rector of Avila, Gonzalo de Avila, who desired her to write a peremptory refusal to Salazar, and send a mandate to the heads of her Order not to receive him, she returned a reply so *aigre douce*, and withal so powerful and convincing, that it would seem to have deprived them of any further wish to return to the subject.

> I have [she writes] read the father Provincial's letter twice over, and still find in it such a want of consideration for me, and himself so convinced of what has not even entered my thoughts, that his paternity need not be astonished that it gave me pain. This of itself is of little consequence, since if it were not for my imperfections, I ought rather to be gratified that his paternity should mortify me, as it is in his power to do with one who is his subject. And as the father Salazar is his subject also, it seems to me that it would be more efficacious for you to stop him than for me to write what your Grace desires to those who are not under my control; since it is the duty of his superior to do so, and they [her friars] on their side would be perfectly justified in paying scant attention to what I said to them. . . . Judging by what he says, I know he will not take such a step without the Provincial's knowledge, and if he does not speak or write to his paternity, it means that he will not. And if by refusing him his permission his paternity can prevent him taking it, I should injure so grave a person, and so great a servant of God, in defaming him throughout the Order (even supposing they paid attention to me); it being a grave libel to say that he wishes to do what he cannot do without offending God. I have spoken to your Grace with all truth, and in my opinion I have done what I was obliged to do in honour and in Christianity [we may be certain she did]. The Lord knows I speak truth in this; and to do more than I have done, would be to act contrary to both. . . . I am almost sure that if the business does not turn out according to your Grace's wish, I shall be blamed as much as if I had done nothing; and to have spoken with him [Salazar] is enough to cause the fulfilment of the prophecies.
>
> The Provincial's letter [she writes to Gracian, to whom she forwards it in Alcalá] displeased me greatly, so much so that I would fain have answered him more sharply than I have; for I know he [Salazar] had told him that I had nothing to do with this change, as is true, for when I knew it, I was greatly distressed, and exceeding desirous it should go no farther. I wrote him as strong a letter as I could, using the same words, I swear to you, as in my answer to the Provincial; for they have got to such a pass, that I thought that, unless I insisted on it as strongly as I did, they would not believe me, and it is important for them to do so, on account of the revelations he [Salazar] speaks of, so that they do not think that by that way I have persuaded him, since it is so great a lie.
>
> But I tell your paternity that I fear their threats so little that I am amazed at the freedom God gives me; and so I told the father rector

that neither the Company nor the whole world would make me abandon anything I knew was to his service, and that I had had nothing whatever to do with this matter, nor would I take any part in persuading him to abandon it. He besought me, that although I refused to do this, to write him [Salazar] a letter, telling him what I tell him in this, that he cannot do it without being excommunicated. I asked, if he [Salazar] was aware of these briefs.

He replied, better than I am myself.

I then said, in that case I am certain that he will do nothing that he knows is an offence to God.

He answered, that still his eagerness might be great enough to make him deceive himself and drive him into it; and so I wrote to him a letter by the same means whereby he wrote me this.

Behold, your paternity, what simplicity; for I know clearly by certain indications that they had seen the letter; although I did not tell him so. And I told him therein not to trust his brethren, for they [who betrayed] Joseph, were his brothers also; because I knew they would see it, since his very friends must have disclosed it; and I am not surprised, for they take it overmuch to heart. Their dread must be of ever allowing even the beginning of such a thing.

I asked him if some amongst them had not been Discalced friars.

He said, yes, Franciscans; but that they had been cast out of their own order first, which had afterwards granted them licenses.

I answered; that they could do the same now: but this they by no means agree to, nor do I agree to tell him not to take the step, only to warn him, as I do in that letter, and leave it to God, for if it is his doing they will give way, for (as I tell him therein) I have informed myself, and certainly it can be done in no other sort, because they will appeal to common law as at the time of the foundation of Pastrana, when another lawyer persuaded me to take the Augustinian, and he was in the wrong. That the Pope will give him license I do not believe, for there they will be beforehand with him. Let your paternity also inform yourself and warn him, for it would distress me greatly if he were to commit any offence against God. I certainly believe that as soon as he knows it is one, he will desist. It gives me great anxiety; because if he remains amongst them after they know the desire he has of joining us, they will no longer hold him in the same reputation as formerly; and I ever bear in view what we owe to the Company; for I do not believe that God will let them do us harm. If, being able to do so, we do not receive him, solely through fear of them, this is to treat him badly, and to requite him but ill for his affection. God direct it, for he will guide him, although I fear lest he may have been moved by these revelations [literally "things of prayer"], for they say he believes them too readily. I have often told him so, and to no avail. It also distresses me to think that the nuns of Veas must have had something to do with it, so eager about it was Catalina de Jesus. He is certainly a servant of God, and if he deceives himself, it is because he thinks that he wishes it, and his Majesty will look after him. But he has put us in a hurly burly: and, as I wrote to your paternity, if I had not heard what I did from Josef (Christ), believe me I would have left no stone unturned to prevent it. But although I do not believe these things [revelations] so much as he does, I am loath to put impediments in the way. How do I know if by doing so I am not standing in the way of his soul receiving some great good?

Salazar did not, so far as we can learn, carry out his intention; for we find Teresa regretting afterwards that an undue regard for the friendship of "those of Jesus" may have led her to stand in the way of a veritable vocation.

It is in the letters, unceasingly flowing, spite of broken arm and all, from the active pen of this old woman sitting in her quiet cell at Avila, that we must follow the strange history of the Carmelite Reform. Misty and uncertain as it is; such a faint ghost of the emotions which filled her heart and so many other hearts of friars and nuns, still it is less misty and uncertain than the confused account of the chronicler. We feel that we here grasp the truth, or the reflex of what was once the truth—that is, until some diligent inquirer, losing his time in investigating the obscure growth of an old-world Order in the archives of Simancas and the National Library of Madrid, shall give the result of his researches to a commercial world which will not care for them.

Here, though, we have the visible events as they touched on, and were reflected from, one Teresa de Jesus, the author of them; and can watch her (all other action being denied to this strong and capable spirit by the accident of sex) as she guides that Reform which it has been her Life's labour to achieve through the shoals and pitfalls which at every moment threaten to engulf and bring it to nought. The marvellous clairvoyance, the swift and unerring instinct with which she strips this troublous affair of all its mazes and complications—from the most contradictory reports smelling out the truth, in her grasp of the whole, losing sight of no detail, however insignificant (as no detail if properly considered ever is)—is akin to genius—rather is it the practical essence of genius. A profound psychologist, knowing how the greatest shocks and most violent tempests may be traced to some trifling weakness, some almost imperceptible flaw, she alone can manage the various characters of her headstrong friars, and weld them into harmonious action;

putting at their service her own consummate tact and knowledge of things and people; knowing at once when to conciliate and when to stand firm. They were all good men, might perhaps have been remarkable men—had not their individuality been shadowed by her own—these friars who propped up the Reform, and all as equally convinced that their own methods were the best. All except Gracian, whose fatal ductility made him the easy prey of a stronger will. Differing exceedingly in character, Mariano, impetuous and fiery, with a biting tongue which cut like acid, and made the Nuncio writhe; a *persona grata* with the King; shifting, intriguing, consumed with activity, ever full of new schemes for extending the Reform, and neglecting the most rudimentary precautions to protect its very existence, losing by some headstrong sally the ground gained by painful effort. Fray Antonio de Jesus, full of the peculiar susceptibilities and narrownesses which so often belong to the consciousness of rigid virtue; inclined to small jealousies, itching to take a prominent part in the affairs of the Order; for the most part a shadowy figure in the background. Gracian, the King's secretary's son, sweet-tempered, lovable, fascinating, "who wrote like an angel and feared like a man," of tender and scrupulous conscience, "not fit," says Teresa, "to struggle between the contending forces of contrary opinions," mild as milk, unsuspicious, gentle. If left alone Teresa could have moulded him to her will. As she watches the faltering action of her friars in Madrid, her great spirit chafing often at their blunders, want of tact, adroitness, initiative, and energy, when all depended on it; at opportunities neglected, and made little of, and points by the score given away to the enemy, she feels what she cannot help but feel, that never were the qualities that shone in her so conspicuous amidst all her sanctity so urgently needed by the Reform as now. From the first, when two years ago she had written to the King from Seville, she had foreseen that the only possible solution to end the discords between the two branches of the Order, perhaps the only condition of the Descalzos remaining in existence at all, was to sever the latter from the Observants and erect them into a separate province. A bold and energetic step, which she had proposed in bold and energetic words. "For forty years," she wrote to Philip, "have I lived in this Order, and, all things considered, I clearly know that if the Discalced friars are not formed into a separate province, and that, shortly, much harm will be done, and I hold it impossible that they can go on." But he to whom she wrote was neither bold nor energetic. The letter was read — yes, carefully docketed, we may be sure, probably some foolish remark (for Philip's extreme prudence was of the kind most akin to folly) scrawled on the margin in his untidy handwriting—but that was all; and now the troubles, then scarcely larger than a man's hand, have become so fierce and burning as to arouse the attention of all Spain.

Long before Ormaneto's death we have seen how earnestly she advised—and how her advice was as persistently disregarded—that the Descalzos should strain every nerve to send emissaries to Rome, to countermine the manœuvres of the Observants, already busy poisoning the minds of the Roman Court against them. In her plaintive letter to Roca she mourns that she is not able to get them to write even a conciliatory letter to the General, much less to send advocates to Rome; for to the last the loyal woman clung to the hope that as he had laid the foundation, so he (Rubeo) might conclude this edifice of the Reform. "I tell you," are her heartfelt words to Gracian, the most facile of them all, "I am in despair that I have not the freedom to be able to do what I tell you to do."

Of the expediency of the latter step of sending representatives to Rome, she would seem at last to have convinced them, since at the close of 1577 she mentions Gracian as being in Alcalá, to hurry forward their departure; but the matter languished during the brunt of persecution subsequent to the arrival in Madrid of the Bird of Evil Omen, El Tostado, who had returned determined to crush out the Discalced Carmelites, root and branch. *Re non integra*, the theologians of Alcalá and Madrid, having decided that Gracian's commission was in no way invalidated by the Nuncio's death, Covarrubias, President of the Council, ordered him to continue his visit, when the arrival of Sega, the Papal legate, presents a new and terrible factor in the difficulties which every moment seem to be crowding thicker and faster round the devoted friar's head.

Already violently predisposed against the Descalzos, the Nuncio had barely landed in Barcelona when he was deafened with the loud and bitter complaints of the Carmelites, who had sped thither to meet him and conduct him to Madrid, and all he now heard served to make that prepossession stronger, and to breed a rankling irritation in his mind against the Descalzos that was not slow of manifesting itself. The Nuncio's first act sufficiently showed his intentions as regarded the Reform. The orders of Tostado—his bold assertion of supreme authority—had left the five friars, Gracian and his companions, irresolute as to what steps to take, when the King, who feared neither Pope nor censure where the religious affairs of Spain were concerned, interposed the Supreme Council, and Tostado found himself again baffled in his attempts to stifle the Reform by a royal mandate ordering him to deliver up his commission and the secret orders by which he acted, and he had nothing for it but to obey.

Such was the state of things when Sega arrived in Madrid; Tostado, actively engaged in persecuting and extirpating the Reform, on the one hand stubbornly maintaining the powers given him by the Chapter of Plasencia; on the other, dragging on a slow and lingering suit with the fiscal of the Council. Whilst it was still dragging itself along, the Nuncio landed.

With the train so well prepared for him, the Nuncio had only to light the match,—so he may have thought,—to end the Descalzos for ever. He was destined, however, to find it a tougher business than he had bargained for, and to leave Spain a sadder and a wiser man. From the first Philip's attitude had been anomalous and undecided. Was it that he took a strange delight in watching the bitter struggles going on around him of two branches of the same Order; or that, still desirous of maintaining friendly relations with Rome, he would do nothing to imperil them; or that, engaged in other matters, his interest in this was merely intermittent? Or was it merely another instance of the inherent indecision and irresolution of his character?

None shall ever know. Yet he held the balance, and at the precise moment when the Calzados were surest of their victory, and had their enemies in their clutch, without finally ending the struggle, he gives the Descalzos a breathing space, and gives them just enough strength, and no more, to renew the contest.

The Nuncio's first act was to renew Tostado's edicts against the Discalced friars, forbidding them to make any further foundations without his permission. His next, to summon Gracian before him to deliver up his powers and the papers relating to his visit, especially those relating to his proceedings against delinquents.

And this the friar would gladly have done, if besides the Nuncio he had not had to reckon with the King. As it was, prudently refusing to comply with a mandate which would have left both himself and the Order at the Nuncio's mercy, he shelters himself behind the King, alleging that, since it was by Philip's orders that he had undertaken the office, he could not deliver up his papers without his permission. The Nuncio, not daring so early in the day to provoke an open rupture with Philip, dissembles his anger as best he may, although it is only too distinctly visible to the trembling friar. Retiring in some confusion from the presence of the irritated legate, he takes counsel with Archbishop Quiroga, who, after telling him contemptuously that he has no more spirit than a fly, bids him go to the King, and when the wretched man fears that by so doing he may make the Nuncio more angry still, meets him with the cold response "that to the Superior all may go!" Excellent advice, no doubt, for the High Inquisitor and Archbishop of Toledo; perhaps not so good for the Discalced friar, who finds himself placed between two opposing forces, who would most probably, nay, most certainly, agree in one thing only, in laying the blame and odium of whatever happened on the weakest of the trio. So to the King he went—a brown, white-caped figure, with sandalled feet, brushing for a moment through royal corridors; yet bearing on his shoulders the present fortunes and future fate of a powerful Order; and was bidden by his Majesty (one would have given much to be present at that interview) to retire to his monastery until the matter could be looked into. And during an interval of nine months, whilst the King's secretaries write to Rome, and the Royal Council, bent on foiling the Nuncio, insists on seeing his authorities for interfering with the religious orders of Spain, Gracian remains inactive at Alcalá, or concealed in one of the caves on the hillside of Pastrana.

As for Tostado, the Royal Council makes short work with his Vicar-Generalship, the Fiscal Chumacero opposing him at every turn, until, baffled and worsted, he once more disappears as he had come, some said to Portugal, others to Rome; his destination a matter of indifference to the Descalzos, so long as they are rid of the shadow of his presence.

In February Gracian emerges from his cave to preach his Lenten sermons. "For God's sake, take care that you do not fall on those roads," warns Teresa, thinking ruefully of her own broken arm, "still swollen, and the hand too, and with a bandage on like a coat of mail," besides the danger of travelling in such troublous times, except in a case of the greatest necessity (for the Carmelites are now so blinded with rage as to dare anything). "I know not what tempts you to go from place to place, since there are souls [to look after] everywhere."

At last, driven to extremities and wellnigh desperate, the Descalzos resolve to convoke a Chapter and elect a Provincial of their own. It was a step fraught with the most important consequences. To elect a Provincial meant the erection of the Reform into a self-governing province, and its complete severance once and for ever from the main body of the Carmelites. Such is the scheme that the prior of Mancera, Fray Juan Roca, as he passes through Avila, breathes into Teresa's ear. Anxious is the consultation that takes place, when he is gone, in that little dark locutory of San José. From the great leathern chairs, polished by age, which still stand before the grating, the Doctor Rueda, "a great man of letters," and good Master Daza, gravely proffer their advice—advice which she embodies in that memorable letter she sends to Gracian early in April, in which she does her best to dissuade him from an ill-considered and illegal action, whose consequences must recoil upon himself and lend colour to the calumnies of their enemies. Both, she writes (for she characteristically suppresses herself), unite in saying that it is an arduous thing to attempt, unless Gracian's commission contains special powers to that effect ; the more difficult, inasmuch as it involves a question of jurisdiction,—the power to elect a Provincial being exclusively confined to the Pope or General. Thus not only will their votes be worthless, and the whole proceedings null and void, but the Observants will need nothing more in order to appeal to the Pope, and cry out loudly that the Descalzos are openly rebellious, and arrogate to themselves an authority they have no right to,—" which would have an ugly sound." Moreover, any election they may make will have to be confirmed by Rome, and it will be far more difficult to get the Pope to sanction it after it is made than to get his license in the first place to make it ; for he has only to see one word written by the King to his ambassador to give it willingly, especially if he is told how the Descalzos are faring at the hands of the Observants. " It might be," she adds, " that if the matter was brought before the King he would gladly do it, since, even as regards the Reform, his favour would be of great assistance ; as it would make the Observants hold us in more esteem, and think twice about undoing us."

From a few passages in this letter we can see how she laid her delicate intuition and woman's wit at the service of her rougher-handed friars ; indirectly bringing before us that strange world of superstition and conviction,—we of a modern age have kept the superstition, but lost the conviction,—in which Teresa de Jesus the Carmelite was such a prominent figure.

If the King is to speak that saving word to his ambassador in Rome, he must be got at through his confessor, the wills of the great Roman princes and ambassadors of the Church conciliated by a judicious tickling of their palms.

I know not whether it were well that your paternity should treat of it with father Master Chaves [Philip's confessor aforesaid], who is very judicious, and would perhaps, if we get him to use his influence on our behalf, get the King to do it ; and if so, the same friars [the ones already fixed upon] must at once set forth with his letters to Rome . . . for, as Dr. Rueda says, the direct road and way is through the Pope or

General. I assure you that, if father Padilla and all of us had joined in effecting this matter through the King, it would have been accomplished now; and moreover, your paternity yourself might bring it before him and the Archbishop (Quiroga); for if, after the Provincial's election is made, it has still to be confirmed, and you need the King's favour for that purpose, it is better to secure his protection now; and even if you effect nothing, you will not incur the stigma and disgrace that you will if, after making the election, you cannot get it confirmed, and it remains a lasting blemish; and your paternity is discredited for having done that which you had no power to do, and for not having known it.

The mere thought that they will lay all the blame on you, and with some show of reason, makes me become a very coward, which I am not wont to do, rather does my boldness wax greater when they act thus without any; and so I have lost no time in writing this, so that you may look well to it. Do you know what I have thought? That perchance some of the things I have sent our father General are being made use of against us (for they were of great esteem) and have been given to cardinals, and it has occurred to me to send him nothing until these matters are settled; and so it might be well, if occasion offered, to give something to the Nuncio. I see, my father, that when your paternity is in Madrid you do much in a day, and that, what with speaking with one and another, and the efforts of your friends in the palace, and father Antonio with the Duchess [of Alba or Pastrana?], much might be done to induce the King to grant this, since his desire is to preserve the Descalzos; and as father Mariano speaks with the King, he might bring it before his notice and beseech him to do it; and remind him how long that "Santico" of fray Juan has been a prisoner. In short, the King gives ear to all; I know not why he should not be spoken to about it, nor why father Mariano especially should not urge it.

But alas! alas! what can a woman do, tied to a quiet cell in Avila, except pray and mourn, whilst her friars blunder for want of capable personal direction. In spite of all Teresa's remonstrances and cogent reasoning, the Chapter was held a few months after. Its immediate results were disastrous, but indirectly the Descalzos owed their deliverance to this bold act of rebellion.

That word from the King to his ambassador, which would not only make them rise in the esteem of their enemies, who in the face of it would no longer dare to urge their extermination with such animosity, but would give them a fresh lease of existence, was never sent; and two days afterwards she again implores Gracian not to risk the danger of being taken prisoner by the Carmelites, "since now they are all on the look-out for your paternity," by accompanying his mother and sister to Avila on their way to Valladolid, where the latter is about to enter Teresa's convent. The visit, which she had not expected so soon, fills her hospitable mind, anxious that her visitors should see her convent at its best, with distress; for the choir is unroofed and full of workmen, and it is impossible for her to salute Da. Juana through the grating as she had hoped. The travellers arrived in Avila at nightfall on the 25th of April. A strange little company, if you could have seen it —but not at all strange then—clattering through those old gray twilight streets on donkeys and mules to Lorenzo's house—Lorenzo himself having gone to Madrid and Seville. They too listen, from some stately old bedchamber hung with arras—we can fancy it,—to the clang of the great cathedral bells tolling out on the midnight air, until falling asleep, the brain still repeating by some reflex action the rhythmical cadence of hoofs sinking in the sand, amidst distorted dreams of mountain passes hemmed in by mountain fastness and boiling river, and parameras green and flowery with the promise of spring, the little world of Avila, and every other world, are blotted out as completely from experience and sensation—as if they had never been. On the morrow Teresa embraces her friend at the convent door, and the day after they set out for Valladolid. "I should have much desired that the Señora Da. Juana had not gone on, but your paternity has made this angel so in love with Valladolid that our prayers were unavailing to induce her to remain here. Oh, how I long for her sister, her of the Doncellas" (the school for noble maidens founded by Archbishop Silicco), "who from ignorance will not let herself be remedied, although she would have a much easier life than where she is." But she at least will have none of Teresa's convents, and eventually marries an honest oidor of Segovia.

On the 7th of May the news that Tostado has left Spain is confirmed—" there is nothing to fear. . . . But oh! my father, I forgot, the woman sent by the prioress of Medina at no small cost to her, as the cure was no less to mine, came to set my arm. The wrist was useless, so the pain and agony was terrible, it being so long since my fall; withal I rejoiced in being able to taste, however little, somewhat of the sufferings endured by our Lord." The nuns remembered other details of this cure, which are diligently set down by Yepes. After sending them all away to the choir to pray for her whilst it was going on, she was left alone with the "curandera" and her companion, a stout peasant woman. The two pulled at her arm by sheer force until the shoulder-bone cracked in the socket, leaving her arm little better than it was, and the sufferer in intense pain. Neither cry nor murmur escaped her lips during the cruel process, and when the nuns returned they found her as tranquil and composed as they had left her. The famous "curandera"—again a picture of manners—lodges in Lorenzo's house, and is sorely put to it by the crowds of people who flock to her to be "cured."

On the 4th of June, a letter—one of those sheets of paper so familiar to us, the large irregular writing become by this time a little tremulous (it may still be seen by those curious in such things in the convent of Valladolid)—starts with the mule train for Seville. In it she thanks Maria de San José for her jars of orange-flower water and conserves: "Do not think, however, I eat such a quantity as you send; but I shall never in my life lose this habit I have of giving." Her arm is better, but she cannot dress herself,—nor will she ever again,—although they assure her that the warm weather will make it well. Maria de San José, too, is in distress—pains in her side, fever, and a mad nun, for whose ravings Teresa recommends a cudgel, "people out of their minds being less sensitive to pain than others." We also learn an important bit of news—a bit of news which shines like a ray of light amidst the chronological confusion worse confounded of the chronicler: "Our father, with the Lord's favour, will go thither (to Seville) in September, and perhaps before, for he has now had orders to continue his visit, as you there will know."

For Gracian has now had that famous interview with Pazos, the successor of the dead Covarrubias as President of the Royal Council. Once more has he pleaded to be released from his commission, which Pazos, phlegmatic, slow-brained, inspired himself by a certain dogged sense of Duty, tells him is impossible, it being God's will and the King's (chiefly, indeed, I think the latter's); that he, Pazos, would also be fain to be rid of the office he holds, if it were not for this same dogged sense of Duty. Gracian despairingly says he will go to the Nuncio; to which Pazos, determined as only phlegmatic people can be, answers "No!" And so, with good store of edicts in his wallet, with which to enlist the aid of secular force if needful, he starts off to commence his visit in Valladolid.

The position of the Carmelite Reformers becomes every moment more precarious. Tostado, indeed, has flitted away; and the shadow of his presence no longer hangs threateningly over them: but Sega, the Papal Nuncio, has himself resolved to take the reins of government into his own hands. Stung to fury by what he chose to regard as his subjects' insubordination, losing sight of all the restraints which prudence and the anomalous attitude of Philip himself imposed, he rushed into a precipitate and ill-considered action—an action which seemed immediately to portend the ruin of the Reform, and eventually proved its salvation.

Heedless that his powers rested on a most tremulous foundation, for he had not yet displayed his warrants to the Royal Council, on the 22nd of July he issued a brief annulling Gracian's visit, and ordering him to deliver up his papers under pain of excommunication *latæ sententiæ*.

On the 9th of August the Royal Council parried the Nuncio's brief by a warrant to the governors of all cities and towns throughout the kingdom to intercept the circulation of the Nuncio's briefs and mandates. And in the meantime, although in March the Count of Tendilla's journey to Rome seemed to afford a favourable opportunity for the friars to travel in his train, March has come and gone, and with it June, July, and August, and nothing has been done to lay the true state of the case before the aged General, or to circumvent the machination of their enemies.

In May, Teresa had written to the procrastinators that the "time is going by without our sending to Rome, and we are all ruined with hoping, and may hope on for a thousand years more. I do not understand it, nor why Nicolas does not go." . . .

Thus with no hope of redress from Rome, the Descalzos had nothing for it but to humbly obey the Nuncio; Mariano even, curbing his hot temper, briefly signified his obedience. The prioress of Valladolid followed his example: Teresa's active advice to all her convents is to obey.

Gracian alone, writing to Teresa from Valladolid, so often changing his cyphers without warning that she can no longer read them, manages to evade the Nuncio's Brief.

For on one of those August nights a strange scene took place in Valladolid. The moonbeams fall full on a band of stalwart monks (headed by Fray Hernandez de Medina, a former Descalzo, "for the worst thief, etc.") battering at the gates of San Alejo, in pursuit of Gracian. As this was going on, Don Geronimo de Tobar (who he may be we know not, nor why he so quixotically espouses a quarrel not his own, although we can see him,—rapier, cape, plumed cap, and all) sets on the friars' following. The street rings for a moment with the clash of swords, and blades flash bright in the moon-rays; whilst the two friars, Gracian's companions, scale the walls unnoticed, and slip away into the neighbouring fields. All Valladolid wakes up. Bishop Mendoza (Teresa's Don Alvaro) sends out his servants with torches to look for the fugitives, and shelters them in his palace—one of the great grim old palaces which have witnessed in those dim days so many strange scenes and notable events. Here from the street before it, through the open door, the notary intones the Brief, presently assuring the Nuncio that he had served it on Gracian himself. Which was false (like most other things done in the name of the law), for, warned beforehand, he had remained that night in the house of a certain "relator," his relative. On the 10th of August the Brief was served on the nuns of San José of Avila. All the Discalced convents are tremulous with excitement and anxiety. Teresa, always self-possessed and tranquil, calmly weighing every issue in that shrewd old head of hers— "To-morrow we will arrange for Julian de Avila to go to Madrid for the purpose of recognising the Nuncio as our head, and pleading with him warmly on our behalf not to deliver us over to the Calzados; and I will likewise write to several people to soften him with regard to your paternity." For Gracian was now a fugitive, giving the slip to his enemies, already on the alert to arrest him. Between the 10th and 11th of August he stole through Avila on his way to the Escorial and Madrid. The sight of the son she loved more deeply than any of her friars, fleeing like a malefactor, afraid to show his face in the light of day, affected the brave old woman deeply. Better could she have borne that the blows should have fallen on herself than on her Paul; but her steadfast confidence in the final issue of the struggle not a whit abated,—Teresa only saw the extreme danger of his position, placed prominently in the breach, ready to fall a victim at any moment to the King's diplomacy or the Nuncio's vengeance. "As far as you can without angering the King, keep aloof from this fire, whatever Father Mariano may say,"—Mariano, the hot-tempered and choleric, whom she still blames for those first disasters at Seville,— "for your paternity's conscience is not for these affairs of contrary opinions, since you are distressed even by that which there is no cause to fear, as has happened lately, and all the world will look upon it as wise: let them settle their disputes themselves. In order, as I have said, to keep aloof, your paternity needs all your wisdom to prevent it looking like fear, except that of offending God." . . . The only remedy left to them is the erection of a separate province. "Treat of the province in every way you can, no matter on what conditions; for all lies in this,—and even the Reform itself. And this ought to be negotiated with the King and President, Archbishop, and all of them, who must be told of the scandals and warfare that have arisen from its not having been done. . . . Your paternity will know how to say it better than I," adds this most consummate of diplomatists and humblest of saints, "and it is very foolish of me to mention it here, except that, amongst your other anxieties, it may escape your memory. I know not whether it will be Pedro who will bear this to you, for he cannot find a mule,"—Pedro being that muleteer whose unseemly jest she had once reproved on one of her journeys by telling him he would yet be a friar, and now her faithful servant. Just now Pedro and his mule (a borrowed one it would seem) are kept hard at it, riding between Madrid and Avila,—and farther afield yet,—for these are stirring times, and Teresa is as busy warning her nuns how they are to receive the Nuncio's Brief as the Carmelites are in serving it.

So daily from her cell in Avila, does her firm and skilful hand navigate this frail bark of the Reform through the storms that lower over it into a calm and peaceful sea.

On the 19th, in five days, Pedro is back in Avila, with a letter from her friar at court, full of buoyant hope. To which Teresa, whom no hopes could elate unduly nor storms cast down, serene and unmovable, answers calmly: "The letter Pedro has brought has delighted us greatly, so full is it of good hopes which apparently will not fail of fulfilment. May our Lord bring it about, according as it may be most to his service. Withal, until I know that Paul has spoken to Methuselah [the Nuncio], I am not without anxiety. . . . By every possible means, or however you can, on whatever conditions, let your paternity effect the matter of the province, for even though other trials will not be wanting, it is important to be in safety. When your paternity shall understand," continues the prudent Teresa, who has studied human nature, and probed its weaknesses far more deeply than her friars, "that it is advisable to make some acknowledgment to the Nuncio, advise us." It would also be well, she adds, that his first visit to the Nuncio should be made in company of that resolute partisan of the Reform, the Count of Tendilla ; and if God should favour them so far as that the Descalzos are made into a separate province, messengers must be at once sent to the General in Rome ; for to the last she clings to the hope that her Discalced friars will still become his most cherished subjects. "Withal, until I know that Pablo has spoken to Methuselah [the Nuncio], and how it has fared with him, I am not without anxiety." Pedro bears other news as he rides into Avila on his tired mule at the close of that August day,—news which has electrified all Spain— the death of the King of Portugal, the brave and quixotic Don Sebastian, the knight-errant of those times, who has been swallowed up in Africa—nay, has been swallowed up so completely and mysteriously, that even to-day strange dreamers on Portuguese soil are awaiting his return !

And Teresa's pen writes on: letters to the Nuncio

(what has become of them no one knows); to the Dominican Chaves, who holds the keys of the royal conscience; to the Jesuit, Hernandez, the countryman and friend of the President of the Royal Council; a whole volume of letters, —so says Yepes, who had seen them,—to Roque de Huerta, his Majesty's mayordomo of woods and forests; to Mariano, whom she beseeches to plead with the Princess of Eboli for the release of San Juan de la Cruz.

But August drawing to its close still finds Gracian hiding like a criminal in the house of Don Diego Peralta, whom Teresa had besought in a former letter not to leave her hunted friar until he had seen him placed in safety and beyond the danger of assassination, "for I am terrified at these wayside murders." Fearful of appearing in the light of day, he has baffled all the efforts of the Carmelites to serve him with the Brief; but the interview with the Nuncio is as far off as ever, and his letter to Teresa is full of gloomy and melancholy foreboding. And Teresa deprecates as folly his placing himself in the Nuncio's power until the latter shall have been smoothed over by the President in whose presence the first interview should, if possible, take place.

In the meantime, Roca, prior of Mancera, going to court to settle some disputes as to a foundation in Valladolid, in doubt whether to apply to the Royal Council or to the Nuncio, was advised by his friends to have recourse to the latter. "Certain I am," he said, "that I shall at once be made a prisoner; but let us go, and rather err by the advice of others." The event proved that he was right. The Nuncio, refusing to listen to him, confined him in the Carmelite convent. At last, in answer to his repeated supplications for a hearing, one day the Nuncio arrives at the convent gates, where he is met by the friars and brethren, all but Fray Juan. It is for him, however, that the Nuncio has come, and he is sent for to the choir. He prostrates himself at the legate's feet, who bids him rise. "Are you that Fray Juan de Jesus who has written me so many notes?" "Si, señor." "Well, what do you want?" "On behalf of my Descalzos it behoves me to speak to your most illustrious in secret." The prior and friars file out, leaving the two alone in the empty choir.

Boldly did good Fray Juan defend the Reform and its originator; but at Teresa's name, the Nuncio, convulsed with rage, broke into violent invectives. "That restless, roving, disobedient, contumacious female, who under the cover of devotion invents evil doctrine; leaving the retirement of the cloister to gad about against the order of the Council of Trent and her superiors: teaching as if she were a master, against the teachings of St. Paul, who ordered that women should not teach."

This was his mildest language. For a moment the friar stood thunderstruck and speechless before the Nuncio's fierce gestures and towering rage; but only for a moment. The "Rock of Bronze" was not to be moved so easily. With warmth and energy he undertook Teresa's defence, endeavoured to show what manner of woman this really was whom the Nuncio abused so roundly; defended, indeed, her and her Reform so eloquently as to leave the Nuncio musing and half convinced. Then, seeing him calmer and more reasonable, he proposed point-blank the formation of the Descalzos into a separate province.

After a long argument, in which Roca displayed all the resources of his wit and ingenuity, the Nuncio rose to go, saying significantly as he did so, "I give you my word not to subject you to the Calzados. Write to all the convents to come to me in all that may occur, for I myself will take charge of your government and increase."

But the warrant of the 9th of August, which intercepted his Briefs and restrained him in the exercise of his authority, changed these favourable sentiments into animosity and anger, and he swore to deliver over the Descalzos bound hand and foot to their adversaries. It was then that the friars, oblivious alike of Pope and General, whose authority alone was competent to such an act, were hurried into the fatal course of separating themselves from the main body of the Carmelites and erecting themselves into a province of their own. We have seen how, so early as April, Teresa had pointed out to Gracian, who would also seem to have conceived some such project,—he, with some show of reason, being still Apostolic Commissary,—that, in the opinion of such learned and capable counsellors as Daza and the Doctor Rueda, the

Pope or the General alone could take a step so decisive and momentous; that for them to do so would only give colour to the reports of their enemies, who would be sure to make the most of their disobedience and breach of discipline; that it would be more difficult to get the Pope to confirm it than to get his consent to the province in the first place.

But now there was no time for reflection: they all seem (Teresa among them) to have been hurried on to the precipice by the turn events had taken.

On the 9th of October, Fray Antonio de Jesus, as Definitor-General of the Descalzos, convoked the Chapter of Almodóvar; and the friars, oblivious of Pope and General, set to work to separate themselves from the main body of the Carmelites. Fray Juan de la Cruz was there, just escaped from his nine months' imprisonment in Toledo—ill, emaciated, his shoulders mutilated for life with the cruel scourgings of his gaolers. "The life Fray Juan has gone through, and that he should have been allowed (being so ill as he is) to go there at once, has distressed me deeply," writes the old saint, whose hot indignation welled forth as she heard the story of his sufferings, to Gracian. "See that they take good care of him in Almodóvar. . . . I assure you that if he dies you will have few left like him." His appearance in the Chapter produced a strange emotion amongst the assembled friars. He, like Teresa, protested against the election of a Provincial, as being a step they had no power to take, and an encroachment on the special prerogatives of the Papal See. But the same malign influence must again have been at work that Teresa mentions so bitterly in her letter to Gracian on the occasion of the General's death; for, in spite of Fray Juan's remonstrances, Fray Antonio de Jesus was elected Provincial. It was then unanimously decided to send delegates to Rome. The choice fell upon Nicolas Doria—the Nicolas, sometimes the "good Nicolao," of Teresa's letters, who on the 24th of March 1577, less than two years before, had received the habit in Seville from the hands of the man whom by a strange contrariety of fortune he afterwards deprived of it. He was now just about forty. A Genoese by birth, a member of that illustrious family "which has filled sea and earth with such victories and trophies that it can rival the most ambitious families of ancient Rome," it was the lot of young Doria to be bred to commerce. At an early age, in the pursuit of the business which generally brought his countrymen to Spain—which business, as far as I can gather from the euphuistic phrase of the chronicler, chiefly consisted in lending money to the Spanish monarch and his bankrupt government at usurious rates of interest—he went over to Seville. Here he became known and respected as a shrewd financier, when, by one of those revulsions of feeling so common in that age, he suddenly turned his back on the world, had himself ordained a priest, and became a diligent student of arts and theology in the College of Sto. Tomas. Nevertheless the priest was still doubled with the financier. The renewal of an old friendship with Mariano, when the latter came to Seville to arrange for a foundation of a Discalced monastery, brought him acquainted with the Archbishop Don Cristóbal de Rojas who, over head and ears in debt, and his papers in an inextricable state of confusion (it is consolatory to know that what the good Archbishop lacked in practicality he made up in charity and piety), entrusted him with the administration of his affairs. And the keen-witted Genoese fulfilled his commission with such dexterity and skill as to earn that prelate's warmest favour and the King's notice. If we may believe the chronicler, it was the advent of Teresa herself in Seville that finally drew him into her Order. Not that he roused in her any such overpowering flush of enthusiasm as had the gentler-natured Gracian. That indeed was an event in her life. She respected Doria for his austere virtues, his evident ability, but when presently the rivalry between him and Gracian grew too evident to be mistaken, it is the latter whom she exculpates, to the latter that her great heart goes out with the wistful affection of a mother.

It was Doria, then, whose talents, birth, knowledge of the country and of affairs pointed him out as the most likely to serve their cause and save it, whom the friars assembled in Almodóvar fixed on as their ambassador to Rome.

The news of the Chapter fell like a thunderbolt in Madrid. Roca, released from his two months' seclusion, rushed off to Almodóvar to see if he could do anything to remedy what he was too late to prevent.

He implored them to reconsider the steps they had taken, the illegality of an election especially reserved to the sovereign pontiff; that the shadow of authority they might have derived from the fact of Gracian's being Apostolic Commissary had ceased from the moment he renounced his powers and warrants into the Nuncio's hands. In vain : he was thrown into prison by the very men he had come to save from the consequences of their folly. Already might be clearly seen the mutual distrust which only awaited Teresa's death to show itself without disguise.

Teresa's attitude in regard to this Chapter is vague. All the blame of this transaction has been hitherto accorded to Gracian. Do facts, do Teresa's own letters, bear out the assertion? On the 15th of October she writes to Gracian, clearly ascribing to the evil influences of "those who care little for your paternity's sufferings" (Fray Antonio de Jesus and Mariano?) the delay that had cost him so dear in giving up his papers to the Nuncio. "I am glad that you will now know by experience how to direct this business in the proper way, and not against the current as I always said." It is not certain, indeed, whether Gracian ever attended that disastrous Chapter of Almodóvar, for which he has hitherto borne all the blame. For she beseeches him and Mariano (and they would both seem to be in Madrid), to send a message to Almodóvar, not to settle the journey of the friars to Rome. "I now see, my father, what a martyr" (it is the renunciation of his papers she refers to) "your paternity has been on account of conflicting opinions, and if they had left you to yourself one can see that you were indeed guided by God."

Again, "I am very glad they are not to elect a Provincial, which, as your paternity says, is very proper; although, as Fray Antonio told me that without risk of sin they could not do otherwise, I did not gainsay him. I thought all had been concluded here; but if it is necessary to go to Rome for the confirmation, they will also have to go for the province."

Thus far the Chapter of Almodóvar; but this old woman,

sick of heart and weary of spirit—" yet strong in desire "—has other news to tell. During these past months the constant burden of her letters has been to enlist the General in their favour. In March, April, May, to the last moment she had repeated it with painful iteration. "I now see," she had written to Gracian, "that your paternity is more anxious than any one [about sending delegates to Rome]; but it cannot in any way hurt to acquit ourselves with the General, and it is a good time now; and if this is not done, I hold not the rest to be lasting. It is never bad to take pains, even if they are many." In spite of all, at the end of September we still find her harping wearily on the same theme. She still hoped that from the General himself might come the solution that would end their difficulties. "For mercy's sake, let us now live no longer on hopes. Every one is amazed at our having no one there to plead for us, and so those others do what they list." But the friars had been too tardy, for the General was dead! To the last she had clung loyally to him, and to the hope that the salvation of the Reform was to be through him—that its first protector even at the eleventh hour would turn and cherish and protect the movement he had inaugurated. No means had she left unturned to win his ear and his heart; the presents she had sent apparently elicited no word of thanks, no sign of softening. Ill news travels fast, and on the 5th of October she writes to Gracian, overwhelmed with sorrow at the General's death, her heart turning to the dead man in a passionate outburst of generous grief almost akin to remorse.

"I am deeply grieved, and the first day I wept bitterly, unable to do aught else. I mourn for the sorrow we have given him, for indeed he did not deserve it; and if we had but gone to him, all would have been right. God forgive him who has always hindered it, for with your paternity I should have had no difficulty, although in this matter you have given me little credit."

The dead General would never now receive those moving messages from the woman so loving and so grateful that a sardine could suborn her; his ears were eternally closed to the old and wearied woman in Avila, oppressed with the sadness and desolation of old age, who prayed him "not to believe what they have told him of Teresa de Jesus, for truly she has never done a thing which did not become a very obedient daughter, . . . and not to condemn without justice, and hearing both sides; and even if only that which they have told him must prevail, let him punish her, inflict penance, that she may be no longer under his displeasure, for any punishment will be easier for her to bear than to see him angered; for even fathers are wont to pardon their children great sins, how much more so when there is none, she, on the contrary, having passed through great trials in the foundation of these monasteries, thinking that she was giving him pleasure; for apart from his being her superior, she bears him a most deep love."

Their reconciliation was indeed to be remitted, as she had unconsciously prophesied three years ago in her letter to him from Seville, to that dim eternity when surely the crooked things of earth shall be straightened, and human misunderstanding vanish under the clear rays of the Sun of Truth.

It was now useless to send friars to Rome, she adds in this same letter to Gracian, which would only be to expose them to the risk of imprisonment, and to the loss of their documents and money. The General gone, they would only find themselves in Rome, utterly inexperienced in the ways of doing business there, wandering about the streets, and finally be taken up for fugitives without any redress.

Useless, indeed! for on the 16th of October, a few days after the Chapter, the Nuncio issues a second Brief more terrible than the first, delivering over the Descalzos to the government and visitation of the Carmelites. His fury, indeed, knows no bounds when he hears of this Chapter of Almodóvar. Ill did the Reform and its authoress fare at the Nuncio's lips, as, mad with passion, he loaded the Descalzos, both absent and present, with opprobrious epithets and insults, "most unworthy," adds the chronicler, "of their persons."

The friars, after the Chapter, had retired to Pastrana, and there, indeed, if they had chosen, they might in the King's name have still defied the Nuncio, his emissaries, and his Briefs; since Mariano had taken care to provide himself with a royal warrant. I think we know what Mariano's counsels would have been; but in this supreme crisis the friars, again forcing on Gracian the burden of decision as to whether they were or were not to accept the Nuncio's authority, once more made him the scapegoat of their rashness or their fears.

Juarez and Coria (the Observant friars sent to receive their obedience) are thundering at the gates; the Governor and an armed crowd are in readiness outside to enforce the royal warrant and hound them from the convent precincts and out of the town. It was a terrible moment for this really good and conscientious man, tormented with many doubts and fears as to what precisely was his duty, tormented with many searchings of conscience. In despair, unable to take a decision, he resorted to the puerile expedient of accepting as an oracle the ravings of a half-mad friar. Instead of resisting, as a bolder and perhaps a worse man might have done, he himself opened the gates to Juarez and Coria; delivered up to them the royal warrant; and in the Chapter, before the assembled friars, placed the Nuncio's brief upon his head in token of submission, causing the rest to follow his example. He has now retired voluntarily from the contest, and so forfeited the favour of the King.

This took place on the eve of All Saints. The three friars were at once ordered to appear before the Nuncio, and complied. The acts of the Chapter were forthwith annulled, and after being publicly excommunicated, the friars were secluded in separate monasteries; forbidden to celebrate or hear mass; to write or receive any communication. The Monastery of Atocha was assigned to Mariano, he being afterwards transferred to Pastrana, the Nuncio fearing his proximity to the King, with whom he was a favourite. Fray Antonio was shut up in the Convent of San Bernardin; whilst Gracian, paying for the faults of all, was condemned by the wrathful Cardinal to chew the cud of bitter fancy in the Carmelite Convent of Madrid.

Doria, too, would have felt the weight of the legate's wrath, and been banished from court, if a Genoese gentleman, the Nuncio's friend, had not pleaded for him to remain to look after the interests of his brother (Horacio Doria). And the wily, capable Italian made the most of his opportunity, secretly working things round in favour of his Discalced brothers with such dissimulation that even his Calced companion conceived no suspicion.

In December the Nuncio's second Brief, by which the Discalced Communities of Castille and Andalucia were rigorously subjected to the Fathers of the Observance, was notified to Teresa in Avila. "It has been a morning of judgment," she writes to Roque de la Huerta; "the authorities, men of letters, and gentlemen who were present, were all astounded at their want of religion; I am in great distress. I would gladly have given them a hearing, but we dared not speak." Peter, the good Peter, was happily at the gate when they arrived, and went to fetch Lorenzo, who presently bustles in with the corregidor—swords, capes, ruffs, velvets, and all. "Little good," she adds, "did those fathers get from their royal warrant [she refers to the submission of the convents of Pastrana and Alcalá to the Observants]. I know not even if they would obey the King, they are so accustomed to do whatever they like." . . .

Never had a darker hour overshadowed the Descalzos. It seemed at last as if the Reform was to be indeed crushed out. Gloom and despair filled every heart—every heart but one. Fray Juan de la Miseria, quietly painting in the cloisters of Alcalá when the Observants made their furious raid,—a fugitive at Rome; her convents at the mercy of the Fathers of the Observance, her sons in prison, Teresa's confidence never for a moment wavered, and her letters bear no trace of discouragement.

"God will do it all," she wrote. She suffered keenly in the sufferings of her children. "I feel little about the rest, for God will remedy it, since it is his business."

A solitary, serene, and steadfast figure, she stood alone, unshaken, braving the tempest which bowed the heads of her friars to the earth. He must be no recreant knight, she whispered to Gracian, sunk in gloom and hopelessness in his cell at Madrid, to desert the banner of his sweet and gracious Lady at the moment of her greatest need. "May God give you strength," she adds in simple earnest words, "to be firm in justice, although you see yourself in great perils. Blessed trials, however great they may be, if they deviate from this in nothing."

"I tell you that there is much to glory in, in the Cross of our Lord Jesus Christ."

Consumed with pain and anxiety at the tribulation of him who was to her far more than a son, she consoled his mother.

"My lady, may your grace know that all your prayer for a long time has been to pray God with great desires to send you trials; I saw that his Majesty was disposing you for those he was about to give you! And such as they have been! Now will you find yourself with so much improvement in your soul, that you will not know it for the same. . . . The pain of your grace has been indeed present to me, but you will also have derived benefit.

"If I only saw them free, I shall be entirely happy, for, as I have said, I hold for certain the principal matter; our Lord will take particular care of it . . . and will do what will be most for his glory and service."

For in the searching radiance of that Glory, fugitive glimpses of which had been revealed to her, Life and this present moment stood revealed to her as it truly is, in all its baseness and weakness and infinitesimal value, its trials and sufferings concealing treasure that pleasure and content are powerless to buy. As for herself, the intimation that she was to be ordered to another convent only elicits the dry remark, "If it should be one of theirs (the Carmelites), what a much worse life they would give me than they did Fray Juan de la Cruz."

Christmas morning again broke bright and clear over Avila, and faded into night. And in one of its many convents, as the nuns sang matins in the cold and shadowy choir, a frail old nun wept bitterly. The tapers quivered in the chill blasts of air, and flickered for a moment on the vague, mysterious outlines of that kneeling figure, and left it vaguer, more mysterious, a shadow amidst the other shadows that filled the icy church and choir.

CHAPTER XXII

LA VERDAD PADECE PERO NO PERECE

It is to this date that I would fain attribute the following story told by Yepes from personal recollection, although,—for even the memory of a bishop is subject to the hazy influences of time—he places the scene in Toledo three years earlier :—

> When towards the years '75 and '76, her Order was in such grave straits that Gregory XIII. sent a very learned and prudent legate to undo it, aided with all his strength by a commissary sent by the General to this effect, and to reduce the Descalzos to the mitigated rule of Carmel, she received a letter from father Geronimo de la Madre de Dios [Gracian], brought to her in Toledo by Mariano; the letter was so hopeless, and father Mariano so despairing, that I (who happened to be present) almost gave up the Reform for lost ; nor was I alone of this opinion, but it was shared by many others, and certainly it was a vehement occasion to lose all confidence, for the friars were very few, and those few there were poor, known to few, looked askance at by many, and without support or influence ; the only assistance the nuns could give, although they were more numerous, was to commend it to God; the Holy Mother Foundress driven to a corner, loaded with abuse ; their enemies many, powerful, and daring, with liberty and power, and the Apostolic Authority on their side. Well, as she was listening to these things, she mused a little within herself, ceasing to speak with us, who left her alone on purpose, as we knew she was communing with God ; and as we continued our conversation, she broke out suddenly, and said, "Trial indeed is in store for us, but the Reform shall not go back." I know not how those who were present answered her ; but from that moment I had no more anxiety about the matter, and nothing of all the things that came to my ears gave me any concern, since I took this for a prophecy. . . . She must at that moment have had some greater light, which reassured her in the greatest peril.

And it would seem, indeed, that the good Yepes was right, and that the Reform was to be wiped out, had it not been for that curious contrariety in things and men which

makes them draw strength and vigour out of calamity, hope
and buoyancy out of total ruin. No man is wise but by
his own experience: it would seem decreed by some obscure
law that no generation can inherit the accumulated experience of its predecessors, can avoid their blunders or profit
by their wisdom. And Persecution, the mainspring of the
greatest and sublimest upheavals, once more in the case of
the obscure Order founded by Teresa de Jesus, saved the
cause it was intended to destroy. For even as she wept,
good news was on the way to Avila. A few bitter words
spoken by a courtier, the Count of Tendilla—that Don Luis
Hurtado de Mendoza, Governor of the Alhambra, who sold
his diamond buttons and his wife's jewels to aid the
Descalzos of Granada,—irritated by the Nuncio's obstinacy,
had brought matters to a crisis. The court itself—was not
the Nuncio a pestilent Italian, and what had Italians to
do with the affairs of Spanish convents?—took the part of
the Discalced Carmelites, and with a happy inconsistency
"forgetting," says the chronicler, "the imprudence of the
Chapter," the cause of all this tumult, "which it set down to
ignorance, not malice," turned round upon the Nuncio.
"And as the victim of persecution," adds this most worldly-
wise of monkish chroniclers, "has generally the people and
those who are disinterested on his side, many there were, and
they of the gravest sort, who in public and in secret defended
the Descalzos, and resented the Nuncio's measures and the conduct of those he chose to execute them." Foremost amongst
these "grave personages" was Mendoza. He appealed to the
Nuncio, if he would do nothing else, at least to hear the
Discalced Carmelites on their own defence. The Nuncio
was obdurate. At last, stung to the quick, the Spanish
noble got to high words, and turning on his heel left the
Nuncio's presence, and went straight to Chumacero, the Fiscal
of the Royal Council. The result of their interview was that
warrant suspending the publication of the Nuncio's Briefs in
Spain, which, as we have seen, the Descalzos were afraid to
use,—all indeed except those of Granada, where the skirmish
between the King's officers and the Carmelites, busy fixing
up the sentences against the Descalzos on the church doors,
ended in fighting and bloodshed.

The Nuncio, still writhing under Tendilla's plain speaking, and bitterly resenting the active part he had taken in the affair of the warrant, complained to the King. Philip heard him with the immovability and impenetrability of a sphinx; gravely assured him of the grief he felt that any one in his kingdom could be found to give cause of complaint to one for whom he himself professed such profound veneration, and offered to reprimand Tendilla; and then making his icy manner still more withering than was its wont, and fixing his cold blue eye on the dismayed prince of the Church, he said, " I hear of the opposition the Calced Carmelites are making to the Descalzos, which may give rise to suspicion, inasmuch as it is against those who profess rigour and perfection. See that you favour virtue, for they tell me you are no friend of the Reform," upon which he turned on his heel, leaving the Nuncio to stomach the rebuke with such relish as he could!

The King has spoken! The fiat has gone forth, and now the game is to be one of skill between King and Cardinal.

Tendilla is reprimanded, as Philip has promised, and, being absent from Madrid, writes to defend himself,—and not himself only, but the Descalzos, from the imputations of their enemies.

A letter which, although written to the President Pazos, is read by the King,—a fact not to be imparted to the Nuncio, to whom he immediately orders the letter to be forwarded, that he might see for himself (perhaps the proof was necessary) that he had kept his Royal Word.

It was the generous and hasty courtier himself who, on his return to Madrid, confident of Philip's approval, first informed Sega that his letter had been seen by the King. The Nuncio feels that he is losing: the Pope, swayed by Archbishop Quiroga, gives an uncertain sound; the King is an immediate and powerful antagonist, and behind him are the greatest nobles in the kingdom and the general feeling of the court.

The Nuncio is in a corner.

" Sir," he says to Tendilla, " to show you how unfeignedly I desire to serve his Majesty, I shall be glad that he should appoint other persons to assist with me in deciding these matters in question, so that with their authority they may settle these differences between the kingdom and the King and me; rewarding virtue and chastising vice."

Ah, ah! I have caught you, old fox! thinks Tendilla to himself, as he answers that, if these words of his most illustrious lordship are not a mere compliment, then nothing can give his Majesty greater pleasure than to hear them; and that no step could better prove his freedom from all passion; and himself offers to carry the note to the King, and bring back the reply.

Tendilla struck whilst the iron was hot. With the letter in his pocket, he left the Nuncio's lodging, himself delivered it to Santoyo, a gentleman of the Bedchamber, who at once took it to the King, who opening it,—scrawled a brief expression of gratification at the Nuncio's zeal on the margin.

But if the Nuncio concedes so much, his wounded dignity demands a victim—who but the man who has so long stood in the way of his exercising his jurisdiction? "I do not complain of the Descalzos," says he; "only of that wretched Father Gracian, who has revolutionised and brought them to nought!"

And seeing that Philip has penetrated the motives of this personal rancour, he makes haste to add, "that it was not because he had prevented him (the Nuncio) assuming his usual jurisdiction over the Orders, oh dear no! but simply because of the serious charges that had been made against him; which made it expedient that he should be tried and sentenced, before he (the Nuncio) could set to work in good earnest to prevail upon the Pope to erect the Descalzos into a separate province: indeed, to prove to his Majesty how little he is moved by passion in this matter, his Majesty may appoint other judges to assist him in the inquiry." Philip took him at his word, and straightway named his head chaplain and almoner Don Luis Manrique; Master Fray Lorenzo de Villavicencio, Augustinian; and two Dominicans, Fray Pedro Fernandez and Fray Hernando de Castillo, whose unanimous decision is that the Community of the Descalzos must be sustained and raised into a self-governing province.

Gracian, however, blocks the way, the Nuncio firmly maintaining that, before anything else is done, he must first be tried and sentenced. He was given the option of being condemned without a trial or of having the matter fully investigated and making a defence.

> This [writes Marmol] was the greatest conflict this servant of God had seen himself in in all his life, since, if, in order that his cause might be tried by dispassionate judges, he allowed himself to be sentenced merely on the evidence of the memorials against him sent from Andalucia, he feared two things: first, the cruel sentence of the Nuncio; secondly, to allow himself to be condemned, and to remain with a slur on his reputation for all his future life,—he being innocent,—thus depriving the Church of the benefits his talents might do her; the more especially knowing, as he was too good a theologian not to know, that for a public man it is a mortal sin to let himself be defamed, and that it is obligatory on such an one to stand up in defence of his honour. On the other hand, if he acted as the Nuncio proposed, which was to ask for a commissary to proceed to Andalucia to sift the charges against him, and defend his cause judicially, there were three very great drawbacks. The first, that he had no money; the friars would not give him any, nor could he reasonably ask his relatives to pay the person sent by the Nuncio to open the suit anew. Secondly, he feared that, on the commissary's arrival, those very people who had calumniated him to the Nuncio would again sign the defamatory memorials; and thus, not only would his innocence *not* be proved, but his reputation suffer more gravely than it had done before. The third objection, and the greatest of all (for the others seemed to me of little moment), was that, if the Descalzos were left subject any longer to the Calzados, after a certain time the King might forget them, and the Nuncio being equally oblivious of the Province and of severing them from the Calzados, the project would be allowed to drop, and the primitive rigour of the Reform die a natural death.

Shall he yield to the instincts felt by every honest man, give his traducers the lie, and assert his own innocence? "If you are desirous that this matter of the Province be effected," counsels Don Luis Manrique, "take your sentence, and make no defence." Which shall he do—sacrifice the Reform or his own fair fame? Can he doubt? "I would do more than this, nay, I would let myself be burned alive, for the sake of the Reform," he answers stoutly; "for, even should they repay this my determination with ingratitude" (and they did, as has been the way with mankind ever since the world began), "I hope in God and the Virgin Mary (whose the Order is) that I shall have my reward, for in this life there remains nothing for me but crosses and more crosses!"

Could he but have looked into the future, he might have thought it well, even in the interests of the Descalzos themselves, to sift, as he could easily have done, those obscure calumnies which were already weaving their dark web about his life.

And so Gracian allowed himself to be sentenced. Deprived of voice and station in the Order, he was bundled off to the College of Alcalá—there to fast and do penance until such time as the Nuncio should soften. Not a word, be it remembered, in the sentence of the real grievance, which was that Gracian had hampered him (the Nuncio) in the exercise of his powers, and brought him into conflict with the King. The Nuncio was far too wide-awake for that; nor did he even listen to the friar's defence, and "he could," says Marmol, "have given an ample one." It is a significant fact that the chronicler, a zealous partisan of Doria and his faction, says nothing of this act of abnegation; the more significant, as his silence proves that the trumped-up allegations against Gracian rested on an altogether unsustainable basis, as he would, if he could (so does party warfare pervert the best of men), have been delighted to show that they were not unfounded.

He does not, however, omit ("indeed, it is not a thing to lose," he says) the following anecdote relating to Doria, which he discovers written by a "person in every way trustworthy, and witnessed by others no less so."

Whilst the Commission thus sat in judgment on the affairs of the Discalced Carmelites, Fray Nicolas de Jesus Maria (Doria), accompanied by another friar, on his way to and from the Carmelite Monastery and the Convent of the Atocha, where the Commissioners resided, was followed by a black and white dog, the symbol of the Dominican Order. "Although they were astonished, they were not afraid," the chronicler remarks. This dog, every now and then turning round his head to look back at them, led them when they got to the Atocha to the cell of the father Master Fray Pedro Fernandez, and then disappeared. This happened several times, until at last it seemed to them so mysterious that they went thither through other streets, but always, when they found themselves at the outskirts of the town, there was the dog waiting to accompany them. When they mentioned the circumstance to Fernandez, he, like themselves, being unable to account for it, nor to guess what dog it was, they came to the conclusion that it contained a mystery; and that the glorious Santo Domingo had chosen that way of showing how ardently he had taken upon himself the affairs of Teresa and her Order, even as he had promised to her when she prayed to him in his house at Segovia.

Let us now leave these grave and reverend signors consulting in Madrid, and proceed to Seville, where an indiscreet confessor—it pains me to say that he was no other than the good Garcí Alvarez—and two melancholy imaginative nuns—one of them that Beatriz de la Madre de Dios whose miraculous vocation Teresa records in the *Fundaciones* —have armed a revolution, and, with the assistance of the triumphant Carmelites, deposed Maria de San José, and elected another prioress in her stead. Very vague these events of Seville—chiefly interesting to us as seen through the vision of one Teresa of Avila. There are denouncings to the Inquisition, who, having learnt wisdom, will have none of them; questionings of trembling nuns for six hours at a stretch—some of weak intellect signing they know not what tissues of nauseous absurdities. Maria de San José accused of illicit relations with Gracian; Teresa figuring as a wicked old woman, who, under pretence of founding convents, carried young women about from one part of the country to the other, —to prostitute them; such, and much more, "unfit to be named in chaste ears," was set about by these Christ-like friars.

"It is a baseness even to disprove such things," exclaimed Teresa; "since if they must lie, it is better that they do it in such a way that no one will believe them, but only laugh at them!"

Teresa enlists the generosity of her countryman, the old prior Pantoja, in favour of her persecuted nuns,—makes him, in fact, her ambassador to them—the bearer of the letter "which I should not be sorry should fall into the Provincial's hands—it being written for no other object."

Brave words they are too which the aged prior of Las Cuevas reads to the nuns of Seville—in some little dark locutory, the sisters rapt in mute attention in the shadow behind the grating. It is the only time in her epistolary correspondence (models of reality, spontaneity, and simplicity) that she rises into eloquence.

> Know that I never loved you so much as now, nor have you had such an opportunity as now to serve our Lord, who bestows on you so great a favour as to enable you to taste somewhat of his Cross, and something of the forlornness his Majesty then suffered. Happy the day you entered that place, since such a fortunate time was awaiting you. Greatly do I envy you; so that when these changes came to my knowledge . . . instead of them giving me pain, I felt an intense interior joy that, without your having to cross the sea, his Majesty has willed to discover to you mines of eternal treasures, with which I hope in his Majesty you will be exceedingly enriched, and share with us here; for I am confident that he will of his mercy enable you to bear all without offending him in aught; therefore do not be afflicted that you feel it greatly; for perchance our Lord wishes to show you that you are not so strong as you thought when you were anxious to suffer. Courage — courage, daughters mine. Remember that to no one does God give more trials than he can bear; and that his Majesty is with those in trouble. . . . Prayer —prayer, my sisters; and let your humility and obedience now shine forth resplendent, so much so that none amongst you is more submissive than the late mother prioress to the vicaress they have placed. Oh what a seasonable opportunity to pluck the fruit from the resolutions you have made to serve the Lord! Consider that he often wishes to prove if our works and words agree. Bring out the Virgin's daughters and her sisters with honour from this great persecution, for if you help yourselves, the good Jesus will help you: for although he sleeps at sea, when the tempest rages, he makes the winds be still. . . . You are amongst your sisters and not in Algiers. Let your spouse alone, and you shall see how before long the sea shall swallow up them that make war on us, even as it did King Pharaoh, and he shall set his people free!

It is no uncertain sound this—this clarion note which rings out so true and brave, bearing on its wings the very spirit of triumphant victory.

In May, however, things have calmed down; the calumnies of the Carmelites have been partially examined by Sega and his colleagues and found destitute of foundation: already the convent has reverted to its usual condition of monotonous calm. What shall be done with the culprits?

Know [counsels Teresa] that there are some persons of such weak intellect that they think they really see all that comes into their head; for the devil must assist them, and my pain is that he must have made that sister think she saw what, as he thought, would bring the house to nought; so that perhaps she is not so much to blame as we think, any more than a madman. ... You must compassionate her as if she were your father's daughter, as indeed so she is of that faithful Father to whom we owe so much, and whom the poor thing has desired to serve all her life.

For many reasons (which I am astonished at your reverence for not having seen), her leaving the convent must not be so much as dreamed of.

Thirdly. Endeavour to forget the thing entirely, each one considering how she would have liked to be treated if it had happened to her.

But here comes in the touch of Jesuitry—the secret of Teresa's strength as an administrator:

I shall be exceedingly angry if you give any occasion for them to think they are ill-treated. *They have already written to me here, that the Company will take it ill if they are ill-treated.* Be careful to be on the look-out.

Neither must she speak to any one except before a third person, or confess except with a Descalzo: bear in mind that these two do not speak to each other in secret; do not press them too hardly, for we women are but weak ... and it would not be ill to give her some occupation, so long as she has no communication with any one outside the house; for solitude and brooding will do her injury. ... Be on your guard, especially at night, for, as the devil is prowling about to destroy the credit of these monasteries, he sometimes makes what appears impossible, possible.

If these two sisters fell out, and could be got to provoke one another, you would get to the root of the matter. ... "En fin, en fin, la verdad padece pero no perece" (Truth may suffer, but will not perish).

On the 28th of June, Maria de San José was restored to her post of prioress, which she refused, perhaps through a mistaken notion of false humility—a vaporous bladder, which Teresa quickly pricks with the sharp old Castilian proverb—"A falta de buenos mi marido alcalde" (For want of a better, my husband the mayor)—also desiring to know whether those nuns have contradicted each other in anything, "as I am greatly distressed about their souls." Beatriz de la Madre de Dios, it is said, wept herself blind, and died at eighty-six in the odour of sanctity: it will scarcely surprise the psychologist to learn that before her death she was taken with the gift of prophecy.

In the meantime, Gracian is in seclusion at Alcalá, Mariano gone to Jerez, commissioned by the King "to extract minerals from certain waters." Events have marched rapidly. Knowing the tendencies of the King and court, it was a foregone conclusion that the accusations against the Descalzos would be found to be without an atom of foundation. On the 1st of April, Salazar was appointed by the Nuncio's Brief Vicar-General of the Descalzos, pending their erection into a province. No better selection could have been made: nor one less obnoxious to the Descalzos, or more so to the Observants. Novices were still to be received in the monasteries; anything that had been altered by the Carmelite visitors was to be restored to its original condition: everything was to go on as before, until instructions came from Rome. For the King and Nuncio had kept their promise and written to Gregory XIII. warmly recommending the erection of the Reform into a separate province. Fray Angel, a man of blameless life and gentle and pacific instincts, was notably prepossessed in favour of Teresa and her Descalzos, especially so of Gracian. Seeing that his term of office must be short, he resolved to let well alone, to make no change in their government, nor to admit the assistance of any other Observant in the execution of his duties. Moreover, he did what he could to get Gracian's sentence revoked, and was so successful that, on the Nuncio paying a visit to the King one day, the latter had only to observe that Father Fray Geronimo had had punishment enough (so powerful were the syllables that dropped from the royal lips), for the Nuncio straightway to revoke the sentence; and, restored to his old rank in the Order, Gracian finds himself once more, so says Marmol, in the thick of sending the ambassadors to Rome. Him too—this later on—did Salazar select as his companion in the government of the Descalzos, or rather on him did he lay the whole weight and burden of it, the Vicar-General confining himself to signing such documents as were required of him. Surely we can imagine Teresa's calm, steadfast joy as she watched the mending fortunes of her Reform, still:—

May he [Salazar] enjoy it only for a short time; I do not mean that his life should be cut short; for he is in truth the cleverest amongst them, and will treat us with consideration, especially as he is so shrewd that he will know how it will end. In some respects it is doing those fathers as evil a turn as ourselves. For perfect people, the Nuncio has left nothing to be desired, since he has made us all suffer.

The auspicious moment has now arrived for sending the delegates to Rome. The first embassy despatched by the friars of Almodóvar had ended in failure, the Nuncio having purposely detained Doria (who had been originally fixed upon to go) in Madrid, on the pretext that he could not be deprived of so sage a counsellor. The mission had then been entrusted to Fray Pedro de los Angeles, who had left the Carmelites to join the Reform, and a lay friar his companion. It was a miserable fiasco. When they arrived in Italy, they found the General dead. They tramped to Naples to report themselves to the new General, Cafardo. He deprived them of their powers, letters, and despatches; but for the rest, treated them benignly enough. Don Bernardino de Mendoza, the Viceroy's son, lodged them in his palace. Fray Pedro's virtue was not proof against the luxurious entertainment of his host. "Weakened by the blandishments of Naples"—I quote the chronicler—"like Hannibal's army with those of Capua," his commission languished, and he returned to Spain and to the Carmelites at one and the same moment. He elected to become a member of the Monastery of Granada, and Ana de Jesus (so the author of her life relates), as she rescued the serge cape from a poor woman to whom he had sold it for swaddling-clothes, is reported to have said that "he who had so basely dishonoured the Virgin's sackcloth would not long enjoy the serge, and that the end of his life was nigh." In vain Fray Pedro sought an interview with the indignant prioress, who resolutely refused to see him. One day as he passed the convent church, it happened to be open, and he and his companion went in to pray. As he did so, the memory of what he had left swept over him, and he began to weep bitterly. "A notable circumstance!" adds the chronicler, to whose garrulity I have owed so much. "Before he rose from the ground he lost the sight of both his eyes, so that it was with great difficulty they got him back to his convent, where in a few days God took him." When

Mother Ana heard of it, she said to the nuns, although why she did not predict it more clearly before we are not told— "I knew it already, my sisters, and for that reason did not care to speak with him; on the contrary, I had counselled him not to come here. But it is good to pay for one's sins in this life, and thus save oneself eternal suffering."

The lot now fell upon Fray Juan de Jesus (Roca), whose fearlessness of tongue and constancy of heart the past had so abundantly proved. He too, for he is one of the marked figures of the Order, merits a few words. A native of Cataluña, of respectable and virtuous parentage, his mother's name of Roca was given him at his baptism, "not without a divine intention,"—I quote the chronicler,—"because he was a rock of bronze in his resistance to relaxation and to every adverse impulse." After taking his degree of Doctor of Theology in the University of Barcelona, he was appointed, on account of his conspicuous talents, to a professorial chair. His learning, however, obtaining for him a benefice, he was ordained a priest. "As he could not be contented with mediocrity," we next find him at Alcalá de Henares, "a place rich in all kinds of learning," competing for one of the university chairs. "In the greatest fervour of his pretension he was distressed to find himself a slave of what his soul despised; and not finding in visible things the wherewithal to fill his aspirations, he thirsted for the invisible." In this frame of mind he happened to hear Gracian preach that famous sermon on the antiquity and glory of the Order of Mount Carmel. Without a sign, without a word, the learned doctor set off straightway to Pastrana and enrolled himself a novice. Thence he wrote to the servant he had left behind him in Alcalá, who, in his turn, had only to receive his master's letter to follow his footsteps and become a Discalced friar,—perhaps fortunately for him, for scarcely had he left the house they lived in than it tumbled down, a circumstance which the devout master and no less devout servant accepted as a celestial warning thenceforth generously to employ their lives in the service of others.

So aptly did the name of Roca typify the firm inflexibility, constancy, and fearlessness of his character, and his unalterable virtue, that amongst his brother friars he was never known by any other. It was Roca who in the Observant Chapter of Moraleja had so stoutly opposed the measures for the destruction of the Descalzos that he forced the Carmelite fathers to desist from their intentions; having on the way thither bolstered up his weaker-kneed companions, the Prior of Pastrana and the Rector of Alcalá, to do the same. A man, too, who loved a joke,—if a grim one. For does not the chronicler, as a proof of the "simplicity and kindliness" of those early days of struggle, relate how, when the three, on their journey back from the self-same Chapter, arrived at Mancera, of which Fray Juan was prior, with great dissimulation, he ordered his monks to throw them into prison, on the pretext that they had not defended the Reform as warmly as they should. The prior and the rector, although astonished (as well they might be), accepted the penance with great humility and simplicity, and were led meekly off to prison. A few hours after, Roca collects his monks,—one of them clad in all the treasures of the sacristy, another two bearing garlands of flowers,— and suddenly opening the dungeon doors, after crowning his captives with the garlands, led them triumphantly to the choir, chanting as they went: *In exitu Israel de Ægypto.*

It is generally the fate of these inflexible characters, however, to find themselves in opposition, not only to their enemies, but to their friends. Nor was the Rock of Bronze an exception. We have seen, when made a prisoner in Madrid, how fearlessly he faced the Nuncio. As fearlessly did he face his own Order in the rebel Chapter of Almodóvar, putting before them such unpalatable truths that they straightway threw him into prison for a month.

In the spring of this self-same year of 1579 in which he started for Rome, an unsuccessful attempt had been made on his liberty. As he was closeted in consultation with Teresa in San José of Avila, the prior of the Carmelites, leaving armed friars below to guard the doors, ascended to the locutory, and with great show of courtesy invited him to accept the hospitality of his monastery, since it was not right that a person of his standing should resort to the "meson." Roca sniffed the danger. The tornera[1] (a woman of action, although her name has not been preserved), seeing the armed friars at the gates, at once sends out to warn certain canons and pious gentlemen of the danger, and the prior, disappointed of his prey, had nothing better for it but to retire as he had come.

Who then more fitted than the Rock of Bronze, bold and valiant and manly, to undertake this difficult and dangerous mission—a mission on which hung the fate of Teresa and her Order?

With the exception of Gracian, who himself seems to have hankered after the journey and to have already dreamt of founding a Discalced monastery even in the sacred city, the prior of Mancera's appointment was warmly approved of by the heads of the Order. Teresa's prioresses warmly responded to the appeals for help, some of them pathetic enough, which now went forth from San José in Avila. "It is only once in a lifetime," she writes to Maria Bautista—only once in a lifetime! "For this reason we all wear one habit, so that we may all help one another, for what belongs to one belongs to all; and he gives well who gives his all. . . . I cannot earn it, for I have only the use of one hand; and more painful is it for me to scrape it together and beg for it: it is certainly a torment to me, that would be unbearable except for God alone." But no! they all give according to their capacity—perhaps beyond it: even the somewhat grasping prioress of Valladolid is moved to generosity, and earns Teresa's warmest gratitude by her prompt response to her appeal for funds to speed on her emissaries at Rome. As for the prioress of Seville, she deposits 600 dollars, a legacy from the Indies; the prioress of Veas contributes 400 escudos, the dowry of a novice; the nuns of Toledo are equally generous; which, together with what she herself is able to scrape together from various noble friends and prelates—besides 8000 reals from Fray Nicolas (Doria) and 400 escudos the gift of their gallant partisan the Count of Tendilla—comes to a goodly sum.

To guard against any unforeseen change of mind on the part of the Nuncio, the utmost secrecy was preserved as to

---

[1] Portress.

the journey and its object, it being considered advisable to keep even the Discalced Communities themselves in ignorance. It is decided too that Roca shall for once at least in his life doff the friar's cowl and sandals for the dress of a gallant of the century, and assuming the name of José Bullon (not quite a borrowed one, for it was his father's), and in such guise, ostensibly bent on a purely secular mission to obtain a dispensation for a gentleman of Avila to marry his cousin, set out for Rome, with his companion the prior of Pastrana. Teresa, when she saw her ambassador, his beard grown, strong, valiant, "a proper man," as, cloaked and booted, his sword and spurs clanked over the faded red bricks of the convent floor, was overcome with joy. His grave and martial aspect was more that of some fire-eating captain than of a subdued and pallid monk, whose awkward air betrayed his assumption of a dress he had forgotten the use of in the cloister. His mule waits at the door. From the frail hand of the great and remarkable woman whom he loved and venerated he receives the final blessing. As his mule's hoofs die away from the convent court, echoing through the narrow streets, she, still motionless and absorbed, breathes silent godspeeds : for on this mission depend the peace, prosperity, and renown of the Resuscitated Order of Our Lady of Carmel. And a hazardous journey it truly was that these two brave friars undertook : " God bring him back safely ; I beseech your grace to tell me on what day he left, and how he was" (this to Roque de Huerta). " I long for the hour for him to leave Spain, for fear any accident should occur to him, which would be a terrible juncture." Small wonder, indeed ! for they had to make their way across Spain, and who knows whether they will not be intercepted, perhaps treacherously poisoned, by those Argus-eyed enemies of theirs, just baffled of what but a few months ago had seemed an easy prey ? Just before they reached Alicante,—the port whence the ship is to waft them to Italy,—they had a terrible fright, for in spite of his disguise the Prior of Pastrana was recognised.

Alternately becalmed and tossed about by fearful tempests ; terror-stricken by the Moorish galeots hovering about on the horizon like birds of prey, the Discalced friars, now transformed into Geronimo de la Vega and the grave and learned Doctor Diego Hurtado de Almazan, at last found themselves at Rome. It is not within the bounds of my history to relate how they sped with Pope and Cardinals. How whilst they were in Rome, the Chapter-General of the Order was held, by the new General and the Master Fray Geronimo Tostado ; how they went about in fear and trembling, their heads ever on their shoulder (according to the characteristic Spanish phrase), lest, the purport of their mission leaking out, they should be caught and cast into prison by the Observants. It is not within the bounds of my history to relate how the King of Spain, although in the thick of his war with Portugal, did not relax his interest in the fortunes of the Reform ; and how the Franciscan friar, Cardinal Montalto (afterwards Pope Sixtus V.), espoused their cause. How, without the timely influence of the Cardinal, Sforza, they were wellnigh outwitted by the wily intrigues of the newly-elected General of the Order, Cafardo, and the Pope's nephew, the Cardinal Buoncampagna ; how glimpses of success were followed by moments of black despair ; how summer wore into winter and winter into summer before Pope Gregory XIII. in full conclave erected the Discalced Carmelites into a separate province by his Brief of the 22nd of June 1580,— in the ninth year of his pontificate,—which sealed and ratified the life-work begun by an obscure nun in a remote corner of Castille,—for is it not all told with much display of superfluous rhetoric in the yellow pages of the Chronicle of Fray Francisco de Santa Maria, where he who runs may read ?

CHAPTER XXIII

DIOS E. VOS

AND so, leaving the Spanish pseudo-gentleman and his grave-browed companion to follow the fluctuating fortunes of the Reform in Rome, let us return to its foundress in Avila, who, looking into the future, foresees the Virgin's Order triumphant, encompassing within its starry girdle distant regions of the earth which were to her a vague dream, but scarcely a reality. She indeed may not live to witness these glorious destinies, but "may his Majesty preserve Paul many years to labour in and enjoy it; for as for me, I shall see it from heaven, if I deserve to go there."

She shall indeed see the Province, and the first Chapter of her Order held on Spanish soil—for three more years of life still remain to her on this side of the grave: three years which, with declining strength, show no diminution of activity and zeal; three more years of labour, weariness, and effort. For to those so heroic of spirit as she, fruition and success bring not repose, but greater responsibility, greater cares; no sinking down in lethargic ease to rest on the laurels so hardly and gloriously earned: "For the night cometh when no man shall work!" Her life will go out like the setting sun of some wondrous day that lives in the memory for ever—most gorgeous and most majestic as its blood-red disc dips behind the shadowy horizon and descends into the mysteries of space.

For in June, when the parameras of Avila wave with flowers, transformed into verdant meadows, where, under the lush grass, trickle a thousand unseen rivulets, Teresa, at the instance of Fray Angel de Salazar, the new Vicar-General of the Descalzos, once more holds herself in readiness to traverse the hot and dusty bridle-tracks of Castille: her ultimate destination Malagon, whose affairs have been gradually going from bad to worse; her more immediate object to visit Valladolid, at the request of Bishop Mendoza and his sister, sorely in need of her consolations— a request which the courtly Provincial, who owes them much, does not dream of refusing: thence to Salamanca, where the need of her daughters is greatest of all, the very silence with which they suffer, the most heartrending of appeals.

"See you now, daughter" (she writes to Maria Bautista) "this poor wretched old woman" (she is 64), "and then to Malagon! I assure you that it has made me laugh; and I have spirit for more. Perhaps, though, before I finish with Salamanca we may have news which would enable me to be with you longer; for as to Malagon, some one else could get it into order." For she saw through the ruse,— never a crafty friar of them all could hoodwink her,—and that the Carmelites are not sorry to get rid of her on any pretext, and out of the neighbourhood of the Encarnacion.[1] "There are indications (it may be suspicion) that these brethren of mine are more anxious to see me at a distance from them than to remedy the necessity of Malagon. This indeed has given me a little concern; since as for the rest, I mean the journey to Malagon, I felt none whatever; although it distresses me to go as prioress, for I am unfit for it, and fear lest I should be wanting in our Lord's service. Let your paternity beseech him that in this I may never falter; and as to the rest, come what may—The greater the labour, the greater the reward."

For no other reason (so rigid the sense of Duty) but that she has become too old and feeble to take more than an intermittent part in the duties of the community, in which she exacted that her prioresses should ever take the lead, she, once the most active of them all, who scrubbed and cooked (and cooked so well, too, that the nuns rejoiced exceedingly when Mother Teresa's turn came round), has become little more than a helpless invalid, with a useless arm, who cannot even clothe herself without assistance. "As for the rest; for the sake of obedience I will go to the end of

[1] Letter to Gracian, 10th June 1579.

the world; and farther than that, I believe that the greater the labour (trabajo), the more joyfully would I do anything, however small, for this great God, to whom I owe so much; above all, I think one serves him most when one does it for obedience' sake alone; for, as regards my Paul, it would be enough for me to do anything with pleasure, for the sake of pleasing him."

Thus heroically she struggled still along the thorny path of which so little remained for her to tread, her great heart yearning for sympathy, longing, as only a great heart can, to lean on the frail reed of human love; to whisper the secrets and sadnesses of her soul into some human ear. "Oh! what solitude every day brings me, and more to my soul, to be so far away from your paternity," she writes to Gracian; "although it seems to it that it is always close to the Father José, and with this I bear this life, although bereft of earthly contents, and with very continuous trouble!"

Salazar yielded to her representations—relieved her of the onerous office she dreaded her inability to fulfil, but still required that she should not fail to visit Malagon and give that convent, gone so wrong, the benefit of her presence.

On the Day of Corpus Christi his mandate for her departure arrived in Avila, "with so many censures that the Bishop's pleasure and the petition he made to his paternity is thoroughly complied with. So I shall set forth one or two days after San Juan" (St. John's Day). Her companion on this journey was Ana de San Bartolomé. She broke her journey, and stayed to rest two or three days at Medina, midway between Avila and Valladolid.

None of her convents more strange and curiously impressive than this of Medina—Medina of the Plains, standing sentinel-like, tall, austere, mysterious, on the very edge of the town, at the entrance to the four cross-roads, along one of which, on one of those evenings late in June of 1579, a country cart, preceded by a white column of dust, crawled painfully up to the convent gates. A palace anciently; its curiously-inlaid roofs still telling a story of ancient splendour and magnificence; outwardly great breadths of walls, stained to many hues—yellow, brown, and red; caked with the universal dust which clings like an outer garment to Castilian man and beast, and veils his dwelling; enigmatic of aspect, for each generation in its passage has imprinted thereon somewhat of its personality—here you may trace in the faded bricks the outlines of a Gothic archway, of a Renaissance window, long ago blocked up to suit the requirements of later inhabitants.

A building whose grim impersonality and expressionlessness fascinates and repels; with nothing to connect the life without with that within; no casement from which the eye may scan the boundless plains that girdle in Medina—in spring and early summer a waving sea of green or golden grain,—as immense, as vast as the great circle of heaven above it. For these narrow rectangular gratings which pierce its surface here and there, as few as may be, are not made for vision, but to admit the air. Outside, the world—the world of Medina—jogs on its way; ragged labourers ride out past it in the gray of early dawn, on donkeys as ragged as themselves, on their way to the fields, and return at eventide in wearied cavalcades, along the brown, dusty road. For in Medina—intensely Castilian as it is,—unlike gray, Gothic, chivalrous Avila, it is the East that gives the dominating note; and the clusters of huts built of mud-bricks baked in the sun bear I know not what resemblance to an Eastern village.

For the glory of Medina has long departed, was departing even in Teresa's time, when the Englishman, the Frank, the German, and the Fleming chaffered and bartered with the taciturn Castilian under the arcades of the market-place; its great warehouses are now empty; the shepherd drives his black merino sheep, or the goat-herd his goats, unmolested through the silent streets—silent except for the tinkling of their bells or the winding of the swineherd's horn. Its stately convents, founded by kings and princes, stand decaying day by day in the stern pathos of past magnificence; and the great old stone palaces,—the coats of arms of their former owners still clinging, defaced and mouldering, to their angles, their carved staircases, once thronged by retainers and men-at-arms,—have now become the dwellings of a rural population of labourers, herdsmen, and shepherds.

On the 3rd of July she arrived in Valladolid. Although

she had begged that she might be spared all tumultuous demonstrations of joy, which rather mortified than gave pleasure to her humble spirit, the more deeply convinced, as life wore on, of her own imperfections, deficiencies, and unworthiness, we may imagine the deep satisfaction of the nuns—nay, after the past terrible year, it was almost a triumph—to look once more, after an absence of four years, on the venerated face of their foundress. "I have been amazed," she says simply to Gracian, "how glad these nuns are to have me with them, and these great people also" (Don Alvaro and Doña Maria de Mendoza)—"I know not why."

The state of her convent under the capable rule of Maria de Bautista leaves nothing to be desired, for years have transformed the gay and giddy girl, who inaugurated in a jest the Reform of the Carmelites, into a grave and sententious prioress—a little too fond of giving advice perhaps, but clever, shrewd, and "a great gatherer for her house." It is said that on the occasion of one of the obnoxious notices being served upon her during the disputes, now so happily drawing to an end, she dictated such a reply to a dull and worthy advocate of Valladolid as left him transfixed with astonishment at the force of a woman's wit. And had not Teresa, too, proud of one whose qualities had been developed under her own training, laughingly and gracefully acknowledged her superiority to herself, when turning towards Gracian, as the prioress was engaged in the occupation which of all others she liked best, that of giving advice, she said, in smiling amazement (not perhaps without its point of irony, which escaped the slower brains around her), "Jesus! how much she knows! I am but a fool before her, confounded at my own ignorance and incapability of any good thing."

Silks and brocades rustled all day long through that little tranquil convent parlour, filling it for a moment with the odour of things and emotions that were not entirely sacred; Doña Maria de Mendoza's coach, a strange structure (Teresa once travelled in it to Madrid), waited for hours before the convent gates, whilst she and the Bishop were closeted with Teresa within. "I was too tired to write, what with seeing so many great ladies (tanta señora)," she adds at the end of an already sufficiently long letter to Gracian in Alcalá—Gracian, with whom the hot summer has disagreed, and made him break out in boils. " Yesterday I was with the Countess of Osorno. The Bishop of Palencia, [the Don Alvaro de Mendoza aforesaid, already Bishop-elect of that diocesis] is here ; your paternity, and all of us owe him much."

Indeed, almost on the eve of her departure, she grudges the time lost in such vain intercourse. " We who should live most apart from the world," she writes to her brother Lorenzo, " are obliged to have so much to do with it, that your grace need not be surprised that, although I have been here the time I have, I have not been able to speak to the sisters (I mean alone), although some of them desire it greatly, for there has been no opportunity."

She is sending him, with the messenger who bears the letter, a chalice, " very good, a better one is not needed, which weighs 12 ducats, and perhaps a real over, and cost 40 reals to make ; which comes to 16 ducats, less 3 reals. It is entirely of silver ; I believe your grace will be pleased with it." (Was it for the chapel at La Serna, I wonder?) " They showed me one here of the metal you mention, and although it is not an old one, and has been gilded, it already shows what it is, and it has got so black inside the foot as to be disgusting. I decided at once not to buy one like it, and it seemed to me not to be thought of that your grace should eat in much silver and use another metal for God." Which little detail paints the somewhat ostentatious and showy character of her brother—as also his thrift—to a nicety ; as also Teresa's healthy hatred of shams, and her honest instincts. " I did not think," she continues, " to get one of so large a size so cheap, but this ' hurguillas ' (huckstress) of a prioress has gone about bargaining for it with one of her friends. . . . The state in which she has this house, and the ability she possesses, are such as to praise God for."

Sometimes she unexpectedly touches the great current of history. Not uninteresting to hear how the course of events then convulsing the Peninsula as it had never been convulsed since the days of the Catholic kings and La

Beltraneja are echoed back from the mind of this old nun.

The old age and decrepitude of the Cardinal, Don Enrique, who succeeded to the throne of Portugal on the death of his nephew, Don Sebastian, had raised up a host of claimants; chief amongst whom were Philip of Spain and the Duke of Braganza, who claimed through his wife, Doña Catalina, Don Manuel's grand-daughter. It is to Don Teutonio de Braganza, Archbishop of Ebora, the Duke of Braganza's uncle, that Teresa writes as follows from Valladolid:

> Your lordship might order word to be sent to me, if in Portugal there is any news of peace, for what I hear here keeps me in great distress; because, if for my sins this business comes to war, I fear that it will do the greatest harm to that country, and even to this it cannot fail to bring great misery. [The people being already groaning under new taxations.] They tell me it is the Duke of Braganza who is at the head of it, and it pains me to the heart, he being such a close connection of yours, letting alone many other reasons besides this. For love of our Lord, since your lordship will naturally be able to influence him greatly, try to effect a settlement (since from what I hear our King is doing all in his power to effect one, and this greatly justifies his cause), and bear in mind the great misfortunes that may come of it; and may your lordship seek the honour of God, as I believe you will, without respect to anything else. May God please to bring it about, as we all here beseech of him; for I assure your lordship that I take it so much to heart that I could wish for death, if God allows it to come to such a pass, so as not to see it. May he guard you with the sanctity that I beseech of him for the good of his Church many years, and bestow on you such a portion of his grace that you may be able to pacify a matter so much to his service. In this country every one says that our King has justice on his side, and that he has left nothing undone to prove it. May the Lord reveal the truth, and we be spared the number of deaths that must take place if it is put in jeopardy; and this at a time when there are so few Christians, that it would be a great calamity were they to shed one another's blood.

A patriotic and single-minded letter. It is perhaps the only occasion on which she enters, however slightly, into the political complications of her country, but when she does, it is to breathe a wider and nobler spirit; to preach a brotherhood *in Christ* (let us doubt it not) that transcends the narrow limits of kinship and nationality. What effect the letter had upon the Cardinal Prince we know not; but it is a fact that at the Cortes of Almerin, where he presided as head of the prelates of Portugal, he preserved, whether from indifference or conviction, a complete neutrality.

The end of July found the intrepid traveller back again in Medina, on her way to Alba de Tormes and Salamanca. She had cut short her visit to Valladolid to prevent any other purchaser snapping up the house, "splendid but dear," that she had fixed her heart on buying for her daughters in Salamanca: but her journey ended in failure, and the only earthly care that troubled her last moments was connected with her Convent of Salamanca.

Oh, my father [she writes to Gracian], how many labours this house costs me; and although all was concluded, the devil has so contrived that we are left without it, and it was the house that suited us best in Salamanca, and a very good bargain for the owner of it. There is no trust to be put in these sons of Adam; for, in spite of his offering it to us himself, and his being a gentleman, and one of the most upright here, as every one says (for all declared with one voice that his word was as good as his bond); not only had he promised, but given his signature before witnesses, himself fetching the notary, and the bargain was concluded. Every one is amazed, except some other gentlemen who persuaded him to it for their own interest or that of their relatives, and had more influence with him than those who would have had him act fairly; and his brother, who negotiated the matter with us with great charity, is deeply distressed. We have commended it to our Lord; it must be that it is for our good. What adds to my distress is that I cannot find a house in Salamanca good for anything. . . . Certainly if these sisters had the house in Seville, they would think they were in heaven. The folly of that prioress [Maria de San José] distresses me deeply; and she has lost greatly in my opinion. I fear me that the Devil has begun in that house, and means to destroy it utterly . . . for I see a slyness [literally, foxiness] in that house which I cannot abide, and that prioress is astuter than her position warrants. And so I fear that, as I told her there, she was never frank with me. I assure you I suffered greatly with her when there. As she has several times written to me in terms of deep repentance, I thought, since she acknowledged it herself, that she had amended. To put into the heads of the poor nuns that the house is such a bad one, is enough of itself to make them all imagine they are ill. I have written terrible letters to her, which have no more effect than if I struck on steel. . . . I believe we shall have to send other sisters there of more weight, who will act in such grave matters as it behoves.

A bitter philippic, perhaps the bitterest and sternest she had ever penned, this written by the old nun in Salamanca, as she compares the position of her sick daughters lodged in a damp and unhealthy house, and now all hope gone of a better, with that of the nuns in Seville where that ingrate, Maria de San José, despising the large and spacious house which had cost her so much suffering and anxiety, was bent, without her knowledge, on leaving it for another—a house, too, with a fairylike patio of alabaster, for all the world like a sweetmeat of white sugar (alcorza), and spacious and delightful views, a matter of great importance to women shut up in such rigorous seclusion! Thus oppressed by anxiety for some of her daughters, and by the ingratitude of others, she was fain to leave matters as they were, and return to Avila. Here she had one of those anomalous attacks of "perlesia" (it may be paralysis—it may mean something widely different). In spite of it she started the day after on a five days' journey to Toledo. For three days the rain fell in torrents, and as it was impossible for the nuns to dry their drenched clothes, it seemed little short of a miracle that Teresa in her delicate state should have received no harm from it. But there is a fund of resistance in the sober Castilian character; regardless of her health (she arrived in Malagon on the 25th of November), she at once plunged with characteristic energy into getting ready for the reception of her nuns the new house, built for them by Da. Luisa de la Cerda on the site Teresa herself had chosen years before in an olive grove near the fortress.

Barely three weeks later, the translation took place on the Feast of the Conception; and for a brief moment the unaccustomed sisters, "looking for all the world like lizards crawling out in summer to take the sun," might imagine themselves a part of the world of men. A moment which to all of them was an era in their lives, the glory of that triumphal procession long one of the most cherished traditions of the convent. But Teresa was confronted with graver cares than these. It was not merely to see the sisters move from one house to another that she had come to Malagon. The rule of a young and inexperienced prioress (for Prioress Brianda was still in Toledo) had played havoc with the discipline and loaded the convent with debt. She was also anxious to test the origin of the dreams and visions of Ana de San Agustin (for if Teresa believed her own visions, she had little faith in those of others), she who was afterwards prioress of Villanueva de la Jara, where her stern and beautifully-modelled face still frowns ascetically from the shadow that envelops it between the grating of the two choirs in the Carmelite Church. A bewitched nun, and a foolish, but well-meaning confessor, added other elements to confusion and anarchy. "The harm a prioress can do is terrible. Things have passed before me which I dare wager do not take place in the most relaxed convents of Spain."

She had come prepared for no half measures, and Jerónima del Espiritu Santo, whom she had brought with her from Salamanca for that purpose, was at once elected prioress. No hint of these scandals was allowed to transpire beyond the convent walls; she dismissed the confessor, but in such a manner as to keep him still a friend. "I have endeavoured to act with all dissimulation; and truly I find him a god-like soul, and that in nothing has there been any malice in him. As he lives at a distance, and has other work, it has been effected without exciting remark; and I got him to preach for us, and sometimes I see him. Everything is now smooth, glory to God!" In less than a month she had reduced the convent to order, without losing a friend or making an enemy!

It is from Malagon she writes that pathetic little fragment of a letter: "Here I find leisure that I have longed for for years, and although I find myself alone, with none to console me, my soul is at rest. And it is because there is no more memory of Teresa de Jesus than if she had never lived. And for this reason I will endeavour to remain here; because sometimes I saw myself in great affliction at hearing so much folly, for there [in Avila?] they have only to say a person is a saint and he must be one without either rhyme or reason. They laugh at me [in Avila] when I tell them to make another, since it costs them nothing more than to say so."

As she had travelled from Avila to Toledo her thoughts had flown back to the occasion when the fatigues of the road were lightened by the presence of Gracian. As Christmas draws near, when it would seem that the flight of time becomes a tangible fact bringing the present nearer to the past in an involuntary recapitulation of our life, she remembers that terrible Christmas night at Avila a year ago, when, bowed by distress, she mourned the captivity of her son and the ruin of her Order,—" God be praised," she writes—and it is to Gracian she sends this, her first Christmas greeting, "who thus betters the seasons. Surely that night was such that I shall never forget it, even though I live many years." And so another Christmas morning rises bright and clear over the bleak sierras, white with powdery snow, which girdle round the little fortress town of Malagon, and fades into night—the night of Oblivion, the end of all men and all things. Be glad and rejoice, ye sisters, as the lights gleaming through the convent corridors reflect a red glow on the snow, and the labourers bar their doors against the wolves driven by hunger from their mountain fastnesses to prowl about the village streets (as was still the case on winter nights towards the middle of this century,—perhaps is so still); sing with clear voices the simple ballads and homely villancicos of the season; for it is one of Teresa's last Christmas-tides on earth, and it is with you she spends it. And as in this dim old convent of Malagon she kneels with her nuns at Matins and Vespers, and their voices now swell, now die away into the vague twilight of the little church, she, this forlorn old woman, so feeble of body and great of spirit, who pulls the strings of the Order, and provides her delegates, her "needy Romanos" (Romans), as she calls them, with money; her brain still pictures a countless series of foundations; immediately Villanueva de la Jara, Madrid, Arenas on the confines of Portugal; and who knows whether, perhaps, she herself may not carry her Order and her nuns to France itself? Maria de San José has been forgiven; for it is not in Teresa's generous nature to nurse resentment; nay, in these January letters, she is sad to think that she should have added to her sick prioress's troubles.

> Your reverence must forgive me, for with those I dearly love I am insufferable, so anxious am I that they should err in nothing. I know not why your reverence should say fray Nicolas [Doria, then in Seville by Salazar's orders, to reinstate Maria de San José as prioress] has been at the bottom of this misunderstanding between us, for you have no

greater champion on earth. He told me the truth, so that, as he foresaw the harm that would come to the convent, I might be undeceived. Oh! my daughter, how little it matters as regards me that you should excuse yourself so much, for I tell you truly that to me it is indifferent whether you pay any heed to me or not, provided I know that you are acting up to your obligations. The mistake, as it seems to me, is that I look on all that concerns you with such anxiety and love, that I think you do not do what you ought if you do not heed me, and that I am only tiring myself out in vain.

Again she refers to Beatriz de Jesus, the author of the troubles at Seville, who is still, it would seem, impenitent :

The Lord often permits a fall, so as to leave the soul more humble. And when repentance is sincere and hearty, it redounds to the greater service of our Lord, as we see in the case of many saints. Therefore, my daughters (you are all daughters of the Virgin, and sisters), endeavour to love one another greatly, and think it never happened. I speak to all of you.

New Year's Day was gladdened by the arrival of a messenger with a letter from the Duchess of Alba. If proof was necessary to show how profoundly a religious creed can distort conscience, and make men perverse and cruel, no two better examples can be found in this grim age than Philip of Spain and Ferdinand of Toledo, the stern Duke of Alba. There is no greater falsity in the world than History, when it goes beyond facts and statistics. When it comes to motives, and would paint the character of the actors in great broad touches, mistrust it as you would the plague. To label this bundle of contradictory impulses and emotions ever in fluidity, undulating, evasive, with one or two adjectives, and so send it down to posterity as the mental category of a man, is the most gigantic of impertinences and lies ; the most intolerable of injustices ! Who would recognise the terrible scourge of Flanders in the old gray-headed man, reading Teresa's *Life*, and meekly listening to the spiritual counsels and comfort of one of her bare-footed friars, professing that nothing could give him greater pleasure, although it cost him many leagues, than to see the Mother Teresa ?

I was almost forgetting about the Duke and Duchess [she writes to Gracian, the bare-footed friar in question]. Know that on New Year's Eve [this with an almost imperceptible tinge of pardonable vanity] the Duchess sent me a messenger with this, and another letter on purpose to know how I was. As to what she says about your paternity having told her that I cared more for the Duke, I would not have it; but I said that as your paternity told me so much of his goodness and spirituality, you must have thought so; but that I loved God only for himself alone, and I saw no reason why I should not love her, and bear her more affection. It was much better expressed, however, than this. I think that book, which she says she made father Medina transcribe, is my great one [her *Life*]. Let me know all you can get to hear about it, and do not forget, for I should be exceeding rejoiced, now that there is no other [copy] but that in the possession of the angels [the Inquisitors], that it should not be lost. To my thinking, the one I have written since [the *Moradas*] is better; at least I had more experience than when I wrote the other. I have already written to the Duke twice.

Intolerance and Religion are twin-born; doubt it not. If the Duke of Alba's name raises a shudder, blame not the man for the cruelty which has made him execrated: blame his age, perhaps blame his own austere virtue, the pursuit of the impossible—of extirpating heresy—the Quixotic dream of him and the master he served, which to my mind casts about them both a certain glow of nobility and greatness. Quixotism—and Fernando de Toledo was a religious Don Quixote, as fruitlessly trying to extirpate his heretics as his prototype tried to overthrow his windmills—always excuses to some extent in a man the excesses to which it leads him. It may be as foolish to compare folly with folly as to contrast beauty with beauty; still, bigotry for bigotry and suffering for suffering, is the intolerance and bigotry on Alba's part so much worse in its results than the modern folly which dooms so many thousands to a long death in life in the thralls of competition and commerce? now and again shooting or hanging a few, in order that the system may not be disturbed? In one case, a sincere desire to save their souls animated the butchers of the Netherlands. In the other, the mainspring is a base greed for money, flimsily veiled over by specious references to Progress and Civilisation. In one case, the epitaph of the victim was the immoral aphorism of the Inquisitor as to the relative importance of soul and body. In the other, the no less wicked maxim of the political economist, that wealth must be produced at all hazards. In the face of so much misery and such lamentable results, who shall award the palm of merit between Alba the Catholic and the countless modern Albas of commerce?

Teresa remained in Malagon till February—as may be seen on the boards hanging in the gateway of the convent, which still perpetuate the memory of her visits. Her task has now been accomplished. "All are now full of contentment, and the prioress such that they have indeed reason to be so.... The house is like a paradise. As to the wasted property, I have been busy planning how they may earn somewhat with spinning and needlework.... Nothing will be wasted in the prioress's hands, who is a great administrator."

No sooner is one duty performed than another imperatively demands the presence of this wonderful old woman.

The hope which now beams radiantly over the fortunes of the Reform once more makes it possible for her to resume those foundations which the events of the last few years have so cruelly interrupted. Three more convents shall yet testify to the unconquerable spirit of this,—the last representative of the virtues and heroism of the old Spain of Ferdinand and Isabella,—this old woman of sixty-five, who still goes forth to found, as Ferdinand of Toledo to fight at seventy, and shall cast their lustre over the last three years of her life.

The origin of the foundation of Villanueva de la Jara is as follows :—

Three maidens, attracted by the fame of the austere Catalina de Cardona, had joined her in the Desert of La Roda ; but soon discouraged by the portentous strictness of a life and rule to which they could not school their weaker natures, they returned home to Villanueva, and, together with four or five others, constituted themselves into a pious community. Assuming the scapulary of Our Lady of Carmel, they took possession of the hermitage of Santa Ana and a small house adjoining. The pious priest, the founder of the hermitage (if we may believe the not very trustworthy accounts of the chronicler, too desirous of casting on his Order such fugitive glimpses of supernatural lustre as he can), had formerly been a Carmelite friar, and on his deathbed left his property for the purpose of raising a monastery close to it. "Either through carelessness or care," drily remarks the chronicler, "the property had disappeared, and the house and a little land was all that remained." But the dream, the unsatisfied aspiration of these worthy women's lives was to enrol themselves in one of the regular Orders; and four years before, during Teresa's residence in Toledo after the conclusion of her Sevilian foundation, a priest arrived with letters from the corporation of Villanueva, together with one from the curate, the learned and virtuous Doctor Agustin Ervias, earnestly beseeching her to accede to their desires. Her first impulse was to refuse.

> On no account did it seem advisable to me to admit it, for these reasons: first, on account of their number, and the difficulty, as it seemed to me, of getting those accustomed to their own mode of life to reconcile themselves to ours; secondly, because they had almost nothing to maintain themselves with, and if they were to live on alms, little enough aid could be expected from a town of little more than a thousand inhabitants, and, although the corporation volunteered to maintain them, it did not seem to me assured; thirdly, they had no house; fourthly, their distance from our monasteries; and, although their virtues were described to me, as I had not seen the maidens, I had no means of knowing whether they were fit for our monasteries or not; and so I decided to reject it entirely.

The end of it, however, after consultation with her confessor Velazquez, who saw a deeper purpose than appeared on the surface in the union of so many hearts together in the same aspiration, was that, without definitely accepting it, neither did she wholly reject it. In any case the storms and tempests which then threatened the very existence of the Discalced Carmelites were scarcely a season for projecting further foundations. Now, however, it was different; and scarcely had she arrived in Malagon when the matter was again earnestly pressed upon her, this time by Fray Antonio de Jesus, who, after the disastrous conclusion of the Chapter of Almodóvar, had been exiled to the Desert of La Roda, about three leagues from Villanueva, where he and the prior, Fray Gabriel de la Asuncion, "a discreet person and a servant of God," often went to preach. A warm friendship sprang up between the two friars and the Doctor Ervias, who made them acquainted with the pious sisterhood, "and being favourably impressed with their virtues, and persuaded by the town and the doctor, they took up the matter as if it had been their own," and at once set to work to besiege Teresa with urgent letters. Fray Gabriel de Asuncion, as he passed through Toledo on his way back from the Observant Chapter of Malagon, where, unheard-of triumph! he, a Descalzo, had just been elected fourth Definitor, finding Teresa gone, followed her to Malagon, where he again pleaded the cause of the Beatas of Villanueva, with right good-will, and promised her, in the name of the good Dr. Ervias, directly the foundation should be an accomplished fact, 300 ducats out of the revenues of his benefice.

"This," writes the shrewd saint, "filled me with uncertainty, it seeming to me that, once it was founded, he (Dr. Ervias) might not be so eager, for, with the little they had, they had enough to live upon; and so I adduced many reasons, and to my thinking very sufficient ones, to the father prior to convince him of the inexpediency of making the foundation; and I said that he and Father Fray Antonio had better look well to it, for I left it on their conscience, what I said to them being in my opinion more than enough to settle the matter in the negative." Moreover, fearing lest her two obstinate friars might, behind her back, wheedle Salazar out of the license, she at once wrote to him not to grant it.

A month and a half passed, perhaps more, and I already thought I had heard the last of it, when comes a messenger with letters from the corporation and Dr. Ervias, in which they bound themselves to provide whatever was needful, accompanied with earnest letters from these two reverend fathers. My fear was, that if I admitted so many sisters together, they were sure, as often happens, to form a faction against the rest, and also the insecurity of the arrangements for their maintenance—for what was offered did not decide me—so that I find myself in sore perplexity. One day, after communicating, as I was commending it to God . . . his Majesty reproved me strongly: With what treasures had that been effected which had been done until now! and that I should not hesitate to accept this house, which would be to his great service, and for the benefit of souls.

Words which to this day are still preserved over the choir of the convent church of Villanueva de la Jara: words which have consecrated that spot as sacred ground for more than three centuries, and are remembered when perchance her heroic exhortations to the strong, tender virtues of her own character, which cast such a lustre over the lives of these first poor primitive sisters, have faded away, and left a languorous atmosphere of somnolent decay, hopelessness, and death. What matters it if the voice heard by Teresa de Jesus was Divine, or elaborated in the depths of her own consciousness —whether it came from above or within,—so long as it was to her the rigid, inflexible voice of Duty? It was in the way that she performed that duty—nobly, fearlessly, uprightly—I had almost said, chivalrously (so far as the term may be applied to a woman, it may be applied to her)—that she teaches us her lesson. There is now neither indecision nor hesitation. She writes for and obtains Salazar's license; orders a solemn procession, in which she leaves it to God to point out the nuns who are to accompany her ("for, oh! my father," she had written to Gracian a month before, "and what anxiety it gives me to find neither a prioress nor nuns to satisfy me"). The lot fell upon Ana de San Agustin and Elvira de San Angelo.

On the 12th of February, the prior of La Roda and Fray Antonio de Jesus, whose miserable jealousy of Gracian and disappointed itch for pre-eminence all melt away in his tender love for her whom they all regarded as their Mother, came to fetch them with a cart and a coach. "The worthy Fray Antonio cannot deny the love he bears me, since, old age and all, he comes so far: he is well and fat—it seems to me as if this year we grew fat on suffering."

On the day following they started. At Toledo the company was increased by two nuns, one of whom she had fixed upon for prioress. She had left Malagon "very old and wearied," as she had written to her prioress of Seville; but no sooner had she started than it seemed as if she took a new lease of life and strength; she had never before, she said, felt so strong or well.

Her journey was one continued triumph. It was as if she anticipated in life the glorious apotheosis which awaited her after death. If honour and fame are to be measured by the applause of men—and by most men, such are the limitations of humanity, they are so measured, except by the noblest minds—then did Teresa de Jesus achieve them during this journey. The Catholic religion has this in it of elevating above its cold and vapid Protestant rivals, that it has always idealised and personified Virtue, and has stirred the crowd to pæans of victory for other heroes than kings and warriors and statesmen—the heroes of Virtue. I doubt, indeed, whether Philip of Spain himself, or his most famous generals, would have been accorded the reception that was now awarded to Teresa de Jesus. From every little town and village the people flocked to catch a glimpse of the aged saint; in Villarobledo it was necessary to post two alguaciles before the door of the house where she was eating; and even then crowds swarmed up the walls in their eagerness to get a peep at the great foundress within; nay, it was necessary to throw some of the most adventurous into prison, to enable her to leave the town. One man, a rich labourer, hearing that she was approaching, in right patriarchal fashion decked his house, made ready a rustic feast, and sent out to gather in his flocks and herds from the neighbouring hamlets, so that they with him and his family might share in the saint's blessing. The saint blessed him indeed, but refused to alight or break her journey, whereupon he brought his whole household out into the road, so that they might all speak with her, and receive her benediction. It was in vain that they set out three hours before daybreak (and that in La Mancha, in winter) to avoid the enthusiastic multitude. Her fame travelled faster than the creaking carts, and moved the same simultaneous impulse of curiosity, veneration, and awe: the people still poured out to greet them. There was also the miracle; at least the driver (a Spanish driver) declared that it was nothing less. For, in spite of her coach (in reality a very sorry cart—the word "coach" in Spanish being applicable to anything slung on wheels) meeting with an accident in the dark, it still managed to accomplish another three leagues, which, when it came to be examined by daylight, seemed impossible. But her greatest triumph is still to come; for her friars—no matter on what pretext, we may be sure it had all been lovingly and carefully planned beforehand—insist on her breaking her journey at their Desert of La Roda, about three leagues from Villanueva, and nearly half-way between it and the town of La Roda, and "it was but right I should obey these friars with whom we travelled, in everything." As they emerged from the path frayed by the bare feet of the monks she had herself conjured into existence, they sallied forth to receive her in procession, and after receiving her blessing on their bended knees, bore her to the church, intoning the Te Deum—ever chanted on great national festivals and rejoicings; on the visits and births of kings—as she crossed the threshold.

The scene and its surroundings affected her deeply. Her friars, with their bare feet and poor "sayal" capes, transport her to the "flowery time" of the solitaries of the desert. It seemed to her that they were but other blossoms, white and fragrant, mingling their perfume with that of the sweet strong-scented aromatic herbs and flowers which peopled this "savoury solitude." "Truly the inward joy I felt was such, that I would have accounted a longer journey well employed . . . although I grieved deeply that the saint through whom the Lord founded this house was now dead, for I did not deserve to see her, although I desired it much."

Strangest of all those strange histories of beatas, or holy women, who flit across the religious chronicles of this age, is that of Catalina Cardona, who had cast round the flowery desert of La Roda the halo of her sufferings and her sanctity, investing it for Teresa with so potent and inscrutable an attraction, that Teresa has sketched her life history in the *Foundations*.

In 1557, when monks and nuns swarmed, and fresh convents and monasteries were being founded every day, a Neapolitan lady had accompanied her relative, the Princess of Salerno, to Valladolid, then the court of Spain. The gay and sprightly Princess, surrounded by her train of Neapolitan courtiers, was virtually a political prisoner; for although, on the discovery of his intrigues with France, the Prince had escaped just in time to save his neck, his vast Neapolitan estates were confiscated to the crown. The continuance in Naples of a woman possessed of rare beauty and a sweet and persuasive tongue, and, what was more dangerous, a quick and lively intellect,—who, on the plea that she had not been privy to the plot, never ceased to reclaim her own dowry and personal possessions,—was not likely to commend itself to the prudent mind of Philip, and he straightway despatched from Flanders a peremptory mandate, ordering her instantly to proceed to Spain.

Concealing her tremors and dismay under an appearance of cheerful alacrity, the Princess determined to obey. At this critical moment of her life, turning aside from the splendid cortège she had gathered round her, she sought for consolation and support from an elderly relative of her own, the most of whose life had been spent in the retirement of a Capuchin convent. This was Catalina de Cardona, the descendant of an illustrious house,—the royal blood of Aragon ran in her veins,—around whose early history the religious chroniclers have woven a tender and superstitious legend. They tell how, when but a child of eight, she is said to have martyred her tender limbs with untold penances, to rescue her father, the fierce swashbuckler captain who had so often led the Emperor's troops to victory, from the pains of Purgatory; how for five years the good nuns laboured to teach her to read, but all in vain, until she was miraculously enlightened by the Holy Ghost; how she made a vow of perpetual virginity, which Heaven itself aided her to keep, for, unable to resist the importunities of her relatives, she was betrothed to a grandee of Naples, who died suddenly on the very eve of his marriage. It was then that the bride of thirteen entered a Capuchin convent, where, without taking the vows, she gave herself up to the life that was most congenial to her.

No better person for the demure and sombre court of Philip II. than this elderly, plain-featured woman, who might to a certain extent sanctify the anything but demure household of the Princess of Salerno,—the merry, beautiful, fascinating Italian, whose youth was to consume away in a bootless suit, and to wither under the frigid blight of Philip's influence.

For a time all went on merrily as a marriage bell in the dark Castilian capital. The Princess's palace was a second court, its grandeur and stateliness surpassed only by the King's, thronged with all the grandees in Castille—princes and ambassadors accounting it an honour to bow the knee before its brilliant mistress. Nevertheless, the Princess's demeanour was scrupulously reserved, and she never left its walls unless accompanied by her grave and elderly cousin, Catalina. Amongst the visitors who thronged her palace was one destined to attain a sad and fearful celebrity, in whose society the Princess took extraordinary pleasure ; and one can well believe the charm that the witty, acute Doctor Agustin Cazalla, with his latitudinarian views and wide experience of men and manners, exercised on the exiled Italian, stifled by the sombre gravity of the Spanish court, and wearied of the dreary and stately ceremony and meaningless grandiloquence of the self-contained Castilians who composed it. But from the first the graver Catalina misdoubted her of the damnable heresy concealed under the Doctor's flowery phrases. Whenever he came, it is noted that, as if to guard her cousin from the fatal contamination of his evil influence, she took her stand by her side, and boldly contradicted his doctrines.

And yet perhaps it was only a question of temperament that separated these two people—the future hermit and the heretic doctor. Catalina had a strain of Aragonese blood, and, strangely enough, nothing is more difficult to eradicate —mix it, strain it, as you will—than even the most distant tinge of Spanish nationality. Uncompromising and severe, accounting the world a delusion, and the body an instrument whereby Satan leads us to perdition, the strange pessimism of her race, which an Italian education had left unmodified, found in her a stern and eloquent exponent. The Kingdom of Heaven must be conquered by blood. Cazalla, of a happier, more buoyant disposition, undervalued the austerities which have as their final result the complete negation of life.

After one of his sermons—the last he was ever to deliver—Catalina told him, it is said, that she had seen flames of fire issuing from his mouth, which smelt pestilently of brimstone.

"Oh, lady," replied the Doctor in Italian, after in vain endeavouring to persuade her that what she had seen was the fevered vision of her own imagination, "speak not such words again!"

But the words had told home, and in spite of the sharp

reproof the Princess gave her cousin for her discourtesy, the discomfited man rose from his chair and left the palace.

Nevertheless Catalina was filled with the same stern and ardent rancour which slumbered in the stern bosoms of the Inquisitors,—men whose moral character, let it not be forgotten, silenced by its rigid perfection the calumnies of their most prejudiced enemies. In her wrath against the heretic, she prophesied that he should preach no more.

On the Saturday following, the church was crowded with courtiers and ladies to hear Cazalla's sermon. The Princess and her attendants were amongst the audience. Just before the Benediction, at the moment when he should have ascended the pulpit, arrived a messenger from the Inquisition, to announce that Cazalla was a prisoner. The Holy Office had done its work stealthily and well!

A year later, the square of Valladolid witnessed one of those fierce and gloomy scenes which exercised so horrible and unholy a fascination on the popular imagination, and ate so deeply into the national character, that in 1762, when it was proposed to do away with the Inquisition, the only reply that could be forced from the king of Bourbon race who expulsed the Jesuits was: "The Spaniards want it, and it does me no harm" (Los Españoles la quieren, y á mí no me estorba). Cazalla, his brother and his sister, after expiating the charge of heresy on the gibbet, were then consigned to the flames, together with the exhumed bones of their mother, who had been mercifully released by Death whilst she was still a prisoner in the Inquisition dungeons.

Already the poor Princess of Salerno was doomed. Her splendour, her beauty, her popularity had drawn to her side warm and eloquent partisans. A perilous litigant this, whose court rivalled the King's. She was dangerous, and must be got rid of. Philip, utterly devoid of the chivalrous feeling or the magnanimity which had characterised his great father, decreed the ruin of the unfortunate woman who had thrown herself on his protection and generosity. She was bidden coldly to leave the court, and retire to Toledo. Mercifully the great Releaser was at hand, and Death stepped in before, like the Princess of Eboli, she found herself a close prisoner behind the gratings of some Castilian fortress. "The tongue of the King," moralises the chronicler, "is penetrating; strong is the breath of his words for those who depend on them, and place their happiness in his discomfiture."

The King, glad at heart, made a hollow pretence of the grief he did not feel. In the general disbanding of the Princess's household, a home was found for the austere Catalina (whose virtues had not failed to reach the monarch's ears) in the household of the Princes of Eboli, and she thus became an inmate of the royal palace, where she had charge of their jewels and wardrobes, and distributed the Prince's alms amongst the necessitous. It is noteworthy as throwing a side-light on the Princess's character, "more spendthrift than generous," notes the chronicler, that the Prince warned his almoner beforehand not to let his liberality come to the knowledge of his wife.

As she grew in years, Catalina's life became still more rigorous. Her fare was vegetables seethed in water; she fasted four days a week; she slept on a straw pallet, and wore unbleached sackcloth next the skin; she scourged herself with pointed hooks. Her body was lacerated with the sharp points of the cilicium, and marked by the weight of heavy chains.

The young Princes, Don Carlos and Don Juan of Austria, all heedless of the gloomy future, conceived a strong attachment for the ill-favoured, homely, solitary woman, to whom they gave the name of Mother. During her absence one day after lunch, the royal scapegraces broke into a chest which contained the sweetmeats. She came upon the culprits amidst a rout of broken jars and syrups spilt upon the floor. "My princes," she said, "this seems to me an omen that some day you will upset the world in defence of the Faith. But I marvel that minds so generous should be employed in such trifles, and that, being able to command, you humiliate yourselves to mischief. A bad example you set the servants to be more daring. It is meet that no one else shall see what you have done, and that your highnesses, with a little more modesty, set to work to put this to rights." When it came to Philip's ears (as what did not?), the grim monarch was delighted with the rugged sincerity with which she had dared to rebuke the Infante of Spain. Don Juan never forgot the woman whom he addressed as Mother; and to her the gallant young hero of Lepanto sent some of his precious spoils: nay, indeed, his leniency to, and chivalrous treatment of, his fallen foe was mainly due, it is said, to her influence and intercession.

But her intercourse with palaces had served to increase, rather than to lessen, Catalina's abhorrence for the world. She was sick of the lies, and the feigning, and the hypocrisy. She fancied she saw the lips of Christ open, and bid her leave the palace, and hie her to a cave, so that she might more freely give herself to prayer and penance.

Encouraged by a Franciscan friar, she accompanied her patrons to Estremera, where a neighbouring priest, to whom she confided her purpose, supplied her with a hermit's habit and hood. Before she started, she left a letter behind her for Ruy Gomez, and another addressed to Don Juan of Austria. It was not yet dawn when, her scanty arrangements concluded, she prepared to leave the house. The doors were barred, but the Christ she wore round her neck rose up, it is said, into the air, and pointing to a low window, bade her follow him. Whereupon, she found herself, she knew not how, standing in the street outside. The priests were waiting for her in the appointed spot, where, after cutting off her hair, she donned the hermit's habit. Well might her great contemporary, lost in amazement, exclaim, " How divinely intoxicated must this Holy soul have been, enraptured [by the thought] that none should hinder her in her enjoyment of her Spouse, and how determined to have nothing more to do with the world, since she thus fled from all its contents!"

So the hermit and her two companions trudged off towards Cuenca. A quarter of a league before they came to La Roda, in the district of Vala de Rey, the hermit said, as she stopped short at the bottom of a sandy hillside: " Here God wills me to take up my abode; let us go no farther."

Catalina, homely of feature but heroic of soul, was forty-three when, leaving behind her the cumbersome ceremonial of the court of Spain, she made her way on foot towards the lonely desert of La Roda, where she buried her life. In that flowery solitude on the banks of the river San Lucar, amidst the pines which murmur mysteriously against the sunset, and all the sweet, strong-scented, aromatic herbs and flowers, so peculiar to the sandy uplands of Spain, you may still see the cave where she hid her existence from the world.

For three years, to the whispered awe and amazement of rustics and shepherds, a hermit, his face shrouded by his hood, who disappeared as mysteriously as he came, eluding all their efforts to track him to his dwelling, knelt at his devotions in the convent church of Fuen Santa. Who he was, or whence he came, none knew, until one day a wandering shepherd discovered him gathering roots and herbs, and followed his trail in the grass to a cave, or rather burrow, hidden amongst the cistus and brushwood of the hillside.

We may not take for granted the chronicler's hyperbolical account of her privations and her sufferings: how she browsed on the herbs and grass which grew around the mouth of her cave, like some beast of the field; how the cruel strokes of scourgings woke the midnight silence; how the flowers hung their heads, oppressed with the weight of the drops of blood which flowed from the hermit's heart; how demons exhausted on her all their malignity, and the angels all their love; how the devil in the shape of a black dog, with matted hair and eyes of fire, sent the kneeling figure rolling amongst the spikes of rosemary; how, as she sank down fainting and exhausted with a fast of forty days, a passing muleteer,—an angel, doubtless, says the chronicler —(there is a strange practicality about a Spanish angel), succoured her distress, her hunger being oftentimes relieved by the like mysterious means. This strange old-world figure, who became at last a part of the universal life of Nature around her,—who, ceasing indeed to move in the world of men, regained instead that supremacy over, and mysterious sympathy with, that other world, which man for his crimes—perhaps also the crime of civilisation (for Indians have it), has lost, needs no such embellishments to enhance its interest. The inhabitants of the sandy hillocks and shadowy pines, seeing a thing as harmless and gentle as themselves, pursued their gambols fearlessly at her feet. The rabbits and partridges saluted her presence with marks of joy, running around her in glad and tumultuous pleasure. She even settled their innocent quarrels, and in the morning lovingly dismissed the vipers and poisonous insects which, attracted to her cell by the heat of a human body, never offered harm to one whom they regarded as their companion. Even the merry insect world, which peopled flower and herb, and filled the sunlight with a thousand strange and confused murmurs; the turtle-dove and the fox, learned to distinguish her presence, and owned her sway. Who shall tell the mysteries of conscience that have been fathomed on this narrow spot of ground; the strange battles fought by the Flesh and the Devil for a tortured soul, through the long winter nights when the wolves and wild boars howled and grunted around her dwelling? Or when winter had given place to summer, and Nature lay hushed in solemn silence under the glimmering stars, who shall tell the mystical harmonies which swept over her soul, as she watched alone, encircled by the solemn grandeur of the night?

At last it got to be whispered about that the cowled solitary was a woman. Some letters written by Don Juan of Austria to her he addressed as mother, found in her cave one day when she was absent, by certain priests, anxious to solve the mystery, betokened that she was a personage of birth and consequence. Her fame spread, not only as a saint, but as one of highest rank. Then the keen eyes of a friar belonging to the neighbouring Convent of Fuen Santa, who went to visit her in her cave, fell on a book of Hours, and as he turned over the leaves, he noted at the end of the book an inscription which the hermit had probably long ago forgotten, stating that it had been a gift from the Princess of Eboli.

Now that her secret was discovered, so great the crowds that flocked to the "good woman" of La Roda, some to cure their infirmities by the magic touch of her hermit's habit, others from curiosity, or to beseech her blessing (amongst them grandees of Spain), that, to prevent them tearing her to pieces in their honest and frenzied devotion, it became necessary to surround her with a guard of armed men.

But it had become the dream of her life to found a convent. Christ himself had held out to her as she prayed in her cave a Carmelite habit, and, on stretching out her hands to take it, she was bathed in a stream of glory; and not he only, but the prophet Elijah, girt about with a hairy girdle. Where, however, shall she find these barefooted friars, with the dark habit, short white cape, and shepherd's crook, of her visions? To every one she addressed the same anxious question, until at length from a labourer on his way home from the fair at Pastrana she heard that there, in some caves on a hillside, lived men clothed even as she described. She at once despatched a letter to her old friend and patron, the powerful and amiable Ruy Gomez, who, pale and worn-out, sought in Pastrana a momentary surcease from the cares and turmoil of the court.

Mariano was sent to fetch her. At the entrance to the town, the dusty friar and hermit were met by the Prince and Princess of Eboli, the Duke of Gandia, and a splendid retinue on horseback. After solemnly receiving the Discalced habit in the Monastery Church of Pastrana, at the request of the Princess of Portugal, she set off for court. Philip sent for her to the Escorial. Although years of unbroken solitude in the desert had set their stamp upon the woman who had once been familiar with the customs of a court, and her appearance was strange and uncouth (she had forgotten, says the hyperbolical chronicler, all the forms of courtesy, and the names of the commonest things), it was noticed that her face, which had never been beautiful, was now transformed by an expression so divine and sweet as to attract all eyes. The Catholic monarch, whom ambassadors and grandees of Spain never addressed but on their bended knees, condescended to lay aside his rank, to discourse familiarly with the simple old woman in the friar's habit, who styled him "my son," and spoke to him in the homely second person.

When she attempted to excuse herself to the Princess for her lack of courtly breeding, the latter embraced her tenderly, beseeching her to make it up in love, and to treat her like one of the countrywomen amongst whom she lived. Would that bigotry and superstition had never any worse results than these!

Don John of Austria, but recently appointed Captain of the Catholic League, promised to transform her hermit's cave into a shrine as precious and renowned as that of Guadalupe; a promise which was never fulfilled.

The Pope's Legate, highly scandalised at a Discalced friar being seen driving through the streets of Madrid with ladies, and scattering blessings out of the coach, although informed by Mariano of her sex, sent for her to his presence. When she gave him her benediction, the Nuncio completely lost his temper. "What! you bring her to me with a hood?" he said to Mariano, adding, as he turned to the hermit, "And by what spirit is it, good woman, that you go about showering blessings broadcast like a bishop?" He ended, however, by beseeching her prayers for the success of the League; and it is said that from her cell in La Roda she watched the progress, and was the first to declare the issue, of the combat which held the whole Christian world in suspense, and made Pope Pius V. groan as he awaited the dubious result. Her return journey to La Roda was a triumphal progress. A cart was laden with the silver vessels, jewels, and chasubles that had been given her as presents. At Alcalá she lodged in the palace of the Marquesa de Cañete; at Guadalajara in the Duke del Infantado's. From Pastrana to La Roda a court alguacil, sent by Ruy Gomez, restrained a crowd so great as to impede their progress.

In April of 1572 a monastery of Discalced Carmelite friars rose upon the spot, the scene of her solitary combats and sufferings, and at her entreaty the church was built over the cave where she had spent eight years of her life. Five years later, in 1577, and a year before Teresa's visit, surrounded by the weeping friars, who besought the dying woman to give them a last blessing, "speaking things of God most moving and devout," Catalina Cardona "entered into her native land," and was buried in the self-same spot where she had lived.

Great is the devotion borne to this monastery because of her, and it seems as if the whole neighbourhood was still full of her presence, especially when one looks upon that solitude and cave where she lived before she resolved to make the monastery. . . . I was profoundly consoled whilst I was there, and still am so, although I was sorely humbled; since I saw that she who had there gone through so harsh a penance was a woman like myself, and more delicately reared, by reason of her station. . . . The desire of imitating her (if I might) was my only comfort, but not so much, for my whole life has slipped away in desires and works I have not done. . . .

And the dead saint, of whose glorified body she had a vision, as she communicated in the church, spoke words of encouragement to the living saint, still struggling, "that I should not get wearied, but endeavour to go forward with these foundations. So by this you see," says the traveller, who was herself so rapidly drawing to her journey's close, and had seen the successful ending of many another toilsome one, "how, her labours being now ended, she enjoys endless glory. For love of our Lord, let us take courage and follow this our sister; and abhorring ourselves, as she did, we shall end our journey; since it is over in so short a time, and everything has an end."

To-day, far away, just on the borders of La Mancha, is a little village, forgotten of men, and baked by the sun. It is La Roda. About three leagues farther on, another little town, buried amongst olive groves—a little town where a population of labourers preserve intact the customs, manners, and dress of their forefathers,—still bears the name of Villanueva de la Jara. Half-way between the two the road passes through a sandy, monotonous tract, sparsely covered with stunted pines. Brilliant and glaring at noonday, when the sun is high in the heavens, and the whole world basks under his fierce light; strangely bleak and impressive in the cold blue light of sunset. A landscape which stirs the imagination, with its tumbled red sand hillocks cut out against the sky in fantastic jags and cusps,—such a landscape as I have seen reflected in the picture of some old Perugian painter, with St. Jerome kneeling in the foreground absorbed in prayer, his lion at his feet. If, turning aside from the road—a track in Teresa's time—you painfully make your way between the sandhills and pines, you come to a sort of tableland. On one side of it, down in the hollow beneath, gliding gently along past its poplar-lined banks, is the broad stream of the San Lucar. On the other a monotonous stretch of plain, broken by weird clumps of pines—now black against the sunset sky—melts into a faraway horizon. On the face of the broken slope above the river, almost hidden in the brambles and thyme, is the entrance to a cave roughly closed in.

"What's this?" I ask my guide, a rough shepherd, who was born close by, and ought to know. "No se sabe" (no one knows), is his apathetic answer. "It is said thereabouts"—with a sweep of the hand that embraces the limitless horizon—"that a woman once lived here in men's clothes. But no one knows, and they say so many things. A few years ago some came to see it—they came of the same family, so they said—and closed up the cave. Up on the top there, by that heap of stones, you see it? is a well, where they say there was once a convent,—but no one knows, and they say so many things."

And so has the very memory of that strange history, this legend of this sixteenth-century Thebaid, completely faded away, and with it the ideas which animated that old, old world, with all its sin, its shame, its chivalrous nobleness, its wondrous virtues, its Inquisition, and its saints, have faded away also. Are the ideas of the new better? Are we, who are still engaged in making history? And as the tall pines sway gently against the evening sky, although the breeze brings back no echo of a convent bell, and the cistus and the rosemary bloom as sweetly at my feet as they once did at those of Catalina Cardona's, and the solitude is full of a vague and mysterious beauty, I wonder whether Nature herself may not keep imperishable records—records hidden to man's feeble and limited perceptions—of the atom of Dust which, calling itself Man, forms part of her for so brief a moment, and is again received by her into her generous bosom, to be nursed into fresh vitalities.

On the morning of that first Sunday in Lent of 1580, an unwonted stir took the place of the apathetic calm and sleepy indifference which was the everyday atmosphere of Villanueva de la Jara—as it is of all Spanish towns, great or small. From earliest dawn keen eyes in the bell-tower scan the white parched track between the olive trees. Presently a little cloud moves on the horizon; the bells swing round in tumultuous volleys of merry and agitated sound which greet the travellers from afar. The whole population of the town streams out into the road—priest, corporation, the "most principal" inhabitants await the coming of Teresa de Jesus, who is to arrive that day. Troops of children, swifter-footed than their elders, have already sped on to meet her, and, falling on their knees beside her cart, their hoods thrown back and young heads bared to the sunlight, fill the air with their acclamations: strangely like another scene, when other children strewed the city of a Syrian plain with palm branches before one Jesus, the son of David, riding on an ass!

The procession swells at every step. People kneel in the road before the mules; swarthy hands steal out from under ragged cloaks to touch the awning, and invoke Teresa's blessing. Muleteers and dusty friars can scarce force a passage through the eager, brown-faced throng which blocks the streets. As she steps over the threshold of the church, the strident notes of the great organ burst forth in triumphant and clamorous sound, and with one accord the people without and within intone the Te Deum Laudamus. A hush of expectation, a momentary lull, falls on the assembled multitude. Then out of the shadow of the open doorway the priests sweep forth, holding aloft the Host on silver "andas." Amidst shouts of joy and muttered benedictions, Our Lady, robed in pearl-spangled velvet, borne shoulder-high, smiles down in the radiant sunlight on the upturned faces of her worshippers. The great cross is raised, the heavy banners are unfurled (for all the riches stored in the dim recesses of the sacristy are displayed to-day), and with one accord the glad procession sweeps through the rush-strewn streets to the Hermitage of Santa Ana. Close behind the Host, under its very shadow, their habits contrasting strangely with the silver and gold-embroidered chasubles and copes of the clergy, follows a little knot of nuns, the black veils which conceal their faces reaching to their feet. They cluster round the bent figure of an old woman, leaning on a staff, towards whom every eye turns in an indefinable commingling of curiosity, veneration, and love.

Before the improvised altars on the way, they halt to chant the praises of the Order of Our Lady of Mount Carmel; and so halting, so singing, the procession at last comes to a stop before the little hermitage. The "servants of God" who waited for their coming at an inner door received Teresa and her nuns with tears of joy.

A day indeed long to be remembered in Villanueva, whose rural population depends for subsistence on the plenty of the seasons. For on that day rain long withheld fell abundantly on its parched and sultry fields—surely a miracle, and as surely worked by the beneficent influence of Teresa de Jesus. And in proof of their gratitude, at the following harvest—an abundant one—the labourers gave a solid donation to the new convent of almost a hundred fanegas of wheat.

Does the dust lie on Teresa's tomb too thick, is our fancy so clogged with it, that we cannot even for a moment, annulling the years and the centuries, stand invisible at the corner of one of those old-world streets of Villanueva de la Jara, flushed with the bright, cold February sun; and watch that memorable procession as it slowly files past us into space and oblivion, and be stirred with its joy and solemnity, its hushed pauses, the glad chant of many voices? And so they pass:—robust, brown-faced Manchegan peasants, in a costume, some relics of which their descendants still retain to-day; hidalgoes and people of consequence in velvet doublet, short cloak, plumed bonnet, and sword (growing a little rusty for want of use); phantoms they, and phantoms we, and the street is empty and silent, except for a dog hunting for garbage in the gutter.

Short as was Teresa's sojourn in Sta. Ana, it left its special legend; and the nuns still tell how, whilst the hermitage was being transformed into a convent, a workman let the wheel he was making for the well slip from his fingers and fall upon her with such force as to fell her to the ground; and she must assuredly have been killed had not St. Joseph (on whose eve it happened) miraculously saved her life.

Five days after her arrival she gave the habits to her new daughters, and apportioned the various conventual offices.

But time pressed ; her work of organisation concluded, her presence was no longer needed. The evening before she again set forth to retraverse the twenty-eight leagues between Villanueva and Malagon, she called together the daughters she had brought with her, and whom she was now to leave behind, exiles and friendless in a strange place, whose life thenceforth would probably be a constant battle against starvation. She gravely and lovingly addressed them, painted the future that awaited them, and its manifold difficulties. Still the Lord had promised her that he would not fail them if they faithfully fulfilled their obligations. If any there were who faltered at the prospect, there was still time, and she begged them even at this last moment to speak out frankly, and she would bear them away with her on the morrow. But they were all brave and valiant souls, these poor, simple, conscientious women, and of the seven none accepted the offer dictated by her tender thoughtfulness.

A last embrace, and before the sun rose over the olive groves of Villanueva, the aged saint had left the town behind her in the chill gray dawn. When she had crossed the threshold, and her voice still lingered in her daughters' ears, a great River rolled between them. For they had seen her face, and listened to her tender farewells for the last time on this side the grave !

CHAPTER XXIV

ANTES QUEBRAR QUE DOBLAR

> "Ca non es la perfeccion
> Mucho fablar :
> Mas obrando, denegar
> Luengo sermon."
>   EL MARQUES DE SANTILLANA.

THE day before Palm Sunday Teresa arrived in Toledo after a thirty leagues' journey from Villanueva de la Jara, which had taken several days to perform. Although she bore the fatigues of the journey so well that she writes to Maria de San José that "for years she had never enjoyed such health," her strength had been sorely tried, and a few days later, on Holy Thursday, she was struggling with one of the sharpest attacks of illness ("of perlesia and the heart") she had ever had in her life.

The brave old woman did not flinch. Accustomed to constant infirmity, she was "up and about whenever able." But she thought she had looked death very closely in the face; and the fear of it that had once haunted her is, as she tells Gracian, now gone; it had mattered as little to her to die as to live. Her weakness, and the secret hope she cherished of being able at last to obtain the desired license for the foundation at Madrid, detained her in Toledo until close on the second week of June. She sought and obtained an interview with the Archbishop himself, when, accompanied by Gracian, she proffered her request in person. He received her kindly, even seemed to favour the project ; but the license was not conceded. His general sympathy was doubtless with the Descalzos, but he bitterly resented his niece's intention of entering the Order at Medina, and attributed it to Teresa's counsels and persuasion. At all events, she now heard for the first time of the fate of the book of her *Life*. Said the grave Archbishop: "Great is the pleasure I receive in knowing you. Thank God, from whom comes all good, and know that a book of yours was presented to the Inquisition, perhaps not altogether with a good motive; but I, together with other very learned men, have read it through; and not only has it not done you harm, but for its sake look on me from to-day henceforward as your chaplain; and be sure that, in all I can do for the Order, right willingly do I offer to help you in everything that may be required." I know not how far these few insignificant words of admiration and empty Castilian offers of service, although spoken by the Grand Inquisitor of Spain himself (however much they might confirm its orthodoxy), consoled Teresa for the years of dreary delay and torture this book, which had been to her "a most great torment and cross," had cost her, or how far they compensated for the refusal of the only thing she desired. If the denouncer was, as has been asserted, the Princess of Eboli (although there is not a tittle of evidence to prove it), Teresa was amply avenged, for she who had once ruled supreme amidst the brilliancy of a court was now close prisoner in her fortress tower of Pastrana, and it was with the utmost difficulty that permission was accorded to Gracian to administer to her such spiritual consolation as he could. There was little pity in the old nun's heart for her fallen enemy: "Fray Hernando del Castillo is here. Report goes that the Princess of Eboli was in her house at Madrid; now they say she is in Pastrana. I cannot say which is true: but either the one or the other is far too good for her."

In spite, however, of the original of her *Life* (thus eulogised by Quiroga) being in the hands of the Inquisitors, who had not yet pronounced a verdict, it was not entirely withdrawn from circulation. A special license had been granted to the Duchess of Alba to retain the copy transcribed for her by that grumpy old Dominican catedratico of Salamanca, Fray Bartolomé de Medina, whose sour dislike Teresa had so deftly transformed into warm attachment. In its perusal the Duke wiled away the weary hours of his imprisonment in Uceda, thus affording to the monkish commentator of Teresa's letters an ingenious comparison with Julius Cæsar engaged in the study of the *Iliad*. He is reported to have said—this fierce bigot who decimated the Low Countries, this saint humble and pious if ever there was one (and, given the fierce grim creed of the epoch, the one view may be as correct as the other),—"that there was nothing that could give him greater pleasure than to see the Mother Teresa, although to do so he had to travel many leagues." It is a somewhat curious circumstance that, although she was brought into such close connection with them, Teresa never saw either the stern Ferdinand of Toledo or his master in the flesh. The Duchess, indeed, was one of her warmest friends, and well did she repay her attachment, since it was as she travelled to Alba to be present at her daughter-in-law's confinement that she met her death.

Amongst the letters written by her during her present sojourn in Toledo is one to Doña Maria Henriquez, Duchess of Alba, congratulating her on her husband's release, and beseeching her to use her influence with her brother-in-law, the Constable of Navarre, in favour of the Jesuits of Pamplona.

It was on this occasion, when Philip was forced to place his prisoner at the head of the troops he was marching into Portugal to pacify the revolts consequent on the annexation of that country to Spain, that the aged Duke (he was then seventy-two) made his memorable answer, "that he obeyed, if only for the sake of its being said that his Majesty had vassals who won him kingdoms whilst they still dragged their chains behind them!"

Touched by Teresa's repeated entreaties for Fray Antonio de Jesus, who had himself been ill, and was still so weak that she feared to go alone with him, lest he should break down on the road, Gracian came from Madrid to conduct her to Segovia; being present, as we have seen, at that famous interview with the Archbishop. It seems certain that she once again passed through Madrid (although by her own desire her visit was kept a profound secret), where she picked up the sister of one Juan Lopez de Velasco, Philip II.'s chronicler, and afterwards Secretary of his Exchequer, who had assisted them greatly during the negotiations now so happily drawing to an end.

Teresa was nothing if not grateful. If for many years she remembered in her prayers a man who had once given her a jug of water by the wayside, what was not her debt to the poverty-stricken gentleman [1] who had aided them so heartily in their struggles? She had therefore willingly consented to receive his sister into the Order. Perhaps it is characteristic of the age that, although the brother had been a brave and devoted soldier, and was, moreover, high in Philip's favour, he was too poor to give her a bed or the modest outfit required by Teresa's rules of the poorest novice.

Not perhaps without some difficulty: "for these nuns make such a pother about anything, unless it happens to coincide with their own wishes, that they are a torment to me!" Nevertheless the prioress of Segovia loved Teresa too well to thwart her; "although I write to her in such a manner that they could do no less than receive her. Little, indeed, was needed for the prioress, who desires to please both your paternity and me!"

And thither the dowerless Juana de la Madre de Dios was now to accompany her. No subsequent prelate dared to take away the black veil which, on her departure from Segovia, Teresa placed over the head of the ignorant novice whom she herself had in vain endeavoured to teach to read, so as to enable her to take part in the choir duties,—consigning to infamy him who should deprive her of it; and, although dedicated to the humbler offices of religion, Juana wore it until her death in 1620.

In Madrid, too, Teresa probably saw for the last time the confessor whose rigours and harshness had only increased her love and veneration for him, Father Baltasar Alvarez, who died two months afterwards in the Jesuit college of Belmonte.

At Segovia the news of her brother Lorenzo's death snapped another of the links which still bound her to life. Since the moment when, freshly disembarked from the galleons, he had come to her like a providence in her hour

---

[1] Besides being a soldier and a statesman, he was also no contemptible scholar, and his erudition may still be seen in Covarrubias' *Tesoro de la Lengua Castellana*.

of utmost need at Seville, they had been united by the tenderest relationship. His admiration and love for her had known no bounds. She counselled, and he meekly besought her direction, not only in the graver matters of conscience, but in the minor arrangements of his household, the education of his children, the management of his fortune. Not only did she regulate his penances and send him hair shirts; but she also decides as to whether or not he shall furnish his house with tapestries and silver, or buy a "good serviceable hack fit for work as well as riding," rather than a mule. "It was strange the confidence he had in all I said to him," she writes, "which proceeded from the great love he had conceived for me."

Of a somewhat full-blooded habit of body, a little vainglorious and ostentatious,—a person of no little consequence in poverty-stricken Avila,—full of old-world flourishes and compliments, such is the faint image of Lorenzo de Cepeda's personality as reflected through his sister's letters. Deeply tinged with that brooding melancholy which in one member of the family at least almost degenerated into madness (even in Seville, Teresa had had some little difficulty in restraining him from entering a religious order), his tastes were those of a sombre recluse, and became more sombre as years went on. No sooner had he taken root in his native town than he bought a property about three miles out of it, a country house with its cornfields, pasture-lands, and belt of scrub-oak, for 14,000 ducats, lying a little to one side of the sandy tract which connects the wind-swept parameras with the cistus-covered prairies of Estremadura. "It is," says Teresa to her prioress, a "*termino redondo*," that is, exempt from all jurisdiction, so that Lorenzo was in fact lord of gallows and knife in his own domain. Surely the worthy Treasurer of Quito has had his heart's desire. Perhaps, who knows but he had by this purchase accomplished a dream, an ambition long nursed in the far-away heats of Peru; that this distant prospect, now fulfilled, of ending his days in Avila in well-earned repose and dignity, ere he too laid down his bones beside those of his fathers and became like them a memory, had shone like a gleam of light through long and weary years of struggle. But alas!

he had there left his youth behind him,—behind him too the wife of his youth; and if the streamlets rushed as merrily through brown paramera or jagged pine forest, alas! they could nevermore be the same to him as in his boyhood. No sooner had he bought it than he found the constant occupations, the supervision it entailed, both irksome and distasteful, and regretted not having laid out his capital in purchasing bonds or mortgages instead—in those days an easy and lucrative source of income. His larger-minded sister[1] did her best to check this growing melancholy, and bring him to a healthier frame of mind. She prays God to help him sell his cattle; his not being able to hear Mass except on Sundays fills her with great concern. She promptly vetoes as folly the vow made by the good hidalgo to refrain from venial sin, and smartly stigmatises his regrets as to La Serna as the devil's doing.

Set your mind at rest that in many respects you have acted for the best, and that you have left more than riches to your children, which is honour. None who hears of it but accounts it a great good fortune. And think you there is no trouble in getting payment of these quit-rents? —a never-ending going about with executions. Be sure it is a temptation: and do not again give way to it, but praise God for it, and do not think that, although you had more time, you would have more prayer. Undeceive yourself about this, for time so well employed as in looking after your children's property does not hinder prayer. . . . Try to find time directly these *fiestas* are over [Christmas and New Year's tide] to see about your papers, and to get them put into the order you intend to leave them in. And what you spend on La Serna is well spent, and when summer comes it will be a pleasure to you to go there occasionally. Jacob did not cease to be a saint because he looked after his flocks, neither did Abraham nor San Joaquin; for, the moment we wish to escape labour, everything becomes a burden to us. . . . It is too great a mercy of God that you are wearied by what to others would be repose. But although it is so, you cannot leave it, for it is our duty to serve God as he sees fit, and not we. What it seems to me you can spare yourself is in this of increasing your fortune, and for this reason partly I have felt glad that you should leave it to God; for even as regards the world one loses somewhat in its esteem. I think it is better to be more

---

[1] Teresa in her convents conserved the ideas of an older age. To her it seemed a distinct dishonour to live on interest,—"a breed of barren metal," as Shakespeare has it. Agriculture, on the contrary, involved no such stigma. To Lorenzo, who had lived more in the world, and was better up to date, it involved none. These quit-rents of which she implies her disapproval were fast becoming one of the curses of Spain.

chary in giving, since God has given you enough to live on and to spare, although not so much [as you would desire]. I do not call what you are thinking of doing in La Serna gaining money, which is very well, but I speak of that other point of adding to your income.

As time went on, in spite of his sister's counsels, Lorenzo became a confirmed ascetic, and again her wholesome restraint was needed to temper the ardour, which her own example, perhaps, had chiefly been instrumental in exciting, of the self-concentrated and morbid man. Guided by her, he gave himself up to the strange train of mystical emotions she knew as the Prayer of Union.

A dangerous exercise—these vague explorings into the abyss of conscience, with reason tottering on the brink. The eminently practical side of Teresa's nature had proved her salvation, but few indeed are those who can attempt to explore the hidden recesses of their inner consciousness with impunity. The following passage in one of her letters to him will perhaps explain my meaning, and may not be without interest either to the psychologist or to the physician :—

"Pay no attention to those afflictions you mention ; for although I have never suffered it, since God in his goodness has always preserved me from these passions, I think it must be that, as the delight experienced by the soul is so great, it reacts on the body. It will wear away gradually with God's favour, if you pay no attention to it. . . . The tremors will also disappear. . . . As to the warmth you say you feel, it is of no consequence ; still, if it is excessive, it may be hurtful to the health." She sends him a hair shirt "extremely efficacious in awakening love," with minute directions when and how to wear it. When winter is over, she will send him some other "trifle" more. "I laugh that you should send me comfits, presents, money, and I—hair shirts!"

But amidst all these vagaries of mysticism, Teresa's habitual good sense and discretion never deserted her. She sternly discouraged visions amongst her nuns, and, as to their writing down their experiences, she would have none of it. So too her brother's health is with her the supreme consideration, and she insists on his following advice which her letters show she too often neglected in her own case He is to sleep not less than six hours, "since we elderly people must so treat our bodies, that they shall not play havoc with our spirit." He is not to wear the hair shirt without a fold of linen underneath to protect his stomach, and if he feels pain in the kidneys, he is at once to leave it off, as also the scourgings, "since God cares more for your health, and that you should obey him, than for your penances." He is also to eat a sufficient supper, and not to deprive himself of sleep.

At first Lorenzo, perhaps for the sake of the education of his sons, who pursued their studies under the Jesuits of San Gil,—and not averse to dazzling his townsmen with the spectacle of his wealth and prosperity,—had taken up his abode in Avila with no little show and pomposity, as is proved by the tapestries and silver, the master of ceremonies, to whom laughing allusion is made by his sister, and the page who accompanied his children to school. Latterly, however, surrounded by a crowd of hungry and out-at-elbows relatives, his circumstances would seem to have got somewhat embarrassed, and he retired to La Serna. " He spends much," she writes ; " and as he is accustomed to want for nothing, and has no stomach to beg from any one, he is very depressed." Nor was the constant presence of a brother, a melancholy soldier of fortune,—who, lacking advancement in the Indies, had returned to his native country as poor as he had left it, to live on Lorenzo's charity,—best calculated to dissipate the good hidalgo's spleen. Indeed Pedro was a source of considerable disquiet to them both. Soured, atrabilious, exacting, and disputatious before she left for Segovia, he had turned up in Toledo much to Teresa's dismay, having quarrelled with Lorenzo and left La Serna in disgust, stating his intention of starting off for Seville on the morrow with a muleteer. " But I know not why, for the wretched man is in such a state that one day of sun might kill him, and he arrived with a pain in the head, and in Seville there is no help for it, but for him to spend his money, and beg in the name of God." I misdoubt me, indeed, whether the luckless adventurer thought much of mass or sanctity, for the rigid old Castilian nun displays but small sympathy for the graceless brother, whose "terrible condition" she charitably ascribed to "melancholy, which grips him fiercely."

Although Pedro's unexpected apparition in Toledo was anything but an unmixed pleasure, she at once induced him to wait, until she could patch up a reconciliation between him and the long-suffering Lorenzo in Avila.

She feels little charity, indeed, for the wretched man whom God seems to have sent to tempt them both, in order to see how far their charity can reach. Even, as she writes to Lorenzo, if he were only a neighbour, much less a brother, she would have little enough to waste on him. In any case Lorenzo must never have him in his house again, and Pedro also swears he would rather die than go back. Still, he is now penitent, and if Pedro is mad, which she believes he is on this point (that of returning to La Serna), "it is clear that your grace is only the more obliged, according to the law of perfection, to do what you can for him, and not to let him go away to die." Indeed it is clearly Lorenzo's duty to diminish his other charities for the sake of giving to his brother. Supposing he were to die on the road, she adds, such is Lorenzo's condition that he would never cease to bewail it. If Lorenzo would give him 200 reals a year to keep him in food over and above the 200 he has hitherto allowed him for his clothes, he can live with his sister (Da. Maria de Guzman), who, he says, has already asked him to do so, or with her son, Don Diego de Guzman.

Even this modest stipend, however, must not be given to him all at once, but doled out to those who give him food and lodging, "for, as far as I can see, he will not stay long anywhere." Five days after, she wrote again, anxious to have the matter settled before she left Toledo. Pedro has got still leaner. "The poor man is here spending his money, and, judging by his thinness, he must be in great affliction."

One thing she stoutly vetoed: Lorenzo's suggestion repeated to her by Pedro, that he might find a convenient asylum in one of her own monasteries. "How would one," she writes, "who refused to eat the meat provided for him at the inn, unless it was tender and well cooked, rather preferring to cheat his hunger with a pie (con un pastel se pasa), put up with the scant fare of a monastery? besides which, it was strictly forbidden to receive laymen as inmates. When I can, I send him some little trifle, but very seldom. I do not know who is to endure him and give him everything done to a turn; a terrible thing," she adds mournfully, "is this humour, which does harm to himself and every one else. God deliver you from taking him again into your house. I wish that every other means should be tried, so that, if he dies, your grace and I should have nothing to reproach ourselves with."

It is to be supposed that a reconciliation was eventually patched up between the two brothers; for Pedro, it seems, returned to Avila, where we shall presently find him fighting tooth and nail with the curator of his dead brother's property.

Nor even in Segovia did the saint forget her brother's interests, for there we find her busying herself in negotiating a match for her nephew Francisco,—for Lorenzo's sons were now young men, and Lorenzo, the second one, had already been provided for in Quito. A strange occupation for a saint and her prioress: "looking about how to sound the intended bride indirectly, so as to see if it is possible for your grace to treat of it!"

But neither marriage nor giving in marriage was to employ Lorenzo much longer. His last letter to her was so full of gloom and dark forebodings that she wrote towards the end of June: "I do not know whence you have it that you are to die soon, nor why you should think such nonsense, and be oppressed by what is not to be. Put your trust in God, who is a true friend, and will fail neither your children nor yourself. I wish, indeed, that you were disposed to come to me here, since I cannot go to you there. At least it is very ill of your grace to go so long without paying a visit to San José, for, since it is so close, the exercise and a little company will rather do you good." His daughter Teresa was a novice in San José, and Teresa fondly hoped that her sprightly sallies and the conversation of the good nuns might rouse him out of his depression. She had ended her letter by requesting him to despatch a messenger, "as a point has been gained in that business, and it has not been taken ill."

A messenger that was never despatched; for, seven days after his sister traced these, her last words to him, after a brief illness of six hours, Lorenzo died suddenly at La Serna, choked by a rush of blood to the mouth.[1]

About three miles from Avila, at the foot of a tumbled, pine-clad hill, down whose face, sparkling in the sun, a streamlet rushes tumultuously, the long, low, rambling country grange still stands in which Lorenzo de Cepeda elected to end his days. Here, at least, is a veritable relic of his life, the mute witness of his goings-out and comings-in,—a real thing, which greeted the eyes of one Lorenzo de Cepeda as familiarly as it does mine, and which, though he paid for it in good store of ducats, is now mine as much as it was ever his. Here, at all events, we touch the past. Here it has not quite faded away into night, like her father's house, where Teresa and these brothers of hers played and prayed away their childhood, and to which they bade farewell, she to found, and they to fight in those far lands beyond the seas—some to win the guerdon of victory in broad pieces of eight,—the most of them to find a nameless grave. Here, at all events, the hand of the barbarians that reared a tawdry church within the walls of what was once Alonso de Cepeda's dwelling, destroying all its most intimate charm and sentiment, has happily been stayed. And here before this gray country house of the Serna, facing brown paramera and blue sierra, with the same dumb impassiveness as when the good Castilian hidalgo weaved part of his existence into its stones, it is the present that becomes unreal and strange, ourselves the unfamiliar figures in the landscape. What, indeed, have modern life and modern ways to do with it? Here along the front is the quaint solana, or open gallery, supported by slender granite pillars, where once a melancholy gentleman, in trunk-hose and doublet and short velvet cloak, gravely took the sun, as his eyes wandered over the tawny landscape of winter. The courtyards, spacious and even stately, surrounded by colonnades of granite pillars, are empty and lifeless. A donkey is tied to a ring in the outer court, where so many years ago Lorenzo, booted and spurred, bestrode his little well-knit Castilian hack (in whose purchase Teresa took so large a share), with

[1] It is worthy of note that Teresa also died in the same way.

its high-peaked saddle of embroidered cordoban. At nightfall, and how often, did not he and his master clatter in and out of the ponderous gateways of Avila—its rider thinking thoughts and living a life all so dim and strange to us. The little chapel where he so often knelt at his devotions, and where Teresa took it so ill that Mass should only be said on festivals, hears Mass no longer. For times have changed, and men with them. Here is the kitchen, sombre, low-roofed, which Teresa would fain have shut off from the rest of the house on account of the noise made by the ploughmen who gathered round its roomy hearth. Thus a few scattered remarks in a nun's letters give us a faint reflex— but still a reflex—of the manner of life lived by this sixteenth-century gentleman in his dignified and rustic solitude. Yet, amidst much that has lost all shape and meaning, and has become even to fancy a mere floating image of mist, the sun setting in the west was once as much a fact to Lorenzo as to me. The stream caught and fixed his declining rays as merrily then as now ; the austere walls of the Gothic city in the distance flushed as redly against the evening sky : but the granite cross at the edge of the sandy road,—time has long obliterated the devices on the sculptured shield at its base,—remains to me what to him was none, an enigma as impenetrable as the Sphinx.

A plain granite urn in the little church of San José of Avila contains the ashes of Lorenzo de Cepeda, lord of La Serna ; and in the chapel opposite, under their marble effigies, rest other and later lords of La Serna, Francisco Guillamas Velasquez[1] and his wife, ancestors of the Dukes de la Roca, and patrons of the church, to erect which they devoted no inconsiderable portion of their fortune.

Teresa acquaints the prioress of Seville of her loss in a tone alike subdued and pathetic. Her grief was the calm, self-contained sorrow of one advanced in years, who must speedily rejoin the beloved traveller who has ended his journey first.

"I repay him his love and confidence," she writes, "in being glad that he has departed from so miserable a life and is now in safety. And these are not mere words, but I truly

[1] Master of the Bedchamber to Philip II.

rejoice whenever I think on it." As some return for the kindness and sympathy he had ever shown the nuns of Seville, she impresses on them that they must now commend him to God, "on condition that if his soul should not need it (as I believe it does not), and according to our faith I can believe it, that it may be directed to the benefit of souls whose necessity is greater. It seems to me, my daughter, that all passes away so quickly, that we should fix our thoughts rather on how to die than how to live. Please God, since I remain here, that it may be to serve him in somewhat, for I am four years older than he, and death never seems to end me."

And then she turns off to occupy herself with the affairs of her dead brother's succession, for he has left her executrix of his will, and the day after to-morrow she must be on her way back to Avila. He has left the 400 ducats he lent to them to San José of Avila. These, she gives them warning, must now be paid up: adding that it might not be amiss to take a "good nun" if such an one should offer.

On the 6th of August, a month later, she writes to the same correspondent from Medina del Campo. She and her nephew Francisco are on their way to Valladolid on legal business, to draw up the documents connected with her brother's succession,—" until I see how he is to be left ; for I assure you that he does not want for trials, nor I either ; so that if it were not that I was assured I was serving God greatly in helping them, such is the reluctance with which I act in this business, I should already have entirely abandoned it : he is very virtuous." But to the duties imposed upon her by her dead brother she brought the same conscientious care and business acumen, the comic side of which in a nun she so thoroughly appreciated.

Years ago Teresa had laughed heartily at herself for being such a " baratona " in the affairs of her Order. Years had not blunted her capacity ; and although she did not succeed in carrying out all her schemes—we shall see what they were presently—and she failed of getting for San José as fat a slice of her brother's inheritance as she had anticipated, the business talent and shrewdness which she displays in such profane matters is truly wonderful.

The prioress of Seville is instructed to find out on the

arrival of the fleet if it brings any money for her dead brother—" may he rest in glory "—so that steps may be taken for its payment. Her reverence is also to discover whether Diego Lopez de Zuñiga, a gentleman of Salamanca living in Lima, is alive or dead. If alive, she is to be told when the armada is starting, so as to send him messages; " but as he is sixty-five years of age and more, and very infirm, it seems reasonable he will now be in heaven." If in heaven, however, a certificate of his death, signed by one or two witnesses, must be got and sent to her with the utmost secrecy and despatch, for " in case he should be dead, I have already settled with his heir to buy some houses of his for the nuns of Salamanca; for their sufferings in the one they are now in are most pitiful, and I know not how it is that it has not killed them."

Lorenzo has left the 400 ducats owing to him by the Convent of Seville for the purpose of building a chapel over his tomb in San José. Teresa reminds them that the debt must be paid. " As I am the executrix, I must now, reluctant as I am, take steps to secure its payment; for which reason it would be well your reverence should see about it. Both as regards this and what you have given to the Order, it might not be ill to take a nun, if you can find a good one." In this letter she encloses one from the Bishop of Canaries to his friend the President of the Contratacion of Seville, so that, in case of money arriving from the Indies, he might take charge of it; " and do everything well, my daughter, in return for what I am going to tell you." The piece of news so ushered in is the crowning triumph of Teresa's life. " Fray Geronimo de Gracian, who is now here in Medina, and has done these journeys with me, and been very useful to me in this business, received a letter five days ago from Rome from Fray Juan de Jesus, in which he says that the Brief has been given to the King's ambassador." The triumph of Teresa's Reform was now complete, for, nine days after this was written, on the 15th of August, the King from Badajoz advised his agent at Rome, the Abbot Briceño, of the receipt of the duplicate of the Brief, which had cost Teresa and her friars so many months of suspense and trembling uncertainty.

Teresa remained in Valladolid until the end of the year.

This year—1580—was long celebrated as that of the universal catarrh, an epidemic which, like the recent influenza, and strangely resembling it in character, swept the whole of Europe, and numbered countless victims. Teresa was amongst the sufferers, and escaped narrowly with life. "The illness has been such," she wrote to her prioress of Seville, "that no one thought I should live." She recovered, indeed, but never again regained her former health and strength. Hitherto, in spite of the continual strain upon her energies and her frequent physical infirmities, she had been comparatively robust, and retained an appearance of youth; but now for the first time it was borne in upon those who loved her that she was failing, and very changed and thin. The good Gracian's heart was filled with anxious forebodings which she, unable to write to him herself (for she now leant more and more on her secretary, and few of her letters after this date are written with her own hand), endeavoured to dissipate through Ana de San Bartolomé. "Little by little," she assured him, "I shall get well. Let not your paternity be distressed at my illness. My own distress is enough." In spite, however, of her enfeebled health, she never once relaxed in the supervision of the financial and spiritual concerns of her convents, still busy as she was with the administration of her brother's estate. To the last, the first offspring of her labours was the most dearly loved; and the material prosperity of San José would now seem to have become the main object of her life. Francisco had returned to Avila—not alone, for Gracian was there also, his mission evidently being to keep a sharp look-out on Francisco and his affairs. Francisco had inherited, together with his property, some share of his father's religious melancholy. He had delighted his aunt at Medina del Campo, where he took the Communion with his servants, by his devout demeanour, and she had written to his sister Teresa (who in the meantime has also learnt the terminology of mysticism—what progress she made in it we know not—and corresponds with her aunt as to her "drynesses," "delights," and the like) that "in goodness he was an angel." For the rest, he seems to have been an amiable, colourless, unstable youth, easily led by a stronger will. We have seen how Teresa and the good prioress of

Segovia had occupied themselves in finding him a bride—a project which had been abruptly ended by Lorenzo's death. It had now been arranged that he was to enter the cloister. It being Teresa's sincere conviction that the monastic was the best and most desirable of all lives; also, as she more than once indicates in her letters, the easiest; and that, indeed, the constitution of all society should be formed on monastic models, we cannot be surprised, or imagine her capable of sacrificing her own nephew for the sake of enriching San José of Avila; that is, supposing any such inducements had been at the bottom of his resolution.

Under these circumstances, then, she despatches her instructions to Gracian in Avila. Perhaps none of her letters so thoroughly as this shows the acute attention to detail, the shrewd, worldly wisdom which were so strangely—perhaps never more strangely—doubled in this extraordinary woman with enthusiasm and mysticism.

A mere single-hearted enthusiast is apt either to despise reality or most singularly to distort it. This Teresa never did. If anything, she carried a certain practicality, a certain very keen perception of things as they were, into her vaguest visions. She was a true daughter of the "Tierra de Avila," and never has the Castilian character been represented in sharper outlines.

Pedro de Ahumada has turned up once more in Avila, as quarrelsome and restless as ever; likely to prove as great a thorn in Francisco's flesh as he had ever been in his father's. Of one person only did Pedro stand in wholesome awe, and that was of his sister. "Francisco will not protect himself from him unless he entrusts his business affairs to me, for I am the only one for whom he has any respect." For Pedro has again taken up his abode at La Serna and refuses to be dislodged, having got possession of the famous hack, the purchase of which Teresa had long ago advised, instead of a mule. "If Pedro de Ahumada should come in on the hack" [from La Serna], writes the wily old nun, "Don Francisco had better keep it and send him back on a hired mule; but he is so cunning that I do not think he will. He has no use for it except to make expense; and so Don Francisco had better tell him, as also that he is not to have house-room at La Serna, so that he will have nowhere to go to or come from; and he must manage him as best he can, without giving him anything, nor signing anything in his favour. He must be told, that he shall always have what my brother left him, with which he is well provided for." ... Pedro has also come to words with Perálvarez, an old soldier who loved arms better than affairs, whom Lorenzo had appointed his children's guardian; and their disputes as to the management of the property led to nothing being done by either of them. As to which Teresa is fain that Francisco should pluck up courage, and speak his mind out sharply to Pedro de Ahumada. It may be doubted whether the poor weak-kneed youth who had already been so completely entrapped could speak out his mind sharply about anything. On one point, however, he is to be especially determined, to let Pedro de Ahumada see no signs of wavering, "rather all the mind he has (and more, if more he can) as to the change he contemplates in his condition." For "that wretched little page," we hear, has let the cat out of the bag, and Francisco's intention is now no secret in Avila, "and since it is already decided on, there is no further need to keep it quiet. So far as he is concerned, it does not seem to me that it will make any difference. He has written me a letter which has made me praise God."

Almost immediately after this Gracian and the would-be novice started off for Pastrana, the former no doubt obedient to Teresa's directions to "sell the hack, and buy a good mule instead of that machuelo [small he-mule]." We may be sure that he was equally attentive to her caution "not to buy something that will tumble my father off, for the other, as he is little, does not give me [you] so many falls," and that Francisco, as she also suggested, bestrode something, not of such value but that he could leave it with an easy conscience to the convent where he took the habit.

Having thus disposed of her nephew, what were Teresa's intentions? A document addressed to the prioress and nuns of San José, and which was long guarded in the treble-locked chest of that convent, reveals them clearly enough.

"The documents which concern the inheritance of that

house are signed and sealed, and are very binding. God knows the care and trouble that it has been to me, until I saw it at this point. God be blessed, who has thus accomplished it: they are most binding. . . . If God be pleased that Don Francisco should profess . . . the property will be at once divided between Don Lorenzo [the second son, then in Peru] and Teresa de Jesus [his sister]. She can dispose of it as she likes until she professes," but "it is clear that she will do what your reverence tells her; and it is right that she should remember her aunt Doña Juana, since she is in so much want. When she professes, all will become the property of the convent." The same steward who administers her share will also administer Lorenzo's, "giving a separate account of the whole expenditure." The chapel over Lorenzo's tomb is to be commenced forthwith. "Whatever shall be wanting of the 400 ducats owing by the nuns of Seville is to be made up out of Don Lorencio's share. I think it is stated in the will (although I do not remember very well) that, in the distribution of Don Lorencio's portion of the estate, I should act in certain things as I thought best. Since, therefore, I understand that it was my brother's intention to build the arch of the chancel (as you all saw that he had already planned it), I hereby declare by these presents, signed with my name, that it is my will that, when my brother's chapel (may he be in glory) is made, the said arch of the chancel should be erected at the same time, together with an iron grating, not of the most costly, but well-seeming and sufficient for the purpose. If God should be pleased to carry off Don Lorencio without children, then the chancel must be built as directed by the will. Take heed not to trust too much in the steward [the saint, in Spanish phrase, was wiser than seven notaries put together], but take care that your chaplains, whoever they may be, go frequently to look after this of the Serna, to see if it is well cultivated, for it is a property that will be valuable; and without great care it will soon go to ruin, and you are obliged in conscience not to let it diminish." "Oh! my daughters," says the shrewd saint (this most delightful of saints and women), as she lays down the pen which reveals a grasp of temporal matters that would scarcely discredit a pious family solicitor in full practice, "what weariness and disputes these temporal belongings bring with them! I always thought it, and now I have seen it by experience; for, to my mind, all the cares I have had in the foundations have not in many respects vexed or wearied me so much as these; I do not know whether it has been caused by my great infirmity which has added to it. Praise God, your reverences, that he has been pleased to accept of it, for you are the chief reason why I have so taken it to heart, and commend me greatly to his Majesty, for I never knew how much I loved you. May he guide everything as shall be most for his honour and glory, and let not temporal riches deprive us of poverty of spirit."

Sentences dictated indeed by a most intimate satisfaction in the conscientious, and, above all, successful, discharge of duty. Nevertheless, man proposes and God disposes. All these plans, which cost her so much weariness and contention, ended in nothing. Francisco at length found a will of his own, and in less than a month the novice, as sick at heart as he was of stomach, resolutely turning his back on Pastrana, made his appearance, shamefaced and discomfited, in Valladolid, in such wholesome dread of Discalced friars and nuns that "I believe," says Teresa naïvely to Gracian, "he would fain set eyes on none of us, and least of all on me." adding, "it is reported that he says that he is afraid of the desire taking possession of him again. In this is seen the great temptation! . . . He is now looking out for a bride, but not outside Avila. It will be a poor marriage enough, for he is full of troubles. Your paternity and Father Nicolao must have been at the bottom of it, for having left him alone so soon; also that convent of Pastrana cannot be very greedy." Nevertheless in Avila Francisco exonerated Teresa from the charge of having forced his inclination, and contritely enough offered to take a wife of her choosing. "But I fear that he will have but little contentment; and so, if it were not for the sake of my seeming vexed at the past, I would not meddle in it at all. . . . A brave temptation it must have been; . . . in my opinion with saints he would have been a saint."

A month later, he married a young lady of Madrid, Da.

Orofrisia de Mendoza y de Castilla, related to half the grandees of Spain—a marriage which, in spite of the bride's dower of 400 ducats, was more productive of honour than profit. The bride was fifteen. "I see nothing against it," writes Teresa to his brother Lorenzo in the Indies, "except Francisco's poverty; for his property is so embarrassed, that unless he gets speedy payment of what is owing to him there (in Quito), I know not how he is to live. On which account let your grace see to it for love of God; so that, since God has given them so much honour, they may have the wherewithal to sustain it." In spite of his thrifty mother-in-law, however, and in spite of his showing himself a shrewd financier of his slender fortune, Francisco was eventually forced to return alone to the Indies, and died in Quito a broken-hearted and poverty-stricken man.

Not without bitterness does Teresa inform her prioress of Seville that "all her plans fall to pieces," and that she is not to send the money (the 400 ducats) to Francisco but to her, "for fear of his spending them on something else, especially now that he is married," adding as her reason, that she is "so wearied of her relatives since her brother died, that she wants no contention with them."

The 400 ducats, however, were never fated to find their way to Avila, and it may be doubted whether the nuns ever saw a farthing of Lorenzo's legacy. In spite of her repeated instructions to Maria de San José to get "some nun to pay the money for my brother's chapel, which can no longer be deferred," almost a year passed before it was at last, regardless of Teresa's injunctions, paid into the hands of Fray Nicolao Doria, who at once appropriated it to paying off the debt owing by the community of Seville to his brother, Horacio Doria.

We have seen how hitherto she has advocated, in eloquent and touching words, the utmost leniency to the two culprits who had been at the bottom of the disturbances in the Convent of Seville. Under all her kindliness and lovableness, there was a stern inflexibility which it was not well to trifle with. She held her convents in such complete submission by other than the bond of love. It had been politic to dissemble—dissimulation was then inseparable from the art of government, and Teresa was a born casuist—whilst the Descalzos were still in mortal fear of their enemies; now that their position was entirely altered, and the Brief from Rome was hourly expected, there is an ominous change of tone. The rigid old disciplinarian had neither forgotten nor forgiven the grievous scandal and shame that Beatriz de Jesus had brought on her sisters of Seville, nor was her attempt to lay the blame on Garci Alvarez, whom Teresa believed to be more misled than misleading, calculated to soften one who could not away with meanness or subterfuge.

A frank confession would have touched the heroic chord in Teresa's nature and melted her heart at once. Not so now. "That which appears to you very well," she writes to the nuns of Seville, "that she should condemn Garci Alvarez, appears to me very ill, and I should believe little of what she says of him, since I hold him to be of good conscience, and I have always thought she made a fool of him." Still, any confession was better than none. "Although it is not what we wish, I have been exceeding glad. Here we have offered up great prayers for her: perhaps the Lord will have mercy. Since I saw the papers, I have been greatly distressed that she should have been allowed to communicate. I assure you, mother, it is not right that such things should be left without chastisement, and it were well that she should not be freed from the perpetual imprisonment, which you say was already decided upon here." Whether this merciless sentence was ever carried out we know not. Maria de San José herself received a somewhat sharp rebuke for lending too indulgent an ear to the culprit's tardy excuses. "I cannot stand those excuses," writes Teresa, "for she cannot deceive God, and her soul must pay for it, since she made the accusations before you all, together with many others you have written to me. Either you speak truth or she;" and yet, in the same breath, she regrets that they have not a larger orchard for the sake of giving her more occupation.

I have dwelt on these details of Teresa's correspondence at this period, as they reveal a side of her character—and not the least important—which must not for a moment be lost sight of. I have left it to others to paint a false picture of an enraptured mystic. Had she wandered into the world to found convents led by mere enthusiasm for an imagined mission, she would most probably have been burned at the stake by the Inquisition, or incarcerated for life like Magdalen de la Cruz. Catalina de Cardona, impelled by religion to make the sacrifice of her life, and to live alone in the rude desert with the beasts (who learned to love her) and the flowers—too harmless to be dangerous—she at least was a one-idea'd enthusiast; but her very name has sunk into obscurity, and to-day her dim legend lingers—a trail of light across the pages of one of the many religious chronicles of the age. Teresa was fervid with enthusiasm, but it was the enthusiasm of a calm, self-reliant, courageous nature; and it was certainly the least factor in her success. Men felt in her that indefinable thing which for want of a better term we will call authority. She was her "own star." Hers was neither a sanguine nor a poetic temperament: she never overstepped the limits of dull reality; she saw it under no false colours. A leader is rarely imaginative; if he is, it is not to success he marches, but to the scaffold and posthumous renown. Teresa worked with the instruments she had: she was a keen reader of character, and knew how to make its foibles, weaknesses, petty vanities subservient to her purpose. She never dreamed of the impossible, and for that reason she came nearer to achieving it than most. Untiring constancy, indefatigable patience, ceaseless energy, a mind wonderfully even and serene, unelated by success; tranquil and steadfast in the face of the greatest reverses—these are the qualities, dull and prosaic as they seem, which move the world, if, as in her case, they are associated with genius and purpose.

Dry, didactic, thoroughly materialistic in her views of life, she possessed, too, a rare flexibility, perhaps more apparent than real, which served her in good stead. Stately and grave we may be sure she was, for such was the bearing of the time; but there was something more, which drew bishops and nobles and the greatest grandees of the land to her feet and kept them there enthralled, through the course of a long life. It was not her sanctity—for that as yet had not been conceded—but the wonderful charm of her personality: a sharp and ready wit; courtly and fascinating manners; a wonderfully persuasive and eloquent tongue, and merry too, "her very laughter was contagious"—these were the outward and visible means whereby she intrenched herself so firmly in the affections of all, and overcame the enmity of the few. Truly a strange mixture, and one rarely seen, of great and little qualities; of nobility and rectitude joined to wily adroitness, much casuistry, rapid insight; a profound knowledge of all the keys of the human heart—such was Teresa de Jesus. For my mind I love her as well when she haggles over ducats (for her convents be it remembered), and circumvents quarrelsome Pedro, and busies herself in all the little minutiæ of life, monastic and otherwise, as it was lived in Avila three centuries ago—and perhaps better—than when she is engaged on bigger matters. For her success in the one arose from the same qualities (and perhaps defects) she displays so eminently in the other.

*   *   *

To her severe illness in September, from which she was still not altogether recovered, and her consequent decay of strength, may be attributed her strange discouragement and reluctance in making the foundations of Palencia and Burgos. Her spirit, too, seemed to have greatly failed her, and for the first time she shrank feeble and wearied from the task she felt scarcely able to perform.

In vain her niece, Maria de Bautista, entreated; in vain the Jesuit Ripalda (her old confessor) told her that her cowardice came from old age; "but indeed I saw it was not so, for I am older now and have none . . . although I heeded the latter greatly, it was not enough to decide me. . . . Now comes the true fervour, since neither men nor God's servants suffice, whereby many times it may be seen that it was not I who effected anything in these foundations, but he who is all-powerful. As, after taking the Communion one day, I was full of doubts, and irresolute whether to found at all, . . . our Lord said to me, like as in reproof: What dost thou fear? When have I failed thee? The same that I have been, I am still: fail not to accomplish these two foundations."

Before this still small voice which has ruled her life so far, and will rule it to the end, hesitation is no longer possible.

Still ailing, the last days of December therefore found her braving the frost and intense cold of a Castilian winter, on her way to Palencia, accompanied by Ana de San Bartolomé, her devoted secretary and nurse, four other nuns, and two priests. A gentleman living in Valladolid had given her the use of his house in Palencia until June; and well did the good Canon Reinoso, to whom, although personally unknown to her, she had written on the strength of a friend's assurance that he was "a servant of God!" to get it ready for their coming, fulfil his mission. For when they arrived, hungry, weary, and perishing with cold,—the heavy rains had made the cart-tracks almost impassable, and the fog had been so thick that they could scarce discern each others' faces,—they found that his thoughtfulness had provided them with beds and many other sorely-needed comforts.

Nevertheless, let her be as wearied as she might, there was little rest that night for the little old indefatigable nun. Her arrival, by her own desire, had been kept a profound secret, and before there has even been time for the whisper to get abroad that she and her nuns are there, the morning's light will find the fourteenth convent of her Order an accomplished fact!

At daybreak Mass was said by one of the priests who had brought them to Palencia; and a message sent to the Bishop, Don Alvaro de Mendoza, who, no less surprised than delighted, presently speeds to the extempore convent, full of kindness and generous gifts, binding himself and his successors to provide it perpetually with bread.

Two days after, at nightfall, Teresa hung up the cracked bell, the unfailing signal of possession. The Bishop's support must have gone for a great deal, but even a bishop is powerless to ensure such an outburst of popular generosity and enthusiasm as her mere presence excited amongst the honest inhabitants of Palencia. Each one endeavoured to outrival his neighbour in showing honour to the guest whose sojourn in their town was felt to be a benediction and a privilege. Warm and ardent was her gratitude. As for the Bishop, "such is the debt this Order owes him, that he who reads these *Foundations* is in duty bound to commend him to our Lord, alive or dead, and so I beg of him for charity;" and to this day the Palencians quote with pride, as a brevet rank of glory, the words in which she has handed down to all time their nobility and benevolence.

I should not wish to leave unsaid many praises of the charity I found in Palencia, in particular and in general. It is true that it seemed to me a thing of the Primitive Church (at least not much in vogue at present in the world), when they saw that we had no endowment, and that they had to maintain us, that not only did they not forbid it, but said that God did them a most great mercy. . . . [Adding in a letter] It is a charitable and frank people, without deceit, which gives me great pleasure.

For at last the unflinching tenacity of this old nun, so feeble of body and so resolute of will, has told home. The Dominating Idea of her Life, followed with a chivalrousness and dogged resolution worthy of her knightly ancestors, has won its way, and she has herself become one of the most distinct personalities in this old world of Spain. Those who were inclined to doubt her sanctity, and there were few who did, were touched into acquiescence by something perhaps better than sanctity—too deep for words, but which imperiously demanded respect and admiration.

"Go, father," said the unwilling corregidor of Palencia, half-angrily, to the supplicant Gracian, who had already, whilst Teresa waited in Valladolid, sued in vain for his license to found—"go, and let it be even as you desire; for the Mother Teresa de Jesus must bear in her bosom some mandate from the Royal Council of God, so that in spite of ourselves we are all forced to do even as she wishes." Her very presence is now enough to ensure success. "Already I am fit for nothing," she writes, "but only for the noise made by Teresa de Jesus."

Never once through the whole course of her career has Teresa felt a doubt as to her mission being the special care of the Divinity. She would fain annihilate herself, so that all the honour and glory may be his. One of the most conclusive proofs, as it seems to me, of the nobleness and purity of her character, of the loftiness of her motives, is this serene and childlike conviction that she was guided by an exterior power. To superficial minds such a sentiment seems puerile: but it is indubitable that those who have most distinctly moved the world with a lever more powerful than that of Archimedes have felt a similar conviction. At all events it is a magnificent Illusion, whence, as from a fountain of perennial courage, our weak and faltering humanity has drunk such draughts of valiancy and strength.

For Teresa de Jesus, it was the condition of her work—the condition of her ability to perform it—that she should feel brooding about and within her this mysterious Presence, counselling and shaping her decisions even in those temporal matters which we might justly consider to be most beneath the notice of the Deity.

Even in her choice of a convent, she unhesitatingly accepts the inner voice of conscience for mysterious dictates from above. She had been offered, and had rejected, the Hermitage of Our Lady of the Street—a popular and much frequented shrine—in favour of another house found for her by the friendly canons Reinoso and Salinas, when:—" I begin to feel a great anxiety and uneasiness which would scarcely let me sit still through Mass; I drew near to receive the most holy sacrament, and, immediately I received it, I heard these words in such a way that I resolutely determined not to take the one I had intended, but that of Our Lady: 'This is the one for thee.' It began to seem to me difficult to draw back from a business so far advanced, and so much to the liking of those who had been so active in bringing it about: the Lord answered, 'They know not the great offence that is offered to me here, nor the remedy this will be.' It crossed my mind that it might be a snare, although I could not but believe it, for I saw well in the operation it worked on me that it was the spirit of God. He then said: 'It is I.' . . . It seemed to me they would think me vain and flighty when they saw such a sudden change, a thing which I greatly abhor. . . . To avoid this, I confessed it to the Canon Reinoso. . . ."[1]

[1] According to Isabel de Jesus, this injunction was repeated more than once,

The good canon, who was still but a young man, willingly accepted (indeed he could do no less, for who could question it?) a special intervention of Providence, in a matter which seemed to them of such supreme importance ; and the return of the messenger sent to conclude the bargain with the absent owner, with an altogether unjustifiable demand for 300 ducats more, providing them, as it did, with a most convenient excuse, confirmed and strengthened these tender and credulous souls in their superstitious awe and reverence. From the first, the two canons took up the business as warmly as if it had been their own, or even more so. They bargained for the house, provided money, became surety for the price. On the owner demanding further security, they at once went in search of the Bishop's Vicar-General—one Prudencio. Meeting him on the way, and being questioned by him as to whither they were going, they replied that they were in search of him to sign the bond. Whereupon the good Prudencio laughed, and said : "So lightly do you talk of guaranteeing such a sum as this !" and, more lightly still, at once signed it without dismounting from his mule ; "which," adds Teresa, "for these times is greatly to be pondered on."

Yet verily they had their reward! Reinoso's kneeling effigy still adorns the chapel which bears his name in Palencia Cathedral ; his only claim to the notice of posterity, his brief association with the great Teresa de Jesus.

Towards the close of a hot June day, a marvellous procession swept through the white mediæval streets of Palencia, bound for Our Lady of the Street. The Bishop came from Valladolid to take part in it, and Gracian journeyed all night to gladden the Mother's heart by his presence in the imposing ceremony. The famous Virgin Our Lady of the Street herself descended from her pedestal that day, and was carried forth to welcome and bring her daughters home. On they come through narrow, sun-baked streets strewn with flags and rushes, preceded by the blare of trumpets and triumphal music. First, amidst the loud

for when Sor Isabel, who was prioress, asked how she could hear the divine voice amidst the noise they were all making at recreation, Teresa answered : " That the voice of God so transfixed the soul's attention that all the turmoil in the world did not suffice to shut it out."

reports of fireworks and low murmurs of admiration, leading the way as was most meet, Maria Santissima; behind her, Bishop and Chapter, grave hidalgoes of the municipality, fine gentleman, and hungry rascal. But who is this,—this nun, somewhat bent and stooping, leaning on a staff, who walks in the place of honour between the Bishop and Canon Reinoso,—whose face they cannot see because of her long black veil? As she passed, a strange hush fell on the tumultuous happy throng—a strange thrill shot through their hearts. For even as they look she has faded from their sight, and others take her place; but all have felt that a solemn and memorable moment of their lives has come and gone; and they who are then youths, grown old and garrulous, as they sit in the sun weaving long-winded stories of the past, will speak of it as marking an epoch in their lives,—for they had even seen Teresa de Jesus for the first and last time! On they sweep, this fantastic, incongruous medley of sixteenth-century folk. Friars white, black, and gray, with shaven crowns, and faces on which the cloister has set its indelible and mysterious seal;—on they sweep, these dark-browed priests and stately gentlemen, these fat-faced, broken-winded canons of the Cathedral Chapter; monk and nun and priest and layman, conjured thither by the indomitable will of an old woman with a broken arm, whose steps they follow. Quickly it passed away, that procession as strange and varied as the vanishing colours of a kaleidoscope, fading away, even as one looked,—into dusty oblivion and indistinctness.

Let me not forget, however, that a blast of wind blew out all the tapers except those carried by the nuns, which alone arrived burning at the church—a notable instance, in favour of these holy women, of the vicarious suspension of the laws of aerostatics!

CHAPTER XXV

EL ORO FINO SE ECHARÁ DE VER EN EL TOQUE

But this triumph had been preceded by a still greater one, for the famous Chapter—famous at least in these partial annals—has been convoked and dissolved, and the existence of the Descalzos has been assured for all time by the decree which has erected them into a separate province.

We have seen how warmly Philip had taken up their cause. It is said that one of those rare moments in which that monarch gave unmistakable signs of joy was as he read the Brief for the convocation of the Chapter, which was given into his hands at Badajoz on the 4th of August 1580, as he was preparing to enter Portugal. A month later the news of its arrival reached Teresa in Valladolid. The convocation of the Chapter was, however, delayed until March of the following year. The death of the Archbishop of Seville, who was to have presided at it, necessitated further recourse to Rome to confirm the appointment of his successor, Teresa's Fray "Pero" Fernandez—an appointment which proved equally unfortunate, for the good friar was lying on his death-bed in the peaceful cloisters of Salamanca, and his days for chapters were over. The news affecting an Order whose welfare he had ever had so nearly at heart, only served to cheer the last moments of the dying man. "Tell the King," he said to Gracian, who had rushed off in hot haste from Seville to Salamanca, "that I am setting forth for Heaven, whence I will assist by my intercessions, since I can no longer be of any use on earth."

Gracian arrived at Gelves with the news of Fernandez's death on the very day that Mariana of Austria (according to the euphonious phrase of the chronicler) "passed to a better life." Perhaps to divert his thoughts from his great loss (I still quote the chronicler), the royal widower sat himself down forthwith and penned a letter to the Pope, proposing the famous Dominican Juan de las Cuevas, prior of Talavera la Reina, as the dead friar's successor.

The third Brief confirming this appointment reached the King, who was still at Gelves, on the 4th of January. In spite of the rains and impassable roads of winter, the good Gracian at once rushed off to Talavera to acquaint Cuevas with his commission, and from his wretched inn (for he refused to accept the hospitality of the stately monastery) he was busy day and night penning letters of convocation to the distant monasteries and convents of Castille for Cuevas's signature. Exactly two months afterwards, on the 4th of March, at Alcalá de Henares, the Chapter was convoked which erected the Descalzos into a separate province of their own, and for ever severed their connection with the Carmelites.

It was the crowning mercy of Teresa's life.

> Being in this foundation (of Palencia) [she writes, in simple and touching language], our Lord concluded a thing of such importance to the honour and glory of his glorious Mother, since it belongs to her Order, she being our Lady and Patron; and to me gave one of the greatest joys and contentments that in this life I could receive; for, for more than twenty-five years the trials and persecutions and afflictions I had passed through would be long to relate; and only our Lord can understand it. And to see it now ended, none but he alone who knows the labours that have been suffered can understand the joy that came to my heart, and the desire I had that all the world should praise our Lord, and that we should offer up to him this our holy King Don Philip, through whom God had brought it to so good an end; for such the malice of the devil, that all was on the point of destruction had it not been for him. Now we are all in peace: Calced and Discalced; none of us are prevented from serving our Lord. For this reason, brothers and sisters mine, since he has listened to your prayers so well, haste to serve his Majesty.

Teresa in Palencia worked as hard as any of her friars; to her were remitted the memorials of her prioresses and convents of nuns. With few of them was she satisfied; that sent her by San José of Avila with the petition for the whole community to eat meat filled her with horror. Already her Order has attained such growth that it is slipping from her control: the child she had reared and nurtured with her heart's blood has grown in stature, and now attempts to stand alone.

"In this question of nuns" (for she does not attempt to interfere with the government of the friars) "I at least can vote," she writes to Gracian. Her great object was to unify her Constitutions, in which hitherto the caprices of a prioress or a visitor have introduced many variations, so that all her convents might be solidly knit together under the same rule. For this object a nun's coif, whether it shall be made of linen of first or second quality, becomes a question as important as any other.

It is her last effort for her Carmelite daughters, the last stone that still remains for her to add to the fabric she has reared. She would fain control the future by her wise and careful direction, and the experience of a lifetime; fain protect her nuns from the incompetent bunglings of incompetent confessors; fain surround them with a potent barrier against which man and devil, human malice and all other, must be for ever powerless. Time has shown her many weak points in the armour which must be forthwith guarded against; her foresight endeavours to penetrate the dark cloud of Time, to obviate every danger, to meet every (as yet) invisible peril, to prevent any misconstruction in the meaning of her Constitutions, which must be so firmly written, so clearly unmistakable, that none can change or gloss them over. Strange and pathetic, are they not, these efforts of frail humanity to bend the inevitable to its will; but it was the last legacy, the only one, that Teresa could leave to her daughters.

Castles in the air, and ropes of sand! Even this short history will see all her sagacity frustrated,—not by devils,—but by her own friars.

On one point she is explicit, nay, almost solemn—that the nuns must be allowed a certain latitude in choosing their confessors and preachers: "We are not only to have in view, my father" (this to Gracian), "those who are now alive, but also that those may become prelates, who will interfere in this and more." On this point she is firm. If the Commissary gives an uncertain sound, the decision is to be got from Rome.

Profoundly has she studied the temper of her nuns; perhaps also the weaknesses of human nature. Coercion is dangerous; "and when they have freedom they care little about it and do not want it." It would almost seem that Teresa succeeded with those sharp eyes of hers in piercing the future, and it is strange that she is the most earnest on those very points for defending which Gracian and Maria de San José were afterwards disgraced, and the former ignominiously expelled the Order. Most anxiously did she seek to close the door against any confessor interfering with the domestic affairs of her convents or the prerogatives of her prioresses. No confessor was to be perpetual, or to exercise authority. Neither must the nuns be subject to the priors of the Discalced monasteries. Well did she know the dangerous snare laid on the threshold of the confessional. "For none of them," she adds, "is like my father Gracian, and we must bear in mind the times to come, and learn from our experience of the past, to remove all opportunity, since the greatest benefit you can do these nuns is to see that they have no further intercourse with the confessor beyond confessing their sins. . . . It is always necessary to look to the worst that may happen, in order to take away this opportunity; for by this road the devil enters without being noticed. This alone, and the taking of too many nuns, I always fear as being the means whereby much harm may come to us; and so I beseech your paternity to be careful that on these points the constitutions are made most firm; as you love me, do me this favour."

Her words leave us no doubts of her intentions; that she never for a moment dreamt of subordinating her nuns to her friars; still less that she meant to limit the former to choosing their confessors from amongst the latter; her object from the first was to secure to her convents a healthy autonomy in these matters as well as in all others, and to restrict the intercourse of any confessor, whether friar or outsider, with her nuns to the confessional pure and simple. It would be well to bear this in mind when we come to the further development of this history.

Perhaps with a touch of the superstition that still in the minds of the vulgar attaches to anything in print, she is desirous that the constitutions be printed—for when they are in writing prioresses there are who take from and add to them what they choose. "Let a great injunction be added that they may know that no one shall either take from or add to them."

Cleanliness is not as a rule a monastic virtue; godliness, it would seem, is more easily practised, for, as regards this at least, Teresa mourns that her nuns are too much for her. "For the love of God, let your paternity be careful that they have clean beds and table-cloths, even although it is more expensive, for it is a terrible thing not to be cleanly: indeed I wish it might be made a Constitution, although, such are they that even then I do not believe it would do much good."

It was to Gracian, never doubting that she wrote to her future Provincial, that she addressed these long and minute directions as to the drawing up of the Constitutions. Long before the Chapter of Alcalá, Teresa had warned Gracian of the existence of an adverse faction, headed by Fray Antonio de Jesus, sourly jealous of Gracian's pre-eminence not only in the Order but in Teresa's affections; himself ambitious, and straining every nerve to secure the coveted distinction. Amongst his supporters was Mariano. How Teresa regarded him and his pretensions may be seen from the following:—

> I spoke much with Mariano on the temptation he is under to elect Macario, who has written to me about it. I do not understand this man, nor do I wish to have any understanding with any one about this matter, except with your reverence. On this account, let what I have written about this be for yourself alone, as it is most important it should be; and do not fail to take counsel with Nicolao (Doria), and let them see you are not anxious for it yourself: and indeed I know not how those there can conscientiously vote for any one else but either of you two.... Know [she again writes a few days after having penned the foregoing passage] that I have been warned that some amongst those who are to give their votes are anxious for the success of father Macario. If after so much prayer God should so will it, it will be for the best; and it is his doing. I saw that some of those who now say this were well inclined to father Nicolas, and if they change, it will be for him. God guide it, and keep your paternity. If the worst comes to the worst, after all, the chief thing will have been accomplished.

Already, then, in these long and confidential letters to Gracian—the intimate outpourings of her heart—letters which she asked him to destroy (although it was well for him that he did not obey her, since they form the completest and most decisive vindication of his reputation), it is too transparent that animosities and mutual jealousy had already parted the men whom hitherto difficulties and trial had united only the more firmly; already the demon of faction and party strife had shown the cloven hoof, and the fuel was already smouldering which was to break out into so fierce a flame, the moment she was laid to rest in Alba, and her presence controlled them no more.

Gracian *was* elected Provincial, and perhaps it would have been well for him if the lot had fallen on peevish, ambitious old Antonio de Jesus. From that moment dates the hostility of the harsh, dogmatic, austere Doria, as antithetic to his own gentle, easy-going, benevolent temperament as fire is to water. Now indeed are we in a position to assign its true value—in a word of three letters—to the calumny attributed by Doria to Teresa on this journey to Soria; and to the bitter and heart-broken complaints of Gracian's conduct to which, according to Fray Antonio de Jesus, she gave vent on the last journey she ever took when she travelled to her death-bed in Alba. How deeply her heart was set on the election of this beloved son is shown most transparently in these letters. She used all her influence to secure it by writing to and petitioning Cuevas in his favour. It was the theme of her prayers and of those of her nuns: "Oh, how anxious they are for you to be elected Provincial. I believe that nothing else will please them."

In her opinion he alone possessed the requisite experience; he alone knew how to disarm opposition as well as to impose his will with gentleness and decision. We may be sure that, in this supreme moment, she sank all personal affection and preference in the greater claims of the general interests of the Order. If at times the wish sweeps over her to see him delivered from the perplexities and difficulties of such a post, "I see," she writes, "that the love I bear you in the Lord, is more powerful than the good of the Order, and from this springs a natural weakness and so deep a feeling that any should fail to see how great a debt they owe your reverence, and how you have laboured, that for the sake of not hearing a word against you, I can scarcely bear it : but when it comes to the point the general good still weighs more heavily. Please God, my father, that so much harm does not come to these houses as to find themselves without your paternity, for they require most constant and minute supervision, and one who understands both."

Such, then, is Teresa's opinion of the man whom she is said to have accused to Doria on her way to Soria of " poca religion." His enemies have heaped every calumny on his memory. In vain the faction who rose to power on his disgrace have mutilated Teresa's letters, and hidden others, in their attempt to rear this monumental lie against a good man's memory. Posterity, in face of irrefragable proof, has at last reversed the sentence of his contemporaries, and the fame of the poor, gentle, long-suffering friar shines brighter to-day than it ever did before.

In her opinion there were two men,—and two men only,—capable of governing the Order. The first was Gracian, the second Doria, " that is, if your reverence goes with him as companion, on account of your experience and your knowledge of the dispositions of the friars and nuns." But lest it should seem that she unduly favoured these two to the exclusion of the rest, she included in the list she sent to the Commissary Cuevas the name of Fray Juan de Jesus (Roca), who, although he lacked the gift of governing, would, if accompanied by Gracian or Doria, naturally abide by their advice ; "and so I believe that if your paternity went with him, he would do all you told him, and so would do well. However, I am sure he will have no votes." As to Fray Antonio de Jesus, she absolutely vetoes him as unfit for the office.

The Chapter met on the 3rd of March in the Discalced Carmelite College of Alcalá. It was attended by Don Luis Hurtado de Mendoza the Count of Tendilla, and by various dignitaries of the university. All expenses connected with it were, by the King's express command, paid out of the Royal Treasury. Strangely enough, the first two friars of the Reform—one of them the greatest of all—Fray Antonio de Jesus and San Juan de la Cruz, were not present. In the first session, Cuevas, after formally pronouncing the separation of the Descalzos, gave vent to a learned and heavy harangue stuffed with Scriptural quotations, intended to prove that division is not discord.

The second session opened with an elegant Latin oration composed by Mariano, on the words *jam hiems transiit, imber abiit et recessit ; . . . surge amica mea et veni.* [Cant. ii. 11, 13]. This concluded, the Chapter proceeded to the appointment of four definitors, Doria, Fray Antonio, San Juan de la Cruz, and Fray Gabriel de la Asuncion. They then came to the election of the Provincial. The voting was divided between Gracian and Fray Antonio de Jesus, the former gaining the day by one vote only. Amidst acclamations and rejoicing and the chanting of the Te Deum the new Provincial was borne in triumph to the College Church. The day after, a brilliant procession, graced by the authorities, the heads of the Universities, and the religious Orders, took their way to the magnificent church dedicated to the martyred children San Justo and San Pastor, where Fray Antonio de Jesus celebrated Mass, and Gracian preached. In the afternoon there was trying of conclusions between pupils and graduates, ex-professors and catedraticos, on various knotty points of theology. All this took place on the Sunday. On the Monday following, it was unanimously decreed by the Chapter to offer up perpetual prayer for the soul of the Catholic King ; some of the weekly scourgings in community were to be devoted to the same purpose. On the 13th of March, the Constitutions were finally drawn up, and in the spring of the following year, in deference to Teresa's wishes, they were printed by Gracian in Salamanca, preceded by a few loving words of dedication to her who was alike his daughter and his mother.

It was one of the notable joys of Teresa's life, although it seems, she writes to Gracian, "somewhat of a dream ; for however much we had wished it, we could never have succeeded in doing it so well as God has done it."

A dream indeed !—but surely not a dream, Teresa, those long, laborious years of your life ; surely not a dream those wanderings over the length and breadth of Spain ! Nay, these too are but a dream, like all the evanescent forms which contain man's fretful and agitated life ; and perhaps in that region of changeless repose—if there be any such—she too has realised that the Reform of the Carmelites was a vanity like the rest. Nevertheless, woe for the world when the dreamers are extinct and cease to dream these dreams which fling some strange glow cast off from the Divinity over the sordid details of ordinary existence, and fill them with a perfume of Idealism. Greater than the Gods of Greece which personified the forces of nature—although their brows may not be so serene—these other Gods personifying other forces, the moral forces of heroism, self-abnegation, disinterestedness.

In spite of all, however, this dream of life seems a real enough thing whilst we are in it, and its current whirls us irresistibly along. The messengers are already in waiting to bear Teresa off to Soria, and, the instant she has walked in the procession with her daughters and seen them finally established, she hastens to be gone.

Her original intention had been to found at Burgos after she had concluded the foundation of Palencia, but how could she, who had never yet been able to resist the claims of gratitude, refuse the pressing appeals of her old friend and confessor Velazquez, now Bishop of Osma, unfeignedly anxious to grace his diocese with one of the Discalced Foundations of Teresa de Jesus? A wealthy widow of Soria, Da. Beatriz de Beamonte, daughter of a captain of Charles V.'s bodyguard, having resolved to devote half her fortune to the endowment of a convent, the Bishop's warm eulogies of Teresa and her daughters had decided her choice in favour of the Barefooted Carmelites. Every arrangement had been made for her comfort. The Bishop's letter was followed by the arrival of a coach sent by Doña Beatriz for the convenience of the traveller. With it came her household chaplain, and a chaplain sent by the Bishop, together with an alguacil to go before them, and to provide for her comfort and accommodation on the road. The Bishop of Palencia, not to be outdone, told off the Racionero Pedro de Ribera to travel in her train, and the little company was swelled by Fray Nicolas de Jesus Maria (Doria), and his companion, Fray Eliseo de la Madre de Dios, besides five nuns and a lay sister chosen from amongst the convents of Salamanca.

Medina, and Segovia. So that in all it was a goodly bodyguard that mustered round her coach, in attendance on the aged traveller—so near the end of a longer journey—and sallied forth from Palencia at daybreak of one of those early days in June of 1581.

But her heart was sore as she noted the absence of one who, she felt, alone understood her, and whom she loved so well that it was enough for any one to show him favour to be loved by her. In spite of his capacity and personal prestige Doria could ill fill the void he had been sent to replace. The absence of Gracian, whose company she had fondly hoped for, cast a deep shadow over the journey and even over the joy she felt in the final triumph of her Order.

> Now do you not see [she had written to him a few days before] how little my content has lasted me? for I was already looking forward to the journey, and I believe that I should have been sorry when it ended, as on those other occasions when I travelled in the company which I had looked for now. God be praised, for now, indeed, it seems to me that I begin to be weary. I assure you, my father, for, in short, the flesh is weak, and so it has saddened me more than I should wish, for, indeed, it has done so greatly. At least your reverence could have put off your departure until you had left us in our house, for a week more or less would not have mattered much. I have been very lonely here, and may it please God that he who was the cause of taking you away succeeds better than I think he will. God deliver me from such haste. . . . Truly, I am not able to say anything to the point, for I have no heart to say it. I have only one consolation, and that is, I am relieved from the fear I might have had, and did have, that they would touch me in this Santo Santorum [her Sancto Sanctorum being Gracian], for I assure you that, on this point, I am strongly tempted; and on condition that this is not done I will be contented that everything should rain on me, and it rains much. At this time I have felt it, and I shall have no heart for anything; for, in short, the soul is sorrowful at being deprived of him who governs and comforts her. May God accept all; and so long as this is so, we have no cause to complain, however great our grief.

Never was reproach more tender, plaintive, and gentle! And yet she is charged with having also in the same breath accused Gracian to his enemy Doria of his "poca religion." The reader will at least be now in a position to appreciate the value of the future charges,—charges made by Doria and his party,—brought against the devoted friar. Charges which, as often as not, rested on the distraught ravings of some visionary nun; charges which made it necessary to mutilate, destroy, or hide Teresa's letters; and to forge letters and documents purporting to come from Ana de San Bartolomé, Teresa's most constant companion in the last moments of her life,—full of the saint's bitter complaints of the failings of this her so-dearly-loved son. To make up for his absence, however, Gracian had sent Doria in his stead, and Teresa is grateful for even so slight a proof of affection. "Too great a favour did your reverence do me in sending him (since you could do no more); a youth would have been no good, only one who can speak and has an air of authority (parecer más)." But none can fill the void his absence causes, none can bring relief to the weary heart of this poor old woman, aching for this, her only earthly consolation. "Oh, my father! praise God, who made you so agreeable to all who know you, that it seems that none can fill this void. Oh! how wearied is the poor Lorencia with everything. She says that there is neither peace nor rest for her soul except with God, and one who, like yourself, understands her. As for the rest, no words can express how great a cross it is to her." Once more she gives a note of warning, which, seen by the light of after events, would have sounded ominously on any other ears more suspicious and less kindly than the sweet-tempered Gracian.

I was delighted with fray Juan de Jesus. Each time I see the love he bears you it makes me love him well. Do not show him disfavour, *for, as times go, a good friend is to be held in much.*

In spite of fatigue, Teresa took a more than usual delight in the changing aspect of the country through which she passed; and one of the few remarks which show that she was not insensible to the beauties of natural scenery, she made in connection with this, one of her last journeys: "These journeys," she writes to Maria de San José, "are very wearisome, although I cannot say the same of that from Palencia to Soria, which was rather indeed a delight to me, because it was level country, and often in sight of rivers, which was great company for me." At five o'clock on the evening of St. Anthony's Day, from amongst the heathy hillocks and moorland which surround the city on that side, the travellers saw gleaming before them the picturesque towers of gray, old-world Soria. On the outskirts of the town the little cortège was swollen every moment by parties of grave ecclesiastics and magnificently-attired gentlemen on prancing horses, who had ridden out to welcome her. The roads and streets were lined with joyous crowds, and the air was rent with acclamations as the coach slowly jolted along the dusty track ; for all delight to honour her now.

As they passed before his palace, where the Bishop was standing at a lower window in expectation of their coming, at a word from the saint the curtains of the coach were drawn back, and she and her daughters besought his benediction on their knees. They then moved on to the house of Doña Beatriz, who was waiting in the gateway to receive them. But no sooner did they escape from the eager throng of spectators outside than the wearied and travel-stained nuns found themselves the centre of another within, for they had now to run the gauntlet of the inquisitive gaze of all the great ladies of Soria, who were gathered together to do them honour. When at last they found themselves in the great and magnificently-decorated room which was to serve as their oratory whilst the church was being got ready, the Mother and her daughters, falling down upon their knees, kissed the ground, and remained a while absorbed in silent prayer. Their orisons finished, Teresa rose, and turning to Doña Beatriz, embraced her with great kindness and affection, thanking her for the favour she had shown them. Doña Beatriz would fain have kissed her hand, but the courteous saint forestalled the movement, and kissed her hostess's instead. She then conversed with the other ladies, " with great discretion and pleasantness," not forgetting to address a few words of thanks to the knot of gay gentlemen around her for the honour they had done her habit. But if they were all astonished at the exquisite tact and judgment which permitted her, without infringing the dignity and reserve she owed her habit, to render with such polished urbanity the barren compliments of the century, they were not less so at the firmness concealed under those courtly and fascinating manners. For when the gentlemen were gone, and the ladies begged that the nuns might be allowed to raise their veils, Teresa refused to gratify their curiosity,—although, indeed, she gave them leave to converse; and not until they found themselves alone with two near relatives of their benefactress did she withdraw her prohibition. In the course of the evening a page arrived to warn her of the approach of the Bishop and Don Juan de Castilla. After a few words of welcome and inquiry, during which every veil was lowered,— not, indeed, it may be supposed, on account of the prelate, who was blind, but of his secular companion, Teresa answering for her silent and motionless nuns,—his lordship left them to their sorely-needed repose; not, however, before he had promised to return on the morrow to celebrate Mass, and to administer the Communion to them with his own hands, Fray Nicolas and his companion returning with him to his lodgings.

On the morrow (it was the 14th of August, and the Feast of Saint Elisha), after the Mass, which was the solemn signal of possession, the deeds of endowment were drawn up by a notary who remained behind in the oratory for that purpose, in the presence of the Bishop, the saint, Da. Beatriz de Beamonte, Doria, Don Juan de Castilla, the Canon Diego Vallejo, the Racionero Ribera, and the Dr. Cebrian of Cuenca. In addition to the 500 ducats she had already promised, and the house they were then in, Da. Beatriz now offered to spend 3000 more on enlarging it. She imposed, however, certain conditions, which, being found incompatible with the peace and retirement of the community, were eventually withdrawn. The church alone was wanting, and this they owed to the generosity of the prelate, who gave them one close to the house, and which could be easily connected with it by means of a corridor. The saint at once gave the patronage of the High Altar to the munificent foundress, to be bestowed on whom she pleased. The writings finished, Teresa paid a visit of inspection to the church, and her busy brain at once set to work to plan the details of her corridor. Almost two months, however, slipped away before the preparations were finally completed; and on the day following that which brought her labours to an end, it being the 6th of August, and the Feast of the Transfiguration, the Host was solemnly placed on the Altar of the

Church of the Discalced Carmelites of Soria, the sermon being preached in the Bishop's absence by the Jesuit, Francisco de la Carrera.

One there was, however, who did not share the universal content. Doña Beatriz had a nephew, Don Francisco Carlos de Beamonte and Navarra, who considered himself unjustly defrauded of the greater portion of an inheritance he had already looked upon as his own, for the sake of a pestilent community of nuns. Teresa and her nuns were alike abhorrent to the graceless youth, who abused them roundly in no measured terms, although, for the sake of not losing the remainder, he took care his words did not reach the ears of his aunt.

For fifteen years, long after Teresa was dead, he still nursed a bitter anger against the woman who had robbed him of his fortune, until one day—I quote his own duly signed and attested testimony, to be found in the evidence for her canonisation—as he was lying on a sick-bed, from which there was little hope of his recovery, he saw her once more, standing close beside him. "Greatly hast thou doubted of my sanctity," he thought she whispered; "yet consider what the Gospel says, that the tree is known by its fruits; think on those that I have given." Then it flashed across his memory how, when he was still but a gay and thoughtless youth in Soria, she had told him certain things which had since come to pass. "Unstrung nerves" was a term not yet invented; no one then dreamt that those attacks of brooding melancholy and unnatural elation—the ordinary symptoms of "conversion"—might have their origin in physical causes alone. Never doubting that they listened to something outside and beyond themselves, the people of this century acted with a grand simplicity. An incident like this decided the course of an entire life; and rarely was there any looking back from the plough to which they had once set their hand in some such moment of intense and inexplicable sensation. So with Don Carlos. He rose from his sick-bed a changed man, entered the third order of the Order he had once so virulently abused, and retired to Arévalo, where his life thenceforth was one continued example of edification to his neighbours.

Before Teresa left Soria she received a visit from the Jesuit Ribera, her biographer, who happened to pass that way on his return from Rome. On his way thither he had paid her a visit in Valladolid, where she still lingered irresolute before the foundation of Palencia. But this last visit has a peculiar and mournful interest, for it was the last time on this side the grave that the good Jesuit looked on the woman whose history he afterwards related in a work which for its simplicity, its candour, and its evident sincerity deserves a place amongst the best biographies of the age. He too was amongst the number present at the inauguration ceremonies of her convent on that day of the Transfiguration. "But of this visit of Soria," he writes, "I remember more on account of its being the last, for I never saw her again, and also for the sorrow I felt afterwards that I should have been four days in the town without knowing she was there until the last, during which I might have been benefited and greatly consoled by her holy conversation."

He has left us a famous portrait of Teresa, the only one that has been painted worthy of her. For the hard-featured woman immortalised by poor Fray Juan de la Miseria, from whose gloomy countenance we turn away with impatience, can have had but little resemblance to the mobile and lively lineaments of life. A modern Spanish engraver, by modifying the original, by suppressing certain features and accentuating others, has indeed managed to give us a more sympathetic presentment. It may be that her beauty, as in the case of many intellectual people (for I think it may be accepted as an axiom that except in the case of a privileged few, beauty and genius do not often inhabit together this frail tenement of mortality), was of that peculiar kind which depends on the strange and potent irradiation of moods or expressions. Thought must have stamped her brow with its majestic touch; her deeply-sunken eyes, which looked away so far and yet so near,[1] must have flashed every movement of irony, kindly satire, unaffected mirth. At times she assumed

[1] This thought was suggested to me by a Spanish peasant, to whom I once showed a picture of the saint. His remark was (and in it he summed up what on my part it has taken a whole book to set forth), "Cara de pensadora. Tiene la vista para aquí y para otra parte." (A thoughtful face. Her eyes are fixed on earth and far beyond it.)

an almost unearthly aspect of beauty : her face was suffused with a radiance which astonished those who looked upon it. Ribera's account at least would serve to show that Teresa shone in physical as well as moral beauty ; and if the alabaster effigy of her sister Juana, whose exquisitely fair and chiselled face still lies cushioned on her sepulchre in Alba de Tormes, affords any criterion, then must Teresa have been singularly beautiful.

In men it is often seen that to those whom the Lord chooses for his sublimest grace and greatest supernatural gifts, he also gives a more perfect and excellent disposition, as is well seen in that he gave to the Mother Teresa de Jesus. She was of very good stature, and in her youth beautiful, and even after she was an old woman of very good seeming, her body large and very white, her face round and full, very well-sized and shaped, her colour white and red, and when she was in prayer, it lit up and became most beauteous, absolutely clear and placid ; her hair black and curly, her brow broad, even, and beautiful, her eyebrows of a red colour, somewhat approaching to black, large and somewhat thick, not very much arched but somewhat level. Her eyes black and round and somewhat heavy lidded (papujado), for so they call them, and I know not how better to explain it, not large, but very well placed, and lively, and so merry, that when she laughed, every one laughed with her, and at other times very grave when she was serious. Her nose small, the bridge not very prominent, and the point round, and slightly curved downwards, the nostrils arched and small, her mouth neither large nor small, the upper lip straight and narrow, the lower one thick and slightly pendulous, its shape and colour excellent : her teeth very good, her chin well-shaped, her ears neither small nor large ; her hands small and very beautiful. She had three small moles on her left cheek which became her much, one below the bridge of the nose, another between her nose and mouth, and the third below her mouth. These details [adds the scrupulous biographer] I have received from those who had more opportunity than I to look at them often. Altogether she was very comely, and walked gracefully, and was so amiable and "*apacible*" that she generally pleased every one who looked at her.

Skilfully brushed in ; but not yet so skilfully and delicately as the slight sketch he has painted of her character :

A most healthy keen and clear judgment, a great discretion and singular prudence, a very cheerful and gentle disposition, an excellent temper and absolutely void of melancholy . . . as is well known by those who knew and conversed with her. . . . And what shall I say of the humility which shone in her so resplendently that it made itself felt even from a long way off.

We have now followed Teresa through the various phases

of youth to old age; we have endeavoured to show the various and contradictory impulses and emotions of a strong and vigorous intellect and character which was led away, but never wholly vanquished, by the tremors of mysticism. A dreamer and a schemer in one,—she was never entirely the one or the other; but through all, and in all, whether she thought she was accompanied by the subtle presence of the Son of God, or anxiously planned how to bring good store of ducats to her poverty-stricken convents, she shows such an honest rectitude, such an inherent love of truth, such a just perception of the realities of men and things, as must alike excite the admiration of him who condemns the first as fanaticism, and the second as a blemish unworthy of a character otherwise so disinterested. Up to a certain point her judgment prevented her becoming the victim of delusion, and she was never sure herself of the reality or origin of her visions, and never ascribed to them any other than a very minor importance. It has been to the interest of her idolaters, however, to gloss over those passages in which she distinctly refers to them as the effects of ill-health, and to pretend to veil their faces as they enter with her into the tabernacle of the transcendental and supernatural.

Towards the close of her life, however, a notable change takes place, and one which now demands our attention. On the eve of her journey to Soria she wrote a paper to the Bishop of Osma, which may be considered as a species of general confession or review of her spiritual life. In such a document it is almost impossible to be perfectly ingenuous. The votaries of a religion which presupposes the suppression of all reason to faith, which itself rests on a long chain of impossibilities and crudities, are never quite free from deception and involuntary exaggeration. Teresa with all her sanctity was perhaps freer than most. At all events, whatever the unconscious exaggeration into which she was betrayed by the almost total absorption of her own personality into her mission, it is a precious revelation.

Her doubts and fears have long been laid at rest; and the imaginary visions which inspired them have now ceased, and their place has been filled by the sublimest of intellectual visions—a constant sense of the abiding presence of the three Persons of the Godhead, and of the Humanity of Christ.

Perhaps the keenest mental sensations and emotions are, as in the case of physical ones, gradually blunted and deadened by use or abuse: she may, with the decay and weariness of old age, be no longer capable of those old impetuses, whose sharp and delicious pain had so often pierced her heart; of those melting moods of tenderness in which the spouse struggled in the amorous embrace of her lover. For all this is gone, leaving behind it a profound and uninterrupted peace,—a complete lordship over the castle of her soul, and perfect security as to the future. Indeed it would seem that the soul has lost all consciousness of self, so complete is its absorption in the Divinity. She can no longer feel the same pangs as of yore at the transgressions of heretics and the sight of souls going to their perdition. Those poignant desires to mortify the flesh and suffer for the Lord, which made her long, rather than fear, that she might be taken and chastised by the Inquisition, have long ago passed away. Nay, rather at this point of her career, according to Yepes, did she take a *naïf*, and perhaps touching pleasure in the esteem accorded to her writings, and the veneration rendered to her Order and convents throughout Spain. She listened delighted to Yepes's praises of the *Camino de la Perfeccion*, and said to him with great satisfaction, "There are grave men who tell me that it seems like the sacred Scriptures." It was no mere personal (and pardonable) vanity that animated her—her, of all women the most humble and least vainglorious—but because she feared lest any smirch falling on her faith or reputation should fall also on her convents; in short, the esteem and honour she enjoyed were grateful to her, for, so it seemed to her, it was more to God's glory and the profit of her children. If she loved to be honoured and esteemed, it was for their sake and their sake alone. Once she had prayed God to take away the opinion entertained by people of her sanctity, but now that she had been so favoured as to have been the instrument of resuscitating the great Order of the Carmelites, her only care was that she should be free of any, even the most trivial, imperfection. She had once asked the Lord, "How dying it was possible to live?" and he had answered, "Daughter, by remembering that, this life ended, thou canst serve and suffer for me no longer." She had had her share indeed of service and of suffering, but verily, and it is with profound satisfaction I say it, in these last years of her troubled existence she tasted of the serenity and absolute tranquillity of a conscience at peace with itself and the world: her work had been so well and thoroughly done; the sacrifice of herself and life had been so complete, that there was no room for aught but joy. Full of celestial peace and calm, bathed in all the glories of sunset, she surveys with unclouded brow the long and weary ascent behind her, in the full assurance that God alone was the author of the visions which He had sent her as being the only means of leading and guiding a weak and troubled soul into security and rest It is full of such tranquil confidence that her life draws unto its close, and some reflection of it lingers in the couplets ("Letrillas")—to my thinking the best she ever wrote—which she left behind her as an imperishable legacy to her daughters of Soria. It is impossible in a foreign idiom to render the quaint lilt and peculiar rhythm which give them such a simple charm. The spirit, indeed, may be rendered; so tender, valiant, steadfast, and true. She composed them for the Festival of the Exaltation of the Cross, on the eve of her departure for Avila; and on that day of every succeeding year until now they are still sung during the midday hour of recreation, the traditional and simple ceremonies she inaugurated being still adhered to. After adoring the Cross, the community, each nun bearing an olive branch, proceeds in solemn procession to the burial-place, filling the cloisters as they go with the strange old-world sound of their foundress's hymn. When the last strains have died away in the stillness, they murmur a response for the souls of the dead, leaving the boughs to wither on the tombs until another year shall renew the same simple rite.

---

[1] En la Cruz está la vida
    Y el consuelo;
    Y ella sola es el camino
    Para el cielo.

---

[1] In the Cross all life is centred
    And consolation;
    And it alone to Heaven the road is
    For us below.

En la Cruz está el Señor	De la Cruz dice la Esposa
De cielo y tierra,	Á su querido,
Y el gozar de mucha paz	Que es una palma preciosa
Aunque haya guerra:	Adonde ha subido:
Todos los males destierra	Y su fruto le ha sabido
En este suelo,	Á Dios del cielo,
Y ella sola es el camino	Y ella sola es el camino
Para el cielo.	Para el cielo.

On the same page which bears her verses, her nuns have set down her last charge to them and their successors. "My daughters, inasmuch as I love you, I leave you to bear in mind three things: the first, regular observance; the second, obedience to your superiors (prelados); and the third, to be charitable to one another; and if you fulfil them, I assure you that God will renew your spirit, even as he did our Father Saint Elisha, for the sake of this house having been founded on his day."

It is curious that at Osma, through which town she passed on her return home to Avila, she should have met her other biographer Yepes—then prior of La Rioja, and afterwards Bishop of Tarazona. He too had heard of her being in Soria, and being informed by the Bishop the day before that she was expected at Osma on the following night, he waited to see her. It was eight at night when she arrived, and the prior went to the door to meet and salute her as she alighted. She asked him who he was, and on being told, she was silent, and he feared that she had forgotten him, or that his presence was unwelcome to her. When they were alone, and he asked her the reason of her silence, she answered, "I was a little startled,"—and then correcting herself as if she had used too strong a phrase, "and indeed the surprise was not great, for it only lasted a moment,—because two things occurred to me,—that you were leaving your Order to do penance; and whether our Lord had not

---

In the Cross is he, the Lord of	Says the spouse to her beloved,
Boundless realms of earth and heaven,	A palm the Cross indeed is
And midst the strife which rages	Which I have climbed,
round us,	And its fruit to me has tasted
In its shadow there is peace.	Of glorious sweets;
From earth it banishes all evil	And it alone to Heaven the road is
And it alone to Heaven the road is	For us below.
For us below.	

wished to reward me for the labour of this foundation by finding you here. This favour consoled me." She also prophesied the duration of his penance, and told him that he would be ashamed, when it was ended, for having been discomfited by such a trifle.

During her sojourn at Osma she twice made confession to him, and received the communion from his hands; of this he has left us some personal details, far more valuable than his biography, in which the figure of Teresa, the woman, glimmers here and there but faintly. As she drew nigh to take the consecrated wafer, he saw—and as it would seem for the first time—her face uncovered. He noted that it was "the colour of earth," which she ascribes to her age (she was then sixty-seven), continuous infirmities, trials, fasts, and vomitings, from which last she suffered for more than thirty years; but in the moment that she received the Lord into her mouth, it became most beautiful, and of a transparent colour, and impressed with so solemn a majesty and gravity "as showed how worthily the Guest was lodged."

He observed, too, that, although her teeth were worn, black, and decayed, her mouth smelt like musk; a circumstance which greatly astonished and scandalised the good friar, who thereupon thought to himself that she could not be so saintly and mortified as she said, since she used odours and comforting things; but when he afterwards asked the nuns if she used perfumes, they told him that she shunned them like the plague, as they gave her intolerable headache, and that when there were spiced biscuits for supper, she went without, as they deprived her of sleep.

It is an old legend in Osma that she was lodged in the Bishop's palace; the old gray pile which still rises grim and menacing on one side of the long, narrow arcaded street. It is more likely, however, that she took refuge in the little dark "meson" close by; a meson now, as it was then—for the centuries have brought little difference to the popular life and patriarchal customs of this old town, stranded far away from railroads in the very heart of Castille,—still consecrated to, and redolent of her memory. On the 19th she continued her journey to Segovia,—a journey of six days—by San Estéban, Ayllon, and Sepulveda. Her travelling companions were the Racionero Ribera of Palencia, that "sanbenito" who had earned her gratitude by helping her in the construction of the corridor between the Convent and Church at Soria, and of whose modest virtues she speaks in enthusiastic praise; and Ana de San Bartolomé, her nurse and secretary. Others had not been wanting who would have accounted it an honour and a privilege to escort the aged saint, but the little meagre Racionero (I think he must have been a young man) seemed to her quite enough; "for the less the noise the better do I fare on these journeys."

In spite, however, of all Ribera's care, it was a rough and fatiguing journey enough for this brave old woman of sixty-seven. The roads were bad—too bad even for the rough country cart in which they travelled—and the heat intense.

> On this journey [writes Teresa] I paid for the comfort I had had in going; for although he who went with us knew the road to Segovia, he was ignorant of the cart track, and so this lad took us into places where we had often to alight, and go on foot, whilst the body of the cart hung suspended over the edge of deep precipices; if we got guides, they guided us to where they knew the road was good, and a little before we got to the bad places, they left us, saying they were busy and could go no farther. Before we got to a posada, as we were uncertain of the road, we had suffered much from the sun, and the danger of being often upset in the cart. I was sorry for him who accompanied us [Ribera;—characteristic this of the old woman, so valiantly trudging along under a blazing sun, that she should still think first of the distress of others], for just when he had told us we were on the right road, we had to turn back again, and retrace our steps: but his virtue was so well rooted that I think I never saw him vexed, which filled me with great amazement, and made me praise the Lord; for where virtue is so well rooted as this, provocations matter little. I praise Him for the way in which He was pleased to deliver us from that road.

Characteristic too, the merry, pleased exclamation—for as firmly rooted as her own virtue was the almost childish prepossession which never left her, that a foundation accomplished without suffering augured but ill for the future—with which she welcomed one of her falls from the cart on this occasion: "At least I have had a fall and hurt myself."

On St. Bartholomew's Eve, they arrived at Segovia, where they found the nuns greatly concerned at their non-arrival; "as the road was such, the delay was much." After a week or more of rest, in which her daughters vied with each other in ministering to her comfort, she set out for Avila. From some little obscure wayside posada in Villacastin, six leagues from Segovia and five from Avila, where she passed the night, whilst the cart was waiting at the door in the first glow of a September morning, she wrote to her prioress of Seville ("For the Mother prioress of the Discalced Carmelites at the back of San Francisco of Seville"—such is the address): "I arrived last night, weary enough of travelling, for I am returning from the foundation of Soria, which is distant from Avila whither I am now bound, forty leagues." (It was in reality forty-three; but when did ever a Spaniard not miscalculate distances?) At length, on the 6th of September, she once more found herself, after a year's absence, amongst her nuns of San José. Even during her lifetime she was saddened and mortified at the spectacle of the dissolution and relaxation of the convent, which she may have been said to have founded with her heart's blood. For long it had been going from bad to worse, and she had declared in grave anxiety at Soria, that, if no other means could be found, she would go to Avila on foot. And, indeed, she alone could unravel the tangled skein of temporal difficulty and spiritual disorganisation. The convent was on the brink of starvation, for with Salcedo's slender legacy (which was not enough to provide them with a daily dinner, let alone the supper, that is supposing it to be punctually paid, for as yet, the nuns were still waiting for the first instalment), the alms on which they had hitherto subsisted, ceased. "They have made me prioress," Teresa wrote to Maria de San José, "from sheer hunger." The stern and rigorous discipline had been greatly relaxed through the foolish weakness and leniency of the chaplain—we are sorry to learn he was no other than our old friend, Master Julian of Avila. It was sorely against her will that she was elected to the office which she already felt too much for her failing strength, and doubted her ability to fulfil. It was the most amusing scene in the world, writes Gracian, she scolding us all for not letting her rest; and as she was about to reason us into electing another prioress, I bade her place her mouth to the earth, and when she was prostrate I began to sing the "Te Deum Laudamus"—and on the 10th of December, in obedience to Gracian's command, she was elected prioress by the unanimous voice of the community.

Avila was no longer the Avila of her youth. The absence of the old familiar faces which had passed out of her life for ever had left a melancholy void in her heart never more to be filled up. The brother to whom she had been knit by the tenderest ties of affection was sleeping tranquilly,—Avila, Peru, La Serna, to him now as if they had never been. Good old Salcedo, too, was gone, leaving a last legacy to San José; and Baltasar Alvarez, at the age of forty-seven, had tranquilly passed away a year before, whilst making his provincial visit to the Jesuit College of Belmonte; and "the worst is" (she refers to Pedro and Francisco), "that those are left who are!" It is the sad penalty of a long life to be gradually deserted by those who have accompanied it for so long; to watch them one by one fall out of the race and disappear, and to be left alone, stranded as it were, the last of a generation, amid things which have grown strange and pathetic memories of past affections. "The more I go," writes Teresa, "the less do I find in life wherein I can take consolation." A little while, O brave and valiant soul! and you too shall lay down the burden which oppresses you, leaving an immortal memory—it may be less imperishable than your sanctity—of courage, devotion, and constancy of purpose, rarely, if ever, equalled amongst women.

Well may she complain to Maria de San José that the loss of so good a brother was as nothing in comparison to the trials caused her by those he had left behind. Her family only added to her anxieties, and was even worse to manage than her convents. Scandal, justly or unjustly, had made itself busy with the fair fame of her niece Beatriz, the daughter of Juan de Ovalle and her sister Juana. The honour of her family was very dear to this rigid old Castilian saint. Her nephew Francisco,—she sums up his character in the phrase, which was surely not meant to be contemptuous, although it strikes the ear with a certain ironical echo, "that he was only fit for God,"—had deluded his wife and his clever mother-in-law as to his income; he had told them he had 2000 ducats, and spent accordingly; the real state of the case being that the provisions for his younger children, and pious legacies, had absorbed Lorenzo's fortune, and left his heir little or nothing to live on. He now sought to annul his father's will, and made some fruitless efforts to withdraw his sister from her aunt's control. There were also symptoms —they were but momentary, however—that Teresa, now a woman herself, the girl whom she had brought up from childhood, and probably dreamt of as her future successor in the Order, was on the point of wavering,—a gloomy foreboding justified by the former conduct of her brother. Casilda de Padilla, "whom some devil must have deranged," had listened to the persuasions of her relatives, and was bent on deserting the Order she had entered in a fit of childish and perhaps temporary enthusiasm. The moral to Teresa's mind is obvious—"that it cannot be his Majesty's will that we should be honoured with the great people of the earth, but with poor folk like the apostles, and so there is no need for this to trouble us. . . . The answer I make here to the remarks of the world is, that, as regards God, it is perhaps for the best, so that we should look to him alone. May she go with God. May he deliver me from these gentlefolk who are all-powerful and have strange turns of temper."

In spite, too, of her express and often-repeated injunctions to Maria de San José to send them to no one but herself; in spite of her direct negative in Palencia to Doria's request that they might be paid to him, the latter, with flagrant bad faith, had induced the prioress of Seville to deliver into his keeping the 200 ducats, the payment of which had been the subject of such anxious correspondence on Teresa's part. The wily friar (perhaps his conduct might merit a stronger term) had at once handed the money to his brother in payment of the sum advanced by the latter to defray the expenses of the delegates to Rome, and the chance of accomplishing her brother's last and sacred behests before her own death seemed to melt farther and farther away. Teresa was justly indignant at such double-dealing, and told her prioress bluntly that they must have schemed it together (not the first time that she alludes to the "*raposería*," the foxy slyness of her favourite prioress, so fit to treat with Andaluces). "I feared it would happen, and it has seemed to me in no way well; for I like frankness." She observes that, if María de San José gave them to Doria to transmit to her, the fact of his having handed them to his brother cannot justify the latter in keeping them in payment of his debt without her prioress's leave, who well deserves, since it was not for want of being warned, to have to pay them twice over; "and so you will, if they do not give them to me," adds the decided old saint.

The chapel is not even begun, and if it is not done whilst I am here (at least commenced), I know not how or when it will be, for I hope, if it be God's will, to go from here to the foundation of Madrid. . . . You may well believe that if the money were mine, or if it was in my power, I should be better pleased not to have anything to do with it [her brother's will]. If you could only see how his fortune [Francisco's] is being wasted; it is a pity, because this boy was only fit for God. Although I wish to withdraw myself entirely, they tell me it is my duty: . . . for I know not how it can end.

Again she recurs to the faithless Father Nicolas—

What has displeased me most is his having set his will against mine; and, in short, that your reverence and he should have acted against my desire . . . his brother was better able to wait than the chapel entrusted to me by my brother; and if I die it will be left, such are his son's necessities, and the money perhaps spent: and this, from what I can see, we may be sure of.

Such were the cares and thoughts which haunted the brain of the old foundress in sixteenth-century Avila; and pursued her as, far away to the west, she watched from her narrow casement the last sunlight fading away over the brown uplands towards Sonsoles, or hobbled through the convent corridors in the gathering gloom, through which the piercing cold of that upland winter had now begun to creep, until she sighed, like many another, before and since the Idumean of Chaldea made a similar plaint, that "God rained everything upon her at once." With these mingled dreams of other foundations,—that of Madrid haunted her to the last. It was indeed to be accomplished, but, as she had all too truly foreseen in Soria, not by her. She had waited on in Soria in the hope of inducing the Cardinal of Toledo to give his consent. But the proud prelate had been deeply stung by the resolution of his niece (that rich widow of Medina, Doña Elena de Quiroga, to whom Teresa had years ago owed so much in the foundation of Medina) to leave the world for the obscure retirement of the convent she had helped to found. In spite of the prudent assurances of the saint (who would really seem from other motives to have opposed that lady's entrance into the Order), that she would not be received without his consent, the Cardinal still withheld the desired license, and she was obliged to return to Avila. She now began to fear (and feared rightly) that her cherished scheme would never be realised. Neither her submission nor her promises seem to have had any effect, although a private and confidential letter to Gracian (which, like so many others she wrote to him with the same request, was not torn up as she desired, but piously preserved) remains to prove her entire sincerity:—

I have sent you these letters from Toledo, so that you may see how grievously the Archbishop takes it, and I see that on no account will it do for us to make him an enemy. And, apart from this, whenever this entrance has been mentioned, I have always been greatly averse to it; for wherever mother and daughter are together with so many of their family, I fear from what I have seen of this lady, that there is sure to be great inquietude, and little peace for her; and so, before I spoke to the Archbishop, I had begged father Baltasar Alvarez to prevent it, and he promised me to do so, for his opinion was the same as mine, and he knew her well. From this you can see how likely it is that I should have persuaded her! I have written to the Cardinal that I will warn your reverence, and that he may be easy that she will not be received, and it would pain me greatly if it were otherwise. Your reverence already knows what secrecy this letter demands: in any case tear it up, so that no one may think he is the cause of its not being done, but that it is solely for her benefit and that of her children, as is true; we have more than enough experience of these widows! . . . The hour cannot have arrived for this foundation [Burgos]. That of Madrid is what is wanting now, and I believe that when the Archbishop sees that we are acting according to his wishes, he will give it at once; and the Bishop here, who is bound thither in October, tells me that he will procure it.

But the resolution of Doña Elena herself defeated Teresa's decision. Her threat that, if she was not admitted into the Carmelites she would join the Franciscans, extorted the Archbishop's tardy and perhaps reluctant consent, which for over twelve years he had so obstinately refused.

Gracian himself went from Salamanca to Medina to celebrate the taking of the habit by so illustrious a novice; and Teresa's last letter to Don Gaspar de Quiroga was one of heartfelt thanks and humble gratitude for so great a consolation and favour. But as to the foundation of Madrid, the last anxiety of these closing years of her life, he remained inflexible, and she still waited for that license which never came, and never was to come, although so long and eagerly expected.

And so the year wears on to its close to the morning and evening clang of the cathedral bells, and the gray streets look grayer against the film of powdery snow, and, "quite a prioress," as she writes laughingly to Gracian in Salamanca, she fights the wolf from the doors of San José, as she had done years ago from those of the Encarnacion. Little, perhaps, to record; little to attract the attention in the actual events that took place in that obscure convent, and yet the nunnery too is thrilled or shaken as profoundly as the world outside by its humble joys and sorrows. A sermon preached by the Doctor Castro, the worthy canon, whom Teresa, true to the instincts of her life, has transformed by her magic influence, and perhaps a dose of that deference and delicate flattery which none ever wielded so dexterously, from an impartial disbeliever in visions into a partial believer in her own; his visits to the little dark locutory,—for the mere fact of his having been a fellow-student of Gracian's when they were lads together in the University of Alcalá had been enough to win him her heart,—were the most stirring events which diversified the sordid cares (for no life is heroic in its details) of her laborious everyday existence. There we may fancy them sitting, she lost in the darkness behind the grating, he in the twilight gloom of the locutory. Occasionally a messenger from the Duchess of Alba or the Marquesa of Villena alights at the convent gates, and blows a worldlier whiff through the quiet precincts. And yet this austere rigid existence differed very little,—except in the regular recurrence of choir duties and a stricter seclusion,—from that which went on in the gray old palaces of Avila, stuck over with armorial bearings, or in the houses of the greatest grandees themselves. If to-day we would form some vague conception of the life our forefathers lived; of its sombre, dignified, changeless repose, we shall find it alone in these Castilian convents where the passage of the centuries only touches the walls without, tinging them with a deeper hue, but the atmosphere within in its smallest details is that which lapped about Teresa. What they then were, they still are ; and as one talks through the grating with the prioress and her nuns, and the quiet murmur of voices fills the silence,—the world outside fades away,—perhaps also the worldliness from one's heart, and one longs for the peace of the cloister,—the peace of a quiet conscience and the humble discharge of Duty,— of practising, folded close to the bosom of the Divinity, those great Ideals, Poverty, Self-sacrifice, Serene Humility. Sombre and dignified even in their poverty, they carry us back, they make us touch the very essence of a century which is fast fading away even in Spain : in them alone lingers a faint transcript of the medium, the thoughts, the internal history of the age. When they have gone, the past will be swept away for ever before the growing vulgarity, the flashy tinsel, a uniformity that is odious without being stately,—the shams and falsities of modern life. Nay ; we have even forgotten how to be merry ! And oh, what mirth and gladness filled the convent when a novice took the veil or made her profession ! What feasting outside and in ! outside, the family of the would-be nun making merry on capons and partridges in her honour ; inside, a warmth of welcome, of lighted tapers, of triumphant joy at the entrance of another spouse of Christ, and perhaps also a good share of the partridges and capons found its way to the " torno."

At least such is the scene that Teresa shows us in the letter she writes to Gracian at two in the morning, as taking place in San José on that 28th of November at the profession of Ana de los Angeles. The Mother's heart had also been cheered by the presence at the ceremony of Fray Juan de la Cruz, sent from Baeza by the Provincial of Andalucia to fetch her to the foundation of Granada, with the comfort and care befitting her age and person. But either because she had not lost all hope of the license for Madrid, or because she was dismayed at the length of the journey (for we cannot imagine her refusal to proceed from the rooted prejudices she as a Castilian entertained against the cheating, mischievous, dangerous Andaluz,—nay ; so far was it from being so, that she had even held out a faint prospect to Maria de San José that she might even yet before she died see her face again in Seville), she resigned the honours of this foundation to Ana de Jesus, prioress of Veas. And on the morrow following, after she had bidden farewell to the nuns whom she had herself carefully selected, and who were to join the foundress at Veas, and thence go with her to Granada, she felt sad and lonely enough.

Other little details in her letters paint her thrifty, struggling life. Her poverty made it impossible for her to assist Gracian with his foundation in Salamanca, "so advantageous to the Order, that truly all should contribute." To this end even Fray Juan de la Cruz had turned out his wallet and counted and re-counted his scanty store of ducats, to see if any could be spared,—but his desires proved greater than his ability. "But she had got," she writes to Gracian, with all her old merry vivacity and shrewd humour, "four crowns out of Antonio Ruiz," who had paid her a visit two or three days before; "and I do well in not keeping them, for, as things go, it would not be wonderful if the temptation came upon me to steal."

Once more the powdery snow covers the neighbouring sierras with a veil of white, and lies in masses in the narrow tortuous streets; once more the wind howls with a strange and dreary sounding, bearing on its wings the secrets of vast and desolate solitudes, of mountain tops untrodden by foot of man, of savage recesses inhabited by the wolf and the wild boar,—of that great white world which lay beyond the grim mediæval town. In the country hamlets no one stirs; and flocks and herds are all under shelter, and packs of wolves scour the streets at midnight. The very shepherds cower over the blaze and listen in awe-struck wonder to some strange, fantastic legend of that wild, stirring past, which was even yet to them a real thing, whilst the door, barred and bolted, creaks and shakes in the fierce blast.

And once more in midwinter Teresa prepares to travel to Burgos. Once more! For she is nearing her journey's end. Once more she shall hear the dull clang of the great cathedral bells as they usher in the most solemn and joyous night of the year, stirring in her all the recollections of her childhood; far-away reminiscences of those with whom she had listened to their strident voice long years ago; some of them now slowly mouldering to dust in the great Franciscan monastery below the walls; some of them on the battlefields of the Indies,—that country vague to her with all the vagueness of immensity; and one in the little monastery church of the convent which owed its existence to her own hands and constant will. As they clang and clash through the stillness of the upland town, above the moaning of the wind, does their tongue convey any note of warning to the little old woman who has listened to their language from childhood to youth, from youth to age? But no! Oblivious of the near as of the distant future, when she shall have so set the seal of her identity on her native town that it shall no longer be Avila of the Knights, but Avila of Teresa de Jesus, she spends her last Christmas-tide on earth; arranges with loving care the little chamber where Gracian, who is on his way from Salamanca, to accompany her to Burgos, is to sleep: "although I do not believe that Doctor Castro, also anxious to have him for a guest, will consent to it." All has been arranged; family difficulties patched up for the present as well as may be. As for her niece Beatriz, much sound advice has been despatched to Juan de Ovalle in Alba, to get his daughter out of harm's way as soon as may be— by spending the winter, as was his usual custom, in the little hamlet of Galinduste:

I shall not be easy so long as I know you remain in Alba . . . since the occasion is by no means dead. For love of our Lord, take heed; for winter is now so far advanced, that it will do you no harm to go where you can have good fires, as is your custom; for, according to the warnings that have been given me, be sure that the devil is not asleep. . . . And surely, señor, putting aside such important matters, which it is impossible to lay too much stress upon, the course which has been suggested is necessary for your daughter's remedy; for she cannot remain with her parents for ever.

In another letter written five days after, she indicates the "remedy" more clearly,—a "remedy," indeed, which does not seem to have commended itself to, or to have been much relished by, the patient. She is about to found at Burgos, and thinks it would be a good plan to give Beatriz the habit in Avila and take her with her ("it will amuse her to visit these convents"), and she might afterwards accompany her to Madrid. But what seemed to Teresa the most powerful of inducements, namely that of being a foundress before she professed, did not rouse any corresponding enthusiasm on the part of those to whom it was proposed, and although she did, after her aunt's death, become a nun, she seems for the present to have preferred the hamlet and the good fires. "God be with them," sighs Teresa; "what a life they give me!"

One of her last letters of the old year was addressed to her nephew Lorenzo in Lima (or, as she styles it, "the City of Kings")—he whose picture still hangs in the ruined old manor-house of Hortigosa. He at least is rich and flourishing, and has made a wealthy marriage. His Indians—poor Indians!—bring him in a revenue of 7000 ducats; and Teresa, who has already had experience of one needy brother, sends a word of warning to Agustin de Ahumada, who was on the point of sailing for Spain in the fleet, to seek a pension for his services from the King. "I assure you that, if he does not bring enough to live on, he will have hard work enough, for no one will give him anything to eat, and for me it will be a sore trial not to be able to assist him. . . . It is an arduous thing for a man of his age to expose himself to so perilous a journey for the sake of fortune, when our attention ought rather to be set on getting ready for Heaven."

CHAPTER XXVI

THE CROWN OF THORNS AND ROSES

AND now we come to the foundation of Burgos, which the chronicler has styled not inaptly—for he too sees dimly into the tragedy of the last act of the drama of a human life—her crown of thorns and roses. Up and gird thy loins, O Teresa! for one last glorious effort; for the Night is coming when Work and Time shall for thee be swallowed up together in darkness, and when no man shall work, whatever may have been his mission. Lay aside the instinctive reluctance, the weariness of body and spirit which tempts thee—if only for a moment—to leave this foundation to stronger arms, but surely not stouter hearts than thine. Away, away there, wrapped in the sunset glow, lies the city, the Home, which thou hast seen glittering before thee from afar even from childhood. This life of thine; this weary laborious life, which seemed unending in the acting, has been but a dream; its griefs, and struggles, and spiritual darknesses but a mist, obscuring for a moment its brightness. Thou art fast approaching the Reality, thou who lovedst the Real in life; thou who even caughtest some dull glimpses of the Eternal Reason on earth, however falsified by the petty dogma of a creed. Bound in thy creed, its darknesses and its miserable prejudices, thou hast arisen far above it, and hast embraced and felt the Infinite striving within thee. Turn and look for the last time, before the city fades away for ever from vision -on the old gray city, storm-tossed and turbulent of look and outline, which has shut in with its changing imagery of day-dawn and sunset so much of thy existence. There lies the Encarnacion, sleeping in the hollow below the frowning battlements; away to the sunset stretches the bare, stone-strewn, rosemary-grown moorland, hiding a thousand crystal streamlets in its bosom. There, too, on the edge of the town, still distinguishable from the dusty Medina track amongst the red roofs and high walls of other convents,—the Gordillas and Sta. Ana of the Bernardines,—is that other convent which owes its existence to thy hands, which have fashioned it within and without to thy own spiritual seeming. O brave old woman! one last lingering look; and Avila for thee has faded away; nay, as completely faded out of thy life as if it had never been; although thou shalt shed over it a posthumous renown and the deeds of the caballeros who sleep in armour in the cathedral shall be forgotten; its heroic past and history be no longer remembered except inasmuch as their traditions nurtured the childhood, and inspired the womanhood, of the great Teresa de Jesus.

Her daughters of San José long remembered this her last residence amongst them. The magic touch of Death alone is wanting to such tender credulity as theirs (there is an element of greatness, let it not be forgotten, even in credulity) to see a miracle in many trivial actions—then unheeded, afterwards invested with a strange significance. It is not until the great curtain shall have rolled between them for ever, and Teresa shall have disappeared into the impenetrable shadow, that, vaguely realising how great had been the figure that had passed from amongst them, the imagination pursuing an inevitable process, lends her that vague supernatural atmosphere, which still shrouds her to-day as with a veil, and obscures the real aspect of the woman.

One might have thought that the last foundation, this crowning act of her career, would have been a continued triumph,—that she had silenced opposition, that she would have found her path cleared of all difficulties, and that she had only to appear in Burgos to make a project an accomplished fact. Such would indeed have been the dramatic ending to her sufferings and struggles; but, alas! human life in the acting rarely preserves the unities, and such was not Teresa's fate. Foiled in her darling project—the foundation at Madrid—she had at sixty-seven, during the last months of her life, to fight as keenly as she had ever done twenty years ago at Avila and Medina, before she added the last to the list of convents which hailed her as their foundress. For more than six years the idea, first suggested to her by some of the Company of Jesus, had lain dormant in her brain. It had been stirred into development by the newly-elected Archbishop of Burgos happening to pass through Valladolid during her stay there previous to the foundation of Palencia. She knew him well, for, like herself, he was an Aviles by birth, and sprung from one of its noblest and most ancient families. As long as Avila had been Avila, no skirmish, no sally after the Moors in the mountains, but some stout Blasco or Nuñez or Vela had had a share in it. What more natural than that he should help a countrywoman, whose struggles in her first foundation, when the whole town had risen against it, had been actually witnessed by him, and were still fresh in his memory? Whilst the two Bishops feasted and ate together in the old Jeronimite Convent of Valladolid, he of Palencia, proffering the request in Teresa's name, had little difficulty in extracting a verbal promise to admit and favour the proposed foundation. Nevertheless, on account of the distance, and of the climate of Burgos being so cold and rigorous, as well as to do pleasure to the good Bishop of Palencia, the former was deferred until the latter should be concluded, and when Soria interposed a still further delay, he sent a canon expressly to Burgos to sound the Archbishop as to his intentions. The Archbishop now, however, imposed conditions; the convent must either be endowed or sanctioned by the city. Teresa received this answer in Soria. The Bishop of Palencia, on the contrary, irritated at his episcopal brother's ambiguous answer, was for her setting forth at once. Teresa, however, was not to be deceived by fair words and reluctant promises. Loath to stir up strife between these two holy men, her ill-health and the approach of winter furnished her with an ostensible excuse (for with exquisite prudence, so as not to set the two friends by the ears, she refrained from assigning the real reason—the conduct of the Archbishop himself), and she quietly returned to Avila.

Nevertheless, a rich and influential widow of Burgos, who, getting acquainted with Teresa in Palencia, whither she had brought her two daughters to take the veil (two of them had already done so four years before in Valladolid), had set her heart upon this convent; and it was owing to her devotion, and not to any Archbishop of them all, that this of Burgos at last became an accomplished fact. She it was who, by generously volunteering to provide the house and sustenance, if needed, overcame the objections of the Corporation.

When she had begun to treat of it, she wrote to me that she had set about the negotiations. I took it as a jest, for I know how hard it is to get them to admit poor convents, and as I did not know, nor did it cross my mind, the obligation she had taken upon herself, it seemed to me that much more was needed. Withal, as I was commending it to the Lord one day in the octave of San Martin [the middle of November], I thought on how it might be done if the license were given : for that I with my many infirmities should go to so cold a place as Burgos (the cold being very hurtful to them) seemed to me impossible, and that it was a temerity to take so long a journey when I had just concluded so severe a one as I have spoken of in my coming from Soria; nor would the father provincial Gracian allow me. I considered that the prioress of Palencia would do as well, since, everything being smooth, there would be nothing to do. Whilst I was thinking this, and being very determined not to go, the Lord says to me these words, and by them I saw that the license had already been granted: Fear not the cold, for I am the true heat. The devil puts forth all his strength to prevent this foundation: put forth all thine for me to accomplish it, and fail not to go in person, for it will be of great benefit. . . .

Once more—for the last time—does the monitor of her life inspire her feeble frame with strength and courage. The natural reluctance of old age and infirmity to brave the snows and rains of a winter journey through Castille vanishes like a cloud before the sun; and when, a few days later, her prevision was justified by the arrival of the license, if she had had her will, she would have set out at once.

Gracian asked indeed whether she had the Archbishop's license in writing, but she quickly inspired him with the same generous confidence that she possessed herself.

The things of God [she answered] need not so much prudence, nor can weighty matters importing his service be undertaken if we wait for everything to be as smooth as we would wish. That foundation [Burgos] will be greatly to the service of God, and if it is put off any longer, it will not be made. Let us risk it [the license of the Archbishop], and keep silence, for the more we suffer the better it will be. And know that the devil is doing his utmost to prevent it; but, nevertheless, let your reverence consider your decision, for that will be the safest.

On the 2nd day of January 1582, Teresa set out for Burgos. Gracian,—to whom she had written with her usual loving solicitude, that, if he preached the last day of the Festival (Advent), he was not to set out without taking a day's rest, for fear the journey should hurt him,—came from Salamanca to Avila to accompany her, partly, she says, because he had to go to visit Soria, partly to look after her health on the road, as the weather was so severe, and she herself so old and infirm, "it seeming to them that my life is worth somewhat. And it was certainly a providence of God; for the roads were such, on account of the heavy rains, that he and his companions were indeed wanted to pick out the road, and help to drag the carts out of the quagmires, especially from Palencia to Burgos."

And so the little caravan took their way over that wild wintry world of Castille to Burgos. A covered cart, followed by a few straggling figures on donkeys, or it may be mules, appeared on one horizon, mingled for a moment with its white immensity, and faded into black dots on the sky-line. As in the Pampas of La Plata, or the sandy deserts of Arabia, on these upland plains, such objects as there are take an altogether disproportionate magnitude and importance, and for miles the ragged shepherd, standing motionless against the sky, noted their approach and watched them disappear. The melancholy and desolate charm of these upland plains is an indefinable impression rather than a positive perception. The earth as limitless as the sky, the sky itself the dominant note in the landscape. At mid-day, under its glittering brilliancy, the earth sinks into insignificance; until it too, as the sun grows low in the heavens, flushes with strange lights and symphonies of colour, and the stony stubble is turned into a glorious palette,—beyond all telling weird and mysterious at nightfall when the long low lines of the horizon darken against the pure green light, and a bunch of thistles looms tragical and ominous against the vast immensity of earth and sky.

Now and again the bell-tower of a church, some flat-roofed, smokeless village breaking for a moment the uninterrupted plain, rather increases than lessens the oppressive sense of solitude.

It is little more than a day's journey, as the crow flies, from Avila to Medina, and on the 4th of January, the day before the Eve of Twelfth Night, the grim Castillo de la Mota, flushed with the evening light, keeping watch and ward over the still invisible city at its base, rose before them above the level of the plain. To us it recalls nothing but historic facts diligently dug out of books: *sic transit gloria mundi:* but to these travellers it recalled personages and events which were still living images in their memory, events which had been enacted by, and in which their own fathers had taken part. Isabella and Ferdinand still cast a gigantic shadow over this their fortress palace; hidden in the plain a few miles distant was Madrigal, the birthplace of the Catholic Queen. Old men still living had seen them both; could remember the slightest detail of some faded pageant; had listened to the sound of their voices.

As the mules' hoofs rang over the frost-bound earth, and night fell slowly over city and plain, these and a hundred other memories evoked by that stern old building in the distance must have been uppermost in their thoughts and on their tongues.

We can fancy their entry into Medina, for the stage is unaltered,—the actors alone are gone. There are the four cross-roads by which they arrived that January night of 1582; here at the angle where town and country meet and blend so strangely is the tall square building of the Discalced Carmelite nuns of Medina. The last lingering strokes of the Ave Marias vibrated just as sadly through the keen wintry air; the pungent smoke of burning straw betokened then as now that the labourer had returned from the fields, and that for him one more day of his life's long labour was done. A cart stopped for a moment before the convent gates; a few figures scarcely more palpable than shadows moved confusedly hither and thither; the clang of a bell woke the echoes of the silent street; some footsteps shuffled through empty passages within; the gates swung open, and then closed; and cart and figures are engulfed in the shadow behind them, and the street is silent and tranquil as before. Nothing to attract more than a momentary movement of curiosity on the part of a passer-by,—except that it took place on one January night of 1582,—and no record remains of it, no record of how these dead people moved and felt, or how they thought and lived, beyond a passing reference to it in a nun's letters. It is because of these gaps that no human ingenuity can fill up—that never can be filled up—that so trivial an occurrence rouses an intense, nay, almost a solemn, interest.

They found the prioress Alberta Bautista ill in bed with high fever. "Jesus! daughter," said the saint, passing her hands gently over the sick woman's face, "and are you ill just when I am here. Come, get up, and have supper with me." And so she did, for as she rose in obedience to Teresa's bidding, she felt herself suddenly relieved, and at once set about ministering to the necessities of the beloved guest.

Oh, the joy of loving hearts, which seasoned the frugal meal that night, and had the virtue of transforming crusts of bread and draughts of water into some high festival! She stayed with them a few days, and on the eve of her departure addressed a letter to the Archbishop of Toledo's chaplain, the licentiate Peña, informing him of the health of Da. Elena Quiroga, the Archbishop's niece, "whose joy is so great, that it has made her praise God, and who has thriven so well on convent fare that she has even grown fat. Indeed she might have been a nun for many years, so versed is she in the 'cosas de religion.' I did not think to leave Avila," she adds, "until I started for the Foundation of Madrid." (I wonder if a pang of remorse smote the Archbishop's heart when the light of death had given to these words an echo of reproach—the more touching as it was unspoken). "Our Lord has been pleased that some persons of Burgos were so desirous that one of these monasteries should be founded there, that they procured the Archbishop's license, and that of the corporation, and so I am going with some sisters to effect it, for so obedience demands, and our Lord wills that it should cost me more labour ; for being so close as is Palencia, it was not his pleasure that it should be done then, but afterwards when I was in Avila, for it is no slight labour now to take so long a journey."

At Valladolid they were detained four days on account of Teresa's health, who, besides having caught a bad cold and sore throat with the severe weather, had had a slight stroke of paralysis.

> Withal [she writes to Catalina de Tolosa], I set out as soon as I was a little better; because I am afraid of your grace, and these my ladies, whose hands I kiss many times. I beseech their graces not to blame me for the delay, nor your grace either, for if you knew in what a state the roads are, perhaps you might blame me more for having come.... They say that the road between this and Burgos is very irksome, and so I do not know if the father provincial will be willing to set out until I am better, although he desires it greatly.

Her arrival at Palencia was a veritable triumph—her last. So great the crowds assembled to see her alight and to hear the sound of her voice—so soon now to be stilled—and seek her benediction, that they had much ado to get the travellers out of the carts. As the cloister doors opened to receive her, she was met by her nuns chanting the Te Deum, as was the invariable custom of all her convents, when she arrived. In token of their joy and delight the good souls had swept and garnished the convent patio, and decked it with altars and images, "which inspired great devotion." During the few days she spent with them, however, she was very ill, and they tried in vain to induce her to remain until the severe weather had moderated, and the heavy rains subsided. To set forth in such weather they all said was impossible, for they ran the risk of perishing on the way; but, brave to the end, nothing they could say was of any avail, and she insisted on proceeding. A man sent to report on the state of the roads, returned with the news that all the rivers were up, and the bridges washed away. For a moment the saint was dismayed, but not for long: "Fear not," whispered the mysterious voice, "for I will be with you"; whereupon, "although it seemed a foolhardiness," she at once started. "Although I did not tell this to the father provincial then, nevertheless it consoled me in the great labours and perils in which we saw ourselves, especially in a crossing near Burgos, called the *pontones*, and the water was so high that the bridges were completely covered, and very deep. In short, it is a great temerity to cross it, above all for carts, which, should they swerve ever so little, would certainly go to the bottom, and in this way one of the carts saw itself in great peril. . . . As we could not do a day's journey on account of the bad roads, for very often the carts stuck fast in the mud, and the animals had to be taken out of the others and yoked to each one by turns so as to drag them out, the fathers who accompanied us had their hands full, for our muleteers chanced to be mere lads, and careless. The presence of the father provincial was a great comfort, because he put his hand to everything, and, besides, his temper is so sweet that he does not seem to mind any labour; and thus what was a very great one he lightened, until it seemed but little, although not that of the pontones, which none of us could help dreading." For they were merry souls, these friars and nuns, making light of the perils of the road as soon as they were over. And perils indeed there were on those wintry Castilian tracks. Now the carts stuck fast on the banks of a river, and the nuns, tucking up their habits, were forced to flounder through the mud on foot. At another time, as they were going up a hill, to Teresa's horror, who was behind, the front cart with the nuns upset, and they were like to have fallen into the river, had not one of the muleteers observed the danger, and seizing the wheel, kept it from falling,—" it seeming almost impossible he should have been able to hold it unaided, unless God had come to their assistance." Thenceforward she insisted on always going in front, so as to be first in danger.

"And oh! the posadas!" she exclaims, as well indeed she might. For they at least are in no way altered—this link, at all events, between now and then is not missing. You can see it any day, the wretched wayside venta, dark as a cave inside, its mud floor trodden into a puddle by the passage in and out of men and beasts. A little straw or dried dung, perhaps, if a little better-to-do, some dried vine shoots, burn in the midst of the floor, the smoke going out through a hole in the roof. The misery of the roads and weather nothing to the intolerable misery, fleas, and dirt within.

But the worst was yet to come. The dreaded pontoons or floating bridges still lay between them and Burgos,—at the best of times so narrow that a false step would have sent the unwary passenger into the river,—now completely submerged under half a yard of water. "We took a guide in a venta, on this side," writes Teresa,—the venta where the night before they had not been able even to get her a bed,— "who knew the crossing, but certainly it is very perilous."

"Now then, my daughters," said the intrepid old woman (she was sixty-seven, and moreover paralytic),—"what greater privilege do you desire than (if it should be needful) to become martyrs here for the love of God? Hinder me not; for it is my desire to cross first, and, if I am drowned, I beseech you earnestly not to attempt it, but to return to the venta."

Saying which, and concealing a momentary qualm,—"for to see oneself without a road or boat, for all the Lord had emboldened me, even I could not but feel afraid, and what would not my companions do,"—she boldly plunged into the world of waters, and restored confidence to the trembling nuns, who stood confessing their sins and mumbling credos on the brink. Truly the old spirit of adventure that had made Spain great, the militant instincts of her race, beat true and strong in this old nun's bosom, who quaintly adds, "that a bad[1] sore throat and continuous fever did not allow her to enjoy the zest of these incidents of the road as much as usual. They all—the nuns—(she writes oblivious of herself) travelled cheerfully enough, for, the danger over, it was an amusement to talk of it. It is a great thing, for those who practise it as often as these nuns, to suffer for obedience."

It is said that, when she found herself on the opposite brink, she was heard to mutter, "It seems impossible that, after having consecrated my existence and dedicated all my labours to thee, thou shouldest treat me thus." Whereupon a voice answered from above (doubtless Christ's): "Thus do I treat my friends!" To which she no less promptly rejoined, "For this reason hast thou so few." An apocryphal anecdote which may not be true, but which, like such anecdotes, paints the woman; for there is a spice of wisdom even in folly. It

---

[1] Ribera mentions that she was very ill, and that the paralysis had affected her tongue. He adds that, as she heard Mass and communicated in a village they came to after crossing the pontoons, she recovered its use, and felt better, although the fever never left her.

was also on this journey that she is reported to have said to a monk who accompanied her (Gracian?), as he talked to her of the reputation she was held in as a saint: "During the course of my life they have said of me three things: when I was young that I was fair to look upon; then, that I was witty; and now some say I am a saint. The first two things I once believed in, and have confessed myself of having given credence to this vanity; but in the third, I have never deceived myself so much as ever to have even begun to believe it."

What did Burgos look like to these old-world travellers, when travelling was travelling indeed, and towns and cities dawned on the traveller from afar, and grew larger and larger on his vision, as tired mule or donkey flagged wearily across the plain;—not as now when you whizz into it in a railway train? Then he saw, what the nuns now saw as they pulled back the awning (for they were but women), a city such as you may see drawn by some monkish draughtsman in the vignette of an old missal, or some old, very old engraving. An irregular conglomerate of serried roofs and monastery towers; girt in with turreted walls and bridges, even as the race of fighters had fashioned it, jagged of outline, a little grayer than the sky, it looked as if it had lain there for ever—a small oasis of life cut out of the vastness of the plain. Ragged sky torn by the tempest; lace-work spire shooting up against it; smokeless, stately, and grim, the city lay dripping in the rain, moss-grown, gray, and faded on the low-lying banks of the Arlanzon. Away to the left, overlooking the water-meadows where the stork mused gravely on the landscape, Las Huelgas, the proudest convent in all Spain,—its aisles lined with tombs of kings and queens, above them the silken banner of Miramamolin rotting proudly to dust. Facing them an old tower on an eminence, mouldering even then, overshadowing the city as was but meet,—as its owner had overshadowed it in life, even the Cid, the great Cid Campeador.

And Teresa, as she watched it growing on her vision across the flooded water-meadows, little recked that as Burgos the capital of Spain long before Valladolid, the chiefest jewel in the Castilian crown—then lived on his memory as if he, the stern old Gothic knight, had been its only *raison d'être*, so too that wild old fortress town amongst the moorlands, which she had beheld for the last time, was to live on hers for all eternity. For these two, so far apart in years, were to be alike in this, that they are the two types in which the Castilian character and its tendency have most distinctly embodied themselves, and been made visible to the world.

It was still light when they reached the outskirts of the town—too light to enter Burgos. For it was no small matter in those days for a band of strangers to run the gauntlet of the hostile gaze and excited curiosity of an unknown—and, being unknown, inimical—town.

They had now got to what is to-day a lonely and deserted suburb, cut in two by railway lines and telegraph posts, crossed by a sandy lane. This sandy lane was then, when honest muleteers and booted and spurred cavaliers rode in and out, as muleteers and gentlemen should, the highroad to Madrid, and the principal entrance on that side to the city. It wound before the high walls of stately hospitals and monasteries, which had spread from the town and invaded this strip of low-lying ground on the right bank of the Arlanzon, and was connected with the city by St. Mary's Bridge. Before the gates of one of these monasteries the travellers alighted. It was the famous monastery of the Augustinians, renowned throughout all Spain as the shrine of one of its most famous images—the celebrated Christ of Burgos. They thus achieved a double object: they put off the last moments of daylight until they could enter Burgos under cover of night; and Teresa and her nuns would also be privileged to make their orisons before the marvellous Christ of which they had heard since childhood.

It is true: there is no more wonderful image—one in which the elements of sublimity, terror, and profound pathos are so eloquently combined as in this Christ of Burgos. The Spaniard is not imaginative. His rigid matter-of-factness penetrates even into his religion. To him every object of his faith is a living concretion; not a nebulous phantasm floating in a remote limbo. He blocks out his Virgins and Images to represent the colour and aspect of life. The Christ—it still hangs terrible and pathetic above the aisles of Burgos Cathedral—is one of the most striking examples of this. It imposes on and thrills the imagination with its grim realism, and startles the gazer into the momentary belief of his forefathers that the rigid form may at any moment rouse itself into movement and volition. It was generally ascribed to Nicodemus, and supposed to have floated all the way from Palestine to Spain, and to have been picked up on the high sea by a pious merchant of Burgos. Others, not satisfied with so prosaic an explanation, will have it that it came down from heaven itself: they are perhaps not altogether wide of the mark, for the obscure carver has indeed, like Prometheus, filched the creative fire. However it may be—and I shall leave it to the pious reader to choose whichever hypothesis commends itself to him most, for all is possible (to faith)—it was and still is the supreme glory and boast of Burgos. Around it, as around other images which deeply affected the national imagination, clusters a circle of legend—terrible, pathetic, always picturesque, strongly tinctured with the character and peculiar characteristics of the Spaniard himself.

Had not the holy head shaken off the golden crown, placed by piety round its pallid brow, and, faithful to the crown of thorns, spurned it to his feet, where ever afterwards it found a resting-place? When stolen by the jealous monks of a neighbouring convent, had not the image straightway returned to its accustomed shrine, and when again wrested from its guardians by main force, appeared in its place next morning as if nothing had happened?

The light of day has ever been unpropitious to religious mysteries. Proving on the one side the reality of the devotion which resolves itself into a cult so splendid and so grand; on the other, the universal acknowledgment that the bulk of men are governed rather by appearances than reason. The perpetual and mysterious twilight was lit by the glimmer of a hundred gold and silver lamps,[1] and sixty silver candlesticks. As the last of the three curtains, embroidered

[1] These lamps were of so extraordinary a size as to cover the entire cupola of the chapel in the cloister devoted to the image. The sixty candlesticks were taller than a good-sized man, and it took three workmen to lift them.

with pearls and precious stones, was drawn apart, and the Man of God stood revealed, the bells clashed loud in the tower above, and all present fell on their knees. "Certainly," says Madame d'Aulnoy, who visited the shrine a century after Teresa, "that sacred spot and divine image inspire religious awe"; and if the brilliant and vivacious Frenchwoman confessed to such a feeling, we may judge of the emotion felt by these simple Castilian nuns and friars of a former generation with their *naïf* belief in a positive faith.

Let us follow them across St. Mary's Bridge. The city is lost in the night. A feeble oil light flickers here and there, a red gleam from an open casement, blurred by the drenching rain. The river lies dark and silent below. All sound has faded from the street, except the pelt, pelt of the rain, the heavy pour of water from the leads on the causeway below; for in a moment the gates will be shut for the night, and no one may go out or in until the morning. In the middle of the bridge an oil lamp gleams before the image of the Virgin, who, wrapped in the rigid folds of her stone raiment, extends a silent benediction to the outgoing or incoming traveller. So they enter the soaking streets of Burgos, and, frozen to the bones and drenched to the skin, at length find themselves under the hospitable roof of Catalina de Tolosa, where they dry their wringing habits before a blazing fire. During the night, Teresa was seized with giddiness of the head and vomitings, and spat up blood, which she attributed to her having remained longer before the fire than was her wont. Nevertheless, next day, stretched on a pallet placed close to a grated window which gave on to a corridor, and concealed by a curtain, she received the visitors who thronged to salute her. The corporation sent to assure her of their goodwill, and to place themselves at her service. This pleased her greatly, since, if she had entertained any misgiving at all, it had been on account of them.

One of these visitors, Don Pedro Manso, Magistral of Burgos Cathedral, and afterwards Bishop of Calahorra, testified nearly thirty years afterwards that, such was the fear and respect that thrilled through him, and made his hair stand on end with awe and reverence, as he drew nigh to speak with her, he indeed knew he was in the presence of a great saint, destined to be a notable pillar in the Church of God. He it is also, who, after a business interview with her, is recorded to have exclaimed, "God help me! I would rather argue with all the theologians in the world put together than with this woman."

During the course of the morning, Gracian returned from his first interview with the Archbishop. His news were anything but reassuring. The capricious prelate he had found "so changed and angry at my having come without his license, as if he himself had neither ordered it nor had anything to do in the matter, and so spoke most furiously against me to the father provincial." When pushed into a corner by Gracian's ingenious arguments, and forced to concede that she had come at his bidding, he took shelter in the quibble that he had meant herself alone ; " but to come with so many nuns, God deliver us from the trouble it gave him !"

In vain the good friar urged that they had complied with the only condition he, the Bishop, had insisted on, viz. that they should obtain the license of the corporation, and that there was nothing more to do but to found forthwith ; and that if they had not given him notice beforehand of their coming, it had been by the advice of the Bishop of Palencia, who, confiding in his metropolitan's word, had seen no need for it. "It was," adds Teresa, in an undertone, so keen to gauge hidden motives, " the will of God that the house should be founded, for had we frankly told him our intentions, he would have ordered us not to come." The long and short of it was, that on no account would he grant a license unless they could endow a house of their own, and they might return as soon as they liked. "A pretty state indeed the roads were in, and the weather also !"

But the old saint was nothing daunted. She had conquered archbishops before—nay, even had them on their knees before her—" Teresa the omnipotent." She was not going to be beaten now. All was for the best. Let the devil lay as many snares as he liked to circumvent it, God was bound to bring his work to a triumphant ending. Gracian too was cheerful, until his patience oozed away with the sickness of hope deferred and the equivocal paltering of the Archbishop. Nor did that prelate confine himself to paltering. He refused the request—it seemed modest enough, but was indeed equivalent to taking possession—made to him by two friendly canons, that the sick woman consumed with fever might hear Mass in a room of Catalina's house—a room which had already been used as a chapel for more than ten years by the Jesuits on their first establishment in Burgos. She might found there, he answered, if she liked, provided always that the endowment was forthcoming, and she could give security for the purchase of a house.

When, after a month's delay, this was finally arranged, and security had been found and given, and the Archbishop professed himself satisfied, his Vicar-General stepped in, interposing other difficulties. He pretended that Catalina's house was damp, and in a noisy street; they must even look out for a house of their own, more to the Archbishop's liking; and "as for the security for the money," adds the perplexed Teresa, "I know not what twistings and turnings." Still she hung on; until at length she determined to seek the Archbishop in person, and to plead with him face to face. The first, and perhaps the only, time in her life that the magic of her presence and simple eloquence signally failed. She obtained nothing, and her nuns scourged themselves in vain,—although I know not by what mysterious chain of reasoning their bleeding shoulders were to turn the fate of the interview. Nevertheless, her companions noted that she returned to them as gay and cheerful as if all she wished had been accomplished. And indeed she has need of all her cheerfulness, for despondency has begun to invade that little band. Gracian and his companions lodged in the house of Canon Manso, an old fellow-student of his at Alcalá,—Gracian, baffled by futilities, begins to despair; the nuns also; and they would all willingly have abandoned the foundation and returned as they had come.

Yea, their spirits shrink away under the touch of adversity; hers only waxes greater. If the good Gracian's distress troubles her, and she wishes he had not come, it is for his sake, not her own.

"Now, Teresa, hold firm!" These words, which she

attributed to God, are but the faint echo of her own indomitable spirit and unflinching resolution. She persuades Gracian that they can do without him. Lent was approaching, and he had to preach his Lenten sermons in Valladolid. He was easily persuaded, but before he went he and his friend Canon Manso did what they could to make the position of the nuns more tolerable. Until now they had been the guests of Catalina de Tolosa, but owing to the Archbishop's refusal to let them hear Mass in a room of her house on Sundays and festivals—for the rest of the week they went without—they were forced to go trudging ankle-deep in mud to a neighbouring church. A small matter, say you? But not so small to women whose life of seclusion had made them peculiarly sensitive; to whom it was positive torture to mix even for a moment with an outside world so strange to them. One nun there was who trembled from head to foot when she found herself in the street. Nor must we imagine that the streets of Burgos were at all like what they are now. You may still see a mediæval Spanish street in some forgotten hamlet of the Vera of Plasencia. A narrow causeway of rough pebbles, barely wide enough to allow a passage for a mule and rider, shut in on either side by the frowning fronts of palaces or hovels, but all alike solid, impenetrable, gray, and moss-grown; the timbered eaves of the roofs shutting out the daylight; and underneath, running in the centre of it, sometimes to a considerable depth, either an open sewer or stream of water. A jostle in such circumstances as often as not led to the flash of swords. Through this shadowy, mysterious street, often ankle-deep in mud, did Teresa and her nuns fleet at earliest dawn to hear a mass,—and she also met with her encounters. As she was crossing one of these places one day, a woman whom she asked to make room for her replied with scorn, "Let the old relic-monger pass," and pushed her violently into the gutter. "Silence, my daughters," she said, as she picked herself out of the mud, to her indignant companions—"silence, for the woman did exceeding well."

Nor was the church itself free from some rough insult. We have seen how at Toledo a woman had stoutly belaboured her with her chapins. In Burgos some men administered a few such hearty kicks to the kneeling saint, for not having got out of their way as quickly as she might, as sent her sprawling on the floor. When Ana de San Bartolomé flew to raise her up, she found the old saint full of laughter, and highly delighted with the incident.

At all this the good Gracian had been greatly distressed, and although not without great difficulty (for local prejudice was strong in those dim far-away days, and those from a neighbouring city were mistrusted not merely as aliens and strangers in the gates, but exposed to suspicion and active hostility, a sentiment which in a less degree is distinctly discernible in the Spain of to-day), he found them a lodging in the Hospital of the Concepcion, a few paces from the monastery of the Augustinians, where they had made their orisons to the famous Christ of Burgos on the night of their arrival. It still exists, this Hospital of the Concepcion, a great walled building in the low-lying sandy suburb outside the town, on the opposite bank of the Arlanzon—it still exists, although modern life has ceased to have any use for anything so spacious and so stately—still exists, its beneficent purpose being put to the uses of a wood-shed. A great, old, rambling place; echoing and empty, with granite staircases of enormous size and massiveness; a white-washed refectory hung with famous Flemish tapestries (they too have gone within the last three years). Here, then, he hired for them some rambling lofts under the roof. "This gave him some satisfaction," says Teresa, "but he went through not a little before he got it for us; for a good room there was there had been hired by a widow of Burgos, and (although she did not require it for half a year) not only did she refuse to lend it to us, but was vexed that we had the rooms under the roof, one of which communicated with hers. And not satisfied with locking it on the outside, she nailed it up inside as well. Moreover, the confraternity thought we were going to take possession of the hospital—which was ludicrous—only that it was God's will we should deserve more. They make us promise the father provincial and me—before a notary, that the moment they tell us to go, we do so at once."

You may still see if you will the lofts under the roof

where Teresa and her daughters dwelt; and the gallery surrounding the humid patio, whence (for in those days it looked down upon the chapel altar) they once heard Mass. There you may fancy them huddled together under the tiles in the winter cold, they and the rats; startled by all the ghostly echoes that haunt the silence of empty and desolate space. Ana de San Bartolomé firmly believed it was haunted by evil spirits—at night things were violently thrown down overhead—and she affirmed to her dying day that she had seen Satanic imps appear through a hole and push one another about. Her nuns suffered from the cold, filth, and evil odour left behind them by generations of poverty-stricken sufferers; Teresa alone was unfeignedly happy, and accepted everything as better than she deserved. "Oh, my Lord, what a luxurious bed is this, in comparison with thine on the cross," she said, as the nuns made up her miserable straw pallet. "Do not pity me," she told the nuns, their compassion aroused by the sight of the sufferings of the brave old woman, who could scarcely swallow without drawing up blood from a wound in her throat—"do not pity me, for the Lord suffered more for me when he drank the gall and vinegar."

One day she longed for an orange, and a lady (Catalina de Tolosa?) sent her some very good ones. What does she do? Shall she eat oranges when others perhaps need them more? So, telling the nuns she was going down for a moment to see a poor man who was complaining greatly—oh, innocent deception! she puts them in her sleeve; hobbles down to the hospital and divides them amongst the sufferers. "I want them more for them than for me," she answered to the reproaches of her companions when she returned; "and I am very glad, for I left them greatly consoled."

Another time, at the sight of a present of some limes, she exclaimed, "Blessed be God for giving me something to take to my poor."

They are little incidents, but paint the nobility of the woman. Who shall tell the ray of light she left behind her, as in her patched old habit (for, ragged as it was, we may be sure it was clean and most neatly patched) she moved amongst those wretched beds.

"Son," she said to a wretched man whose groans and cries disturbed the repose of the other sufferers—"son, why do you complain so, and not bear this with patience for the love of God?" And presently his pain left him, and with it his complaints. And thenceforth, however intolerable the operations he underwent, he bore them in silence. The very sight of her consoled those poor sick folk, and they besought of the infirmarian to bring them that Holy Woman often. And when she left the hospital she left behind her mourning hearts and streaming eyes.

Daily were they cheered by the visits and presents of the generous Catalina de Tolosa. Indeed, without her they could not have lived. She too displayed much courage and valour in facing the criticisms and the sharp tongues of her townsmen. Not but that they wounded her so sorely that, however much she sought to hide the wound, it could not be concealed from the sharp and sympathetic vision of Teresa. And yet verily, according to the verdict of that day, she had her reward—her two sons became Discalced friars in Teresa's Order, she and all her daughters nuns in the convent which she was mainly instrumental in founding. And her children rose up and called her blessed!

It was now the Eve of San José. The confraternity had warned them that they must out of the hospital by Easter. What was to be done? All Teresa's efforts and those of her friends had been fruitless; and they were still as far off as ever from getting a house of their own. She now bethought herself—was it not the Eve of San José, her loyal patron?—of one which, having been successively rejected by three Orders on the same mission in Burgos as herself, had till that moment almost faded from her memory.

Being one day with the licenciado Aguilar [can you not fancy him, this good medical man of Avila, with his gloves and his tasselled cane and his pompous strut?], who, as I have said, was a friend of our father's [Gracian], and went about looking for a house for us with great solicitude, as he was telling me how he had seen some, and that there were none to be got in the place, nor did it seem possible to get any, according to what they told me I remembered me of this, which as I say we had already rejected, and bethought me that even though it be so bad as they say, it might tide us over our necessity, and that afterwards we could sell it: and I asked the licenciado to do me the favour to go and see it. It did not seem to him a bad idea; he had not seen the house, and, in spite of its being a stormy and tempestuous day, he started off at once. It was inhabited by a tenant who had little wish it should be sold, and would not show it; but he was greatly pleased with the site and all he could see, and so we resolved to buy it. The gentleman it belonged to was not in Burgos, but had entrusted the sale to a priest, a servant of God, whom his Majesty inspired with the desire to sell it to us, and to treat us with great frankness. It was arranged that I should go and see it: I was so pleased with it that it would have seemed to me cheap, even had they asked twice as much more as what I understood they were willing to give it to us for; nor was it much for me to do, for its owner had been offered that price two years before, and would not take it. Presently next day came the priest and the licentiate who, when he saw the price he asked, was for settling it there and then. [One may be sure, being Spaniards, that there was much bargaining.] I had mentioned it to some friends, who told me that if I gave it, I gave 500 ducats too much. So I told him, but he thought it cheap even if I gave the price he asked, and so did I, and I would not have hesitated, for it seemed to me given away; but as the money belonged to the Order, it made me scrupulous. This meeting was on the Eve of the glorious San José, before Mass: I told them we would talk the matter over again when Mass was over, and then decide. The licentiate is of a very good understanding, and saw clearly, that if it got wind, either it would cost us much more, or we should lose it altogether. He was therefore very earnest about the matter, and made the priest promise to come back after Mass. We went to commend it to God, who said to me: And dost thou hesitate because of money? showing clearly what we ought to do. They all pressed me to conclude the bargain. The sisters had besought San José greatly that we might have a house on his day, and although we did not dream we should have it so soon, he brought it about. They all pressed me to conclude it, as was done, for the licentiate found a notary at the very door—which seemed a dispensation of Providence—and came with him and told me that it was best to settle it, and brought a witness; and the door of the room being shut, so that nothing should transpire (for this was his fear), the sale was concluded with all firmness on the Eve of the glorious San José, by the kindly diligence and understanding of this good friend. No one thought we should get it so cheaply, and so when it began to get wind, forthwith came forward other purchasers, who said that the priest who sold it had let it go for nothing; and that the sale should be undone, because the fraud had been great: the good priest went through much. The occupants of the house, who were a principal gentleman and his wife, were at once notified; and so delighted were they that their house should become a convent, that they sanctioned it, if only for that reason, although, indeed, they could do nothing else. Immediately the next day the deeds were drawn up, and the third of the price of the house paid down, all as the priest had bargained for.

After some little difficulty in getting rid of a troublesome occupant loath to go, Teresa and her nuns moved into their new house. With the help of the good licentiate, and at no great cost, in little more than a month it assumed the appearance of a monastery.

"Truly it seemed as if our Lord had kept it for himself, for almost everything seemed to have been done beforehand. It is true that immediately I saw it, and everything as if it had been done on purpose for us, it seemed to me somewhat of a dream to see it so quickly ready. Well did our Lord repay us for what we had gone through, by bringing us to a delightful spot; for with its gardens, views, and water, it seems nothing else."

But their difficulties were by no means ended. The cavilling Archbishop was still to be placated. At first he expressed himself highly delighted with their good success; even took the credit of it to himself, but wrathful was he when he heard that they were actually in the house; still more so that they had put up gratings and a torno. "I appeased him as much as I could," adds Teresa; "for, although he is quickly angered, he is a good man, and it is soon over!"

Nevertheless, although he came to see the house, and professed himself pleased with it, for more than a month he obstinately withheld the license. Nay more, he would allow no Mass in the Chapel, although the owners of the house had never used it for any other purpose; and on feast days and Sundays they were still forced, as at Catalina de Tolosa's, to resort to a neighbouring church. Then there were questions as to the deeds. "Now they were satisfied with cautioners; the next moment they wanted the money with many other importunities. In this the Archbishop was not so much to blame as a vicar-general of his, who battled with us so terribly that if God had not taken him away on a journey, when his charge devolved on another, I think it never would have ended." Canon Manso put in a word whenever he was able; but at length Teresa as a last resort appealed to the Bishop of Palencia. Already deeply offended at his archiepiscopal brother's paltering, and at the treatment she had received, he at once sent her an open letter for him "in such wise that to have delivered it, would have been to ruin everything."

Indeed the unpalatable home-truths it contained were so unequivocally and frankly expressed that Canon Manso advised her not to deliver it, and from what I know of Teresa I doubt whether it was ever seen by the touchy and irascible prelate to whom it was addressed. Again she wrote to his Most Illustrious of Palencia, and this time D. Alvaro de Mendoza, making a heroic effort to swallow his wounded pride and indignation,—"all he had done for the Order," he averred, " was as nothing to that letter "—took a more conciliatory tone. The good Hernando de Matanza— let his name be remembered, at least, if we know no more of him than that he was in his time "a good servant of God " —sped with the missive to the Archbishop's palace. The night before, for the first time during all these weary months of waiting and delay, Teresa herself had given way to the general despondency. Oh! now, Teresa, on the eve of victory hold firm, hold firm! How blessed are the feet of him who brings good tidings! Hernando returns in triumph ; and, with a joy too deep perhaps for words, announces it to those within by quietly setting to work to ring the convent bell.

Ring on, oh bell! fill the convent corridors with thy feeble tinkling. Thou commemoratest a victory bloodless, indeed, but one in which human strength and endurance have been strained to their utmost limits! Let thy echoes ring on for ever ; let them vibrate for all time in the memory of Burgos ; in the memory of all who love her,—for it is the last thou or any other shalt celebrate, won by Teresa de Jesus. Nay, not the last! There is still one other, the greatest of all to be fought and won—one that is very near now.

Next day—it was the 19th of April 1582—the Host was solemnly placed on the altar. The first Mass was celebrated by Canon Manso; High Mass by the Dominican prior of San Pablo. It was a solemn and gorgeous scene. The musicians and minstrels of Burgos spontaneously offered their services, and their bursts of minstrelsy swelled through the humble little chapel. Great joy was there that day in the ancient capital of Castille ; for the Archbishop's petty tyranny had in a lesser degree the same passive virtues (the only ones) as persecution, and rallied all hearts to the brave, undaunted old woman. And the good Catalina de Tolosa, the worthy matron who had stripped her own house of its beds and furniture (for " she was very much a daughter of some one ") to administer to their necessities, she too is full of gladness.

"Of those who have founded our monasteries," says Teresa in her history of this foundation, written during this last year of her life, "others have given very much greater wealth ; but to none has it cost one-tenth part of the trouble." Let her too be remembered. And verily, according to the judgment of her epoch—it may have shifted since ; but what matter?—she had her reward. Before Teresa left Burgos her daughters received the habit from the saint's own hands —a ceremony actually graced by the Archbishop himself, who, tardily repentant, now publicly from the pulpit sang the praises of the Discalced Order of Carmelites, and expressed his sorrow for the delays there had been in the Foundation.

Two of Catalina's sons became Discalced friars, and worthy ones. Her daughters all entered the same Order ; she herself took the habit in Palencia, "thereby fulfilling "—it is Ribera who speaks—" the words of David, that the generation of the just shall be blessed." Even for those days presenting an unparalleled example of a family of nine persons moved by the same impulse, entering and dying in the same Order !

Yet let us not forget that the salient events of life —what in the conception of the vulgar alone constitute the history—are in reality very few. Teresa's triumphs lasted but a moment : were but the pearls, stringing together long intervals of obscure labours, in which there is little to attract the shallow mind. Detail and more detail ; humble duties ; cares often wearisome, and sometimes sordid. Such is the obscure undertone of all lives ; tragic enough, too, if we could but see it with a larger vision. One day witnessed the triumph which all men could see and wonder at, which forms the exterior and tangible part of her history ; but labour, cares, sordid or otherwise, humble duties,—formed her *life*. And to me he is greatest and lives his life most worthily, although no triumphs smile upon his efforts, to whom no trifle is too small, no detail too sordid, if it enshrines and consecrates a daily sacrifice to Duty.

In the meantime, however, the good Catalina is sorely perplexed and troubled of conscience. She had bequeathed her fortune after her death (that part of it at least which such of her daughters as had already entered the cloister had renounced) to the Jesuit College of Burgos. This she had now legally transferred to Teresa's convent. The fathers of the College, who were moreover her confessors, naturally regarded these fresh dispositions sourly, and gave her no peace. They accused Teresa of being at the bottom of it all; and the quarrel between her and her old friends promised to be a bitter and fierce one. Anxious to avoid a rupture with her old friends and supporters in many an emergency, as well as to release the generous widow from a false position, she and Gracian formally resigned the gift in presence of a notary, and returned the deeds to Catalina de Tolosa. This was done with great secrecy lest it should reach the Archbishop's ears; since he had granted the license on the express condition that the convent was endowed, and might have conceived himself aggrieved, although as Teresa says, the loss was not his but the convent's, which was now left in a most precarious state, and in danger of perishing from hunger. For since every one supposed (and it was not wise to undeceive them) that the nuns had enough to live on, they were shut off from the ordinary resources of those founded in poverty, viz. the alms of the faithful. Yet Teresa knew neither doubt nor fear.

They will not want [she writes]; for the Lord, who provides alms for other monasteries dependent on them, will arouse up some to assist them here, or will show them some way by which they may maintain themselves. Although as not one of them has been founded in like sort, I sometimes besought him, since he had willed it to be made, that he would devise some means for their assistance, so that they should not want for the necessaries of life, and I felt reluctant to leave them, until I saw whether or not some nun would enter. And once as I was thinking on this after I had communicated, the Lord said to me: Of what dost thou doubt? For this is now concluded; thou mayest indeed go! thereby assuring me that they would not want for anything needful. Because it was in such a manner that I never again felt the least anxiety any more than if I had left them with an excellent income; and immediately I set about the arrangements for my departure, since it seemed to me that I was no longer of any use, except to take my ease . . . and that elsewhere, although with more labour, I could do more good.

Yea, Teresa, now thou canst go, for thy mission in Burgos,—nay, thy mission on earth also, is well-nigh done. Not, however, before a grateful town acclaims her as its deliverer, so keenly has her personality entered into the hearts and touched the imagination of its inhabitants, in whom the old chivalric spirit of the Cid still found a distant echo. For on Ascension Day the river rose and flooded the city. Houses were swept away; the monasteries were abandoned by their inmates, but not the little monastery on the low-lying ground down by the river,—the most exposed of all. For Teresa refused to fly; carrying the Host before them, she and her nuns took refuge in a room at the top of the house, and there repeated their litanies until the danger was over. And the Archbishop declared, and with him many of the city, that God had spared it because of the presence of Teresa de Jesus.

Towards the end of July,—the 26th according to Ines de Jesus,—Teresa set out on her last journey, leaving behind her an imperishable memory. Yes! There in the distance, before it fades from her sight, she looks back on the stork-haunted towers of Las Huelgas, founded by kings,—the scene of strange pageants, which even to her are more an old-world pageant than a reality. The monarchs who have for a moment filled the throne of Spain, and then departed like shadows, have one and all visited Las Huelgas. Once in the life of a king is that bricked door in the cloister opened to welcome him in his pride of triumph. Once more it may be opened to receive his bones. The visit of one Teresa de Jesus, shall, like that of kings, be long remembered in the annals of Las Huelgas; nay, she has left behind her a more abiding impression than any king. For of that venerable community, ruled by their mitred abbess, where the daughters only of the proudest nobility of Spain are allowed to dedicate themselves to God, four of its titled nuns—amongst them the daughters of the Count of Aguilar—presently abandon its delights and privileges, to assume the sackcloth, and share the privations of the Barefooted Carmelites.

And not on that stately monastery alone, but on the Hospital de la Concepcion, has she set her indelible seal. There, enshrined in the hearts of those humble, bed-ridden folk, whose sufferings she had consoled, casting over poverty and rags the tender radiance of sympathy (although she too, Teresa the Omnipotent, is as poor and ragged as they), will she, the very sight of whom had soothed them, and whose absence, when she left the Hospital, they had wept so bitterly, be long remembered and long mourned.

CHAPTER XXVII

NOT TO A STRANGE COUNTRY, BUT TO HER NATIVE LAND

> "It will be a great thing at the hour of death, to see that we are going to be judged by one whom we have loved above all things. Securely may we set forth to answer for our sins: for it will not be to set forth to a strange country, but our own native land, since it is that of him we love, and who loves us."
>
> CAMINO DE PERFECCION.

PERHAPS it was well the end was near; that her death came when it did; that she should have been spared the last and bitterest of all disillusions—that of watching what she had built up by the efforts of a lifetime crumble away under her eyes. Already the fervour of her convents has begun to decay; her prioresses are openly rebellious and impatient of her authority; her friars are divided by jealousy and ambition. Warned, perhaps, by some obscure presentiment, she had in vain begged of Gracian, her favourite son, to postpone his journey into Andalucia, and to stay by her side a little longer. The last pathetic appeal she was to make to him (alas! he knew not it was the last) remained unheeded. Doria was in Genoa, sent thither by Gracian—so said his detractors—that he might be rid of an inconvenient censor, but in reality because his birth, ability, and intimate connection with Genoa and Rome alike pointed him out as the most fitting person to entrust with the important mission of laying the submission of the Descalzos at the General's feet, and procuring his confirmation of the late Chapter of Alcalá. She has been disappointed in her hopes of founding at Madrid, which still haunts her, will haunt her to the last. Let her only accomplish this one foundation, no more,—let her establish her Order in the Court of Spain,—and her days for journeyings are done; for now as she writes, before she left Burgos, to Peña (the Archbishop's chaplain), who she still hopes may touch his master into acquiescence,—" she is very old and wearied. Confident that his Majesty will enlighten his Most Illustrious as to what is best, and that he desires to show her favour, she therefore would not be importunate ; except that as his Most Illustrious has so much to think of, and that she knows that this is for our Lord's service, she would not wish it to be lost sight of, for any want of diligence of hers ; and so she reminds his lordship of it, being very certain that God will give him light, and all will be done for the best and at the most fitting season." Her pathetic entreaties were of no avail. The Archbishop deferred giving the license until the King returned from Portugal ; and when the King returned it was too late, for she was dead. What, however, she failed to achieve in life, she accomplished in death ; for four years afterwards, as Yepes described to him the scene when her body was exposed in Avila, smitten perhaps by remorse as he remembered how often the great and heroic spirit had sued in vain, he exclaimed : " Let it be done forthwith ! "

She had been wounded too—how should she not—by the conduct of Ana de Jesus in Granada, who, in her newly-acquired importance of foundress, had shown a disposition to shake off all control, and to act without consulting either herself or Gracian,—showing how correctly Teresa had gauged her character when she had written to Gracian from Avila, a few months before, that her fault was an itch for command.

But Teresa was not to be trifled with, and, old and feeble as she was, she at once asserted her authority in as stern and austere a reprimand as she had ever penned.

You have set about your disobedience so cleverly, that this last [specimen of it] has given me no little pain, for it cannot but appear very ill to the entire Order, and furthermore on account of the evil example which it may have left behind for other prioresses to act in the same way, who will have no lack of excuses either. And now that you give those gentle people such a character, it has been a great indiscretion your having been so many . . . for in the same way as you sent those poor women back so many leagues, when they had barely arrived (for I know not how you had the heart to do it), you might also have sent back those who came from Veas, and even others along with them, for your having been so many has been a terrible discourtesy, especially when you felt you were giving trouble.

For let it not be forgotten that Teresa was a lady of delicate instincts and perceptions, and had never, though often sorely pressed, infringed the unwritten laws of good breeding.

> I have laughed at the fright you give us that the Archbishop will do away with the monastery. . . . But if it is to go on as it is doing now, introducing the beginnings of disobedience into the Order, it would indeed be well it should not exist, *for nothing is to be gained by founding many monasteries, unless those who live in them lead saintly lives.*

Without saying anything to Gracian, or consulting him as to their choice, the wily prioress had taken with her from Veas those nuns most partial to herself. On this point Teresa's commands are peremptory. With the exception of Ana de Jesus herself, they are all to return thither without delay:

> Since any kind of attachment, even though it be to their prioress, is utterly against the spirit of the Descalzas, and checks all improvement in the spiritual life. . . . It is the beginning of faction and rivalry, and of many other calamities, if it is not checked at the commencement: and for this once at least, for mercy's sake, be guided by me; and afterwards, when you are more settled, and they more detached, you may have them back again if you think fit. Truly I know not who they were you took, for with great secrecy have you kept it from me and our father [Gracian]; nor did I think your reverence would take so many thence; but I imagine that they are those most affected to your reverence. . . . I beseech your reverence to consider that you are bringing up souls for spouses of the Crucified; and that you crucify them in rooting out their will, and putting an end to these childishnesses. Consider that you are carrying the Order into a new kingdom [Granada], and that your reverence and the rest are obliged to act like valorous men and not like weak women. What matters it, my mother [Ana de Jesus has been hurt in her dignity by having been addressed by Gracian as president instead of prioress], whether the father provincial calls you president or prioress, or Ana de Jesus. . . . Of a truth, I have been greatly put to the blush, that after so long the Descalzas should pay attention to these mean and paltry things. . . . Either your sufferings have deprived you of your wits, or the Devil has begun to work his infernal machinations in this Order. Here until we made our election, when our father came, such was the name we gave her, and not prioress, and it is all the same. . . . Whenever I think on the straits you are

putting those gentlefolk to, I cannot but feel it. I already wrote to you the other day to get a house, even though it should not be very good and reasonable; for however ill you may be in it, you will be more at your ease. And if you were not, it is better that you should suffer rather than those who show you such charity.

Besides the disobedience and offended dignity of Ana de Jesus, which so justly roused the ire of the high-minded old woman, the disquietude and disorder which filled the Convent of Alba had transpired to the outer world. The nuns were on bad terms with Teresa de Laiz, who, infringing unduly on her character of foundress and benefactress, interfered in the affairs of the community.

But however despotic, or whatever her faults, it was impossible for Teresa to speak out her mind so frankly to Teresa de Laiz as to a misguided prioress. Ostensibly she laid the blame on the nuns, but, with great adroitness, she let that lady clearly perceive that she was not blind to the real cause of these dissensions.

Tomasina Bautista, prioress of Burgos, trembles from head to foot at the very idea of going back to take that post in Alba, and "the reasons she gives are such, and so important for the peace of her soul, that no superior will order it. She has now a good house and is very happy."

If your grace loves her well you ought to be glad of it, and not wish for one who does not care to be with you. God forgive her, for so greatly do I desire to please you, that I would fain it were possible to do so in everything. . . . If your grace is distressed at the thought that the Mother Juana del Espiritu Santo is to remain as prioress, it is needless; because she has written to me that for nothing in life will she again accept this office. I know not what to say of those nuns: I fear that none of them will be prioress long, for all flee from it. I beseech your grace to consider that it is your house, and that with such inquietude they cannot serve God; and so it is exceedingly necessary that you show them favour in nothing, for if they are what they ought to be, what matters it who is prioress? but it is all childishness and partiality . . . and I guess pretty nearly who they are that make the others restless, and if God give me health, I shall try to go there as soon as I am able, to get at the bottom of the mischief; for I am deeply pained to know for a fact that things have been told to friars of another Order, which ought to have been kept strictly private, and it has got wind amongst secular people beyond the town. . . . They must not think that it is a trifle thus to disturb a monastery, and to communicate to people outside, things so prejudicial to those on whose virtues the eyes of the world are fixed.

In Salamanca things were even worse. The prioress, Ana de la Encarnacion, Teresa's cousin, had, all unknown to her, craftily set about the purchase of a house. This manœuvre Teresa quickly intercepted. As good fortune would have it, Pedro de la Vanda y Manrique, the owner of the one they occupied, happened to be in Valladolid, and she hired it from him for another year.

> I assure your reverence [she writes to Gracian] that she holds me bewitched. Such a brave woman is it that she transacts business neither more nor less than as if she had already your reverence's license. To the rector she says, although he knows nothing of her purchase, and disapproves of it, as you know, that she does everything by my orders; to me that the rector is doing it by yours. It is some devil's mischief, and I know not what she goes upon (for she would not tell a lie); only that her great anxiety to get this wretched house has deprived her of her wits. Brother fray Diego de Salamanca came yesterday (he who was here with your reverence during the visit) and told me that the rector of San Lazaro had been forced into this business for my sake, until he told her that every time he had anything to do with it he got absolution, it being altogether so against God; nevertheless, on account of the importunities of the prioress he could do no more, and that all Salamanca was talking about the purchase . . . and from what I can gather they have set about it with artifice so as to prevent it getting to my knowledge. . . . I wrote to Cristóbal Juarez [the owner of the house which the prioress was bargaining for], to beseech him not to do anything further about it until I went, which would be towards the end of October. . . . I told Cristóbal Juarez that I should first like to see where the money is to come from (for I was told he was the surety), and that I should be loath any harm should come to him, giving him to understand that the money to pay him was not forthcoming. . . . God has willed [she adds piously] that they [the nuns] had lent the money to your reverences; for, if not, it would have been paid down together with Antonio de la Fuente's; but now I have just received another letter from the prioress, who tells me that Cristóbal Juarez has got some one to advance him the 1000 ducats until he can get them from Antonio de la Fuente, and I am afraid they have already been deposited. . . . And another evil is that, so that they may move into Cristóbal Juarez's house, the students must go to the new house of San Lazaro, which is enough to kill them. I am writing to the rector not to consent to it, and I will keep a sharp look-out about it. As to the 80 ducats you owe the nuns, do not let it trouble you, for Don Francisco [lord of Coca and Alaejos, to whose generosity the friars were already greatly indebted for the foundation of the College of Salamanca] will pay them to the nuns in a year's time from now; and the best of all is that he has not got them now to give. No fear that I shall assist them. It is of more importance that the students should be accommodated than that they should have a large house. Where are they to get the money

from to pay the "censo"? As for me, this business has driven me distracted. For if your reverence has given them license, how is it that you refer them to me after it is done? If you have not, how is it that the money has been paid—for they have given 500 ducats to the daughter of Monroy's brother-in-law? And how is it that they look upon it as so finally concluded, that the prioress writes to me that it cannot be undone? God remedy it, for so he will. . . . For the love of God, let your reverence see well to your doings there [in Andalucia]. Put no faith in nuns, for I assure you that, if they want a thing, they will not stick at trifles. . . . If your departure could have given me any joy, it is to see you quit of these vexations, for much rather would I suffer them alone.

And lonely she is, in very truth, and full of many troubles. "You would be amazed," she writes from Valladolid to her prioress of Toledo, "if you knew how overwhelmed I am with trials and business."

Has not Gracian gone to Andalucia, where the plague, which still stalks terrific and menacing over Seville, has already carried away one of her friars? Might he not have stayed by her side a little longer? Could not those monasteries have spared him to her at least two months more, whilst he helped her to put some order into those of Castille?

I know not the cause [she writes feebly and sadly—and we have never before seen her so discouraged and despondent], but so keenly have I felt your absence at such a moment, that it took away all my desire to write to you; and thus I have not done so until now, when I cannot help it; and as to-day is full moon, I have passed a wretched night, and so my head is very bad. Until now I have been better, and tomorrow I hope (when the moon wanes) my indisposition will have passed away. My throat is better, but not well.

Already Doria and Gracian represent two adverse factions in the Order; already the duel has commenced which can only end in the downfall of one of them. "I do not understand," she had written to Gracian from Avila in December of 1581—only a few short months ago, and if the words refer to Doria, as has been supposed, they deserve attention,—"some sanctities: I say this for him who does not write to you,—and the other who wishes everything to be done, as he thinks fit, has tempted me. Oh, Jesus! how little there is perfect in this life."

The mutual antipathy of these two men,—the only two

of ability in the Order,—could not long be concealed from those sharp old eyes. The buzzings of Gracian's enemies filled her ears. Gracian, it was said, had sent Doria to Rome to get rid of him, and was not averse, it was said, to keep him there on the pretext of founding a monastery.

There is still time enough to found a house in Rome [she writes] ; for your reverence is in great want of subjects, even for those in Spain ; and Nicolao you need greatly, for in my opinion it is impossible for you to attend to so many things unaided. So fray Juan de la Cuevas told me, with whom I often spoke about it. His earnest desire is that you may do well ; and he has a great affection for you, for which I am indeed grateful to him. And he told me, moreover, that your reverence acted against the rules, which were, that should you be left without a companion (I forget whether he said the priors had anything to do with the choice) you should elect another ; and that he held it impossible to do without one ; that Moses had chosen I know not how many to assist him. I told him how there was no one, that we were even scarce of priors : he replied that the latter was the most important. Since I came here, I have been told that it has been remarked of your reverence that you do not take about with you a person of any weight. Indeed I see that it is because you cannot help yourself ; but as the time for the Chapter is drawing near, I would fain they had nothing to allege against you. For the love of God look well to it ; and how you preach in Andalucia. I never like to see your reverence remain there long ; for as you wrote to me to-day of those who have been in trouble there, I pray God not to do me so much evil as to see you suffer ; and, as you say, the devil does not sleep. Believe, at least, that I shall be wretched as long as you are there. . . . Do not now think of making yourself an Andaluz, for you are not of the temperament to deal with them. As to the preaching, I beseech your reverence again earnestly, although you preach little, to be exceeding careful what you say. . . . In Alba it has done them much good my writing to them to say how angry I am. All will be well, with God's help, and we shall be in Avila at the end of this month. Be sure that it was not fitting to drag this child [her niece Teresa] about from one place to another any longer. Oh, my father, how distressed I have been these last few days ; it went away when I knew you were well. My respects to the Mother Prioress and all the sisters. I do not write to them, for they will hear of me from you. I was glad to know they were well, and I beseech them earnestly not to break your heart, but to make much of you. . . . Our Lord protect you, as I implore him, and deliver you from dangers. Amen. To-day is the first of September.

For three centuries his enemies have triumphantly pointed to this letter,—the last she ever wrote to him,—as a proof of Teresa's estrangement from, and censure of, this her so-dearly-beloved son. So little does it take for a pious order to condemn a man to all eternity, if only sufficiently backed up by a distracted woman's "visions" and flagrant ill-faith. It is fair to state that his own party had their visionary nuns who undertook his vindication. But in such cases might is right, and exile and banishment triumphantly decided the question as to which set of visions was more worthy of credence.

Such is the letter in which only malice and a foregone conclusion could see anything but the tenderest solicitude and concern for Gracian's welfare and reputation. No comment of mine is needed; but it may be well to turn to it when we come to the causes which drove him from the Order.

It would seem that during these her last weeks of life, not only her prioresses, but her own family, had conspired to fill her heart with bitterness and sorrow. "Indeed—indeed she is full of trials of a thousand shapes!" and in truth she is very lonely. If she had not long ago learnt the lesson which it would seem the only object of life to teach, she learns it now;—that man's hopes and efforts and work, and all he does and is, are but a floating quicksand, and that no faith can be placed in the son of man.

She would fain have inspired all the world with something of the gigantic spirit that burnt within her: it remains a dead letter, even to the prioresses she had trained. In Valladolid her own family threatened her with litigation. Lorenzo's will had been found open, and they sought to annul it on that account.

> Although she is not in the right [she refers to Francisco's sharp, decided mother-in-law], she has great valour, and some tell her she is; and to save Francisco from utter ruin and ourselves great expense, I have been advised to come to an agreement. San José will lose thereby; but I trust in God, if only our claim is properly secured, that it will eventually inherit all. I have been, and am still, broken-hearted about it, although [it is always to Gracian she writes] Teresa is all right. Oh, how she has suffered from your not coming! Partly I am glad that she may begin to see how little we can trust in any one but God; and even to me, it has done no harm.

It was on this occasion that a notary forced his way into Teresa's presence and covered her with abuse. No trace of anger or vexation crossed her face. When he had finished she answered calmly, with a characteristic touch of quaint irony, "God reward your grace for the favour you have done me." The ingratitude of her prioress, however, was harder to bear. Maria de Bautista sided with her enemies. Deeply wounded at her niece's coldness and evident desire to get rid of her, she at once prepared for her departure. Before she took her leave she called the nuns together—those daughters who shall never look on her face again or hear her voice except in celestial dreams, a fading and radiant vision—and bade them a tender farewell. "My daughters," she said, in the touching words which have been handed on from one generation of nuns to another to this day:

"My daughters, I leave this house greatly consoled by the perfection I see in it, and the poverty, and the charity you bear one another; and if it continues as it does now, our Lord will help you greatly. Let each one do her utmost that through her not a single imperfection enters into the perfection of the Order; and alas for her through whom this shall happen! Do not let your prayers become a mere habit, but day by day make heroic acts of still greater perfection. Accustom yourselves to have great desires, for out of them great benefits may be derived, even if they cannot be put into action."

But the bitterness of this last journey, which was fated to be her *via crucis*, was not yet over. As they were going the prioress caught hold of Ana de San Bartolomé's habit and bade them return thither no more. Nor did she meet with a warmer welcome at Medina, where, if Ana de Bartolomé is to be believed, she suffered keenly from the insubordination of the prioress. "How true it is," Teresa had once written to Maria de San José, "that our nature loves to be requited." Amongst the many fine qualities of her nature, a keen and ardent sense of gratitude, and a tender sensitiveness to affection were the most conspicuous. She reproved her prioress for some small matter which had gone amiss and was met with insubordination and insult. Had it come to this, then, that after all these years her daughters openly defied her? She ate nothing that evening, and lay awake all night. On the morrow she set forth for Alba. Her intention was to have gone straight through to Avila, whence she hoped, after giving the veil to her niece Teresa, to go and put things to rights in Salamanca, and thence to Madrid. In this—her last desire—she was also doomed to disappointment. She found Fray Antonio de Jesus waiting for her in Medina with the Duchess of Alba's coach. The young Duchess was on the eve of her confinement and the old saint's intercessions were sorely needed. Broken in spirit—too old and feeble to resist—although sorely against her will, so she, whose whole life had been one long obedience, "like him who was obedient unto death, and that the death of the cross," obeyed once more. It is to Ana de San Bartolomé that we owe the account of this last journey; and it is strange to see what accents of amazing accuracy, delicacy, and heartfelt pathos this didactic and somewhat prosaic Castilian finds in which to relate these closing scenes. None of them knew she was dying. Teresa least of all. Sor Ana must have penned these notes in the first moments of her bereavement, when every little circumstance relating to the Dead is invested with a heart-moving and solemn interest.

"On the morrow we set forth," writes the venerable Ana, for a shred of Teresa's mantle fell also upon her, and she has been beatified if not canonised—" without bearing anything with us for the road, and the saint stricken down with her last sickness, and I could find nothing on the way to give her; and one night—we were in a poor village—Peñaranda de Bracamonte—where we could get nothing to eat, and finding herself exceeding weak she said: 'Daughter, give me something, for I am fainting,' and I had nothing but some dried figs, and she suffering from fever. I gave them four reals to get me some eggs for her, cost what they might. When I saw that nothing could be got for money, which was returned to me, I could not look at the saint without weeping, for her face seemed half-dead. I can never describe the affliction I was in then, for it seemed to me as if my heart was broken, and I did nothing but weep when I saw myself in such a plight,—for I watched her dying, and was powerless to help her." "Do not be afflicted for me, daughter," said the old saint, as she noted her companion's deep distress, "for these figs are very good; there are many poor people who do not get such a treat." The next day they fared even worse, for the only thing they could get for her in the hamlet (Macotera?) where they stayed to eat, was some greens boiled with onions, which she partook of thankfully, although they were bad for her complaint.

At six o'clock on the 20th of December she arrived at the end of her last earthly journey, to the fatigues and sufferings of which, ingratitude and unkindness had not been wanting to add their sting. Did she, as she came in sight of the gray mediæval pastoral town, dominated by the ducal castle of Alba glittering on its eminence, lift up the curtains of her litter, and gaze once more with faded eyes on the tall trees which line the sweep of the gleaming Tormes, the view of which in other days, from the narrow grating of her cell, had so often delighted and consoled her? or did she, already insensible to exterior impressions, descry the first faint outlines of some other Country, some other River, some other City gleaming afar off, but very close to her now, to which she believed that Death was most assuredly the portal?

Just before she reached Alba she was met by a messenger with the news of the Duchess's safe delivery, and she rallied for a moment to say with a gleam of her old, quaint humour, which old age, fatigue, hunger, and sorrow could not quench, "Thank God that this saint will be no longer needed."

It was noticed that, contrary to her wont, she permitted her daughters to kiss her hand, and gave them her benediction with many fond and endearing expressions. As they lovingly undressed her and put her into bed, she said, "Oh! God help me, daughters, and how tired I feel: it is more than twenty years since I went to bed so early; blessed be God that I have fallen ill amongst you."

On the morrow, resuming her accustomed mode of life, and for eight days afterwards with increasing difficulty and pain, she rose, visited the house, inspecting everything, attended the Divine Offices, and communicated with great devotion. After communicating on St. Michael's Day she sickened, never to recover; the heroic spirit could no longer battle against the rapidly declining strength.

She begged them to carry her up to the infirmary, the

grating of which looked on to the High Altar, and whence she could hear Mass. There she lay an entire day and night, absorbed in prayer. Eight years ago she had noted down in her Breviary the year of her death, and when she bade farewell to her daughters of Segovia she had told them that they had seen her for the last time in this life, and that the hour of her departure was at hand. Not until now was it borne in upon her that the time for Rest was come. Gently did she prepare her faithful nurse, Ana de San Bartolomé, for the inevitable separation—which, in spite of the auguries of the doctors, she saw approaching. The nuns began to remember and to repeat to each other, in awe-stricken whispers, how between eight and nine of the morning, a sister had seen a ray of light, clear as crystal, above all conception lovely, pass close by the window of the cell where she afterwards died; how that very summer they had heard close by them as they were at prayer a soft and tender moan, and how the Mother Catalina Bautista, the infirmarian, looking up at the heavens as she prayed before the crucifix in the convent patio, had seen a star larger and brighter than the rest alight and stop stationary above the roof of the central nave of the church, bathing it in bright effulgence.

Patiently and obediently she suffered all the remedies applied by her afflicted daughters. The cruel blistering of the doctors drew from her lips no murmur of complaint. Three days before her death she sent for Fray Antonio de Jesus, her first Discalced friar, to hear her confession. Bound to her by the ties of a lifetime of affection and common anxiety, intensified by the memories of the struggles and hardships of other days, he exclaimed broken-hearted, as he knelt before her bed, and realised the prospect of the so fast approaching separation, "Mother! pray God not to take you now; leave us not so soon." "Hush, Father," answered the dying woman,—and who knows but the very sound of her voice had power to soothe the old man's sorrow,—"and is it you that speak thus? I am no longer necessary in this world." Almost as she was speaking she grew suddenly worse, and the doctors, who were sent for with great haste, ordered her to be carried down to the cell in which she was before, on account of the coldness of the infirmary, and applied cupping glasses to the scarified flesh. Although she smiled, aware of the inefficacy of the cruel remedy, she suffered it to be applied obediently and cheerfully.

Her daughters remembered every detail of those last painful moments, which they watched with such solicitude; how that a medicine of evil-smelling oils, ordered by the doctors from the drug shop, was spilled by accident on the saint's bed, at the moment of the visit of the old Duchess of Alba, who came constantly to tend and feed with her own hand one whom she already looked upon as a saint.

"The saint was pained that she had come at such an unpropitious moment, on account of the evil smell, and I said to her [it is the mother Maria de San Francisco who writes]: Do not grieve, Mother, for you smell as if you had been sprinkled with water of angels [an old-world perfume]. And so it was that it had a most fragrant scent, and the saint answered me: Praised be God, daughter; cover it up, cover it up, so that it does not smell ill, and annoy the Duchess, for I should be only too glad that she had not come here at this time.

"When the Duchess entered she at once sat down and began to embrace our Holy Mother, and to draw the clothes over her, and she said: 'Do not do that, your Excellency, for they smell very ill with the remedies that have been given me;' to which the Duchess replied: 'On the contrary, they smell delightful; and I am vexed that they should throw scent on them, for if anything, it seems as if water of angels had been sprinkled here, and it may do you harm.' And hearing what her Excellency said, I observed carefully, and it seemed to me a miracle; since in spite of the pestiferous oils that had been spilt upon them, there was no evil smell, but on the contrary, sweet savours, as has been said."

But the end was drawing rapidly near. At five o'clock on St. Francis' Eve she asked for the sacraments. As she waited for them to be brought, her bed surrounded by the nuns in deep affliction and sorrow, she, clasping her hands, addressed them in tender words of humble supplication rather than the authoritative ones of a last bequest.

"Daughters and my mistresses, I beseech you to pardon the bad example I have set you, and not to follow my example, who have been the greatest sinner in the world, and she who has kept her Rule and Constitutions the worst. I beseech you for the love of God, my daughters, to keep them with great perfection and obey your superiors."

When the Host entered her cell, in spite of her extreme weakness, she rose and knelt, and would have prostrated herself on the ground before it, had they not controlled her. Those watching her saw her face change, and light up with a majestic and resplendent beauty. All signs of age had faded away, leaving behind them the serenity of youth. Clasping her hands together, her soul inflamed with Divinest Love, she murmured gladly sweet and joyous words of welcome. "Oh, my Lord and my spouse, at last the longed-for hour has come ; it is now time for us to see one another. My Lord, it is now time to set forth ; let us go with God-speed and thy will be done. The hour has at last come for me to leave this exile, and for my soul to rejoice, one with thee in what I have so long desired."

In this supreme trance, from her memory slip away all merits of her own ; she sees only a weak and erring human nature darkened by many failings, and clings to Divine Mercy alone. Over and again she repeated, "After all, Lord, I am a daughter of the Church," and asked pardon for her sins, saying that she hoped to be saved through the Blood of Jesus Christ, and beseeching her daughters to pray for her. The pathetic, broken utterances of the Psalmist never left her lips. *Sacrificium Deo spiritus contribulatus : cor contritum et humiliatum, Deus, non despicies. Ne projicias me a facie tua. Spiritum sanctum tuum ne auferas a me. Cor mundum crea in me, Deus.* But the passage she dwelt on most was that half verse, *Cor contritum et humiliatum, Deus, non despicies.* At nine of the same night she received Extreme Unction, and herself joined in reciting the Psalms and Responses. Again she expressed her thanks for having been made a daughter of the Church. Once only did Fray Antonio interrupt her celestial repose, and bring back her thoughts to the Earth which was becoming so dim and shadowy, by asking her whether she wished them to take her body to Avila. "Jesus! Must you ask that, my father? is there anything I can call my own? Will they not give me a little earth here?"

And in answer to one of the nuns who reminded her that our Lord had no house he could call his own, she said, "How well you speak, Mother! You have consoled me greatly." When the morning light penetrated the narrow cell, she moved to one side, holding the crucifix, which never left her until she was buried. So she remained for fourteen hours, in deep peace and quiet, her lips moving at intervals, as if she was speaking with some one they could not see. Towards nine on the night of the 4th of October 1582, her face suddenly became illumined with a great light and splendour, beautiful and radiant as the sun, and in a last aspiration of supreme love, so peacefully and imperceptibly, that it seemed to those around her that she was still in prayer, her soul took flight.

Fain would I believe that before it sped on its last strange journey, she turned for the last time in a mute appeal for human sympathy and love, and died with her head resting in the loving arms of her faithful companion and nurse, Ana de San Bartolomé.

> Largire clarum vespere
> Quo vita nusquam decidat ;
> Sed praemium mortis sacrae
> Perennis instat Gloria.

That self-same night, as the nuns watched round her bed, the infirmarian, Catalina de la Concepcion, sitting close to the low window of the cell which looked out upon the cloister, heard a rustle as of many footsteps, and looking out she saw a great and brilliant throng, clothed in white, which seemed to enter the cell and fill it with their presence. At the moment when the celestial visitors reached Teresa's bed, she expired.

That same night Ana de Jesus, lying sick unto death in her far-away convent of Granada, saw standing beside her bed a Carmelite nun, whose face she could not discern because of its surpassing glory and splendour. And as she looked, saying to herself, "Surely I know this nun!" the face smiled and drew nearer and nearer, until, dazzled by the excessive splendour which encircled the glorious figure, she could see no more. And not to one only, but to many of her children did she appear that night at that mysterious moment when, with three sighs so gentle and so feeble as to be scarcely perceptible, her soul left the bondage of the flesh. "We here in Heaven," whispered the radiant vision to a Carmelite monk, whose name is not given, "and you there on Earth must be one in love and purity: we above seeing the Divine Essence; and you on earth adoring the Most Holy Sacrament. So that you below shall do with it, what we here with the Essence: We enjoying and you suffering, for herein lies the difference between us; and the more your suffering the greater your joy. Say thus to my daughters."

And when the light of another day broke over the little world of Alba, and gilded the pallid features of her for whom the Eternal Morrow had dawned in some other world, Lo, and behold! as the watchers blinded with tears looked through the grating of her cell into the convent orchard, yesterday so familiar—to-day and for all days henceforward so strange and unlike—to their amazement, for it was old and cankered, and the season for flowering long past—an almond tree that grew in a little plot of ground before the window was covered with beauteous and fragrant blossom!

From nine in the evening she lay until next morning, surrounded by her afflicted nuns. Some rays of the glory, which had been revealed to her dying eyes, still lingered around the lifeless clay, touching it with an unearthly beauty. The benignant touch of Death had smoothed out all the wrinkles, and her face, set in the majesty of its passionless repose, regained the serene beauty of its youth; her hands and feet, "transparent like mother-of-pearl," and her limbs, flexible and supple, retained the beauty of the innocence and sanctity they had guarded during life.

A strange and undefinable fragrance, unlike any earthly perfume—a fragrance which even in life had been perceptible, and clung to the articles she used most—issued from the body as they performed the last duties and prepared it for the grave, filling the entire convent with its odour. At times it seemed to come in waves of renewed sweetness and fragrance, which at last became so overpowering that it was necessary to open the casement. Nor was this all. Those who were then present testified . . . years after, in the evidence for her canonisation, to the miracles worked by the dead body of Teresa de Jesus. One sister recovered her sense of smell; another suffering from violent pains in the head and eyes felt them swiftly removed as she embraced the transparent feet. As Isabel de la Cruz passed the Mother's lifeless hands over her brow, she regained her failing sight. And who shall say that, by some strange psychological process dimly to be defined—some loosening of the flood-gates of the heart and conscience—some extreme tension of spirit when her sick daughters kissed her feet in a last solemn embrace, and passed her dead hands over the aching brow and failing sight,—who shall say that their simple faith and supreme emotion did not effect what they ascribed to the miraculous virtues of that sacred and beloved body?

It is a strange coincidence that she died on the same day of the year as San Francisco de Assisi. On the morrow following she was buried. The Bishop of Salamanca, the Duke of Huescar,[1] and many gentlemen and monks belonging to other religious orders, having heard the news of her death in Salamanca, arrived in all haste to take part in the hurried and simple funeral. And so, stretched out on a bier covered with cloth of gold,—as so many years before she had foretold it would be,—did the Form of the great woman upon whom they now looked for the last time as they had seen and known her in Life, receive the last marks of veneration and love from these great lords and simple neighbours of Alba. Amidst sighs and awe-stricken whispers they kissed the feet which had wandered so far, and were now for ever stilled, and the patched and faded habit of the Mother Teresa de Jesus. He who succeeded in touching the sacred body felt

---

[1] The Duke of Huescar is the second, as that of Count of Lerin is the third title of the Dukes of Alba. This Duke of Huescar was that D. Fadrique de Toledo who accompanied his father, the great Duke, to Flanders. His wife's delivery had been the cause of Teresa's coming to Alba.

that he bore with him a talisman through life, and to that never-to-be-forgotten moment will his thoughts cling as the clouds thicken in death, be he Duke or Bishop or Peasant.

Her body, clothed in its habit, was then lifted off the bier, placed in a coffin, and buried in a hole in the wall beneath the arch and grating which separated the Coro Bajo from the church, so that both those within and without might rejoice in it alike. In order the better to preserve their sacred treasure, and to secure it from being robbed and carried off to Avila, at the instance of Teresa de Laiz, the foundress, a mass of bricks, stones, and lime was hurriedly piled on the coffin lid. The workmen and the nuns, who all lent a hand, spent two days blocking up the grave before it was accounted sufficiently safeguarded and secure. But the memory of the dead woman, so near and yet so far, still haunted them. Strange knockings were heard inside the grave itself. An indescribable fragrance issued from it,—a fragrance varying not only in degree, but in nature; sometimes like lilies, at others like jessamine and violets: sometimes impossible to define. They began to reproach themselves for not having given a more reverent and honourable burial to the foundress, whose virtues and character, seen through the perspective of death, grew daily more beauteous and wondrous. They longed, the poor women! to probe the mysteries of that blocked-up tomb in the choir wall; to look once more on what was left of the mortal remains of Teresa de Jesus. At length, nine months after her death (she who might bitterly have opposed it, Teresa de Laiz, could oppose it no longer, for she too was come to her long home in the walls of the convent church), Gracian, who in his capacity of Provincial was visiting the convent, acceded to their prayers that the body might be exhumed. With the utmost secrecy, lest any inkling of it should reach the Duke of Alba, he and his companion, aided by the community, set to work to remove the stones and rubbish. This took them four days, the coffin being opened on the 4th of July 1583. The lid had been broken in with the mass of building material. It was half rotten, and full of mould and damp. The habit too was rotten and smelt of damp and decay. But the body, although it was covered with the earth which had fallen through the lid, was as sound and entire as on the day it was buried. They removed the mouldering clothes (for according to Spanish custom she was buried fully dressed in the habit she had worn in life), washed the body and scraped the earth off with knives, and after putting fresh clothes on her, wrapped her up in a sheet and placed her in a chest, which was again deposited in the same place as before, and which may still be seen by the devout or curious visitor to Alba. It was noticed, however, that the scrapings of earth (which were piously preserved as relics) were impregnated with the same indefinable odour as pervaded the tomb itself. They did not remark (however strange it may appear), what it was reserved for a future occasion to demonstrate, that both earth and cere-clothes were saturated in a fragrant oil which exuded from the body, and communicated itself to everything it touched, "so that if the Lord (I quote Yepes) had not declared it afterwards by a thousand ways, they were so blinded with joy that they would not have seen it."

Those to whom her wonderful life may have said but little knelt in silent and reverent veneration before the miracle of the incorruptibility of her body. This indeed proved her to have been a saint in very truth. This was the immediate cause of the first steps being taken by the miracle-loving and superstitious Philip II. to secure her beatification and canonisation. Human nature, eternally unchanged and unchangeable,—the same in the nineteenth century as in the sixteenth,—as throughout the ages, crying like Thomas incredulously for the sign, blind to the greatness and mystery of the life which has passed before their eyes, and they have touched and failed to apprehend. For the opinion of the old Archbishop of Florence, San Antonino, was held by few:

"As for us whose path is surrounded by shadows, to whom it is permitted to judge of the saints by what we know and presume of their works, I think that none can doubt but that many of the blessed men and women, who have not been canonised by the Church, nor even mentioned by her, have not been less worthy nor less glorious than many who are canonised. For the canonising of them does not make them more worthy, nor give them more essential glory, neither does it determine the degree of sanctity, but only that temporal honour and glory that may arise to them from the solemn celebration of their office and festival, which without this cannot be done."

Before, however, the body was replaced, Gracian cut off the left hand, and bore it with him to Avila in a locked casket. All of which took place on the 4th of July 1583.

Two years later, in the second general Chapter of the Order held at Pastrana, Gracian, no longer Provincial of the Order, pleaded the prior claims of the convent of Avila to the possession of the body of its foundress. Avila, which had been not only her own birthplace, but that of the Reform, had undoubtedly the best right to the mortal remains of its illustrious townswoman. It was by the merest accident that she had gone to die in Alba, instead of in the Convent of San José, where she was still prioress. There was another and a more urgent reason. Before Teresa's death Gracian had given a signed and written promise to the Bishop of Palencia (Don Alvaro de Mendoza), that her body should find its last resting-place on the right side of the altar opposite to the sumptuous tomb he had built for himself to the left of the High Altar of San José. Through his secretary, Carrillo, who was present at the Chapter, the Bishop now demanded the fulfilment of this promise.

On the 24th of November 1585, Fray Gregorio de Nacianceno and his two companions, the Bishop's secretary, and Master Julian de Avila, arrived in Alba on their secret mission. Gracian arrived at the convent on the same day. To the prioress alone, and to two or three of the oldest and most venerable of the nuns, did they confide the object of their coming. The Convent Church of Alba has witnessed strange sights,—but never one more strange and weird than that which took place at nine o'clock of that November night of 1585. So as not to excite suspicion, the nuns were sent to sing Matins in the Coro Alto; and then, whilst the dreary monotone of their voices rose and fell through the vaulted roof, the two friars, together with the prioress and such of the nuns alone as had been taken into the secret, set to work to open the tomb once more.

The clothes which enveloped the corpse were rotten; the sheet saturated with the oil[1] that distilled from the body; but the body itself, in spite of its being somewhat shrivelled, they found as intact and fragrant as before. It was noticed that a small serge cloak which had been used to stanch the blood which oozed from her mouth (her death, like that of her brother Lorenzo, was due to a broken blood-vessel, or according to the expression of her biographers, "a flux of blood") was saturated with blood, which still after the lapse of three years and two months, retained its natural colour.

When in fulfilment of his orders, Fray Gregorio, overcome by emotion (he afterwards told Ribera that it was the greatest sacrifice of himself God had ever called upon him to make), drew the knife which hung at his belt and severed the left arm from the body, that they might leave it with the nuns of Alba—so the Chapter had decreed in order to mitigate their grief—the bone was as sound, and the flesh as soft, and its colour as natural, as if she had but just died. Then wrapping up their precious burden as best they could, they bore it from the convent.

In the meantime the strange odour peculiar to the relics, which invaded the choir and kept increasing in intensity, roused the suspicions of the nuns in the choir above. Stricken with a sudden and woful foreboding, heedless of Matins (to remain for ever unsaid,—but I am confident that the saint forgave them that one breach of discipline), and guided by the celestial fragrance, they rushed to the porteria,—to find their treasure gone and the gates shut. Then they remembered, as, stricken with grief, they looked on the severed arm and a bit of the blood-stained cloth—all that remained to them of the sacred body of their foundress —how one day during recreation, whilst they talked of what was going on in the Chapter of Pastrana, they had heard three knocks twice repeated inside the grave, on the same

---

[1] It is strange that Ribera, whose *Life* was written in 1590, should not mention the fact of the oil. Yepes, on the contrary, who insists upon it, wrote in 1614, the year of her beatification. The judicious reader may draw from these facts whatever conclusion he chooses.

day and hour when, according to Fray Gregorio Nacianceno, the warrant for the translation had been signed at Pastrana.

At earliest dawn the friars and their mysterious burden were already traversing the wild track over the uplands to Avila—the road Teresa had so often travelled in life, and was fated still to travel again before her bones and mutilated body were allowed once more to rest in peace at Alba. Although the arrival of the body in Avila was kept a profound secret (it was feared that the Dukes of Alba might get wind of it, and insist on its instant restitution), it was impossible to prevent some notice of it transpiring to the outer world. A secret rumour reached Yepes in Madrid—the good Yepes, now Confessor to the King, and in the way of obtaining a fat bishopric. Provided with the Provincial Doria's license, who easily granted it to one whose express object it was to lay before his Majesty an account of its marvellous incorruptibility, the Jeronimite friar sped to Avila as fast as his mule's hoofs could bear him. With him went the Bishop of Cordoba and Don Francisco de Contreras, Oidor of the Royal Council, "with the devout intent of visiting the holy body, and seeing that new marvel." They arrived in Avila on the last day of the old year, and were lodged in the palace of the Bishop, to whom they confided their purpose. On New Year's Day some twenty people,—including the most famous doctors and notaries of the city,—to testify to all that passed, and a few "principal" gentry, assembled in the porteria of San José of Avila. All fell on their knees in silent adoration as the body was brought out into the gateway. Then rising, they stood bare-headed, some amongst them moved to tears at the sight of the rigid mummy before them. The body was entire—no sign of corruption could be discovered—and gave forth a fragrant smell; the bones and nerves so firmly knit together that, when they lifted it out of the chest, it conserved its rigidity, and stood upright with very little support. The flesh was soft and flexible; they could lift the head by the hair; the bones and flesh of the shoulder whence the arm had been severed by Nacianceno retained their natural colour; and withal it did not weigh more than a child of two years old; "so that," concludes good Bishop

Yepes, "herein appear three miracles—incorruption, fragrance, and agility."

It was impossible that an event so transcendental should not get wind. The Bishop of Avila threatened excommunication on all who should divulge what they had seen, but was forced to raise it, so intense was the excitement. So went events in Avila; but in Alba they were far otherwise. It is said that a lay sister, on the supposition that she was not included in the censures of the Chapter, asked the prioress's leave to present a pie she had made to the Duchess. Inside the pie she placed a paper giving a full account of what had happened. The old Duchess, deeply moved, rushed out into the streets screaming like a madwoman—"They have taken Santa Teresa from me! They have taken the saint from me!" The old Duke of Alba was dead; also his son—the Duke of Huescar, who had been present at Teresa's funeral,—and the then representative of the House of Alba was that Don Antonio Alvarez de Toledo immortalised in Lope de Vega's sonnet:

> Belardo que á mi tierra hayas venido
> A ser uno tambien de mis pastores.

He was absent at the time in Navarre, of which he was hereditary Constable; but his uncle, the Prior of San Juan, who managed his estates, one of the saint's most ardent devotees, at once used all the powerful influence of the House of Alba to secure its return to their ancestral town, of which it had now become the chiefest treasure. A brief was despatched by Sixtus V. to his Nuncio in Spain, ordering its immediate restitution.

Without a moment's delay, Fray Nicolas de Jesus Maria (Doria), the Provincial, set out for Avila to arrange for the translation. At dead of night two friars, bearing between them their strange burden, issued from the gates of Avila, crossed the bridge, and took the hilly path to Mancera. And so for the last time did Teresa bid a long farewell to her native town. In a small town half-way between Duruelo and Mancera,—La Boveda,—some labourers, who were threshing at night, attracted by the unusual and peculiar odour which issued from the remains, left their threshing-floors and followed them, in order to discover what it was that caused it.

At Mancera, where they stayed in the monastery for the night, a sick monk, suffering from tertian ague, was, "to console him," bidden by the prior "to make haste and rise to keep watch over the holy body." He too smelt the strange and peculiar fragrance. He remained by her side until midnight, and for that night at least he was free from the ague, the attack of which should have come on at nightfall. On the morrow, when they bore her away, his tears fell fast as he bade her farewell, and prayed, not that he might be rid of his infirmities, but that she would help him to suffer them; "and that same day the ague left him and never again returned."

They arrived at Alba early in the morning of the 23rd of August of 1586, but so cunningly concealed the nature of their burden that none might know what they carried; and at eight o'clock in the morning, a little before or after, they deposited the body in the convent. Great was the rejoicing that day in Alba! Arrangements had been made to meet and bring her into the town in solemn and triumphant procession, to the sound of music. But the downcast friars, bent on fulfilling their ungracious and distasteful mission, sternly discouraged any attempt at festivity. The Provincial's orders were decisive, and obeyed to the letter. He had not placed the body there to remain, but merely as a loan, in obedience to the Pope. There was to be no rejoicing. The friars were to deliver it up, and receive an acknowledgment that it had been done.

In the presence of the Duke of Alba and the Countess of Lerin, and the crowd which filled the church, it was uncovered, so that all could see it. The Prior of Pastrana briefly asked the nuns whether they recognised the body as being that of the Mother Teresa de Jesus, and if they accepted its delivery. Their answer was swelled by the unanimous response of the crowd, and it was duly attested by a notary. Guards were placed at the gates of the church to secure the safety of the relics, which, after so many vicissitudes, and nearly a year's absence, had been at last restored to their safe keeping; for no one believed in the friars' faith, or that they would not get them away if they could. An injunction was also served on the nuns not to give them up. It was well that the body was in safety behind the grating, for the excited crowd, in their eagerness for relics, would have torn it to pieces.

Ribera, on his way from Salamanca to Avila on purpose to visit the body, "which I greatly desired to do," arrived at the monastery very little after the friars, so that, had he (he notes regretfully) got there a moment before, he would have found it in the porteria, and had his desire gratified.

It is to his pen that we owe the description of the strange scene which took place that August day within the convent walls of Alba. The body lay all exposed to view behind the grating of the low choir from early in the morning until nightfall.

"The whole afternoon the church was so full of people come to see the marvel, that neither could they be put out nor could those who were farther inside get out, until very late, for none could gaze at her enough. . . . Of all this I was a witness, and saw her at my leisure through the grating and afterwards, though hurriedly; for, although it was night, and the doors of the church were being shut, those behind us would not let us do so. That same night, before the friars who had brought her started on their journey, they came to sup at the posada, and brought away with them the habit in which the body had been wrapped, to take it back to Avila, for in Alba they clothed it in another. It was wrapped and tied up in a blanket, so that the folds came out at the sides, and I drew near to smell it, and it had an excellent odour; it remained there about three-quarters of an hour, and when the friars were gone I went to the room where they had been, and even from the short time the habit had lain there, it had left a perfume in the chamber, which at once I smelt and recognised. In a little while my companion returned, and I asked him if he smelt anything; and he said he did, and that it was very perceptible."

Ribera has left us a minute description of the body as it was in 1588:

"I saw the sainted body, greatly to my satisfaction, on

the 25th of March of this year of 1588, as I examined it thoroughly, it being my intention to give the testimony I give here. I can describe it well. It is erect, although bent somewhat forward, as is usual with old people; and by it, it can well be seen that she was of very good stature. By placing a hand behind it to lean against, it stands up, and can be dressed and undressed as if she were alive. The whole body is of the colour of dates, although in some parts a little whiter. The face is of a darker colour than the rest, since, the veil having fallen over it, and gathered together a great quantity of dust, it was much worse treated than other parts of the body; but it is absolutely entire, so that not even the tip of the nose has received any injury. The head is as thickly covered with hair as when they buried her. The eyes are dried up, the moisture they possessed having evaporated, but as for the rest entire. Even the hairs on the moles on her face are there. The mouth is tightly shut, so that it cannot be opened. The shoulders, especially, are very fleshy. The place whence the arm was cut is moist, and the moisture clings to the hand, and leaves the same odour as the body. The hand exceeding shapely, and raised as if in the action of benediction, although the fingers are not entire. *They did ill in taking them, since the hand that did such great things, and that God had left entire, ought for ever to have remained so.* The feet are very beautiful and shapely, and, in short, the whole body is well covered with flesh. The fragrance of the body is the same as that of the arm, but stronger. So great a consolation was it to me to see this hidden treasure, that to my thinking it was the best day I ever had in my life, and I could not gaze at her enough. One anxiety I have, lest some day they should separate it, either at the request of great personages or at the importunity of the monasteries; for by no means should this be done, but it should remain as God left it, as a testimony of his greatness, and the most pure virginity and admirable sanctity of the Mother Teresa de Jesus. To my thinking, neither he who asks it nor he who grants it, will act like true sons of hers." . . .

CHAPTER XXVIII

THE PATRON SAINT OF SPAIN

> Her life was marvellous, you say, Lorenzo, and so her Death,
> And what o'ertook it passing marvellous.
> Where'er she trod they say the roses blossomed,
> And lilies breathed strange fragrance.
> Nay more,—I've heard it said that o'er her sepulchre they catch the gleam of
>   angels' wings,
> And hear faint strain of voices chanting throughout the silent Night.
>   OLD PLAY.

IN 1594, twelve years after Teresa's death, Ana de Jesus, on her way from Salamanca to Avila, procured leave from her superiors to visit the remains of the Mother she had so venerated, and by her disobedience so pained, in life.

In 1598 the body was removed to a worthier burial-place to the left of the High Altar, above the choir, where a sort of little chapel or niche, as in the case of all famous Spanish shrines—that of Our Lady of Guadalupe, for instance—had been built for its reception. On the side next the convent a little door gave admittance to the nuns who decked and tended it; towards the church it was protected by a gilded grating. Here, then, they placed the chest —the gift of Teresa's friend, the old Duchess of Alba— which contained her remains. The walls were hung with cloth of silver, the gift of a later Duchess of Alba, Doña Mencia de Mendoza; and the silver lamp which burnt before it day and night was the offering of the Duke, her husband. The rich baldaquin of cloth of gold which canopied the coffin was sent by an Infanta of Spain, Doña Isabel Clara Eugenia, afterwards Archduchess of Flanders.

For the three short years that had come and gone since Teresa's death had worked a mighty change. It was no longer a mere tribute of sorrowing veneration for the virtues of

the woman whose like they should never look on again, but
of adoration to the saint. By a process easily understood
in ardent and self-concentrated minds, amidst the silence and
mystic repose of the cloister, the real Teresa who had lived
and moved amongst them became dimmer and dimmer; as the
successive layers of atmosphere between her and them grew
thicker and thicker, so she too gradually faded away. In
like proportion as she had impressed them in life, so did
she beset their imaginations in death; and the counterfeit
image they were fabricating in her stead—Time and they
between them—loomed day by day larger and more glorious,
more fixed in outline, more ethereal and unearthly. The
miracles attributed to her relics grew in magnitude and
wonder. But I would note one fact: that the miracles said
to have been worked at this period are widely different in
character from the crude inventions of the following century
which canonised her. They do not outrageously offend
either our sense of probability or the canons of good taste.
They are all directed to beneficent ends, and not to the mere
wanton laudation of the saint herself. They are the spontaneous outcome of genuine simplicity and faith; and however *naïf*, however much they show that humanity loves to
deceive itself, only a fool or a person entirely devoid of the
finer instincts could find it in his heart to laugh at them.
Nay, some of these cures, marvellous as they are, are steeped
in so strange a pathos, and old-world and stately dignity, that
we almost find ourselves deploring as a loss to humanity
the disappearance of the good faith, the tenderness and passionate Belief, that made such things possible. Even the
relation of them as told by Ribera, with that strange blending
of matter-of-factness and simplicity and gravity which is
the peculiar characteristic of the Spanish character,—and
peculiarly his, rouses no mental protest, but rather holds the
mind in a sort of tender fascination.

There were doubtless other motives—motives of which
those who acted upon them may have been dimly conscious,
or even altogether unconscious (for it must be remembered
we are not dealing with a century of charlatanry, but of one
which esteemed Truth, or what it conceived to be Truth, as the
most precious of its possessions). The miracles worked by

the sacred relics so jealously guarded in the Convent of Alba undoubtedly shed a reflected lustre on that community—a lustre which it was to their glory (not interest) to enhance; but no less certain is it that the body of legend which clustered around them was most firmly believed in by those who unconsciously helped to weave it.

In 1603, in order to put an end to the ravages of the relic-hunters, the General of the Order commanded the chest to be nailed down, so as to make it impossible to open without breaking. On this occasion the body was again uncovered in the presence of the Duke and Duchess of Alba, and the entire community. Before, however, Fray Tomas de Jesus accomplished his behest, he still further mutilated the body he had been sent to preserve more barbarously than any of his predecessors. He distributed bits of flesh amongst the bystanders,—and besides the fair portion he reserved for himself, tore away a rib "with more devotion than piety."

On the 13th of July 1616, two years after her beatification, on the occasion of some alterations being made in the disposition of the tomb, the body was again discovered, and from that date, for more than a hundred and thirty-four years, it remained "in safe custody and concealed from human vision."

In 1750 the tomb was again opened in honour of Ferdinand VI. and his wife, Maria Barbara of Portugal; and, although the royal visit never took place, owing to the Queen's illness, the General of the Order, Fray Nicolas de Jesus Maria, and the Duke of Huescar, as representing the House of Alba, proceeded to Alba, to make the necessary arrangements. The stone sepulchral urn in which the chest was laid was then once more brought to light. The chest itself was found to be of wood, and secured with nine bars of gilded iron. The lock was also gilt, but as the key was lost, it had to be forced. The chest was lined inside with crimson velvet, as fresh and lovely as if it had been but newly cut from the piece. The body—what little of it was left—showed no signs of corruption, although sadly mutilated by a mistaken and irreverent piety. The right foot, the left hand and arm, and the heart; a portion of the upper jaw, the left eye; several of the ribs, and various pieces of flesh and bones, had been carried away by the relic-hunters. The flesh, skin, and bones of the rest of the body were intact and uninjured; the head was severed from the bust, and a great part of the neck missing. The pupil and lashes of the right eye were distinctly discernible; the right arm as flexible as if still imbued with life. In the place where the hand had been forcibly wrenched off, the bone was still white and beauteous. The toes and nails of the right foot could be clearly distinguished. The body itself was covered with a fine linen sheet; over this was laid a second covering of thin crimson silk. A leaden casket which lay in the coffin beside it contained a parchment deed testifying to the condition of the body when last it was exhumed in 1616.

As the Duke of Huescar was unable to assist at its formal restitution to the urn—having been recalled by the King to the Escorial—he solemnly made oath before he left Alba that the body was the same he had seen taken out of it little more than a fortnight before. This was on the 18th of October, and on the 29th it was again replaced in the chest, which was nailed round with nine bars of gilded iron as before, locked with three keys, and once more deposited in the urn.

In 1760 the tomb where she had rested so long was pulled down to make way for a sumptuous chapel reared in her honour by those Catholic monarchs, Ferdinand VI. and Maria Barbara of Portugal. The whole disposition of the church was then entirely altered. A new choir was built at the end opposite the High Altar; the altar-pieces were torn down or renewed. The little, dark, rustic church as Teresa had known it disappeared; one by one the old landmarks sacred to her memory were done away with; the grave and dignified century of which she had formed a part was for ever effaced under the mole of jaspers and marbles laid on it by the cold, gaunt, inartistic hand of the eighteenth century, which produced nothing—could produce nothing, and, utterly barren and impotent itself, was only the more eager to destroy what it no longer understood.

On the afternoon of the 13th of October of that year (Ferdinand VI. was king no more, and Charles III. reigned in his stead), the body, which, whilst this profane work of destruction was going on, had been guarded in the cell where she died, was solemnly conducted to the Camarin Bajo.

There for the fifth and last time—for it has never been opened since, and most probably never will be again—the chest was opened, and the identity and incorruption of the body once more solemnly verified. On the morrow (how far away are we from dear, good, old, simple Ribera—Teresa herself is becoming very shadowy!) the worthy inhabitants of Alba and the surrounding district were once more admitted to look their last on the poor mummy which had once enshrined the great Teresa de Jesus. From earliest morning to three o'clock in the afternoon, there it lay exposed in the Low Choir to the gaze of the curious and excited multitude. For seven hours the Carmelite friars were unceasingly engaged in touching it with the crosses, medals, and objects of devotion handed to them for that purpose. Then, borne shoulder-high by six monks, and followed by a solemn procession of prelates, friars, and veiled nuns, carrying lighted tapers, it was taken to the Camarin Alto, the little chapel above the High Altar, which had been prepared for its reception. The rigid limbs were clothed in a rich habit; a collar in the form of the Golden Fleece, from which depended silver hearts equal in number to the donors,—the Carmelite nuns of Sta. Ana of Madrid,—was hung round her neck. Thus decked out, she was laid on a cushion of crimson satin bordered with gold lace; the pillow on which her head —it was severed from the trunk—rested was of the same material embroidered in silver. A martyr's palm was laid across her breast. The silver chest—the gift of the Kings of Spain—was then locked, and the four keys given into the keeping of the General of the Order, the prioress, the representative of the Dukes of Alba, Don Alonso de Oviedo, and she was left to repose—a repose which I hope will never again be broken—in the spot where she now rests above the High Altar of Alba.

The old chest, the gift of the Duchess of Alba, in which she had first been placed, was offered by the Duke of Alba to the King in the name of the General and Definitory of the Discalced Carmelites, and accepted with pious satisfaction by his Majesty, who ordered it to be placed in his oratory. Where it may be now I do not know.

For me Teresa's life is now finished. I have still to follow the successive steps of her beatification and canonisation, but they are events in which she had no part either dead or living. I would fain bring my history of her to an end in the words of the simple old Jesuit, whose loyalty and affection for her shines so transparently through every line of his biography—a work which for purity and simplicity of style, and downright, old-fashioned directness,—deserves to take its place as a classic in the literature of the period.

"With these, O Lord my God, who makest saints and crownest them, will I bring to an end the history that I took upon me to write of thy faithful servant, so that the world might know the treasures thou didst place in her, and all may praise thee without end. And since thou art the beginning and end of all sanctity, Saviour of the world and our Lord, and these fragrant and beauteous flowers which have been born and are born in thy Holy Church would not have been roses, but thorns and briers, had they not been watered with thy most precious Blood, may thou be praised eternally in thy saints, the most perfect work of thy fingers. May it please thy eternal bounty that this slight gift I offer thee may ascend before thee with a sweet perfume, and that because I, unworthy and miserable sinner, have spoken of so much sanctity, it may not cause thee to remember my sins anew, on account of my deeds being so different from those I have related, but on the contrary that through her intercession they may be forgiven me, and mayest thou place within me a new heart and a new spirit, so that I may indeed appear like her thou lovest, and I love. And if it were not an over-boldness, I will speak to my Lord, although I am but dust and ashes, and beseech him that all those who out of devotion to his servant shall read this true and faithful history, although ill written, may draw from it, by thy mercy, lively desires to praise thee always for the grandeurs thou workest, and to imitate these so sovereign virtues, and serve thee with all their heart. The works at which they marvel, Lord, are thy gifts; the truth, no matter whence it comes, is thine. These powerful deeds cannot in very truth but move, and great indeed is the force thou givest them ; deliver me, Lord, from this fear, the only one can I have, that its efficacy may not be lost because of my having been the instrument of this writing. And thou, holy mother mine, for whose glory and memory I have laboured, although I was not worthy to relate thy praises, well dost thou know how willingly I have done it, and what thou hast done in order that it might be effected. I said ill that I have laboured, for I have not felt it labour, rather has it been to me a consolation and a joy to write this, although my time was very much occupied. I have desired that the memory of thy glorious deeds should not be lost, and to this end have I done all I could, so that thou mayest be for ever known and imitated, and in thee and for thee that this great Lord who made thee so marvellous may be praised. Pardon the slowness of my genius and the poverty of my words, since thou knowest that my will to serve thee has been neither slow nor poor. And since the Lord favoured me so greatly as to let me know thee in this life, and thou didst love me well, and wast careful to commend me to his Majesty, obtain from him what I have besought of him, and never neglect this thy miserable son who loves thee so dearly, until by thy merits I reach the blessed sight of our Lord and Creator, where with thee and all the saints I may rejoice in him and praise him for ever and ever. Amen."

*　　　　　*　　　　　*

In 1595, thirteen years after her death, Philip II., moved thereto by the miracles reported to be worked by her relics and the prodigy of the blood which still oozed from the body, and dyed everything it came in contact with, set on foot, through the Nuncio Camilo Gayetano, the preliminary inquiries necessary to her beatification. Her manuscripts were collected and taken to the Escorial, where they lie beside those of St. Augustine and St. John Chrysostom, religiously preserved as the chiefest jewels of that great and magnificent foundation. The Spanish Ambassador at Rome, the Duke of Sesa, was urged to push forward the process of canonisation with all the speed and warmth possible ; but in spite of the feverish desire of the Catholic king, it was reserved to his grandson to see this crowning glory cast a lustre on his reign. Things went slowly in those days, and it was not until 1614 that her beatification, so ardently prayed for, not only by the monarch and kingdom of Spain, but by the rulers of Europe, was decreed by Paul V.; two Popes having filled the pontifical chair and passed away whilst the negotiations dragged on their weary course of official delay.

On the 7th of May 1614, the first news of her beatification was brought to Spain by no less a person than Don Carlos Doria, General of the Genoese fleet, and Duke of Thursis, who arrived in Barcelona with a squadron of seventeen galleys. The news spread like wildfire; although the rejoicings were postponed until it was solemnly confirmed by the General of the Order. The couriers with his letters and a copy of the Brief reached Barcelona at seven o'clock on the evening of the 30th, as the friars had just concluded Matins. The bells were at once set in motion, informing the city of the great event with glad and joyous peals. The monks, headed by their prior in cope of cloth of gold, descended to the body of the church, and in voices broken and tremulous with emotion chanted the Te Deum. On the morrow, after placing Teresa's picture covered with a rich canopy of brocade in the midst of the High Altar, the Prior sallied forth on a visit of ceremony to Prince Philibert, to the Marquis of Almazan, the Viceroy of Cataluña, and the great dignitaries of the city,—to all of whom he imparted the triumphal tidings. Two monks sped on the same mission to the Tribunals of the Chancelleria, the Inquisition, etc.; whilst two others were sent to the different monasteries and convents of the city.

On that same day the friars celebrated Vespers with unusual pomp and splendour. The church was hung with damask; the floor strewn with broom and lovely flowers; the altar buried beneath roses, lilies, and orange-blossom, and, sparkling with tapers, "seemed like a picture of the paradise of God." Incense and perfumes floated into the streets; the merry bursts of minstrelsy summoned the worshippers from afar. In they streamed from three in the afternoon until eleven at night: Prince Philibert—it was noticed that his devotions to the saint took him half an hour—the Viceroy, his wife, and all the nobility and authorities of Barcelona. I should like to have been there—to have wandered unperceived amidst that obscure, unchronicled multitude of craftsmen and minor folk ; to have heard the squibs and crackers hiss and crackle in the air over the sombre walled old town, lighting up all manner of strange angles and projections, gleaming out seawards, revealing in a flash turreted walls and cathedral towers ; to have listened to those old-world minstrels posted on the church roofs, tripping up one another's heels, in all manner of quaint, forgotten snatches, trills, and sonorous madrigals, until it was (affirms the narrator) "a glory to hear them " ; to have watched the torches on the Rambla blaze redly into the hot summer night ; and have shaken at the volleys from those flint-lock muskets, as they rolled through the narrow echoing streets.

The general feasting was, however, appointed for the 4th of October. Nothing like it had ever been seen before in Barcelona since the entry of Columbus : no prince's entry had ever been celebrated with such magnificence and splendour. It was preceded by an eight days' fast, from the 26th of September, on which day the saint's flag was unfurled high above the bell-tower of the Discalced Carmelite Monastery, where it remained to the vigil of her festival.

At three o'clock on the 2nd of October, Don Geran de Guardiola, in gala suit of silvered white, and cape and cap of black velvet lined with the same, and glistening with diamonds and precious stones (the dried old counsellor dwells on the details with the unction of an artist),—his horse was also white, and as magnificent as himself, in silver trappings and velvet housings which swept the ground,—Don Geran de Guardiola, I say, escorted by all the young nobles of Barcelona, no less splendidly accoutred, arrived at the monastery gates. A mounted troop of trumpeters and minstrels stationed in the plaza are awaiting their approach ; amidst the blare of trumpets, and the roll of kettle-drums, they dismount and enter the church. Flanked on either side by Don Juan de Boscardos and Don Miguel de Moncada, who hold the pendent tassels, Don Geran hoists aloft Teresa's white silk banner, and marches proudly into the sunshine. Again they remount—the minstrels, the trumpets, and the kettle-drums more strident and triumphant than before—and then, in the silence which suddenly invades the little plaza, a herald proclaims Teresa's festival before the gates of her monastery church.

At twelve o'clock at noon on that 4th of October, as the clock struck the hour, the thunder of artillery and the clashing of the cathedral bells announced the commencement of the festival. From every church and convent tower in the city clamoured the peals of merry and deafening sounds. "All Barcelona," says a contemporary witness, "was in revolution." Never before had such seething multitudes of people been gathered together within its walls. From her lofty perch on the tower of the monastery church,—her image, clothed in silk and covered with pearls and precious stones of inestimable value,—Teresa beamed a mute and benignant welcome to her votaries. At six o'clock, as the last stroke of the Ave Marias pealed through the air—the religious ceremonies being now concluded in the friars' church—the bonfires were lit and the whole city became a blaze of light. Lanterns, some green like emeralds, others like rubies or topazes, sparkled from every battlement, from every turret and gate. Great cressets full of pitch burnt in every street and plaza, converting night into day. The Carmelite Convent was like "a starry heaven" with fireworks and illuminations. From church tower and battlement floated a continuous stream of minstrelsy. How those minstrels played that night! drawing the soul out of those archaic instruments of theirs, the very names of which in their Arcadian simplicity have become unfamiliar to us. But the great spectacle of the night was the return of the saint's image to the convent, after being borne in solemn procession round the city. It was not until nearly ten that the expectant multitudes in the plaza opposite the monastery caught sight of the saint's ship. On it sweeps, the grand and imposing spectacle; first the heralds, trumpeters, and drummers on horseback; then the minstrels in a triumphal car drawn by powerful Flanders horses; and last of all, surrounded by a guard of nobles,— a splendid vision of silver cloth and orange-tawny, and plumed hats—their horses in silver trappings adorned with knots of orange-tawny—the image of Teresa, raised far above the crowd from the stern of a mimic ship, receives the homage of her worshippers. Four little children at her feet represent the four cardinal virtues, and twelve boy-friars, clad in the diminutive habits of her Order, are scattered about her on the deck.

Presently the people surge backwards like a receding wave, as the master of ceremonies rides forward to clear the way. The ship is brought to a standstill in front of the gate of the Boqueria, whilst the cavaliers enter by the opposite gate (the Puerta Forriça); "putting their horses through their paces in most lovely seeming and knightly and gallant fashion," they made their obeisance to the saint, and broke each five lances in her honour. The saint's ship then advanced and engaged in a mimic combat with a ship supposed to represent apostasy, already stationed in the plaza for the purpose. She then opened fire on a castle which, with its elaborate outworks and tower of homage, represented the "obduracy of the heretics against the Catholic Church in those times when, by the providence of God, our saint was sent to illumine it." A dead crocodile, blazing with fireworks symbolical of the devil, flew through the air to defend them. Apostasy and heresy fared ill that night; being utterly routed and consumed with fire, and when the smoke cleared off, the saint, "exceeding triumphant and glorious," was left mistress of the field.

When this was over the monks in solemn procession came forth to welcome her, and bear her shoulder-high in triumph to the church. As the deep strains of the Te Deum grew fainter and fainter and the last taper disappeared within the shadow of the gates, the populace, profoundly moved, broke into tears and sobs.

Placed on a silver pedestal in the centre of the High Altar of the monastery church, she then received the last farewells of her votaries until close on midnight.

Nor was the rest of Spain behindhand, as the accounts which lie buried in the dust of public libraries still remain to prove. In Valladolid the festival was celebrated by a great bull-fight in the plaza—the bulls being from the famous Xarama,—in which the Marquis of Aguilar and other noble hidalgoes displayed their courage and the swiftness of their horses. The greatest poet of his day, Lope de Vega, penned sonnets and villancicos in her honour. Perhaps more touching than in the great cities of Salamanca, Madrid, and Cordoba, the demonstrations of joy she received in Alba, where her body lay enshrined. There, by the unanimous voice of the people, she was elected patron saint of the province, an example which was followed by Salamanca.

The whole history of Spain records no more simultaneous and splendid fervour of national rejoicing. It may be doubted whether the conquest of Granada evoked such a thrill of triumph as the beatification of this Castilian gentlewoman. It is impossible to read the faded accounts of these old thanksgivings without being stirred by a strange emotion. For the old forms of the world in which Teresa had lived, and of which she formed a part, were even then passing away; the glory of Spain was on the eve of its extinction. Mediaevalism was emerging into more modern forms of life and thought. The spirit that informed it was gone, but never had its outer manifestations been more brilliant: the life so fast ebbing away clung jealously and with a sort of desperation to the minutest forms and ceremonies and splendours which had clothed it. The feasts and rejoicings which welcomed Teresa's beatification are especially noteworthy, inasmuch as they were the last lingering remnants of a former age, whose vitality had been consumed in the general decadence of the nation. It was the ghost, decked out in rags and finery, of the great impulse of mediaeval chivalry,—which special causes had rendered inseparable from Religion, and whose last throbs were still distinctly to be felt in Spain, when the brilliant light of the Renaissance had illumined and revivified the rest of Europe with new and fresh forms of thought.

Let Don Geran de Guardiola, with gala-suit of silvered white cloth, and cape and bonnet of black velvet, studded with diamonds and precious stones, prance once more on his white charger, with its velvet gualdaropa and silver trappings, through those dim old-world streets of Barcelona, to the honour of the Castilian saint. Let bands of gorgeously attired youths break lances for the favour of their lady: let the feathers wave once more from jewelled caps as they passage their steeds in stately joust along the Rambla of

Barcelona—for it is a most fitting ending to all that was so grave, so stately, and so chivalrous in the past. Let the bells ring and clash from the great cathedral and the countless towers of monasteries and churches; for they, although they know it not, are ringing out old Spain,—the period of great thoughts and greater deeds,—and Teresa was the last of it!

On the 12th of May 1622,—eight years after—she was publicly canonised in Rome together with other three Spanish saints, San Isidoro, Ignacio de Loyola, and San Francisco de Xavier; when the Roman senate in their official robes and insignia, the Pope's brother the Duke of Trano, and more than fifty bishops, all carrying white torches, accompanied her banner to the Discalced Carmelite Church of La Escala. The previous scene in St. Peter's is not without a certain smack of Paganism. The Pope seated on his throne in St. Peter's was appealed to by his nephew, Cardinal Ludovisio, to canonise the saints. When the request had been thrice repeated, the Pope's secretary rose, and, in a brief oration, defined and declared them saints. Then began the Mass of St. Gregory, in which special mention was made of each one of them according to the order of their canonisation, their names being drowned in the roar of cannon and volleys of artillery which, at a given signal, poured from the Castle of San Angelo.

At the offertory the Generals of the different Orders to which the saints belonged made offering to the Pope in the name of each one of them, of two small pipes of wine, two silvered loaves, and three baskets covered with a network of gold and silver. In the first were two white doves; in the second two turtle doves; and in the third a number of little birds, which, on being released, happy to regain their liberty, flew chirping into the roof, whence they sang through nearly the whole Mass.

In 1732, Benedict XIII. instituted the Feast of the Transverberation of her Heart. It is strange that until this year we hear nothing of this mysterious and miraculous wound. And yet, according to the Discalced Carmelites, the heart had been cut from her body between 1582 and 1586. Ribera knew nothing of such a wound,—for if he had, he would certainly have mentioned it; Yepes still less, although the former wrote his *Life* in 1590, and the latter died in 1613. Fray Francisco de Santa Maria preserves the same significant silence. The wound—according to the evidence of various doctors and surgeons present at the judicial examination of it in 1726—was burnt at the edges, and presented all the symptoms of having been effected by a red-hot instrument—"evidently with great artifice"; and we are fain to agree with the good surgeon Miguel Sanchez, in his conclusion, in spite of the different interpretation we attach to it.

The mysterious thorns which seem to grow upwards from the dust at the base of the heart were first observed in 1836. In 1872 they were visited and examined by a commission of professional men appointed for that purpose by the Bishop of Salamanca. Although they came to various opinions and conclusions, they all confessed their ignorance of the nature and causes of so remarkable a phenomenon. It would be interesting to know how and in what way their observations were conducted; and how closely they were allowed to inspect and examine them.

Teresa was solemnly voted patroness of Spain by "Parliament in High Court" assembled, on the 30th of November 1617,—a decision, however, which was not confirmed on account of the violent opposition of the Archbishop of Seville and others, who would admit no rival to contest the ascendency of Santiago over the national fortunes. The King (the weak and pious Philip III.) bent to the storm, and the execution of the decree was suspended. Philip IV. again attempted to carry through what his father had so signally failed in accomplishing. He succeeded indeed in obtaining a Brief from Rome, declaring the saint Patron of Spain, but did not find it so easy to bend the stubborn wills of his subjects. The brief and stormy controversy it provoked is chiefly remarkable for the conspicuous part played in it by Quevedo—the last of the great Spanish writers, who could still wield the Spanish tongue with the force and sincerity of a Sta. Teresa, and the grace and richness of diction of a Fray Luis de Leon. The paper he addressed to the King on this occasion—rather in the capacity of a Knight of

Santiago to the Grand Master of his Order, than of a vassal to his ruler—is a model of learning, brilliant antithesis, and nervous eloquence: the reasoning (limited as is its scope) being precise, clear, penetrating, and logical. The canons of Santiago appealed to Rome. The Discalced Carmelites, instead of boldly seconding the King, remained inactive, and refused to appear. The Spanish Ambassador, without the royal instructions,—the King's letters were, it is said, intercepted on the road,—was powerless to act. The Pope withdrew the Brief; the King was beaten, and Santiago triumphed.

In a codicil to his will, the last King of the House of Austria (the weak and drivelling Charles II.) left it as a solemn charge to his successors to do their utmost to ensure the "compatronato" of Teresa. At least, so late as 1812, under Ferdinand VII., her claims to the patronship were again urged by the Carmelites, and confirmed by the Cortes of Cadiz, but again the decree was never carried out—owing to the opposition of the Rigid Catholics,—and it remains to this day a dead letter in the "Diario de las Sesiones."

Nor were these the only honours decreed to her by her enthusiastic and admiring countrymen; and it must not be forgotten that to the dignity of a doctor of Salamanca she adds that of a colonel of artillery.

CONCLUSION

INVENI PORTAM

It would seem to me that I had ill fulfilled my task if I did not carry the extraordinary history of the Reform a little farther, and follow to the end the fortunes of those whose lives had been so long bound up with Teresa's; the men into whom she had breathed somewhat of her own marvellous spirit, and who had followed the banner she had held aloft so fearlessly through the dark and stormy years which preceded the triumph of the Reform. I am inspired too by a wish to do tardy justice to the man who, of all others, most contributed to it; on whose memory calumny still rests black and thick,—her favourite, the most tenderly cherished of all her sons; he of whom she wrote, that there would never be such another as her "greatest Prelate."

After Teresa's death, the same fate overtook her immediate followers, those she had most thoroughly saturated with her spirit, as befell those of San Francisco of Assisi. Their very loyalty to the traditions of their foundress; their determined resistance to any innovation in the institutions and government she had left them, inevitably doomed them to destruction. Gracian—he who had filled the highest offices in the Order, and Teresa's own letters prove how worthily and well he did so—was expelled from it with disgrace; the last days of San Juan de la Cruz were embittered by persecution; and Maria de San José of Seville died of a broken heart eight days after her arrival at La Cuerva, whither she was banished.

The jealousy against Gracian began from the moment he entered the Order, and had slowly gathered volume. Teresa herself had watched its progress (for nothing escaped those keen eyes of hers) from the very first; and during those black and miserable years, when the fate of the Reform hung trembling in the balance, it had added to her anxieties. The discontented and ambitious friars never forgave the brilliant young monk, fresh from the university, for having, when scarcely more than a novice, risen to the head of the Order. They never forgave him the undisguised partiality and preference ever shown to him by Teresa from her first interview with him at Veas to the hour of her death. The gray-headed Fray Antonio de Jesus nursed, with all the concentrated venom of a brooding and suspicious mind, a bitter resentment against the man who, he conceived, had not only supplanted him in the Order, but in the affections of their foundress. He took refuge in a sulky and obstinate silence—refused even to answer her letters. She had even suggested to Gracian, from Malagon, in January of 1580, more than a year before the Chapter of Alcalá, that Fray Antonio should be elected Provincial: "If only to let him die in peace, now that his melancholy has taken this form . . . and to be rid of these rancours . . . since so long as he has a superior over him he cannot do any harm."

And so the storm brewed. Gracian's opponents were not slow to perceive the advantages to be reaped from espousing the cause, and seconding the pretensions, of the peevish, discontented old man, who, the first and oldest of her friars, had seen himself relegated to a secondary place in favour of an upstart, young enough to be his son. And at the Chapter of Alcalá—the crowning glory of Teresa's hard and laborious life, when the Papal decree was confirmed, and the Discalced Carmelites for ever separated from the main body of the Observants,—he willingly became the cat's-paw of Doria and his party. There the muttering of the distant storm made itself more distinctly heard. It needed all Teresa's influence, it needed all the determined efforts of the Dominican Cuevas who presided, to secure Gracian's election, and one vote alone stood between him and defeat. Even then his rivals asserted that he, a raw novice, had been chosen over their heads, before he had had time to prove his vocation, to become, barely a few months after he had made his profession, Apostolic Commissary, and the central figure of the Order. He had shown, said the jealous friars, a disposition to command rather than obey. He had ever paid more attention to the exterior and secular part of his calling than to silence and prayer. He had deviated from the Rule and Constitutions rather than risk the loss of his popularity. But what they laid particular stress on was the allegation that from the first he had entirely overlooked the spirit of the Rule, which was contemplative and eremitical, to devote his energies to the confessional and the pulpit. In spite, however, of their determined opposition, to Teresa's fervent joy, her Eliseo was elected. During her life she stood an impregnable wall of defence between him and their miserable jealousies and disappointed ambitions. Her letters to him are full of the warning notes of danger. She protected him from the open and occult attack of his enemies. The moment she was dead he was left defenceless against the storm.

The tone of the Chapter was not long of asserting itself. The whispers began to grow ominously in volume. They disturbed the last moments of the dying saint; but there is not a shadow of proof, as has been asserted by Doria's fierce partisans, on the partial and unreliable evidence of Fray Antonio de Jesus himself, and of Ana de San Bartolomé (afterwards Gracian's most prominent accusers), that her confidence in and love for him suffered any change. His every action was submitted to the fierce scrutiny of a thousand peering eyes. The leniency of his government, the breadth with which he interpreted the spirit rather than the letter of the Rule (for in intellect and grasp he was far above his fellows, and his aims were wider and more universal), were interpreted against him by the narrow zealots who rose to power on his ruin. Doria was a very different antagonist from the weak, sour old man whom Teresa had treated with the same tender indulgence one accords to a spoilt and wayward child. The very antithesis of Gracian, from the first there was little sympathy between them. A man of undoubted power and ability, of iron capacity, this Doria; rigid, unrelenting, narrow, despotic—ready to sacrifice everything to his gigantic personal ambition. A foe indeed to be feared,—this austere, ungracious Genoese, who would neither conciliate nor be conciliated—the descendant of those stern old sea-wolves who for more than a century had led the galleys of Spain to victory. Teresa summed up his character shrewdly enough when he first entered the Order: "He has certainly seemed to me sensible, and of good counsel, and a servant of God, although he does not possess that grace and gentleness which God gave to Paul, for to few does He give so much together; but he is certainly a man to be esteemed, and very humble and penitent, and knows how to conquer wills; and he will thoroughly recognise Paul's worth, and is very determined to be guided by him in all things; for in many things (if Paul agrees well with him, as I believe he will, if it is only to please me) it will be of great advantage for the two of you to be always of the same opinion, and to me a great consolation." It would seem as if already she had a distinct prevision of the incompatibility of these two men, whom she would fain have linked together in the government. They were as unlike physically as morally. Their portraits still hang side by side in the peaceful cloisters of Pastrana; the one handsome, beaming good temper and benignity, his blue eyes as ingenuous and frank in expression as those of a child—already partially bald, with a tendency to obesity. The other vulture-faced, beak-nosed, eagle-eyed, thin-lipped, all muscle and sinew, not an ounce of spare flesh; full of the grim intensity and suppressed ferocity of a bird of prey about to spring on its quarry. A countenance which inspires one with repulsion and even dread.

The very year after Teresa's death, at the Chapter of Almodóvar, Doria, breaking through all restraint, gave vent to the undisguised animosity against Gracian which had long been slumbering in his breast. In view of this approaching Chapter, as if she already foresaw what was about to happen, Teresa, in her anxiety to shield him, had written little more than a month before her death, to warn him as to certain complaints which had come to her ears, and which she feared might give rise to imputations in the Chapter. It fell out even as she had feared; and Doria, throwing off the mask, declared that his rival's complacency and want of rectitude had brought destruction on the Order. It was seriously debated whether or not Gracian should be deposed from the provincialate. But the time was not yet ripe for action, and in an invidious and artful apology, even more dangerous and inflammatory than the attack, Doria contended that Gracian should be allowed to conclude his term of office. Thus commenced that mortal duel (if the term duel can be applied to a combat so unequal, where the aggression was all on one side) which ended in Gracian's final expulsion from the Order.

And yet, two years later, in the Chapter of Lisbon (1585), by a strange irony of fate, Gracian himself nominated as his successor the man who was to work his ruin. Already Doria's mingled hatred and ambition, which had grated so unpleasantly on his brethren's ears at the Chapter of Almodóvar, were sufficiently palpable; so palpable indeed as to alarm the high-minded, pure-souled, angelic San Juan de la Cruz, who exclaimed with a flash of prophetic insight: "Your reverence has elected one who will some day deprive you of the habit." In that same Chapter, Gracian defended himself from the attacks that had been made on his character, affirming them to be false and calumnious. The Chapter was then suspended until the arrival of the new Provincial, when the sittings were renewed at Pastrana in October.

On this occasion Doria introduced various changes into the government of the Order, and proposed the division of the Province into four districts, each governed by its separate vicar. This step was, as Gracian too clearly foresaw, the prelude to the elaborate scheme, the details of which had already been carefully matured. He made a marked allusion to Gracian. "Let us," said he, "pluck up the barren fig tree and cut off the rotten limb, and the body will recover its health."

Doria showed his hand still more clearly in the Chapter held in Valladolid in 1587, where his proposal to associate the Definitors with the Provincial in the government, and to give them a decisive vote, met with universal disapprobation. He would still seem to have wavered between removing his rival from Spain, and thus destroying the undeniable influence he wielded in the Order, or his total extinction—for Gracian was appointed Provincial of Mexico. But the friars were no match for the austere, eagle-faced Genoese. Without consulting them, which would have been to risk a certain defeat, he acted boldly, promptly, and alone, if we except his two coadjutors, Mariano and Fray Juan de Jesus Roca. A memorial was laid before the King, of whose support they had previously assured themselves. Philip warmly seconded them with the Pope, through his ambassador Olivares. It was not without difficulty the Brief was granted, Doria having inserted a clause, unheard of as yet in the history of the Mendicant Orders—with what object will presently be seen,—to give the Order authority to expel any rebellious subject from its bosom. The first portion of his scheme was now achieved, and henceforth the Descalzos were virtually at the mercy of the Provincial and his Definitors.

On the 25th of November of the same year, Doria and his Definitors met in council in Madrid to receive the Brief which was to revolutionise the government of the Order. It is worthy of remark that in this Council none of those men sat or had a voice who had struggled hand in hand with Teresa through the blackest hours of the Reform. Only one figured amongst the names of the unknown friars, the creatures of Doria,—one whose little jealousies and peevish character she had long ago seen through—Fray Antonio de Jesus. It was decided to convoke a General Chapter, to read the Brief before it, and either to force it on the whole assembly, or on a majority.

There was one man—and one man only whose presence constituted a formidable menace—who might even yet defeat all these schemes, and turn them against their very author. It was not to be expected that Gracian would sit by and quietly watch the whole constitution of the Order, which he, together with Teresa, had been mainly instrumental in establishing, subverted and scattered to the winds, without making an energetic protest. Had he not already written a pamphlet sufficiently indicative of his sentiments, entitled " An Apology in Defence of Charity against some who, under the cover of obedience to discipline, have been the means of relaxing it and disturbing orders"? A man like this—a man who promised to disturb all Doria's carefully-elaborated schemes—must be got rid of before anything further could be done. But how? It is easy for malignity to find a motive. An indiscreet observation—or one which seemed so to a jealous and vindictive mind—in a book on Missions to the Heathen, which he, in unison with the Franciscans, had written and printed without first obtaining his superior's sanction, afforded a plausible pretext. In spite of all, several of the conclave espoused his cause. But Doria carried the day.

That old rivalry ; that jealousy of the power and preference so long enjoyed by Gracian—the love and confidence shown him by Teresa above all others—still stank in the nostrils of the harsh, imperious monk, and were now to be revenged a thousandfold.

Gracian was deprived of all voice active or passive in the forthcoming chapters of the Order, and was forbidden even to be present. The notice of this decree reached him in Irun, where he was busy founding a monastery. He hurried to Madrid. In this, of all moments the one in which he should have acted with decision and indignantly repelled the accusations of his enemies—one of these being an undue freedom of intercourse with the nuns,—he humbly avowed himself in the wrong, and made a complete and abject submission. "I have erred," he wrote, " through oversights caused by the frankness of my nature, and not from malice ; nor does my conscience accuse me of any guilt." He proffered complete obedience, offered to resign the post of Provincial of Mexico, and being, as he said, already wearied of the cares of office, only craved for liberty to retire to some monastery, where he could devote himself to a life of contemplation and prayer. So did the incautious man play into the hands of his wily adversary. Had Gracian stood firm on this occasion, and forced his opponents, instead of obscure calumnies (for the book, Doria cunningly allowed it to be supposed, was only a pretext to conceal more serious and graver breaches of discipline), to formulate specific charges against him, he might still have been triumphant, demolished Doria's plans, and completely routed their underhand tactics. He numbered many followers in the Order, who already began to murmur angrily at the determined persecution he was subjected to. They openly declared that the sentence had been dictated by the ambitious Doria to free himself from his rival's presence in the Chapter, and to prevent what he had reason to dread, the election of Gracian himself as Vicar-General; that he had taken advantage of Gracian's ingrained simplicity and ingenuousness to remove a formidable competitor for the Vicar-Generalship. And it is certain that Gracian's appearance in the Chapter would have been the signal for open revolt; and more than certain that Doria and his faction would have been completely routed, and Gracian once more have taken his place at the head of the Order, to which he had consecrated his life.

A few months ago Doria had still hesitated between removing his enemy from Spain in an honourable capacity —making for him a bridge of silver—or his total extinction. He now hesitated no longer. Perhaps with the contempt of a bold, resolute nature for a weaker, he despised any such precautions with one who, being the only man in the Order capable of making front against him or calling in question the autocratic and despotic rule he was on the point of instituting, allowed his wings to be clipped so tamely. The resignation was accepted; the previous sentence confirmed, which, since he could neither elect, nor be elected to any of its posts, stripped Gracian of all voice and influence in the Order. He was taken at his word, and loosed from the Vicariate of Mexico. He might indeed still go to Mexico if he would, but only as the head of a band of friars.

From the first it would seem to have been a deeply-laid and premeditated plan of action on the part of the astute Italian to drag the simple and kindly friar into the meshes of his net. He had now not only succeeded in removing a dangerous competitor from his path, but had at the same time lured him to his ruin. Thenceforth Gracian was doomed.

Having thus, by depriving him of all voice in the Order, swept the field of the only foe he had any reason to dread, Doria proceeded to hold his first Chapter of the Discalced Carmelite Congregation of Spain.

On the 18th of June 1588 the Chapter commenced its sittings in Madrid. The session began stormily. Four or five friars, incited thereto (it is said) by Gracian, boldly condemned the change in the government, and almost revolutionised the assembly. When the uproar subsided, a secret ballot was taken (it was easy for those who destroyed and mutilated Teresa's letters to tamper with votes), and Doria was elected by a majority of twenty-six.

They then proceeded to distribute the congregation into six provinces. Instead of being, as hitherto, under the control of one provincial and his substitutes, who resigned their authority to him the moment he stepped into their respective provinces, each province was to be governed by a provincial of its own. The attendance of priors of monasteries,—who had hitherto had a voice in the government,—was dispensed with at the General Chapters, henceforth exclusively composed of the Vicar-General, and his Council of six, the provincials and their associates, the definitors. The priors were limited to the local chapter of each province, presided over by its provincial. The authority of the Council embraced the whole civil and criminal jurisdiction of the Order—nuns as well as friars—and the appointment of priors, sub-priors, readers, confessors, preachers, was vested in it alone. No monk or nun could change from one community to another without its express permission. It took cognisance of the minutest affairs in the scattered Order. The Vicar-General was elected for a term of six years; he and his Council (six in number) to form a permanent body, residing in Madrid, in a house set apart for that purpose. It will be noted that in this scheme the power of the General of the Order shrank into a mere shadow, and that the real substance of it was vested in the autocrat who, at the head of his Council, pulled the strings from Madrid. Also that the provincials were left little more than the name, they being debarred from all action independent of the central body. Doria, in short, was to be a kind of *Deus ex machinâ*, wielding an irresponsible and incontrovertible authority, similar in a less marked degree to that of the General of the Jesuits, on whose constitutions he had evidently modelled his scheme. It was an innovation that Teresa never would have sanctioned; utterly foreign in its aim and purpose to the spirit of her rule, which was, to grant as large an autonomy as possible to each and every one of her convents. The priors and prioresses were shorn of the authority they had hitherto wielded, and which, in the case of her nuns, she had fought so zealously to obtain and keep intact. Had she been alive it would either never have been effected, or, if effected, it is probable that she would have shared the fate of those who, wedded to the traditions of their foundress, were the most determined in their resistance to any innovation in the institutions and government she had bequeathed to their keeping. Had she been alive Doria might never have dared to bring it forward, or, if he had, with her standing behind him making up for what he lacked by her own strength of will and energetic resolution, Gracian would have strenuously opposed it; and had they not carried the day, the world might have witnessed the strange spectacle of a woman far up in years—banished to, and a close prisoner in some distant convent of the very Order she herself had founded.

It must not be imagined that Doria carried out his projects without opposition. The storm it excited in the Order and throughout Spain was tremendous. It was a *coup de main* cleverly contrived and executed, and he had astutely provided against any resistance on the part of the priors and the provincials by depriving them of all voice in the government, and limiting it to a council of seven.

But he had not reckoned with the prioresses, who bitterly resented this unwarrantable invasion of their liberties—so contrary to all that Teresa had ever thought, or said, or written; and resolved to shake off the tyrannical rule to which it was proposed to subject them. Ana de Jesus, foundress of Granada, and Prioress of Madrid; Maria de San José of Seville, instigated thereto (it is said) by Gracian, with the spirit and energy of their great foundress herself, prepared to make a stout attempt to preserve the ancient discipline of the Order. That all the trifling details of a woman's convent, its weaknesses, its peccadilloes, should be laid before a conclave of seven austere monks, far from the scene of action, and incapable of judging—that they should become a theme for comment throughout the Order—seemed to these brave and independent spirits a monstrous violation of Teresa's Rule. Ana de Jesus resolved to get Teresa's Constitutions—which expressly gave to the prioresses the right of choosing their own confessors—confirmed ; to appeal to the Pope to appoint a Commissary-General, who although subject to the Vicar-General, should alone take cognisance in all matters relating to the nuns ; and who more fitted for the purpose than those well-proved servants and heads of the Order, so dear to their foundress, Fray Juan de la Cruz or Geronimo de Gracian ?

All this she planned in her valorous soul (she might have been disobedient once, but I am sure Teresa would have applauded her now, and blessed the imperious character of her prioress), and behind her stood a serried little group of warm partisans, the best fitted in all Spain to judge of Teresa's intentions, and to guard her Constitutions as she had left them. Don Teutonio de Braganza, Archbishop of Evora ; Fray Luis de Leon, the eminent catedrático of Salamanca, who, "although he had neither known nor seen the Mother Teresa on earth, knew and saw her in the image of her daughters" ; and the great and scholarly Dominican Bañes, one of the most cherished amongst Teresa's confessors, all unanimously signified their approval of this decisive step. Maria de San José of Lisbon and Gracian joined heart and soul with her of Granada. Counting on the support and protection of the King's sister—the Empress Maria,—and of the Archduke Cardinal of Portugal, whom Gracian had enlisted in their favour, they resolved to have recourse to the sovereign Pontiff himself.

Marmol, a priest and near relative of Gracian (whose life and misadventures he afterwards wrote), undertook the mission. He conducted it with such secrecy that it was not until the Brief had been actually despatched "sub annulo Piscatoris" of Sixtus V. that Doria conceived any suspicions as to what was going on. Furious at being defied, and his authority set at nought by a few refractory prioresses, he immediately convoked an extraordinary Chapter-General, which sat in the Monastery of San Hermenegildo of Madrid. It was decided that the Brief appointing the Central Council, and giving it absolute control over the nuns, should be at once enforced, and the provincials entirely deprived of the authority they still conserved over them. And in case the nuns achieved their object, and Doria and his party were

worsted, it was resolved to abandon them to their own devices
—to treat them in fact as if they no longer belonged to the
Order. Since they had appealed to the Pope, let the Pope
manage them in future even as he thought fit. Gracian, too,
must be withdrawn from Portugal, where, protected by powerful friends, he was intriguing with Maria de San José (10th
June 1590). His friends and firmest supporters were no less
anxious for his presence than his enemies, and used every effort
to induce him to obey. In February, four months before the
Chapter met, Fray Luis de Leon had written from Salamanca
to Marmol in Madrid :

> It is necessary not only for him but for his supporters, and the Order,
> that his cause should be tried, and in Spain: and if it should be
> impossible to get the King and the Pope to appoint judges for him here,
> he can do this ; appear before the Cardinal and institute an action against
> these fathers for defamation of character (accion de jactancia), as it is
> called, by saying that it has come to his notice that they have deprived
> him of all voice, both active and passive, on account of the crimes and
> excesses he has committed, and that they likewise say and publish that
> they have other and graver charges against him, and that they give him
> out as being relaxed, and a bad monk, and a criminal. Whereon the
> Cardinal will order them to appear before him to answer it. If they
> appear and answer, the truth must come out ; if not, he will proceed
> against them by default, and they must declare him not guilty, and
> revoke the sentence they have given of privation of active and passive
> voice, and will restore his rights. If they consent to this, they will virtually confess the malice which has actuated them in the past : if they
> appeal, then it will be time enough to go on with the matter, and to
> consult afresh as to what more is to be done.

But Gracian gave no heed to these prudent counsels. It
seemed as if he was obstinately bent on precipitating his
own ruin. Bolstered up by the favour and protection of the
Cardinal Archduke of Portugal, to whom he had rendered
important services during the siege of Lisbon,—when it was
besieged by the Pretender Don Antonio and the English
under Drake,—confident in the protection of his powerful
patron, he weakly closed his eyes to the approaching danger.
The commonest instinct of self-preservation might have
warned even *his* ingenuous simplicity how small is the trust
to be placed in princes.

A month later Fray Luis again wrote :

> I have received yours and seen the copy of the father Gracian's,

which I should have known was his wherever I had seen it, without any one to tell me so. The reasons he alleges for his absence have some colour of religion; but from what I see, and it may be I am mistaken, they arise rather from the natural disposition of the father Gracian, who is by nature indolent in these things, and it is easy to give the colours of religion to what in truth is not so; and the more so in this case, where indolence of soul looks so like modesty, and pusillanimity like humility.

Let us begin with the welfare of the Order, which he puts last, and thence come to the first. And, as to this: first, I am exceedingly amazed that the father Gracian persuades himself that his withdrawal from it will do anything to remedy the present inconveniences which day by day are growing greater, and that those who are now silent owing to his being present will then sally forth in its defence. Because, if we consider it rightly, it is all the other way; for if some have now courage to resist, it is on account of his presence, and if he is not there, the whole thing will be hushed up by force, and all reduced to submission—according to all sound reasoning. It may be that it is not so, but this is to be conjectured; and thus to pursue a most uncertain hope, and on account of it to do immediate and certain harm to the Order.

Two or three things occur to me at present as being of the greatest importance for his Order, the wellbeing of which depends on their being placed on a proper footing. One is, that which calls in question his innocence and that of the nuns he has had to do with; for if they are left under such a stigma, many persons, generally and particularly, will be aggrieved and suffer in their reputations. Another is the government of the friars, which is being introduced, and which, as the father Gracian knows and has written, is so prejudicial; and which, if it is thus established, must destroy the principal virtues, which are charity, *simplicity*, and single-mindedness, which will be to the detriment not of one person, but of the whole Order, and not for a day, but for many years, and an evil that, if once introduced, will bring about the decay of the Order, so that it will be necessary for another Teresa to rise from the grave to restore it. [Such, then, was the opinion of this acute and profound observer of Doria's ambitious schemes]. The third is as regards that which relates to the nuns, on whose destruction they are also bent, by changing their rules, from which they have derived such benefits. . . . This, then, being the truth, it is no less so that he is in conscience bound, to the utmost of his power, to do whatever he can towards this end, and if he fails in this duty, he will be to blame, and offends God very gravely, and all the good he chooses to fancy he will do in the Indies will not palliate it. . . . His Order is in flames and like to be destroyed; and he wishes to turn his back on this, being as he is, or able to be, a party in its remedy, and to go away to seek other benefits and other souls. His duty is to those of his own Order, and not to those of the Indians. . . . God has entrusted him with this office, and tells him almost with audible words to resist the evil that is coming upon his Order. Is it well that the father Gracian should say to him now: You, Lord, will do it, for I wish to go to the Indies to baptize two or three infidels? God will answer him: Unprofitable servant, this I order thee, and this I will that thou shouldst do, and since thou failest me in this, it is certain that thou wilt fail me in the rest. I will confide no more in thee, since I have no lack of persons for these ministries.

. He says that to take action in his defence disquietens his conscience, and gives him scruples. A little disquietude is a less evil than the guilt of not fulfilling what the benefit of his Order imperatively demands of him. What duty of active life would ever be done if we considered this? Let him reassure himself that he is doing his duty, and what God wills him to do. If he defended himself alone, and discovered the faults of his assailants on his own account only, it would be an imperfection; but since it is for the general good, as in fact it is, it is a sin not to do it.

He says that it is to tarnish the reputation of the Order. . . . Which is worse, that ten or twenty persons should not have a good opinion of six or seven friars [the number of the Council], or that all the nuns of the Order should get the fame of loose and abandoned women? . . .

He says that if he goes away others will come forward in their defence. This is laughable: since now, when they are armed and have the captain present, they dare not sally forth, to think that they will sally forth afterwards, when they want the head and his power,—and these others will be left absolute masters of the field. . . .

He says he will be accounted vain if he takes up the cudgels in his own defence? Who but a fool can imagine such a thing? Moreover, he is not defending himself but many others; and, what is more,—the wellbeing of his Order. . . . And if some are scandalised, it is clear that it is the scandal of Pharisees. They will not account him vain if he indeed opposes the evil that menaces his Order; but they will account him chicken-hearted and pusillanimous if at such a moment he turns his back.

And then he says a thing, which is that he has no patience with you for not seeing that it is probable they will face him with two or three companions as witnesses. . . . And without doubt, and if I did not know the father Gracian, and, from many things that have come under my notice, was assured of his virtue, I should conceive an ill suspicion of him, and believe he is afraid because "non est bene sibi conscius."

But March came and went; and in April the old friar wrote again:

The sight of his letter has filled me with a great fear that he will give us the slip either one way or the other . . . and it seems to me I see it is the Devil that gives him such a longing for the Indies.

Once more he wrote on the 18th of July, in answer to Marmol's letter acquainting him with the doings of the Chapter in the previous June:

I received both of yours together, on my way from Madrigal; together with the decree and additions of those fathers, which resemble the quiver whence they come, for their excellent sense can be seen even in the style. . . . God alone knows the end he [Doria] has in view. I am pleased with the constitution to reduce the votes to fifteen, and that those fifteen can exchange their offices amongst one another as they see fit; and I repeat that I am delighted; for, although I had strong suspicions of that father's [Doria's] ambition, still I saw that he concealed it by giving definitive votes to the members of the Council, and I was waiting until he revealed it in some way; and with this he has now done so, so openly that even a blind man must see it; and if this does not open Loaisa's eyes, he will indeed be more than blind. The punishment decreed for the carnally-inclined is admirable; it would have been better if it had been established against the ambitious. . . . Judges are wanted, I repeat judges, and judges a thousand times, and the reason why this is growing every day is because this has not been strenuously enough insisted on. Please God, señor, that these mothers would cut themselves aloof from them and be ruled as was their first monastery, for thus would they preserve themselves in their purity, and live in peace. Here they have been told [the nuns of Salamanca] that their Constitutions have been confirmed in Rome, and that the Pope has given them to the General, and the General sent them to the Vicar; I cannot believe it, nor that the señor Doctor has allowed them to come by any other hand but his own. Let me know what truth there is in it; let me know what goes on in Lisbon; and stir up that fat-brained dolt of a relation of yours [Gracian] to defend himself, and the public cause of the Order; for this they send in the letters is an infernal libel. I know not whether those fathers, by whose advice such things are done and written, have lost their brains or their conscience, for either one or other is lacking, if not both,—so as to hit the mark better.

But neither for this did Gracian awake out of his culpable supineness; and Fray Luis de Leon was left to defend the nuns alone. Nor is it one of the least noteworthy deeds in his career that the noble old man, defying both King and Doria, stood up single-handed in the cause of these defenceless women. Never was right or reason more stoutly maintained; never did weakness meet with a greater-souled or more chivalrous champion. On the 7th of August, Sixtus V. was dead. A fortnight later, before the news of his death had time to reach the shores of Spain, the Brief confirming Teresa's Constitutions, and committing the government of the nuns to a Commissary-General, appointed for that purpose, arrived at Madrid. Its execution was committed to the Archbishop of Ebora and Fray Luis de Leon. The former dexterously withdrew and left his colleague to cope with it as best he might. The latter at once insisted on the convocation of the Council and Provincials to proceed to the election of the Commissary, and boldly proposed Gracian or

Fray Juan de la Cruz. But the learned Dominican was no match for the crafty Genoese, who betook himself to the Pardo, where the King was hunting.

At the very moment the Chapter was about to assemble (Philip had given no sign), arrived an order from the Nuncio to dismiss the conclave until a new faculty could be obtained from Rome. But the brave Augustinian was not to be beaten. In spite of the King and Doria, he again convoked a Chapter, and Doria again appealed to the King. As the monks were filing into the Chapter, appeared a gentleman of the King's bedchamber: "His Majesty orders your paternities to suspend the execution of the Brief for the meantime, and to change nothing until his Holiness, to whom all has been made known, shall decide otherwise." Fray Luis de Leon, a second time outwitted by the Genoese, muttered as he left the council-chamber, "It is impossible to execute any of his Holiness's orders in Spain." The bird of the air, or the curious ear of some sanctimonious friar, caught the bold utterance of the brave old Augustinian and carried it to the King. In the moment which was to crown the labours and the sufferings of a long and laborious life—as he was about to be elected a Provincial of the Order of which he had been the most splendid light, and on which to this day his memory sheds an unfading lustre—the King interfered, and another was elected in his stead. Philip had well learned, in that cold, inscrutable, dogged mind of his, to bide his time, so as to crush the more certainly and swiftly. They say the disappointment broke the friar's heart, but I do not believe that the hand even of a king could break the heart of one who had for five years defied all the horrors of the Inquisition dungeons; and who on the morrow of his release, oblivious of the years that had rolled between, took up the thread of his discourse in the Lecture Halls of Salamanca with the memorable words: "As I was saying." When the dust has cleared off and the shadows dispersed, how small a figure—the mean-souled, narrow-minded, vindictive Philip, the Lord of Spain and the Indies—beside the grand Augustinian monk, whose magnanimous and gentle soul conceived and penned the *Ode to Solitude!*

The nuns had been deprived of their mainstay. But

there was still a man, the most famous scholar of his age—famous in the disputes of the schools (now ancient history) as the opponent of Molina—who dared to lift up his voice with no uncertain sound in defence of Teresa's daughters, as once before he had defied the large and unruly meeting at Avila, when he pleaded for the fate of her first foundation. Bañes unburdened his mind to Doria in no measured terms ; told him plainly that his action in abandoning the nuns,—thus virtually expelling them from the Order,—was infamous, and without a parallel in the annals of the Church. The iron friar remained rigid in his implacability and hate. "Well, then," said the Dominican, "I will induce my Order to receive the nuns you cast off." To which Doria made answer : "I shall keep you to your word, for it will be to our interest and theirs that they should pass to the Rule of so venerable a religion." The King's comment on Bañes's intervention was mordant and concise : "Who brings Bañes into matters that concern him not ?"

On the 1st of June 1591, this being the fixed and regular time assigned for its assembly, another General Chapter was held in Madrid. After various regulations as to the government, it turned its attention to the nuns. Although Doria treated them as already separated from the Order, the King had veered round in their favour, and no decisive step could be taken without a further decree from Rome. It then turned its attention to Gracian, who, still firmly intrenched in Lisbon, had hitherto stubbornly refused to leave Portugal. But the discussion was cut short by a letter presented by the Archbishop of Ebora, indicative of his submission. There was indeed nothing else left for him to do, for the Archduke Cardinal, at the King's desire, had delivered him bound hand and foot, as it were, into the hands of his enemies. A few weeks later he arrived in Madrid. All present at that Chapter knew that over his head the sword already hung suspended. And yet only one man lifted up his voice in his defence. Where was Mariano, his old companion, who had fought with him through those troublous times in Andalucia ? Could he not say a word to avert the doom from one he had known so long and so intimately ; with whom he had shared so many struggles,—so many triumphs ? For the sake of the great woman who had loved him so well, could he not swallow his personal rivalry for a moment, and say if one word only in his favour? Yes, Mariano was there, but he held his tongue! And Fray Antonio de Jesus —what of him? Was it possible that a man of eighty had not long ago buried and cast behind him the memories of those old, unworthy rancours and resentments? What, after all, did it matter that they should speak or keep silence? For one spoke in his favour; the greatest amongst them— before whom they and their jealousies melt into misshapen shadows—a pure and lofty soul who once more reluctantly plunged into those grim and sordid dissensions, arose for the last time at the voice of Duty to speak grave words of warning. They were not to be forgiven him. Fray Juan de la Cruz saw the abyss into which Doria, blinded by his gigantic personal ambition, was bent on plunging not only himself, but the Order. He disapproved the constant and contradictory changes introduced into its constitution, subversive of all discipline, and the origin of confusion. He pleaded,—and we may judge (in spite of the carefully-guarded and biassed words of the chronicler) that he pleaded ably and well,—in favour of Gracian. Forecasting the future, he warned them against taking any cruel and hasty resolution which they must afterwards repent. He pleaded for the nuns, and deprecated the Vicar-General's harshness in chastising all for the fault of one or two—if fault there was. His noble and dispassionate words produced no effect on the passionate and prejudiced audience around him; for since the priors had been deprived of a seat in the Chapters, Doria had no difficulty in filling it with his own creatures, who owed all to him. Suspicious of Fray Juan's complicity in the action taken by Ana de Jesus, knowing that, if the Bull granted by Sixtus V. was confirmed, the office of Commissary-General of the nuns would naturally fall on one of the heads of the Order (and who more likely than San Juan de la Cruz?), Doria hastened to annul his appointment to the Provincialate of the Indies, bestowed on him by that very Chapter—an election which had already afforded a theme for murmuring tongues, so obviously was it an attempt to secure his absence from Spain.

Dragged from his cell, thrust into the fierce faction fights of the Order, he who had ever dwelt so far above the affairs of men, in regions of calm and ineffable peace and contemplation, and had desired nothing better than to leave his country, if only to escape from the tumults and clash of tongues which rent his heart,—he now remembered that he had prayed to die free from the cares of office; and in Doria's paltry vengeance he only saw a sign that his prayer had been answered, and that the end was not far off. But not yet, O valiant soul—not yet! For somewhat has the Church placed thee on her altars as a beacon and a consolation to suffering and weak humanity! The price of sanctity is hardly won! "Would you wish me," he said to his sons, "not to drink of the cup my Father sends me?" And the cup of which he was to drink was verily very bitter! He had scarcely returned to his beloved solitude of La Peñuela—*montes alti et cælo propinqui sunt contemplativi*—than he was subjected to a base attempt to besmirch the dignity and purity of his character. His accusers were Fray Diego de Evangelista (who under Doria's administration had risen to be General Definitor, and whose laxities San Juan de la Cruz as visitor had been called on to reprove) and Fray Francisco Crisóstomo (whom the saint had also admonished for the same reasons). Their names deserve to be mentioned, if only that they may be held up to universal execration.

Fray Diego, charged with the investigations into Gracian's conduct in the convents of Seville and Granada, in his desire to please his master (Doria), outstripped his commission, and spared no pains to blacken the character of him for whom all felt a singular veneration. With perverse malignity, they threatened and menaced the terrified nuns into vague admissions and utterances, which were falsified or embellished by the secretary who took them down; and the Commissary loudly proclaimed that it was his purpose to cast out from the Order him who had founded it, Teresa's first and greatest recruit. The universal burst of resentment and anger which hailed these base calumnies against a man whose life had been so absolutely spotless and free from reproach convinced Doria that there were limits beyond which even he could not go with impunity. It is said that as he read the indictment the paper fell from his hands. Why did he not burn it? The malice of a devil could scarcely go farther than to perpetuate a posthumous libel.

A little while, and Fray Juan de la Cruz will have gone beyond the power of his enemies to defame. A pale diaphanous figure, passionless, serene, he has floated across the pages of this history, leaving little mark and little impress. "The good such men do lives after them!" As the monks watched beside his deathbed, the convent bells rang out on the midnight silence. "What are they ringing for?" he asked; and when they told him "for matins," his eyes encircled the bystanders in one long sweet gaze of mute farewell. "I am going to sing them in heaven," he said, and, kissing the crucifix, he murmured, "Into thy hands, O Lord, I commend my spirit," and died. So died Fray Juan de la Cruz, in the fifty-eighth year of his age, on the 14th of December 1591.

If he, whose character for sanctity was venerated by all about him, did not escape the penalty of his opposition, but fell a victim to calumny, we can scarcely feel surprise at the fate in store for Gracian,—not a vaporous, nebulous essence, but a man of flesh and blood, although a weak one. He arrived in Madrid, says the chronicler, like one desperate, without humility or resignation. There are surprising depths of defiance even in the gentlest natures, when pushed beyond all limits of human bearing. He obstinately refused to clear himself before his enemies. What, indeed, had he to clear himself of? He had, in his letters and memorials to the King, dared to characterise the new form of government instituted by Doria as tyrannical, and more fitted for Court Alcaldes than a religious Order. Certain sick friars had asked him for a license to eat meat one day on account of their infirmities, and he had answered, "Love God, and eat meat or not as you will." A nun, who saw him for the first time after a long interval, knelt down and embraced him, and, kissing the feet of the Christ which hung on his breast, fell into an ecstasy. During the heat of summer, whilst he was superintending the building operations going on in the nuns' convent at Lisbon, they had taken out a mattress for him into the gateway, where he took some repose during the heat of

the day. He went inside the convent to give extreme unction
to a dying nun; the effort of sitting up was too much for
her, and she fainted away, and Gracian threw his arms
around her to sustain her head. One night, when the friars
were gathered together in community, they heard a man
battering at the door with his fists and demanding confession. He wished to go out and shrive the tormented soul,
and on hearing that it was against the rules of obedience
to open the door at night, he said angrily: "Fathers, what
obedience? There is no obedience here. Let us go forth and
hear his confession." These and such as these were the
charges against him, which had so roused the honest wrath of
good old Fray Luis de Leon. That he was able to bear the
fierce scrutiny directed against him by the suspicious malignity
of his enemies so well is in itself significant. The worst
accusations they could bring against him in the crisis of his
fall was his intimacy with secular people; his efforts to fill
the chairs of the Spanish universities with Carmelite friars;
his predilection for preaching and the duties of the Confessional, and the leniency of his Rule and punishments. For
his dream had been to bring the Carmelite Order to a pitch
of splendour; to give it a world-wide influence—had he not
himself, whilst Provincial of Portugal, been instrumental in
its extension to Mexico, Congo, and Abyssinia—to fill the
great universities with its friars, to cover it with an aureole
of learning and enlightenment, and to make it a worthy rival
of the great Dominican and Augustinian Orders? Surely
not an inglorious ambition! He failed, not because he was
not at the height of his *rôle*, but from a certain slackness of
fibre, a lack of certain work-a-day qualities, which, if a man
hath not, there shall be taken from him even that he hath!
He was too gentle and yielding to be a fighter, too unsuspicious to be a good diplomatist. His very virtues became
defects in the circumstances in which he was placed. Had
he been the one, he might have cowed his enemies by the
fierceness of his attack; if the other, have adroitly parried
their strokes and turned the points of their weapons against
their own breasts. As ill-luck would have it, he was neither.
His whole conduct, from beginning to end, was one long
series of mistakes. He temporised when he should have

stood firm; he was firm when he should have temporised. His fatal freedom from suspicion made him an easy prey, and it is surprising how easily he fell into the trap laid for him by Doria. Even his firm friend and supporter, Fray Luis de Leon, was doubtful whether his inexplicable vacillation and supineness arose from cowardice or humility. At all events, in the moment of his fall he plucked up courage and behaved like a man. He knew himself to be innocent. He was aware that his real crime was that he had stood in the way of Doria's ambition. Expecting no mercy, and desiring none, he took refuge in a proud defiance. Neither Doria's hypocritical grief at his victim's obduracy and impenitence, nor all the efforts of his chosen colleagues to make him plead guilty, made any impression on him. In this supreme moment of his life he found that decision and firmness, the want of which had proved so fatal to him. Once only did he relax—to throw himself on Philip's mercy (an unknown quantity in that monarch's character)—and to implore that he might be tried by judges, more impartial and dispassionate than those whose personal enmity against him was so notorious; otherwise he pleaded that he was entirely at their mercy.

But Gracian had once more hindered the plans on which Philip had set his heart (for from the first he had heartily espoused Doria's scheme), and it was but a faint show of justice that he received at the hands of the Jeronimite and Dominican appointed to take cognisance of his cause. They were more intent on watching how the breeze blew at Court than in engaging themselves in a lengthy controversy with the King and Doria. For might was now right; and they themselves feared lest at any moment they might become the victims of the royal displeasure. The result of their investigations was already a foregone conclusion. The alternative was offered to him, which he refused with disdain to accept—correction at the hands of the Order or to be expelled from it. He was then sentenced by a private vote to be disfrocked; forbidden under severe penalties to preach, to write to any nun, or to enter any convent belonging to the Order. After listening to the hypocritical expressions in which the sentence was wrapped up, without a word he took off his hood and flung it from him. Forestalling the officious friars who then stepped forward to deprive him of his habit, he undressed himself with his own hands, and it also he flung from him. He then clothed himself in the priest's robes which had been got ready for the purpose (they were new, and very honourable, remarks Fray Gregorio de San Angelo, who played a prominent part on this occasion); he was then deprived of the tonsure, and went forth into the world a disgraced and homeless man. It is said—and this time at least the miracle does not seem to me so stupendous—that at the moment of his expulsion blood issued from Teresa's girdle, which is still venerated in Zaragoza. Such was the fall of Doria's hated rival, whose resistance to his ambition, and an ardent desire to conserve the Order under the governance instituted by its foundress were the whole head and front of his offending. The most spiritual of her sons, San Juan de la Cruz, that strange and tender personality, had been mercifully released by death from witnessing Gracian's disgrace. As for Ana de Jesus and Maria de San José, women of great talent and discernment, and undoubtedly Teresa's most capable and trusted prioresses,— the one was a close prisoner in Salamanca, the other banished to La Cuerva, where she died of a broken heart. Fray Luis was dead, unable to survive (but I do not believe it, in spite of the affirmations of the chronicler) the loss of Philip's favour for having championed their cause. The Order of Discalced Carmelites is no longer the Order Teresa founded, and those who have fought so tenaciously to preserve her Constitutions in all their purity are accused of fomenting conspiracy and rebellion against its head.

It is perhaps some satisfaction to know that Doria himself was overtaken by death before he could leave his plans established, and that one of his most ardent coadjutors was drowned whilst crossing a stream—a judgment of Heaven, it was said at the time, and I see no reason to contradict it.

Gracian's further adventures—his sickening and hopeless suit for redress in Rome; his imprisonment by Turkish corsairs, steeped in all the romance and movement of that strange century—he has himself related in the form of a dialogue between two friars, who, under the tall chestnuts of a peaceful Neapolitan monastery, discuss the fate of their storm-tossed comrade. Bidding farewell to his mother, and donning a hermit's habit, he made his way to Alicante, thinking thence to take ship for Italy. Whilst he waited he lodged in a meson, and, "since a Simon of Cyrene is never wanting to assist in bearing the cross," it so happened that the mistress of the hostelry, who was well-to-do, had an only son, a lad about to set forth to Milan to see service as a soldier. The mother and son were kindly simple folk. They thought that, if he went with the friar to Rome, with the assistance of the latter, added to his own meagre stock of Latin, it would be easy for him to get ordained and enter the priesthood. In him the lonely gentle man found a companion, counsellor, friend, secretary, and servant, according to his heart's desire. Whilst Gracian remained shut up in his room (he notes that it opened out on a balcony looking towards the sea), as his eyes wandered over the strip of blue dancing against the yellow sand, its surface broken by the tall wand of a flowering aloe, enshrined in a distance of radiant sky, Joaquin charged himself with all the arrangements for their journey. Hearing of a ship in Tortosa about to sail for Genoa with a freight of wool, the strangely-assorted pair made their way thither, spending Holy Week in Valencia to see the sights and attend the services, celebrated throughout Spain for their stateliness and grandeur. The night before they were to sail, Gracian received a letter from a friend, offering him a passage on board the royal galleys, about to start from Vinaroz with subsidies for the French war. The simple friar was for holding to his bargain; the provisions for the voyage had been purchased, and they had met with great kindness both from captain and passengers. No such sentimental scruples disturbed the practical Joaquin, who having been to Rome before as secretary to a bishop, knew what a sea-voyage was.

"Father," he said, "go to sleep and don't trouble yourself, for in these matters I am not going to do what you order, but what is best." And at break of day on the morrow, having sold the provisions, he resolutely mounted the friar on a horse, and bore him off to Vinaroz. He might, indeed, go to Rome. But Philip's shadow stalked after him. "If Father Gracian should arrive there," Philip wrote to the Spanish Ambassador, the Duke of Sesa, "request the Pope not to give him a hearing, nor allow the matter to be reopened." Certainly it was not worth while to quarrel with his Catholic Majesty for the sake of a poor outcast friar; and when the Cardinal Santa Severina interceded in his behalf, the Pope made answer that he showed him favour enough in not clapping him into prison, and bade the Cardinal meddle no more in "that father's" matters, but to admonish him to enter some religious order, as his superiors had enjoined, within eight days' time.

But, alas! no religion would give an asylum to the disgraced and banished man. The Carthusians, Discalced Franciscans, Capuchins, shut their doors in his face; the Procurator of the Dominicans asked the Pope what crime his Order had been guilty of, that it should be forced to receive a man who had been expelled from his own.

From Rome he wandered to Naples to solicit the protection of the Viceroy, who refused to see or hear him: it was not to his interest, he said, to befriend a man who had forfeited the King's favour.

Thence, like "some wandering knight-errant, who looses his horse's reins to go whither chance may lead," he proceeded to Sicily. But here, too, Olivares, the Viceroy, refused to give him a hearing, although his wife, with the noble and disinterested charity of a generous woman (may she rest in peace, if for that deed alone!), found him an asylum in the Hospital of Santiago, whilst she wrote to Rome on his behalf. Here for a few peaceful months—from February to August—he forgot his woes in the composition of various treatises and books, which prove his curious and heterogeneous erudition. Aided by the wounded soldiers, he transcribed the *Mystic Harmony*—its title indicative of its subject; wrote a History of the Carmelite Order; and beguiled his leisure (no doubt to the admiration of his military coadjutors) by lighter treatises on the Art of Warfare, Anatomy, and Arithmetic. He was rudely awakened from this brief interlude of tranquillity by a Papal Brief from Rome, ordering him without delay to join the Order of Augustinians.

When, on the morning of the 11th of October 1593, laden with papers, and 250 copies of his works which he had caused to be printed in Naples, he embarked at Gaeta in one of the Inquisition frigates for Rome, it seemed at last that a gleam of hope smiled on his chequered fortunes. Scarcely three hours after, however, between Gaeta and Monte Sarcoli, as they were standing well out to sea, they were pursued and captured by a Turkish galliot. Stripped to the skin and laden with chains, he and the rest of the crew were flung into the hold; a little while after he beheld his precious MS. of the *Armonia Mystica*, which had cost him so many labours, and was of no little value, being put to the base use of cleaning his captors' muskets.

In a small island,—Ventoten, not laid down in any chart known to modern navigators,—where the corsairs put in for refreshment, they were joined by three other galliots and some brigantines from Biserta.

From Ventoten they made a night attack on Gaeta, but were driven back, owing to a woman who heard them and gave the alarm. Casting anchor between Gaeta and Naples, where they took in provisions and sacked two hermitages, they sailed up the Bay of Naples, swooping down upon more than a hundred barques coming from Castellamare and Torre del Greco. Three galleys from the harbour gave chase to and fired a few shots at the foremost galliot (Gracian's), but not being particularly anxious to come to closer quarters, presently made their way back again into the harbour, and the arraez swore, as he plucked his beard with rage, that had it not been for the two which had hung behind, for the sake of plundering some frigates, he would most certainly have captured them. All of which took place under the very casements of the town of Naples on that October morning of 1593.

They then attempted to surprise Torre del Greco, and to capture the Cardinal Ascanio Colonna; and after plundering one hundred and ninety souls, " with the swiftness of demons " the bold marauders bore out to sea. In spite of its being a dead calm, which forced them to take to their oars, daylight found them in the Straits of Bonifacio, and the next day they anchored at the Island of San Pedro, off the coast of Barbary. Here the captives were set on shore to refresh themselves (literally, "unflea," despulgar) and take the sun. The pots were already boiling on the fire when four galleys belonging to the Duke of Florence hove in sight.

Without losing an instant, the captives were hastily embarked, and the anchor weighed, more than thirty Turks being left behind. The galleys gave hot chase, and escape seemed hopeless, when the wind, freshening up, broke the lateen yard of the Admiral's sail, checking the pursuit, and forcing them to take shelter under the same island which the Turks had just abandoned. It seemed to the wretched captives that they saw the gates of heaven opened, when at last they found themselves in the port of Biserta, and they looked forward to the baths as a sort of paradise. A paradise which soon turned into a purgatory. The captain of the frigate, Antonio de Leyva, died within a few days of landing. The baths themselves were like long, narrow, underground stables or warehouses, with a corn-mill in the centre worked by an ass and an old blind renegade.

Here, in order to exist at all, they had nothing for it but to erect frames or hurdles similar to those used for rearing silkworms, to which they climbed up on sticks. The stench, filth, and darkness such that a Spanish prison (in that century!) was nothing to it.

After setting apart one captive in every ten for the Baxa,[1] Elisbey and Durali, the joint-owners of the skiff by which they had been taken, cast lots for the remainder. Gracian fell to the share of Elisbey, and would have had but little difficulty in effecting his ransom,—for the captain was in want of money,—had it not been for an unfortunate rumour which reached the ears of the Baxa of Tunis, that he was an archbishop with an income of from 10,000 to 20,000 ducats, and was going to Rome to be made a cardinal; moreover, that he was a great marabout amongst the Christians, and a relative of the King of Spain. Now, when any person of consequence was taken, the Baxa could by law either select the prize for himself or the Great Turk. But Elisbey, when summoned to give up his prisoner, pretended that Gracian

---

[1] The names are in the phonetic Arabic of Gracian, not mine. He published an Arabic Grammar, of which I have never been able to find a copy.

did not belong to him, but to Durali, who, from being an Algerian, and an old man of exceedingly savage temper, would be better able to defend him than himself. But the Baxa had no idea of letting so valuable a prize slip through his fingers, and presently despatched his Chauz, or ambassador to the Great Turk, with an escort of mounted soldiers armed with lance and musket, to bring old Durali to reason.

Durali threatened to pitch the Chauz head foremost downstairs, if he repeated his request a second time.

"Look here, Durali," answered the Chauz, by name Caymbali; "this time I forgive thee, for I see that thou art drunk; but by the head of the great Pataxa (Padishah), if tomorrow morning, when thou hast digested thy wine, thou dost not give me up the Papaz, I will drag thee at my horse's tail to Tunis." Whereupon irascible old Durali was convinced.

So in the chill dawn of a cold November morning, mounted on the top of water-baskets, and surrounded by janissaries, huddled in an old striped haik given him by the Christians, Gracian, with his breviary and some of his papers, took the road to Tunis. The wretched man was like to starve, had it not been for a bit of bread given him for the journey when he set out, by a compassionate Christian. At sunrise next day they came to a swollen river, which they could only swim across on horseback. Preceded by a Moor, who bore his clothes and held the reins, those on the brink encouraged him by their shouts. "Grip the mane stoutly, fix your eyes upon the sky, Papaz, and do not heed the water," cried the guide: and all his life long Gracian remembered that the best sermon he had ever listened to came from the lips of an infidel.

For two years—his feet riveted in chains—he lingered a captive in the Baths of Tunis. Apart from the fetters, however, his position seems to have been by no means intolerable. Perhaps what most surprises us in this strange recital is the comparative leniency with which the Christians were treated, and the cordial relations which existed between them and the Turks. Their faith and rituals were not merely tolerated but even encouraged by the Baxa. "Dog," he answered to one of the gaolers who complained of the evil language used by the Papaz to his holy sabi Mahomet—"dog! what business is it of thine to hear what the Papaz preaches. Dost thou want perchance to become a Christian? Leave them alone; are they not within the walls of their dwelling-place, and is it likely they should speak well of Mahomet?" And in the Baths, ill lighted, miserable, and damp as they were, a sort of dark, obscure cave was set apart for the Christians' Mass said by a priest, bought for that purpose by the Baxa, who was free to go and come, and was treated with consideration and respect. Put it down to the meanest of motives—viz. to prevent the Christians turning renegades, and thus becoming unavailable for service as oarsmen in the galleys—the Baxa proved himself a deeper politician than Ferdinand, Isabella, and Philip II., their great-grandson, then by the grace of God burning heretics by the score, in Christian Spain.

The gentle benevolence and transparent simplicity of the good friar quickly won him the hearts of Turk and Christian alike. The Christian captives provided him with food, clothes, and money. The Sultanas, the Baxa's mother and mother-in-law—the latter a Greek from Chio—sent him presents of linen and food from their own table; the Baxa's baker a loaf daily from the batch of bread baked especially for the seraglio.

Priest, confessor, umpire, mediator, all in one, writing letters for renegades, in which, as he naïvely confesses, he contrived to inform the Viceroy of matters affecting the interests of Christendom, so wore away the long monotonous hours of his captivity. The Turks who frequented the little eating-booths kept by the Christians, attracted thither by the Requin or Christian brandy, invited him to eat and drink with them. If they sought a cure at the hands of the Christian barber, they prudently made him the depositary of their fees. "Keep these ten ducats, Father," they said, "and if Maese Pedro cures us within such and such a time, let him have them, and if not, return them to us, for we are not such fools as the people of your country, and give the doctor money not to attend us, but to heal us." Oh, wise Moors! An old man, inspired by I know not what admiration for his harmless character, brought his sick grandchild to receive the miraculous touch of the gentle Papaz. Christians grown old and useless in captivity related to him a thousand curious facts about the country, and these he afterwards embodied in a book.

With a lovable and *naïf* vanity characteristic of the man, he records the notable results of his teaching; and although we refuse to believe that a Moor wept when he heard Christ's name reviled, or that Christmas was kept in more esteem than Mahomet's birthday, he unconsciously shows us that he was himself both loved and venerated. And we see no reason to doubt the somewhat unseasonable devotion of a drunken Turk, who on being shown a crucifix, and told that it was Cidnaiça (the Lord Jesus), and the woman at his feet La Miria, his mother, sallied forth into the Jewish quarter, and, shouting " Chifutiguidi que matastes á Cidnaiça " " Cuckold Jews, who murdered Christ!"—broke as many Jewish heads as came in contact with his cudgel.

So the days wore away in the dark, narrow underground cellar. At daylight the heavy bolts clashed, and the gates were opened for the captives to go to their work. For a brief interval at mid-day, whilst the camels were being watered, the friar was allowed to drag his chains into the sunlit courtyard, hemmed in on one side by the Baths, on the other by the massive walls of the Alcaçava or fortress. Here for a moment, as he listened to the hoarse guttural shout of the camel-drivers, and the challenge of the white-robed sentinels sitting motionless with their muskets; above, great breadths of glistering walls, whose flame-shaped battlements were cut out in a frame of vivid azure, the Castilian monk became a part of that strange Eastern phantasmagoria around him.

And at sunset, when the chains had grated in the locks for the night, for even these poor wretches—not being in an English gaol or workhouse—knew a gleam of joy and brightness, Gracian enjoyed for a fugitive moment his old oratorical triumphs, as perched on a tub at the church door he roused them with words as eloquent, perhaps more so, than those which had made him famous in the universities of Spain. Then, too, you might have heard the tinkle of guitars, and six hundred voices raised in vespers. No matter that they kept but little time or measure. I even think that they reached heaven as nearly, as if they had rolled through the resounding roof of the most magnificent cathedral. On greater occasions, when they celebrated the festivals of their church with lute and zither, the Turks lent them silks and brocades to adorn the church and patio.

Teresa had judged well. There *was* in the composition of the unfortunate friar a heroic strain which, developed under happier circumstances, might have girt his brow also with the aureole of the saints. In the humble, faithful performance of his mission—devoting the gifts that poured in on him to the relief of the sick and the hungry, who were even poorer and more miserable than he himself, he found such tranquillity and happiness that he describes these two years in the Baths of Tunis as the most peaceful of his life.

Twice it would seem that he was in danger of being burnt alive, for the rumour got about that he was an inquisitor, and the fact of his having been captured on board an Inquisition frigate, freighted with instruments of torture, lent it a sinister seeming of truth. The janissaries demanded him of the Baxa to put him to death; but the Baxa had no idea of burning even an inquisitor whom he had decided to be worth thirty thousand crowns at least,—and so the matter dropped. "This inspired Eliseo with such contempt for the Turks, and such daring against them, that in all his sermons he never failed to speak ill of Mahomet, and publicly taunt him as a dog." His conversion of a Christian renegade from Salamanca, who had taught him Arabic, drove the one to the oars, and loaded the other with a hundredweight of iron. Not that the Baxa cared—for it was to his gain, as he frankly confessed,—but Cerberus occasionally demands his sop. "Well! what do I care," he said, "that El Mami has turned Christian? Would that there were more of them, and so for this crime we shall take him from his master, put him in irons, and have another galley-slave the more; and as for the Papaz, put him into the Magyar chains"—these having been brought especially from Constantinople for the use of a notorious sea-captain. In June of 1594 the poor friar discerned a chance of freedom. Six hundred ducats of his ransom were already deposited in Tabarca. The Baxa himself, on the point of leaving Tunis on a naval expedition, and not intending to return, was in terrible need of money. Iafer Bey—the Califa—the supreme head after the Baxa, "an old and very able man;" Caymbali, the Chauz, who had brought him to Biserta, both spoke in his behalf. Gracian was assured by the Baxa's silversmith, Diego Rodriguez, who offered to aid him with 400 ducats more, that if at this juncture he failed to effect his ransom, then he was most assuredly doomed to the Towers of the Black Sea. But the Baxa, who had already embarked, and was on the point of sailing, was inexorable. "Don't talk to me of the Papaz," he exclaimed, "a farthing under 6000 crowns!"

So the friar and an old Genoese were left to the solitude of the empty and silent Baths, their fellow-prisoners having gone with the Baxa. Since the affair of El Mami his confinement had been made more rigorous. Long habit had accustomed him to his former shackles, which he had managed to roll about his body in such a way as not to impede him in celebrating Mass. But now he could scarce crawl out to see the sky and breathe the air. He was closely watched by a sentinel, Mançur, who inspected his irons every night. So through the long summer months he lay stretched on his crib—"and what we suffered from fleas, filth, stench, rats, and fear of phantasms that went about those caves, was of itself a certain kind of martyrdom; so that the worst dungeon of a Christian prison is a delightful garden in comparison to what one goes through there."

In August a dispute about his ransom again dashed the cup from his lips, the very day before that on which he was to have regained his freedom. The 400 crowns lent him by the generous silversmith, and which he wore round his legs concealed beneath his fetters, he now devoted to releasing others, "leaving," as he says, "his own rescue to God; and if he had had in his possession the 600 of Tabarca, he would have spent them in the same way."

It was to the Baxa's need for money to pay his janissaries that Gracian at length owed his freedom. It was impossible to delay their payment even for a day, nor would want of funds be accepted as any excuse. About this time also the Lomelines (?) of Tabarca sent the Baxa a present, and entreated him to accept of the 600 crowns. He rejected the offer with scorn. A day before the janissaries were to be paid, the Baxa in great perturbation sent for one Simon Escanisi, a wealthy Tunisian Jew. Now this Jew had just arrived from a journey to Gaeta, Naples, and Sarcoli, where he had been repeatedly urged by Gracian's friends to leave no means untried to bring about his release.

"I know not how to look for money for thee," said cunning Simon, "since thou wilt not sell this Papaz, whom I know to be a poor friar, and never in his life wilt thou get more out of him than the 600 crowns in Tabarca. Do not lose the money nor the opportunity, for one of these days he will die on your hands, and you will get nothing." At length, after a long dispute, the Jew beat the Baxa down to 3000 crowns. "If we let this occasion slip," said the good Jew to the poor Papaz, "I see no hope of your ever getting free, and one by one we will deliver you from your imprisonment, for after all—God is great." Nor had Gracian any hope either; but he held his tongue that he might not be thought to belittle the God that the Jew called great.

At the critical moment, when the Baxa knew not where to turn to fill his empty coffers, Simon appeared with 600 ducats, and the bargain was closed at 1000. Off speeds good and cunning Simon to the Baths. After two years' imprisonment Gracian's fetters are at last knocked off, and he himself safely lodged in the house of the French Consul. "It was enough to make one praise God, the pleasure shown by many Turks and Moors, who met him in the street after having seen him in chains. Some said, *Zalam alicum Papaz*[1] —God be with thee; others, *Stasaala*—Praise be to God, and like salutations. Others took and entertained him in their houses, or showed him their gardens, and all that there was to see in Tunis."

To the relief of Simon, however (who saw his 1000 crowns in jeopardy so long as Gracian remained in Tunis; for, unable to forget the dialectics of the schools, or the learning whose brilliancy had dazzled his contemporaries, the honest friar could scarce refrain from accepting the

---

[1] Again I must note that the Arabic is Gracian's, not mine.

challenge of the Mofiti and Cadi to enter with them the lists of theological discussion), the beginning of May found him on his way to Biserta.

After a stormy passage and a narrow escape from recapture, he arrived in Genoa and begged his way to Rome, where he took out a brief to beg in order to refund his ransom. The Congregation de Regularibus revoked his sentence and expulsion and ordered the Descalzos once more to receive him into their bosom. But it was not to be. Doria and Mariano indeed were dead, and gone to their account, but the Order was still governed by their creatures. He finally took the habit of the Calced Carmelites, who treated him with every honour and consideration, the General's cell being set apart for him in the Monastery of San Martin in Montibus. For five years he remained in Rome in the employment of Cardinal Deza. Once again he visited the African coast, Tetuan and Ceuta, sent thither by the Pope to preach the Jubilee. In 1601 he returned to Spain, and saw his sister, Maria de San José, Prioress of Consuegra, and his brother, Fray Lorenzo de la Madre de Dios. Thence he went to Madrid to salute his family, and had the supreme consolation of being present at his mother's deathbed. After some other ups and downs he finally drifted to Flanders, and died in Brussels in 1614 at the age of sixty-nine, softly repeating Teresa's couplets, and holding in his hand to the last the image of her he called his mistress.

A man whose learning was rather diverse and curious than deep or extended, full of strange odds and ends; his books, bristling with secular erudition and dialectics, are still among the curiosities of the theological literature of the period. Withal, simple and guileless as a child, and with all a child's *naïf* impracticability, he is certainly the most human and the most lovable, as well as the most ill-fated, of Teresa's friars. Strangely enough he analysed and knew (a knowledge that many of us never attain to) the secret of his material failure. Indecision and want of confidence in himself were the remote causes of his ruin. "One may say," writes his friend, Marmol, "that the very candour of his disposition was the cause of his lacking the malice or caution which is often so necessary amongst the sons of

Adam, and from this perhaps came the greater part of his woes."

From the very outset he became the victim of the strangest caprices of fortune, and if one believed in predestination, in him we might find a startling example of it.

Let us say with the unknown annotator—perhaps a member of his own family—who has written it on the yellow-stained margin of my copy of Marmol's pages, published four years after his death, in Valladolid:

O juicios de Dios! O juicios de los hombres!

*　　　*　　　*

EPILOGUE

Thus fittingly from Avila of the Saints, and no less fittingly from a country where the Church for a thousand years was indeed militant, came the last great saint of mediaevalism, in many respects the greatest of them all.

There will be no more saints. The world will go on producing great people, or rather great people will be born into it, with sympathies as large, as bold to dare, as brave to do, and as little understood as she was. But the world itself has changed; the scene is no longer the same. To idealise greatness to such a superlative degree as it has been idealised in Teresa, presupposes a force and vigour of conviction, a power of enthusiasm, a capability of those very qualities it idealises, which it has ceased to possess. It is the especial grace of these privileged beings to force mankind to shake off its inertia, and for a moment to inspire into it that bright glow, that eager intensity of purpose—the reflection of their own. She died at the right moment. It is the sad privilege of great minds to feel the full bitterness of disillusion, to discover the depth of the chasm between the ideal and reality. The bright and luminous vision so fair in the distance which had beckoned her on to each successive effort, was inexorably destined to lose its beauty and mystery when chained down and shut in within palpable stone walls. To materialise the intangible is a sacrilege punished on the daring and exalted mind that conceives it, as inexorably as the theft of Prometheus.

Teresa's last moments were saddened by some such conviction. As those who continue and bring to its completion some admirable cathedral—that of Avila, for instance—are incapable of understanding or carrying out the grand design of the unknown architect who first conceived it; so too her prioresses, incapable of comprehending, responded ill to the intentions of their foundress. Division had broken out amongst her friars. Had she lived longer she too would probably have incurred the same disgrace that blighted the name and fame of Gracian, and embittered the last moments of San Juan de la Cruz.

Great is the power and majesty of Death. Never greater than in this, that in its cold clear light we read all that has escaped us in the life that has gone. A thousand little circumstances that seemed so insignificant in the acting, become invested with I know not what sudden majesty and grandeur. Imagination endeavours to pierce the thin haze between us and the voice that is silent, the heart that is for ever still. By degrees the loved image, now shrouded in all the mystery of the unknown and the irreparable, becomes a distant and beautiful picture, and every detail, regarded with such slight attention at the time, then reveals to us its hidden meaning. Then it was, but not till then, that those poor coarse alpargatas in which she trod over so many leagues of Castilian tracks; the staff on which she leant in old age, became, and justly, the most honourable of her relics.

Her nuns of Alba buried her with little honour. The mausoleum of religious literature which weighs down her memory bears to me a strange resemblance to the pile of stones and brick and mortar that broke in her coffin lid at Alba. From these I have endeavoured to disinter her with loving and reverent hands, and to paint her, however feebly, as in very truth and seeming she walked in the world of men.

And so Teresa and her friars pass before me into the night. With them goes out old Spain, its gloomy stateliness, its austere repose, its grave interiors, its democratic impulses. She has gone; yet in the convents where she was once a presence, a seat in the choir, a bench at the refectory table, eternally wait for their shadowy guest. Yet, although she has gone, old-world towns and villages still preserve the sombre setting that enshrined her life. In the streets of Toledo, shut in by moss-grown walls of gloomy buildings, blotting out the sunlight; in the gray escutcheoned houses of Avila; in little sun-baked villages lost in the wilds of La Mancha and Castille, far from the turmoil of men, she and the spirit of her age linger flickeringly. A nun's figure—small, indeed, in the immensity of past and future—once knelt for a moment in those great cathedrals, as the roll of Tenebræ or the glad Te Deum of triumph thundered above the aisles—ere she too went her way into space. In remote country districts, a meson, a venta, where she once passed the night in those ceaseless pilgrimages, is still pointed out by the inhabitants, and, without ceasing to welcome the wayfarer now as then, is for ever consecrated to her memory. Perhaps to me, however, she has lived most vividly, I have seen her most distinctly, as the donkey's feet sink noiselessly into the sand of the narrow paths which traverse hither and thither the immense plateaux of Castille. There in the silence of some hot noonday, broken only by the chirp of a bird, or murmurs of myriads of crickets lost in the fine lush grass—around me the paramera strewn thickly with grim fantastic boulders, lit up here and there by bright patches of grain; flecked with masses of scarlet poppies or corn-flowers, whose stars of vivid blue are profiled sharply against the searching sky—there, as the sun lingers high above and the afternoon wears on apace, like confused strains of music which seem to float from space and time, not so perfectly co-ordinated as to form a definite melody,—have I caught those odds and ends of memories, forgotten instincts, a persistent re-assertion of the past, lurking in the brain, and handed on unconsciously from father to son, which first led me to write the Life of Teresa de Jesus.

In upland villages, amongst simple country people have I found the clearest glimpses (if still obscure) of the conditions of her life. Duruelo, still intact, thanks to the laudable incuria of the Spanish peasant, is after three centuries redolent of her memory. Her hand planted the poplars beside the gateway. A skull half buried in the sand of the little graveyard close by is that of some forgotten friar, whose life blossomed for a moment in the desert, and faded tranquilly into night.

Yes! Let me look well on the landscape—photograph it well on the chambers of the brain ; the blue mountains of Piedrahita in the distance still faintly streaked with snow, the brown plain around me ; the streamlet (Rio al mar) winding through its grassy bottom ; the oak glades I rode through in the morning light ; in the background the brilliant sky, framing all as in a picture. For on the same spot where I now stand, she also stood three centuries ago, and blotted out for a moment sky, and stream, and sandy track. Here then ; in Malagon where the rude boards in the gateway commemorate her visits ; in Villanueva de la Jara, buried amongst the olive yards, I find her still, if not in visible presence, in invisible potentiality. The gray, time-stained walls, the humble rustic interior, the rough woodwork, the darkness, the obscurity, the austere repose, the unbroken tranquillity of these old buildings show us what these primitive convents were—what she herself was too, whose life lies imprisoned in them for ever.

Sometimes—so little has all changed—one almost fancies the little procession of peasants one passes journeying to worship at her shrine across the treeless wastes or through the sunlit oak glades, will meet *not* the saint, but the simple Castilian gentlewoman, who three centuries ago journeyed seated on an ass even as they do now.

O! Saint that trodst this earth of thine,
This little speck of earth, this Avila;
All unaware those gray old walls should be the shrine,
Not only of the Ages but of Thee:
O! Thou that fillest this weak brain of mine
With thy great figure, small in huge Immensity of Past and Present,
Stoop down from thy high pedestal and blot whatever line
May be unworthy of Thyself in me.
Nay, as Thou smilest on the kneeling crowd
Who low before thee bow and sing thy praises loud,
Wilt thou not e'en vouchsafe a smile to me,
Who saw thee not, yet seek to know what thou didst not,
What thing it was, so strong, so slight,
Which shone on thee in Death—through thee in Life?

INDEX

ADELANTADO, an, ii. 41
Ahumada, Doña Beatriz de, i. 86
Ahumada, family of, i. 16, 79
Ahumada, Lorenzo de, ii. 340
Ahumada, Pedro de, ii. 288, 296
Alba de Tormes, i. 436, 439; Convent of, ii. 371
Alba, Duchess of, ii. 380
Alba, Duke of, ii. 259, 283
Alba, Dukes of, their castle, i. 438
Alcalá de Henares, i. 353, 400; Chapter of, ii. 315; College at, ii. 67
Alcántara, Fr. Pedro de, i. 188, 258
Almodóvar, Chapter of, ii. 224
Altomira, ii. 68
Alvarez, Baltasar, i. 164
Alvarez, Garci, ii. 105, 153
Anchorites, Early Christian, i. 283
Andrada, i. 382
Angeles, Fray Pedro de los, ii. 242
Angeles, Isabel de los, i. 301, 456
Arriaga, Doña Maria de, i. 448
Avila, i. 2, 24; history of, i. 7; houses of, i. 83; life in. i. 270; opposition of, to Teresa's new convent, i. 271; changes at, ii. 332
Avila, Juan de, i. 70, 160
Avila, Julian de, i. 266, 275, 327, 333; ii. 32
Azaro, Ambrosio Mariano, i. 393, 414

BAÑEZ, Fray Domingo, i. 205, 273, 319, 444; ii. 425
Barron, Fr. Vicente de, i. 137, 256
Batuecas, Carmelite Monastery of, i. 62
Bautista, Maria de, ii. 38, 252
Beamonte, Da. Beatriz de, ii. 317, 320
Beamonte, Don Francisco Carlos de, ii. 322
Beatification of Teresa, ii. 400
Becedas, Curandera of, i. 116
Beltrán, Fr. Luis de, i. 232

Bernarda, daughter of Pablo Matias, ii. 151
Blasquez, Jimena, i. 8
Bolandists, Acts of, i. 280
Borja, Francisco, Duke of Gandia, i. 152
Brazil, Princess of, i. 352
Brianda, prioress of Malagon, ii. 150
Burgos, Archbishop of, ii. 343, 355
Burgos, ii. 351; Convent of Las Huelgas, i. 40; foundation of Carmelite convent at, ii. 341; Hospital of the Concepcion, ii. 358; Teresa's journey to, ii. 345; the Christ of, ii. 352

Camino de Perfeccion, i. 308
Cañada, Castellanos de la, i. 114
Canonisation of Teresa, ii. 406
Capra Hispanica, i. 5
Caravaca, foundation of, ii. 120
Cardona, Catalina de, ii. 29, 266
Carlos, Don, ii. 270
Carmelite Order, origin and development of, i. 280; Rules of, i. 284; Reform of the, i. 227; Reformed Order of, i. 261; ii. 230, 409
Castellanos de la Cañada, i. 114
Castilian, Teresa's use of, i. 68, 198
Castille, travelling in, i. 332; landscape of, i. 334
Cazalla, Doctor Agustin, ii. 268
Cepeda, Alonso de, i. 85
Cepeda, family of, i. 78
Cepeda, Francisca, ii. 294
Cepeda, Lorenzo de, i. 418, *note*: ii. 102, 149, 162, 176, 284
Cepeda, Rodrigo de, i. 88
Cerda, Da. Luisa de la, ii. 118, 150, 248, 358, 380
Charles V., i. 32
Cisneros, Cardinal, i. 12
Concepcion, Hospital of, at Burgos, ii. 358

Constitutions of Descalzos, ii. 311, 316
Cordoba, ii. 94
Corsairs, Turkish, ii. 434
Council of Orders, ii. 53
Cows, Our Lady of the, i. 19
Cruz, Magdalen de la, i. 159
Cruz, San Juan de la, i. 346, 368; ii. 201, 426
Curandera, i. 117; ii. 217

DANTISCO, Doña Juana de, ii. 167
Daza, Gaspar, i. 146, 195
Dehesa, i. 9, *note*²
Demons, belief in, i. 181; Teresa's conflicts with, i. 182
Descalzos, *see* Discalced Carmelites
Diaz, Maré, the hermit of San Millan, i. 161, *note*
Discalced Carmelites, Order of, i. 56; rules of, 291; fame of, ii. 69; feud with the Observants, ii. 75, 108, 132, 187; constitutions of, ii. 311; reorganisation of, ii. 417; separation from the Carmelites, ii. 213, 224, 247, 309, 315
Doria, Nicolas, ii. 224, 314, 333; rivalry with Gracian, ii. 373, 409, 411
Duruelo, Monastery of, i. 368, 377

EBOLI, Princess of, i. 389, 403; enters Pastrana, ii. 27
Eckart, mysticism of, i. 46
Encarnacion, Ana de la, i. 203
Encarnacion, Convent of the, i. 3, 109, 123; life in, i. 132, 228; Teresa, prioress of, i. 460; hostility of nuns of, to Teresa, ii. 1; ruins of, ii. 199
Ervias, Doctor Agustin, ii. 262
Evangelista, Fray Juan, ii. 110

FERNANDEZ, Fray Pedro de, i. 458; ii. 67
Figueredo, "correo mayor" of Toledo, ii. 138
Fundaciones, ii. 166, 170

GABRIEL, Fray, ii. 73
Gaitan, Antonio, ii. 23, 32
Gandia, Duke of, i. 152
Garcia, Antonio Lopez, ii. 55
Gaytan, Antonio, ii. 121
Gracian, ii. 7, 60, 77, 108, 141, 190, 219, 229, 236; history of, ii. 82; his first interview with Teresa, ii. 87; at Seville, ii. 137; elected Provincial, ii. 314, 316; rivalry with Doria, ii. 373, 409, '411; expelled from the Order, ii.' 430; further adventures of, ii. 431
Granada, Fray Luis de, i. 160
Guardiola, Don Geran de, ii. 402
Gutierrez, Nicolás, i. 432

HEREDIA, Fr. Antonio de, i. 330, 345
Hernandez, Fray Pablo, i. 371
Hortigosa, i. 105
Huescar, Duke of, ii. 384

IBAÑEZ, i. 235
Inquisition, i. 34; and Teresa, i. 65
Isabel of Portugal, i. 153

JESUITS, Order of, i. 149; quarrel with Carmelites, i. 280
Jesus, Ana de, ii. 369, 418
Jesus, Fray Antonio de, ii. 110, 146, 209, 229, 316, 379
Jesus, Fray Baltasar de, ii. 61, 68, 198
Jesus, Isabel de, i. 450
Jesus, Maria de, i. 253
Jews, persecution of, i. 13
Juan, Don, of Austria, ii. 270

LAIZ, Teresa, i. 439
La Roda, ii. 276; hermit of, ii. 271
La Serna, ii. 291
Las Huelgas, convent of, at Burgos, i. 40; ii. 351, 366
Leon, Fray Luis de, i. 71; ii. 419
"Letrado," ii. 152
Letters, Teresa's, i. 248, 360, 370; ii. 129
Life, Teresa's, i. 410; ii. 282
Lisbon, prioress of, i. 160
Locutions, divine, of Teresa, i. 155
Loyola, Ignatius, i. 148

MALAGON, i. 353; Monastery of, ii. 160, 249, 256
Mancera de Abajo, ii. 65
Manso, Don Pedro, ii. 354
Mariano, Ambrosio, ii. 61, 76, 99, 209, 229
Marmol, ii. 419
Mascareñas, Da. Leonor de, i. 393
Mateo, the hermit, i. 394
Matias, Pablo, ii. 151
Medina del Campo, i. 326; ii. 250, 346; foundation of convent at, i. 337
Medina, Fray Bartolomé de, ii. 18
Mendoza, Ana de, i. 389, 403
Mendoza, Da. Maria de, i. 351, 366; ii. 252
Mendoza, Don Bernardino de, i. 357

Mendoza, Don Luis Hurtado de, ii. 233
Mendoza, Pedro Gonzalez de, i. 403
Mendozas, the, i. 403
Miracles of Teresa, i. 242, 448; ii. 57; performed by her relics, ii. 395
Miseria, Fray Juan de la, i. 395, 414; ii. 61
Monasteries, i. 37; Spanish, state of, in sixteenth century, i. 323
Monastic orders, i. 34
Monterey, Counts of, i. 447
Moors in Spain, i. 10
Moradas, Teresa's, i. 203, 425
Mudejares, i. 2, *note*
Mysticism, Spanish, i. 44; of Eckart, i. 46; of Teresa, i. 145

NACIMIENTO, Maria del, i. 204
New World, discovery of, i. 16
Nieto, Fray Balthasar de, i. 414; ii. 61

OBSERVANTS AND DESCALZOS, feud between, ii. 75, 108, 132, 187
Ocampo, Maria de, i. 227
Ormaneto, Cardinal Legate, ii. 192
Osma, ii. 328
Osuna, Fray Francisco, i. 45
Ovalle, Gonzalo de, i. 242
Ovalle, Juan de, i. 240, 242, 261, 418; ii. 164
Ovalle, Juana de, i. 240, 261

PADILLA, Casilda de, ii. 41
Padranos, Fray Juan de, i. 151
Palafox, Bishop of Osma, ii. 200
Palencia, ii. 348; Teresa at, ii. 304
Palencia, Bishop of, ii. 343
Pastrana, ii. 27, 62, 389, 401; Monastery of, i. 61; ii. 32
Pazos, President of the Royal Council, ii. 217
Pedro the muleteer, ii. 220
Perez, Antonio, i. 405
Philip II., i. 31, 322, 404; ii. 211, 234
— as V., i. 322
Ponz, i. 24
Portrait of Teresa, ii. 323
Portugal, affairs in, ii. 254
Poverty, place of, in Teresa's system, i. 293
Prayer, Teresa on, i. 206-220; her Treatise of, i. 197
Prophecies of Teresa, i. 245; ii. 55

QUIROGA, Archbishop, ii. 212
Quiroga, Doña Elena de, ii. 334

RAMIREZ, Alonso, i. 372
Ramirez, Martin, i. 371
Reform of Carmelites, ii. 409. *See also* Discalced Carmelites
Reforms, religious, i. 54, 227, 322
Reinoso, Canon, ii. 306
"Relations" of Teresa, i. 190, 450
Religion, Spanish idea of, i. 27, 37
"Reposteros," i. 339
Ribera, Francisco de, i. 69; his description of Teresa's corpse, ii. 392
Ribera, Pedro de, ii. 317, 323, 330
Roads, Spanish, in the sixteenth century, ii. 91
Roca, Fray Juan de, ii. 213, 222, 243
Rubeo, Fray Juan Bautista, i. 322
Ruiz, Alfonso, ii. 150
Ruiz, Simon, i. 417, 456

SACRAMENTO, Maria del, i. 433, 445
St. Albert, rule of, i. 284, 291
Salamanca, i. 432; Convent of, ii. 255, 372; Teresa's journey to, ii. 14
Salazar, Fr. Angel de, i. 232
Salazar, Fray Gaspar de, ii. 2, 76, 204, 241
Salazar, Maria de, i. 253
Salcedo, Francisco de, i. 146, 195; ii. 175
Salerno, Princess of, ii. 266
Saludador (health giver), i. 117
San Bartolomé, Ana de, ii. 377
Sandoval, Catalina de, ii. 50
Sandoval, Don Cristóbal de, ii. 101
San Francisco, Maria de, i. 203
San Geronimo, Maria de, i. 306
San Gil (the Jesuit College), i. 155
San José, Convent of, i. 233; foundation of, i. 257; rules of life in, i. 291
San José, Maria de, ii. 118, 138, 146, 301
San Juan de los Reyes, church in Toledo, i. 428
San Juan del Puerto, ii. 77
San Millan, hermit of, i. 161, *note*
San Segundo, legend of, i. 91
Santa Barbada, story of, i. 92
Santo Domingo, Isabel de, i. 417; ii. 27
Santo Matia, Fray Germán de, ii. 201
Santo Tomás, monastery of, i. 13
Sega, Philip, Bishop of Ripa, ii. 197, 210, 228, 234
Segovia, Teresa at, ii. 24
Seraphic doctor (Teresa), i. 179
Seraphic vow, i. 191
"Serranos," i. 7
Seville, nuns of, ii. 142, 238, 301;

Teresa at, ii. 103; Gracian at, ii. 137
Silva, Ruy Gomez de, i. 389, 404
Sonsoles, shrine of, i. 18
Soria, ii. 320; Teresa travels to, ii. 317
Spain, art in, i. 30; in sixteenth century, i. 21, 35, 157; church music of, i. 31; literature in, i. 30
Suarez, Fray Augustin, ii. 136

TERESA, her brothers, i. 16; mysticism of, i. 48, 73, 145; visions and ecstasies of, i. 52, 162-173, ii. 9; as a religious reformer, i. 54; and the Inquisition, i. 65; autobiography of, i. 66; style of, i. 67, 199; contemporary biographers of, i. 68; the woman, i. 72; birth and childhood, i. 77; her father's house, i. 82; her reading, i. 94; personal appearance, i. 97, ii. 324; enters cloister, i. 111; at Castellanos de la Cañada, i. 114; her return to the Encarnacion, 129; MS. of her life, i. 143, 410; puts herself under the Jesuits' guidance, i. 151; her divine "locutions," i. 155; her detractors and opponents, i. 173; transverberation of her heart, i. 178, ii. 406; conflict with demons, i. 182; her vision of hell, i. 186; her "Relations," i. 190, 450; her treatise of prayer, i. 197; charm of, i. 198; her *Moradas*, i. 203, 425; on prayer, i. 206-220; her miracles, i. 242, 448, ii. 57; predictions of, i. 245, ii. 55; letters to her brother Lorenzo, i. 248; founds San José, i. 257; her doubts, i. 265; her *Camino de Perfeccion*, i. 308; founds Malagon, i. 353; her life, i. 360, ii. 282; her letters, i. 360-370, ii. 129; founds Duruelo, i. 368; founds Toledo, i. 374; founds Pastrana, i. 410; her house in Toledo, i. 424; founds Salamanca, i. 432; founds Alba de Tormes, i. 439; prioress of Encarnacion, i. 460, 462; opposition to, ii. 1; her rule as abbess, ii. 4; travels to Salamanca, ii. 14; at Segovia, ii. 24; her worldly shrewdness, ii. 36; travels to Veas, ii. 55, 58; at Seville, ii. 103; her first interview with Gracian, ii. 86; her arrival at Cordoba, ii. 95; resides at Toledo, ii. 132; her *Funaciones*, ii. 166-170; her bearing trial, ii. 230; triumphant journey ii. 264, 278; her character, 301; at Palencia, ii. 304; care f her nuns, ii. 310; travels to So ii. 317; portrait of, i. *frontispi.* ii. 323; couplets by, ii. 325; last hours, ii. 378; her death, 382; burial of, ii. 384; her bo removed to Avila, ii. 387; her bo taken back to Alba, ii. 390; description of her corpse, ii. 392; miracles by her relics, ii. 395; beatification of, ii. 400; canonisation of, ii. 406; chosen patroness of Spain, ii. 407

Teresian vow, i. 191
Tendilla, Count of, ii. 233
Tiemblo, i. 379
Toledo, i. 250, 384; Church of San Juan de los Reyes, i. 428; Teresa's house in, i. 424, ii. 132
Toledo, Don Luis de, ii. 66
Toledo, Fr. Garcia de, i. 256
Tolosa, Catalina de, ii. 354, 360, 364
Torno, i. 307, *note*
Torquemada, i. 13
Tostado, Fray Geronimo, ii. 125, 200, 211
Traggia, Padre, i. 80
Treatise of prayer, i. 197
Tunis, Baxa (pasha) of, ii. 435
Turkish corsairs, ii. 434

ULLOA, Da. Guiomar de, i. 155, 178, 226

VALLADOLID, i. 366; scene in, ii. 2
Vanda, Pedro de la, ii. 19
Vargas, Fray Francisco de, ii. 71, 9 prior of Cordoba, ii. 67
Vasquez, i. 407
Veas, ii. 49; Teresa's arrival at, i. 58; monastery of, ii. 161
Vejámen, Cartel de, ii. 7
"Vejámen Espiritual," ii. 174
Villanueva de la Jara, ii. 276; foundation of, ii. 261
Visions of Teresa, i. 52, 162-173
Vow, Teresian, i. 191

YEPES, i. 69; ii. 328

www.ingramcontent.com/pod-product-compliance
Lightning Source LLC
Chambersburg PA
CBHW031957300426
44117CB00008B/804